SEXUAL ABERRATIONS ·

SEXUAL ABERRATIONS

The Phenomena of Fetishism in Relation to Sex

WILHELM STEKEL, M.D.

AUTHORIZED ENGLISH VERSION FROM
THE FIRST GERMAN EDITION BY
SAMUEL PARKER, M.D.

INTRODUCTION BY
EMIL A. GUTHEIL, M.D.

VOLUME ONE

LIVERIGHT

NEW YORK

Liveright Paperbound Edition 1971
SBN: 87140-049-9
LCC: 71-149628
MANUFACTURED IN UNITED STATES OF AMERICA

INTRODUCTION

This book deals in a scientific manner with a sexual deviation called fetishism. This deviation involves the attraction to an *object* associated with a sexual partner rather than the attraction to a *partner* as such.

The phenomenon of fetishism has been known to psychiatrists and criminologists for a long time as one of the clinical forms of sexual psychopathology. The first psychodynamic investigation, however, goes back to Sigmund Freud, and the year 1905, when, in his first *Drei Abhandlungen zur Sexualtheorie* (Deuticke, Vienna) he approached this problem psychoanalytically.

Freud recognized the importance of infantile traumatic experiences for the peculiar constriction of the patient's erotic horizon, seen in fetishism, and attempted to explain why these traumatic experiences had become the center of the patient's erotic preoccupation. He thought that it was the specific emotional elaboration of these experiences that kept them alive in the patient's mind. Freud emphasized especially the connection between fetishism and the castration fear, a fact which helps to understand why fetishism is a predominantly "male" disease, and why "female" fetishism is so rare as to be practically nonexistent.

We know now that Freud overestimated the value of the castration complex in the psychopathology of fetishism. Stekel's present volume, which first appeared in 1923, reaches further and digs deeper than Freud's original work on the subject. Stekel attempts to show that the sexual deviation called fetishism has a polymorphous structure and represents—as do all neurotic disorders—a compromise solution and a crystallization point for many trends and many complexes existing in the patient's mind simultaneously; that it is, in fact, a synthesis of the patient's highest as well as of his lowest aspirations.

The great value of Stekel's present book lies in its lucidity

INTRODUCTION

and its broad and undogmatic views, supported by a legion of case histories, some of them presented in minute detail. The volume covers the entire field, and includes alsc material dealing with a special form of fetishism, called transvestitism. As in all of Stekel's books, the general social and therapeutic implications of the disease are discussed extensively. Physicians—especially psychiatrists—psychologists, psychiatric case workers, members of the Bar and officers of penal institutions will find in the present volume valuable clues for the understanding and management of one of the baffling sexual aberrations of our time.

EMIL A. GUTHEIL, M.D.

New York, N. Y.
February 1952

AUTHOR'S PREFACE

For the purposes of this subject, the exhaustive study of the literature was of paramount importance, but I must emphasize the fact that it is not my purpose in the following pages to present a detailed case description of fetishism. The knowledge of many observations by others does, however, enable us to carry out a sort of comparative psychological study which is of benefit to psychoanalysis.

I believe that this book materially extends our understanding of the psychopathology of fetishism, although I am well aware that there are still many riddles left for us to solve. It is unfortunate that the material is not only infrequent, but also difficult to handle.

The following book will deal with sadism and masochism (issued in English by Horace Liveright, Inc., 1929). My readers will already have noticed that each of my works is organically developed out of the previous one. In this respect, Fetishism is a continuation of Impulsive Conduct (it is, after all, an impulsive form itself). As the last chapters of the book, especially, will reveal, it constitutes a transition to the important subject of sadism.

For those readers who are unacquainted with my new terminology as it is uniformly carried out in these volumes, I may say that parapathia stands for neurosis; paralogia for psychosis; and paraphilia for perversion.

I am especially indebted to Havelock Ellis, Ludwig Binswanger and Dr. Sigg for their kind permission to make use of their interesting cases. I must also thank Dr. Anton Missriegler, my industrious colleague, for his many suggestions and the preparation of the indices.

Dr. Wilhelm Stekel.

TRANSLATOR'S NOTE

This book was written by a physician of acknowledged experience in the field of emotional and instinctual disturbances. He has written it expressly for physicians and earnest students, and it is in the interest of making the author's authoritative methods and views accessible to our professional class that the translator has undertaken an English rendition. The exhaustiveness and wealth of allusion are precisely the factors which illustrate how much more we have gained from the psychoanalytical approach to these disturbances than from the purely descriptive treatises which have gone before.

S. PARKER.

CONTENTS OF VOLUME ONE

CHAPTER I

DEFINITION OF FETISHISM

CHAPTER II

ANALYSIS OF AN INDIVIDUAL LOVE CONDITION

CHAPTER III

EROTIC SYMBOLISM

CONTENTS OF VOLUME ONE

CONTENTS OF VOLUME ONE

Wer ist krank? Bin ich genesen?
Und wer ist mein Arzt gewesen?
Jetzt erst glaub' ich dich genesen,
Denn gesund ist, wer vergass.

NIETZSCHE.

SEXUAL ABERRATIONS

SEXUAL ABERRATIONS
VOLUME ONE

I

WHAT IS FETISHISM?

The phenomenon of fetishism is doubtless one of the most puzzling in the whole domain of sexual pathology. Indeed, we have, as yet, no real conception of how widespread or important it is. We all know that every human has individual needs, but we realize that his love-life is nevertheless contingent upon certain conditions. The personal form of sexual attraction varies with different persons on the basis of a kind of fetishism, i.e., everyone prefers certain characteristics or attributes in his sexual objects. As a matter of fact, such attributes are practically the conditions of his attraction. Hands, feet, ears, the voice, the eyes, complexion, odor, bust, and other parts of the body have always been "fetishes." We call them normal fetishes. They become pathological only when they have pushed the whole love object into the background and themselves appropriate the function of a love object, e.g., when a lover satisfies himself with the possession of a woman's shoe and considers the woman herself as secondary or even disturbing and superfluous. I said the possession of the woman and thereby almost allied myself with many authors who forget the fact that there is also a homosexual fetishism. Such is, in my experience, the end of every case of fetishism. Succinctly, the essence of such a condition can be totally explained as a retreat from the female, flight from woman.[1] Fetishism always develops into a depreciation of the female, regardless of the causes, and the same is true of the few cases of female fetishism which I have been able to observe. In the latter type of case, there occurs a deflation of the value of the male and simultaneously the person strives to find a form of sexual gratification which will make

3

the sexual partner superfluous.   This attitude is usually what Adler called the "fear of the sexual partner," a fear which plays an important and even leading rôle in the struggle of the sexes, throwing a bright light upon many a dark phenomenon of our sex life.[2]

Binet has given us an explanation of fetishism which is very seductive.   Krafft-Ebing, Moll and Merzbach are among those who have generally accepted it.   According to this worthy author, every sexual perversion depends upon an "accident agissant sur un sujet prédisposé."   The first sexual impression is permanently soldered to the individual's whole sex feeling; so that only the memory of this impression can provoke passion. A boy sees the naked bust of his governess and thereby experiences his first sexual excitement.   This is the law of the recurrence of identities, a law which plays an important rôle in the parapathias.   We see in this notion of Binet,[3] however, practically the kernel of Freud's well-known theory according to which the trauma becomes the cause of the parapathia if it strikes a predisposed individual.   This theory nevertheless does not explain all the curious traits of the fetish lover.   Nor does it explain the question as to why all children do not react to such impressions with the development of fetishism.

We cannot sufficiently emphasize the fact that all these forms of paraphilia are a part of the make-up of all normal humans. If we examine so-called normal individuals carefully, we find that they all have their predilection points (erogenous zones). These parts of the body are preferred and their irritation intensifies the libido.   I quite agree with Eulenburg[4] who writes:

"Just a general remark by way of introduction.   All the forms of sexual perversion I have just mentioned, much as they differ from each other, have nevertheless one thing in common: their roots reach deep down into the matrix of natural and normal sex life; there they are somehow closely connected with the feelings and expressions of our physiological erotism.   They are only pathologically one-sided offshoots or hyperbolic intensifications, distortions, monstrous fruits of certain partial and secondary expressions of this erotism which is considered "normal" or at least within the limits of healthy sex feeling.   Fetishism thus finds its physiological basis in individual sex conditions, in the conscious or unconscious tendencies to partial attraction which so often obtain in the normal person's choice of a love object (the exhibitionism displayed in the tendency and necessity of shameless stripping even in normal love relations), in the sadism and masochism of certain frequent phenomena associated with the orgasm of the love act (in animals as well as humans), and finally in the voluptuous effect of certain injuries dealt out to the love object or, conversely, of humiliations and even mistreatment suffered at the hands of the partner. The importance of this physiological background of sexual perversions is analogous to a similar situation in the case of many phenomena of the functional psychoses. In the delusions of grandeur and persecution of the true paranoiac, for example, we also frequently find pathological development and intensification of the traits of personal over-estimation and suspicious judgment of others which were characteristic of the individual before the incidence of his psychosis.

"This principle of partial attraction almost invariably plays quite a leading rôle, either consciously or unconsciously, in the healthy love-life of normal individuals. Magnus Hirschfeld has laid especial stress on this point in an interesting monograph on this subject. One man falls only for slender, graceful figures, another yearns for full and voluptuous Rubens' types. The one raves of blondes, the other of brunettes and black- or red-haired women do not lack for admirers—at least no more than the blue-, brown- or dark-eyed women lauded by the poets. Any sensual effect can take on a dominating importance. The way of a walk, the voice, the odor of the body or any part of it, that well-known "odor di femina," these can make themselves effective, can become the basis of a permanent and irresistible attraction (or, contrarily, also of an insurmountable repulsion). How many are susceptible to the chic dress which permits of the plastic emphasis of physical beauty: small feet, narrow waist, proper curve of the hips. Even the whole arrangement, the cloth, the cut, can be provocative, not to speak of the highly seductive and studied effects achieved by the art of the tailor and the designer. We have already arrived at the transitions not only to parts of the body as a fetish, but to the fetishism of clothes and goods. We have passed from the "physiological" to the pathological. The same processes are to be found among women, although in this case the vestigial and transitional forms as well as true fetishism are much more seldom, or at least appear to be so because the personal love conditions of women, their "partial attractions" (and partial repulsions) operate at a deeper level and come to the surface much less frequently. Nevertheless, the preference for bearded or clean-shaven men, big and strong or small and delicate males, the susceptibility of some women to exotic, foreign races, or types of other colors, brown Turcos, black Somalis, yellow Asiatics, etc., these expressions of sex attraction must be reckoned in this class."

Many authors consider "individual love conditions" to be fetishism. Let us examine such a case somewhat more closely. This case was described by Garnier as object fetishism of an inverted person (homosexual).

Case 1. Gustave L., thirty-two, servant, of medium build and normal physical development, was indicted because of an attack upon his faithless love object X. The story of his life mentions the fact that as early as ten years of age he experienced a thrill when embraced by a man whose beard brushed his cheek. He proceeded by all manner of means to achieve the same excitement whenever he could. Shortly thereafter he was so impassioned by the sight of an urinating man that he was impelled to masturbate. At thirteen he noticed that he was sexually excited by the sight of laborers in their working clothes. A well-fitting shirt was sufficient to bring on an orgasm even if only imagined. Any other form of clothing, however, including the military uniform, left him cold. He began to have relations with women, but felt no particular pleasure. His vain desire to imitate his comrades impelled him in these relations more than anything else. Only one woman was able to enchant the twenty-three-year-old boy, and the reason for that was the fact that he was in love with her lover and not with the forty-six-year-old woman herself. This lover also wore a blouse. During intercourse with the woman, he would have a mental picture of her lover and would then have an orgasm. Nevertheless, he tired of the woman, bummed restlessly about searching for his ideal and was unable to remain in any one place. Finally he succeeded in

attracting the friendship of an ideal partner. Seizing upon en-
thusiastic words, he pictured to Garnier the various phases and
practices of his relations with this man (mutual masturbation and
pederasty). But his pain was boundless when he learned that his
friend had relations with women, too. The excitement which this
realization provoked led to jaundice. Following a frightful depression which was complicated by insomnia, and tortured by indescribable jealousy, he threatened his betrayer with a revolver and
was arrested.

This case exhibits only certain features of fetishism. Gustave is restless, changes his female love objects, but he is apparently satisfied with his lover. The blouse is an individual
love condition which is probably a fixation of infantile impressions. When one studies the life histories of normal individuals, one will be surprised to find that such personal love
conditions absorb considerable importance during adolescence,
but that such infantilism is overcome in the course of time and
then these impressions fade. The intellectual and civilized person lays much more weight on spiritual attributes, he enjoys
rather the consonance of ideas and tastes and only unconsciously
does it sometimes appear as if the individual love conditions
have been paramount in determining the choice of a love object. The healthier a person is, the more easily does he conquer the tyranny of symbolism in life. But who can say of
himself that he is completely free in this respect? It would be
gratifying to analyze a number of normal persons with a view
to studying their personal sex foibles.
    Havelock Ellis has already begun with the publication of the
erotic biographies of normal individuals. His cases are very
instructive and have even prompted Freud to change his opinions on the sexuality of parapathics. The parapathic does not
suffer from a pathological sexuality, but rather from his special
relation to sexuality. He fights off his sexuality. I know of
innumerable examples of persons who remain quite healthy
when they learn not to take their deviations from the normal
tragically. I offer the following illustration.

Case 2. G. S., twenty years old, stud. chem. "I first learned
to masturbate when I began cross-bar gymnastics, i.e., at eight

years of age. The special opportunity appeared while climbing on
the hard iron bars, but particularly while on the soft, flexible rope.
That was also the reason why I was the best climber in the class.
As far as I can remember I had only the desire to achieve that
"fine feeling" (as I called it) at any price. That I didn't fall from
the rope during the orgasm is still a wonder to me. Sometimes,
when I had climbed to the top before I had an orgasm, I would
slide back down the rope a distance and then climb back up again
in order to get my thrill. In the courtyard of our former home
there was a cross-bar which was also used as a swing and I
climbed up and down the ropes of this, too, often enough. One
day my eldest brother saw me doing this from a window of his
study and I hardly knew what hole to crawl away to for shame.
I was altogether very careful to cover my activity from the very
beginning (why especially?).

But there was something else besides the climbing which excited
me insanely, and that was riding and anything which was at all
connected with it. In 1897, my parents spent the summer with us
in B. There, we boys were occasionally permitted to ride around
on the beach donkeys and, of course, that meant masturbation for
me, since all I had to do was to press myself a little harder against
the pommel. Yet I was fearfully bashful even so much so to speak
the words riding, saddle, stirrup, spur, riding breeches, riding
boots, and the like.

Subsequently, i.e., at about my fourteenth or fifteenth year, I
began to give up climbing (if only because I was no longer taking
gymnastics), and the riding came to the fore. I still had no idea
what all this interest meant. Nor did I as yet masturbate with my
hands, but rather in the following fashion: I would blow up a rubber air cushion such as I used to sit on, and then I would bend it in
such a way that it would take on about the form of a saddle.
Keeping it in this shape, I would put it on a chair, sit down on it,
brace my hands firmly in front of it, so that the soft rubber would
not be pushed forward out of shape, and then begin to work. I
also used to do it this way with the use of a bundle of towels in the
bath room. Frequently I have also made use of my father's hunting boots or my mother's galoshes to intensify my pleasure. Sometimes I would also masturbate on a saddle which lay in the stables
of a friendly family X (but always with the terrifying anxiety that
I would be discovered). Twice, but with great fear, I got a pair
of riding boots belonging to Mr. X, which also had spurs on them,
and pulled them on in a toilet on the first floor of their house.

The boots I found in a dark corner near the bedroom of Mr. and Mrs. X. I masturbated once or twice a day on the average, always imagined something that had to do with riding, and usually also spoke some words aloud.

Then there were two other things which affected me strongly and those were women's high-heeled shoes and sport breeches which were to be buttoned below the knee. It was the peculiar creasing of these breeches which especially excited me; so that, although I would under no circumstances wear such trousers, I would secretly try to tie them on with garters and string and would then masturbate. In this operation I began to use my hand only after my fifteenth year, but up to that time I would get an orgasm by rubbing my penis against some other soft object.

Once I nearly went wild when I saw a pair of perforated women's shoes with very high heels in a store window. They must have reached to the knees (similar to the shoes one sees in the circus). I nibbled at the memory of this sight for weeks. Indeed, I even thought of stealing the shoes. Frequently I would draw riding boots, women's shoes and the like on pieces of paper in order to titillate myself and achieve satisfaction more quickly. The special female qualities began to interest me after my sixteenth year.

A school-mate afforded me "sexual enlightenment" in a rather gross way as early as my first high school year. I suppose I believed what he said, but it didn't bother me much otherwise. I had no idea at that time that my masturbatory acts had any sexual meaning. Of course, I also joined my comrades in making fun of notorious portions of the "holies" or, pardon me, the holy Scriptures, as well as the book of psalms. But I had no real understanding of why I did it. And then all these things began gradually to appear. I observed how, within me, these "forbidden" things would crop up singly in my lascivious thoughts, would then be held at bay for a while, until, finally, the mental images of the specific female attractiveness gained the upper hand and have retained it. For now neither riding or anything connected with it (unless it be a woman riding in a man's saddle as, e.g., in the Wild West movies and melodramas) nor anything like climbing can give me the least thrill, although—but of this more later.

The period of my most intensive masturbation was during the last three years of high school (I was always a frivolous and lazy pupil, but a good one nevertheless). I masturbated four and five times a day and once established my record of seven times. Since

I never dared to do this during school hours in the morning, I always masturbated in the afternoons. I practised mutual onanism with a cousin, who was living with us, quite frequently and once even tried immissio penis in anum on him, but this was a complete failure.

Since I suffered from this "bad habit," it is understandable that I also tried to give it up. I was once able to withhold myself for a week, but then I had nocturnal pollutions and that was the end of my abstinence. The immediate provocation for the period of abstinence was a lecture by a pastor. The lecture, I felt at the time, quite elevated me. It is not difficult to imagine that this lecture had about as permanent an effect as the faithful promises I made myself. I was always of the opinion that I was committing a fault, if not a sin (although this notion occasionally broke through); that is, if the differentiation I make is permissible. But I was especially affected by the fear that I was ruining my health (which, by the way, is enviably good).

Towards the end of the next to last school year, female images prevailed in my phantasies and replaced all the others. For some time I was unusually tender towards my mother and sisters, especially the eldest, and kissed them whenever I could. My attitude changed abruptly, however, when, during one of my very infrequent nocturnal emissions, I tried in my dream to have intercourse with my eldest sister. In the morning I had such a moral hangover that I summarily gave up my tenderness towards them and have not had a recurrent desire since then.

The following has, however, become the chief source of sexual excitement for me: It is not the naked woman, but rather the barely draped body, especially the breast, delicately indicating or outlining the form, which fascinates me. I'm practically beside myself with passion whenever I see a lightly clothed girl running, her breasts beneath her blouse or dress visibly following her running motions. Well-shaped women's legs (but not at all necessarily clothed in perforated or sheer stockings) and women's feet are also the objects of my phantasies. I must emphasize that I'm not attracted by naked feet, but rather by feet covered with fine shoes carrying half-high or straight heels. I am particularly provoked when a good share of the leg is also visible; the shoe itself would leave me cold. I don't particularly prefer really small feet, but neither do I lay much store by large ones. I can get an erection pronto, e.g., whenever I see a pretty and well-formed girl fighting against the wind, which wraps her dress flatly about her body. But I'm disconsolate if she has a corset on. Corsets can inflame me, and to a considerable degree, but only when I see them in pictures, like the ones in *Lustige Blaetter* and *Jugend*. The pictures by Bayros excite me greatly, but those by Reznicek less.

The slit skirt now in the mode, which often permits of a clandestine peek as far as the knee, frequently gives me an erection. What a start this is for the imagination! Especially when one can picture the leg up as high as one likes. Clothing which has portions cut out catches my fancy only when it is very loose and deeply cut out. Hair or clothes in themselves mean nothing to me.

For some time now I have been masturbating manually once a day. During vacations and on Sundays as well as on days when there is no work, I sometimes make it twice or three times. But I can also leave off for a day or two without afterwards trying to make it up. If I masturbate during the day, I take one of the magazines I mentioned above and enliven the pictures with my imagination, e.g., what I should do were I to kiss the girl, slowly undress her, lay my head between her breasts; and finally she would take my penis and put it in her vagina and then we would expire with pleasure. These are the usual phantasies to which such pictures are subject as I have seen during the day. In my mind, however, the girl must keep her shoes and stockings on, since this promotes my satisfaction. I then picture to myself how she embraces me with her legs and we press body to body and breast to breast. . . .

On the occasion of my second visit to England in the summer of 1913, I had intercourse with a woman for the first time. But when I got home, I was unable to withstand the urge to masturbate, thinking of the prostitute, remembering especially how she stuck my penis in her vagina.

It is true that I went up to the university with the best intentions not to sink into the "cesspool of sin and vice" and to remain "pure." Gradually, however, the more my mind became freed from the bonds of school and church, the more liberally did I look upon sexuality, and I began to yearn for woman with all my thought and feeling. I do so to-day more than ever. Since on Sundays I had to visit my parents who lived not far away, I dared not, especially for fear of my father, try intercourse in Germany. But I don't want an ordinary prostitute, nor did I ever look for such women. I want a sweet, open, refreshing girl who possesses a personality and an interest in the arts and sciences. That's what I've always been looking for in vain, but my fear of my father

and my bashfulness have always held me back. In England—'
thank God—I was far enough away from home. It was there,
too, that I made several friends, thereby losing some of my bashfulness; but one of the girls lost her charms for me, some of the
others didn't keep their dates, and another aroused my pity—but
not my passion.

Back home again, I did not give up my search, although it is
my opinion that there is a dearth of desirable material here.
Furthermore, a rather revolting occurrence banished my interest
in women temporarily. A good friend and schoolmate of mine,
with whom I spend a good share of my time, picked up a gonorrhœa. I have asked surely a dozen girls for a date (quite
a number for my finances), but only one kept her appointment; all
the others turned me down and this one was unable to meet me a
second time, so I let her go.

Nevertheless, I never did and I never will give up my attempts.
I have often run out on the street in the night and fog simply because every fibre in my body cried out for a woman. I never
know where to hide myself. I usually walk about until I am
tired. Often a streetwalker has appeared, but I usually let her
go, despite my terrible need, and return to my "handiwork."

At this point I must interrupt the story of G. S. to point out
that he has found a way to woman, but does not feel himself
to be pathological despite his fetishistic tendencies. His statements about the frequency of his masturbation are worthy of
consideration. If we remember that this is a strong and fine-
looking man, we will realize how little truth there is in the
exaggerations about the ruinous effects of onanism peddled by
even the leading sexologists.

One thing is evident: this man's fetishism lies in the direct
path which leads to the woman, and this point deserves closer
attention. It would probably be more advantageous not to
speak of fetishism in such cases at all. Otherwise we would
have to differentiate between great and small and between false
and genuine fetishism. Eulenburg's term "partialism" would
probably do well enough for such cases. We know now that
every person has his own set of partial attractions or preferences; so that the term genuine fetishism would have to be re-
served for such cases as I have exhaustively analyzed and discussed towards the end of this treatise.

The true fetish lover dispenses with a sexual partner and gratifies himself with a symbol. This symbol can be represented by a piece of clothing, a part of the partner's body (pubic hair, nails, braid or pig-tail) or any object used by the other person (irrigator, prosthesis, handkerchief, apron, petticoat, chemise, brush, etc.).

We thus have three kinds of erotic symbolism (Havelock Ellis).

1. The importance of the partial attraction. The love object must fulfill a certain sexual condition. Sexual intercourse is possible when this condition is met.

2. The paraphilic seeks certain attributes in his love object and finds his gratification at the zone of partial preference (orgasm in nasa, in auricula, inter mammas, etc.).

3. The paraphilic dispenses with the female, satisfies himself with the symbol and uses the erotic symbol to dispense with the partner. We shall reserve the name of fetishism for such cases as these.

I have already stressed the fact that all persons display certain fetishistic rudiments. These vestigial traits are by no means so important in normal individuals as in true fetish lovers, however, because they themselves constitute a means to an end, to conquest of the female and to alloerotic orgasm, whereas in the case of genuine fetishism such traits make the individual independent of his sexual object. He becomes progressively freer and rapidly sinks into a state of autoerotism. Fetishism thus becomes an apparent cause of impotence. I say apparent because impotence springs only from a fear of the sexual act (which is looked upon as sin) or from a fear of the sexual partner. Thus Moll emphasizes the fact that fetishism leads to impotence, but Krafft-Ebing comes somewhat closer to the truth when he writes: "It is thus perhaps better to look for the pathological criterion of the fetishism of parts of the body on a strictly subjective, psychic level. The concentration of the patient's sexual interest in a certain part of the other person's body which (and this is to be stressed) never has a direct relationship with the sex act (such as breasts, external genitals, etc.), often leads this type of fetish seeker to disregard actual intercourse as the goal of his sexual striving, but to find his

gratification rather in some act executed upon that part of the
body which is most attractive."

Here we have two important symptoms of fetishism: A fetish is chosen which possesses but a distant connection with the
sexual act as such (and sometimes none whatever) and, sec-
ondly, with the aid of this fetish the coitus can be disregarded.[5]
By this I do not mean to deny that there are fetish lovers who
have normal intercourse. I myself know such cases, though
they are rare. Nevertheless, in all these cases one can always
find the tendency to pass up coitus and to cohabit with the
woman only under the pressure of social duty.

Despite the numerous case histories of fetishistic patients
which one can read, I can honestly declare that we are as yet
far from understanding the essence of this illness. Fetishism
is a complicated religion, an artful setting, whose structure can
be compared only with the compulsion neuroses. Indeed, we
will probably be nearer the truth if we say that fetishism is an
obsessional neurosis.

It has recently become modish to rant about the dangers and
the disadvantages of psychoanalysis. But there is one good
thing about psychoanalysis which we must not forget and that
is the wonderful opportunity it has given us to deal with the
patients and their parapathias for months and even years at a
time. As soon as we have learned to disentangle ourselves
from the bonds of prepossession, aprioristic theses and definitive methods of approach, we must recognize that such an intensive association with the patient must necessarily afford the
unbiassed scientist an unusual opportunity to become acquainted
with just those intimate and far-reaching details which the patient invariably withholds during the first few visits. Nevertheless, it is precisely in the sphere of the paraphilias that psychoanalysis has advanced the least. Aside from the fundamental treatise on the *Three Contributions to the Theory of
Sex* by Freud, there are only a few studies in paraphilia by
Sadger and some smaller contributions on foot fetishism by
Abraham to which we will refer later. The reason for this is
to be found in Freud's opinion that paraphilia is something
complete; that it is not reducible or analyzable to any further
component elements. According to the well-known statement

of this author, the child is a "polymorphous pervert." If it sublimates these perverse instincts, i.e., if it is possible for the child to transform them into socially amenable drives, then it will develop into a healthy and normal individual. If, however, these impulses are simply repressed, so that they retain their vitality in the unconscious and produce symptoms, then the individual becomes parapathic. Should the original, perverse tendencies persist into adult life, then the individual has become an adult pervert.

In such a system there is nothing to be analyzed. "The neurosis is the negative of a perversion," says Freud. I disagreed with this statement of Freud's when I was yet personally associated with him and worked as a pupil under the tremendous influence of his ideas. At this time I can but repeat what has been so often said: Paraphilia (perversion) frequently shows us nothing more than the well-known picture of a parapathia (neurosis). In many cases the paraphilia (perversion) is a positive of the parapathia (neurosis). I am able to demonstrate this in the case of the fetishist and have been able to demonstrate it in the case of homosexuality. To decide how much of a parapathia is due to the constitutional component and how much of it is a psychic superstructure, that is a problem beyond me. But, in the case of fetishism, I can demonstrate the nature of this emotional superstructure, whereas the "constitutional" element always hauled up by Freudians in their embarrassment fades into the background as an insoluble and hypothetical factor.

Under the pressure of experience, Freud has recently modified his opinions and now concedes transitional types which stand between a neurosis and a perversion. His most recent opinions have been represented by Sadger as follows:[6]

"The purely accidental and chronological contact of the fetish and genital excitement as represented in Binet's explanation is at least not exhaustive or universally applicable. It is also not at all understandable why an accidentally simultaneous occurrence should take on such permanent power. Begging the question by calling it degeneration is only a way out, but not a true explanation.

"It is at this point that the further studies of Freud begin.

He took as a point of departure the notion that one invariably finds an intensification of certain partial instincts in fetishism, primarily the sexual pleasure derived from peeping, but also the thrill derived from odors. One lover of clothing fetishes was found always to have been a witness while his mother was undressing, this even as a little child. Not that anything out of the ordinary had occurred between them. It was only that the woman was so attached to her son that she did not suffer him to be ashamed when she undressed and it was thus that both usually had no scruples in undressing before each other. This naturally increased the constitutionally exaggerated peeping tendencies in the boy until he became a voyeur (peeper). Constitution and bringing-up worked hand in hand. When, later, his peeping impulses were repressed, the boy became a clothing fetishist by the mechanism of displacing his energies from the naked to the clothed. Instead of evincing an interest in the naked female, he developed an interest in her clothing. He also exhibited an intellectual parallel to this emotional one-sidedness. The man became a speculative philosopher, i.e., he turned his interests from the things of the world to words which are, as it were, the mantels of our concepts. This explains the attraction that philosophy held for him.

"The mechanism operating in this case was about as follows: It is a case of an increased peeping impulse which wanted to look and could be gratified by a disrobing person. The repression which followed was introduced by a dissociation of the complex to which this peeping drive was attached. One part of this complex, i.e., the naked body of his mother, was completely suppressed, whereas the other part of the complex, associated with the repressed part in a certain manner, was idealized, surrounded with hyperbolic over-estimation, elevated to the status of a fetish. This is a reaction which stands about half way between complete repression and sublimation. This boy thus no longer had a desire to fill his eyes, nor even to be reminded of this tendency, but he became an idolator of clothing, that which had formerly frustrated his seeing anything. He became a clothing fetish lover after the repression of his peeping tendencies and the dissociation of the complex. The theoretical importance of this explanation is that it shows us how this case of fetishism does not develop on the basis of an early childhood impression, but because of an instinct repression and the dissociation of the attendant complex.

"In another case of foot fetishism Freud nevertheless found precisely this peeping pleasure to be the definitive motive. As a child the patient in question had always looked under the skirts of women. He always began with a close observation of the feet and would then cast his eyes gradually along the leg until he was looking up at their genitals. It was during one of these exploratory trips in sexual provinces that he suffered a severe psychic trauma. He did not achieve a view of his mother's genitals, but the parts of his younger sister. This view afforded him a sudden realization of the possibility of castration which had already been threatened him. This, however, was the culmination of the intimidating efforts of up-bringing. He was greatly frightened and this was the beginning of inhibition. The reaction was at first only a local or geographical one, i.e., he dared no longer look all the way up to the genitals, but had to keep himself back, and thus became permanently fixated to the very beginning of his peeping trip, viz., to the feet. Had the inhibition been a greater one, he would have been thrown further back than the foot. He would have preferred the value of shoes, and in severe cases it is not even necessary for the foot to be in the shoe; the shoe alone is a sufficient sexual object. The choice of the foot in this case was determined by a double motive: geographically and symbolically it was the female penis. It seems apparent that the patient's mother herself formed the condition for the boy's fetishistic development by exhibiting an increased erotism in respect of the foot,[7] as a result of which she doubtless kissed her baby's feet a good deal. Thus again inheritance and the acquisition of a trait work together in this case. During sexual development, there was then a regression due to intimidation and, finally, fixation during puberty. In order that a perversion may take firm root, it is necessary that a repeated fixation during adolescence take place. In short, a congenital predisposition, intimidation with regression in childhood and, finally, a second fixation in puberty which leads to permanent consolidation of the perversion."

Freudian constitution is thus now replaced by the "disposi-

tion of the erogenous zones." That's not progress. It only
states in other words that the fetish lover is predisposed to his
disease by the presence of a higher congenital erogeneity of
certain parts of the body. Paraphilia then arises on the basis
of a preference of certain partial instincts. The fetish itself
replaces the genitals.

Such a description of the facts is one-sided. It embraces
some of the cases, but is by no means applicable to the essence
of true fetishism. The process is also frequently quite the opposite of the one described by Sadger. It is possible that precisely the view of a forbidden part of the body can lead to the
repression of peeping lust and the compensatory intensification
of other sensual reactions. The normal lover looks eagerly at
his love object, he likes to touch her, her kisses taste good to
him, he is thrilled by the special odor his sex object pervades,
her voice possesses for him an inimitable ring, a wonderful
melody. In short, he loves with all his five senses. The emphasis laid on any one of these senses at the expense of the
others may frequently be due to the fact that the other four
senses have been repressed because they were associated with
forbidden impulses.

Sadger's explanation possibly embraces individual cases of
partialism, but it is certainly ineffective in solving the riddle of
genuine fetishism which has nothing to do with any congenital
disposition (i.e., with a stressing of erogenous zones).

Fetishism is a disease and not a fate. It is a parapathia. It
is a construction built by the patient for a particular purpose.
This point of view also permits us to drop all the so-called
"normal fetishes" from our present concept. When a man is
fascinated by small ears and is always looking for girls who
possess them, he is yet far from being a fetish lover in this
sense. He simply expresses a form of sexual variation which
is so infinite in its possibilities that it would be impossible to
describe it. The point is that his variation lies along the sexual
guiding line which leads to the woman, to use an expression of
Blüher as developed from Adler. Normal fetishism aids the
man in the conquest of the woman and even promotes his libido.
These cases have nothing at all in common with the cases of
fetishism as I shall describe them. As a matter of fact, they

are quite the opposite of what we shall call fetishism and we would do well in such cases not to speak of fetishism at all. The true fetishist needs the fetish in order to supplant the female. The normal individual, however, prefers certain erogenous zones in order to make the possession of the female more piquant and valuable. The fetish lover depreciates the woman, whereas the normal person over-estimates the possessor of the erogenous zones he prefers.

This is also demonstrable in most cases of partialism. Thus Havelock Ellis writes rather interestingly of foot fetishism:

"The sexual symbolization of the female foot and its denudation, which we thus find so characteristic of bygone eras of civilization, and also the fascinating effect which such a leaning has, these realizations are of importance to us in explaining the cases of foot fetishism in our own times. Much as this tendency may be eccentric, it can nevertheless be only a recurrence of a sensual or emotional compulsion due to a kind of pseudo-atavism or to a developmental inhibition such as our forefathers probably, and our own small children doubtless, experience. The occasional reappearance of this rudimentary impulse and the tenacity with which it can persist are conditioned by an hypersensitive reaction of an abnormally nervous and perhaps prematurely developed organism to irritations which are generally not noticed or quickly overcome by the average European population. Or, on the other hand, the usual type of person can promptly repress such an abnormal reaction in the maze of highly complicated processes which mark the course of the sexual physiology and tumescence.

"Even if it were considered rash to speak of fetishism as a true atavism, it is still possible to look upon it as a congenital development. It is the infrequent development of a congenital rudiment which frequently had a general and, we might say, normal distribution in earlier epochs of history.

"It may well be that the insensitive and average man never notices such a detail, but for the man who loves with phantasy and rapt attention these susceptibilities become a definite center of gravitation in the highly complex constellation of his passionate feelings. An especially nervous person can find such a symbolism to be an absolutely indispensable element of attractiveness in the women he loves, once the symbolism has taken sufficient root in him. Finally, the fully captivated person looks upon the symbol as the chief thing and the person herself is no longer a source of interest, becomes simply an appendix to the symbol. Or the individual who was the love object passes completely into the background of the fetish lover's mind and the symbol alone becomes the goal and the sole source of sexual gratification. Although we may consider as diseased the tendency to find especial sexual attraction in the symbol of the love object, we must say that the genuine and complete perversion is represented only by the last type of case mentioned above, viz., the case in which only the symbol is capable of affording sexual satisfaction. In the less marked cases of this type of symbolism, it is still the woman who is sought, and procreation is essentially preserved. But if the woman is ignored and the symbol itself becomes an adequate and even welcome stimulus to detumescence then the condition is certainly a pathological one."

Havelock Ellis thus also sees the substitution of the symbol for the love partner as the pathological element of fetishism. He emphasizes the atavistic basis of foot fetishism, a point of view which approximates the sweaty-feet theory of Abraham and Freud. I would rather support the theory of Alfred Adler in the case of foot fetishism: whoever sucked his big toe as a baby will later become a foot fetishist. This point of view is more closely allied to my declaration that the fetish itself is a replica of the person's own erogenous zone. We love in the other person whatever we love in ourselves. We stimulate libido only in those zones of our partner whose activation in us promotes libido, too.

One will find that this law can be corroborated in the whole province of sexual life. There are, of course, all kinds of displacements and substitutions. If a naked foot made us happy in childhood, if we desired only to see the naked foot of another person, then it is possible that in adult life this libidinal charge is passed on to the shoe which clothes the foot. We have already seen, in Case 2, G. S., p. 7, how the fact that the body was clothed constituted the special source of animation. The reason is simply that the draping permits the phantasy to increase the voluptuousness of the draped object many fold.

If we study various cases of fetishism we will ever find that the tendency to flee from the female is of the utmost importance. I recall the well-known case of Moll, who exhibited a case of rose fetishism. The man lived in absolute abstinence. He never had intercourse with women and even declared that he was a mysogonist. One evening he saw a woman who was wearing a beautiful rose upon her breast and promptly fell in love—with the woman, but primarily with the rose. Secretly he soon engaged himself to this woman, but his desire was solely directed to her roses. He never rested until the roses she wore became his property. He would then take them home, smell them over and over again and thereby sense the deepest raptures. He finally collected quite a museum of roses with a deal of industry. I wish also to point out that this is a characteristic which we will observe time and again. This collecting of the symbolic objects is what I have called the harem cult of the fetishist. It never is absent in any case of genuine fetishism. It is a characteristic sign of the true bent and is at bottom the symbolic representation of the individual's latent Don Juan strivings. The fetish lover is a Don Juan type or has, at least, secret appetites of this kind. But they are at war with his inner morality. Instead of collecting women,[8] however, he collects fetishes.

Every fetish adept has his harem of handkerchiefs, drawers, shoes, braids, photographs, hair, corsets, garters, etc., etc. Each single fetish soon loses its enchanting qualities as a fetish and the devotee quickly and hungrily finds himself another sample only to drag forth the old one again after a while; all just like a pasha in his harem. There is always a favorite for the moment.

But to get back to our rose fetishist. Did he marry the woman whose roses he had learned to love so well that he had become engaged to their possessor? By no means. He did as all fetishists do. He gave some lame excuse for breaking off the engagement, gave up the woman and remained true to his roses. The fetish has fulfilled its duty. It kept the man from the woman and took the latter's place.

But behind this apparent paraphilia there is a secret anxiety. This man hides between Scylla and Charybdis, between satanical desires and puritanical tendencies. He is a Don Juan without the nerve to commit sin. The female appears to him devoid of any fascination because the seductive qualities have been violently passed on to a smaller object, the rose. It's no sin to kiss roses. Nor can the rose put his potency to the test. The rose as companion will never force him into the struggle of the sexes, the battle which the fetish lover always avoids.

Now, this also explains to us a form of fetishism which turns out not to be fetishism at all in the sense in which we here use the word. I mean the preference some men have for small, old, crippled, ugly, bent and short women who are cross-eyed and limp; for misshapen creatures, in a word. The famous case of the philosopher Descartes, who was attracted only by cross-eyed women, belongs in this group. I would like at this point also to point out that there are men who choose women who have one leg amputated or who wear crutches. In addition to the well-known and understandable infantile source of these cases (memory of an infantile sexual object), the majority of them probably have another motivation. The man feels sympathetic towards these deformed women. They are not accepted at the full female value. One of Merzbach's cases, of which I shall speak later, corroborates this supposition fully. Destiny has branded them and they are underrated. With such women, it is easier for the man to feel the full importance of his personality, a circumstance which plays a deciding rôle in the business of wooing and wedding a woman. Compared with such half-women, the man feels himself whole. This also gives us insight into the reason why some men are so potent when with prostitutes and such failures with decent women. This type of man so over-estimates the decent female that he feels inferior in her presence and this circumstance often precludes the possibility of any sexual aggression because potency and the feeling of superiority are intimately related feelings. In such cases, then, the man drops to the level of the "branded" woman, he makes her happy with his favor, whereas *he* is otherwise the one who is favored.[9]

We will always find in the cases of fetishism that are described, that the person in question emphasizes the fact that he has always lived in abstinence. Thus, Lippmann says of his case of pig-tail fetishism: "He never displayed the slightest trace of sensuality. Conversation about girls or about sexual matters held no interest for him. At the request of a friend he joined a fraternity which demanded abstinence in sexual matters as a condition of membership. He declared that such a condition was easy for him." But the fact that he was only repressing his sexuality is let out of the bag when we learn that, contrary to his usual habits, he once became drunk and in that condition sprang for the bar-maid, and tousled her hair. Such effects of alcohol, the banishment of inhibitions, apparent changes of character, can frequently be observed in sexual matters. For such persons chastity is practically a necessity for it protects them from such slips of conduct (cited after Merzbach: *Die krankhaften Erscheinungen des Geschlechtssinnes*, Alfred Hölder, 1909).

This patient further stated: "He never experienced any sensual attraction to a person of the opposite sex. This became especially clear to him once when there was a discussion in a society called Ethos on the difficulties of resisting seductive experiences. At that time he was imbued with an honest conviction when he stated that he could guarantee chastity as far as he were concerned, but he had no notion of what temptation meant to the others." We notice here that this patient has avoided women from earliest youth and the reason is palpably that he doesn't even wish to begin the battle of the sexes. He always fears the superiority of the female, just as I have explained it in the discussion about men preferring crippled women. One of Merzbach's patients, who sought out only deformed women as his sexual partners, stated that he was mightily inflamed whenever his partner and he had to go through all sorts of tricks with the cushions and bed linen to get the woman into the right position. "In addition to the sexual lust provoked, such handicapped creatures possessed the added virtue of feeling indebted. . . ." Manifestly, the patient laid the greatest store by the woman's thankfulness and his feelings of superiority. The fact that many men are potent with a prostitute, but impotent with a decent woman even in marriage, is reducible to this fine play of egoism.

I could buttress these statements sufficiently on the basis of many cases described by other authors. Regardless of whether there is a tendency to shoe nails, roses, handkerchiefs or corsets, one will always observe that these persons have a desire to avoid the woman. There is a marked chastity of living in contrast to the extravagance of their phantasies. It is always a battle between the satanic and the religious.

Erotic eccentricities (Eulenburg's "picacism") have nothing in common with fetishism. They are usually fixated infantile habits as I have sufficiently described in "Infantile Psychosexuality" of this series.

In defining the nature of fetishism, I wish to present further some cases from the *Sexual Pathology* of Magnus Hirschfeld. The first case reads:

"In another case a man was plagued with the obsession to sit down on any spot from which a woman had just arisen. He was usually able to effect his purpose even in well-filled street cars and trains and without being suspiciously noticed. The warmth imparted to the seat by the woman's buttocks often provoked an erection in him. But to sit down on a seat which had previously been occupied by a man called forth a wave of unpleasantness in him and finally became impossible. In hotels, trains and otherwise, he usually made use of women's toilets, but this habit not infrequently brought down hard words upon his head."

This man very probably had begun early in life to use the toilet immediately after a female member of the family had been there. The warmth of the seat then provoked pleasure in the boy. The contact with the seat doubtless kindled associations of contact with the female body (the well-known tertium defecations which plays such an important part in childhood). The repressed homosexuality is expressed in his disinclination to sit upon any seat previously occupied by a man. This is a typical case of "psycho-sexual infantilism" with repressed homosexuality and repressed anal sexuality.

We come to the second case of Hirschfeld:

"One of my patients, a Jewish business man, was filled with

a sadistic hatred against red hair. He nevertheless married a woman with fiery red hair. He rationalized this act with two excuses: He thought that he would lose his hatred through constant association with the object of his disgust in marriage. In addition, his wife brought so much money with her that he decided the red hair was worth the price. And, lastly, all those whom he had questioned found red hair rather pleasing if anything. He had come to me because he wanted to have his distaste cured by hypnosis. Before undertaking anything else, I suggested to the wife that she dye her hair, but this she stoutly refused to do. She conceived her husband's distaste as a personal slight or, at best, as a whim which he would easily give up "if he really loved her." Many similar cases occur everywhere, with the public sadly underestimating fetishistic compulsions in its ignorance. The marriage was dissolved."

This is a case of "partialism," a love condition of a highly individual kind, but negative; similar to what Hirschfeld has described as "anti-fetishism." The man evidently fights off an irresistible susceptibility to red-haired women (infantile memory?), and his method is to transform the leaning into its opposite. He nevertheless succumbs to the seductive effects of the red hair and then rationalizes his marriage in a rather sorry way by saying he wants to "accustom" himself to red hair by this marriage. But his inhibitory mechanisms are found to be stronger than his leanings. This man could easily be cured by psychoanalysis, just as psychoanalysis can uncover the psychological background of his conduct. The case does not belong to the group of true fetishism.

Hirschfeld's third case reads:

"I now come to an example of hair fetishism. The patient, who has been under my care for over ten years, is a prominent government official of fifty years. He relates the following:

"When he was seven years old, the children were all in bed one evening when their young governess came to them and embraced them one by one because she was leaving. The moment when our patient held her hair is still clear in his mind. When he began to have waves of sexual appetite during puberty, his passion was always aroused by the sight of a lovely head of hair. From that time on, he was enkindled only by men's hair, whereas women's hair created no stir in him. More, he was interested only in smooth, brown-black hair which was parted. The patient also casts his eyes upon the forelock, but that is not of such importance to him. He is distinctly fussy about how far the part is pulled to one side. He prefers young and bashful men, but insists that they must act naturally. He finds the heights of pleasure and constant sexual provocation in acting as barber to someone. He executes this as follows: Standing behind the man, he moistens the hair with oil and pomade which, along with a comb, he always carries in his pocket, and then he draws a part through the hair. When he has drawn the part back as far as the neck, he gets an emission, but even stroking the smooth hair, smoothing it down, has this effect, especially if he lightly touches the back of the individual with his body while approaching for the operation. He never exposes his genitals for shame, but he believes that this would enhance his feelings. He himself has a part in his hair and very frequently cares for his hair, but he gets much more enjoyment from executing the operation on others. The very sight of a part in someone's hair is enough to cause him to run after that person and speak to him. During the time when he was a young officer, he always drew a careful part in his hair before meeting any girl and having intercourse; and the moment before the orgasm he would picture a very straight and lovely part as the symbol of most acute pleasure. The patient states that he has no understanding for the desire on the part of some to cut off hair and keep it as a remembrance or because of a compulsion, yet he can imagine "that he would cut off a lock from the head of a very dear friend who were dying and would be lost to him forever." His chief associations pass from the sight of a fine part back to the most enjoyable hours he had experienced in parting the hair of young men, "an expression of the highest level of his thoughts and feelings, a world in which he moved as within a charmed circle the center of which was represented by a well-drawn, straight, brown-black part, the very focus of a universe in which but little light disclosed pulsating life shining forth from deepest night." Because of his eccentric habits, the patient had become noticeable and in the places which he frequents he has become known as "the barber." These places, also, by no means reflect his aristocratic origin, but are of a low-grade atmosphere which he prefers."

This case, also, has little to do with genuine fetishism. It is rather a typical case of "psycho-sexual infantilism" with homosexuality.

The reader has doubtless become anxious to read a typical case of true fetishism. Somewhat later I shall produce the exhaustive analyses of such cases, but at this point I wish to insert a very characteristic case of Paul Garnier's,[10] which will serve even further to describe and delimit our subject.

Case 3. The twenty-six-year-old writer, Louis X., had publicly masturbated in the Park of Vincennes and was arrested on a charge of disorderly conduct. The official physicians, Paul Garnier and Legras examined him as to his mental condition and gave the following as part of their opinion:

X. comes of a wealthy family and has a distinct degenerative heredity from his mother's side. He nevertheless discloses no especial signs of degeneracy. On the contrary, he gives the appearance of being remarkably well-kept and elegant. He wears patent leather shoes which are noticeably shiny. He carries a *pince-nez* and a monocle without, however, being near-sighted, but only to affect an interesting attitude. His carriage is quiet and his movements controlled. His voice is monotonous and somewhat feminine. He is tall, slender, and wears a light blonde beard. Because of their excessive cultivation, his hands give the impression of delicate, female hands. His finger nails, lastly, are so long that they incapacitate him for any kind of manual work whatever.

He has always enjoyed the best of physical health, but psychically he shows considerable anomaly. He was always fearful and never manifested any degree of aggressiveness. "We never saw him laugh," said his brother. He lives alone and passes his days behind the locked door of his room. He had always exhibited a flair for the paradoxical, for irony and depreciation. On the other hand, he had never given anyone the slightest cause for censure, neither at home or in school. But this is due more to his passivity than to his ambition.

His habits were always bizarre, and everyone made fun of his manners. He was hardly twelve years old when he was already paying extraordinary attention to his personal care, anointed his body with pomade, powdered it afterwards and was constantly admiring himself in the mirror like a vain woman. It was laughable to see him try to protect his complexion when in the country and he invariably hid himself from the direct rays of the sun. His brother often found him striking a grotesque pose in bed, his head covered with a sheet, lying flat on his belly.

At the age of 13, X. was first introduced to onanism in school. At home he would wait for his parents to go out and then masturbate in peace. From this time on, he achieved an orgasm while masturbating only if he could have a pair of patent leather shoes before him.

This habit of staring at shoes had been present early in childhood, however. With exception of manual masturbation, all other forms of onanism disgusted him. He reached the age of seventeen and still had no noticeable yearning for the female sex. They sent him to the university where he studied law, but his heart was not there. He was, however, attracted to writing and decided to become an author. He then published several pieces of his work, but they were prompt failures. It was during his period of military service that he tried to initiate heterosexual intercourse, especially because his comrades made fun of his girlish bashfulness. He found no gratification whatever in coitus, however, and returned to masturbation. After his one-year term of service he got himself ready for the doctorate and also published two novels which gradually sank into oblivion, unnoticed. His favorite books were the works of suggestive authors.

At twenty-two he felt the first breath of a nebulous desire for passive pederasty and made bashful but fruitless attempts to placate these wishes. He then began to enjoy admiring elegant and handsome young fellows and his raptures were distinctly increased when they happened to be wearing patent leather shoes. He would picture these patent leather shoes to himself when he masturbated at home, and invariably used the most recent example he had seen.

He was always convinced of his powers as a literary possibility and knew well how to pull the wool over his parents' eyes for four years. He declared that he was working in the office of an attorney and would leave the house regularly at the expected hour each morning. He said that he was going to the office and always used all kinds of tricks to keep his mother and his brother off his track. Arrived at home, he would drop remarks about his studies and how intensively he was working. He would even tell the family about the successes his writings were enjoying. When he left the house each day, however, he would actually go to various museums of the city or would go collecting butterflies. On these trips he was vainly in search of his ideal, a creature which he described as follows: "I yearned for the company of an elegant and cultured young man. I desired that we should meet daily and pass many hours together chatting on literature, philosophy, etc. Now and again, during these hours, it was my desire that we should exchange caresses and pet a little, and finally masturbate each other. I would never ask my ideal to gratify my tendencies to pederasty, the disgusting details might wreck our friendship. Nevertheless, I have desired to be possessed by a man at least once in my life, if only to experience the feeling. But none of these dreams are destined ever to come true."

Dejected at the failure of his literary ventures, tortured by the fear that his complicated web of lies would be discovered for what it was, disconsolate over the frustration of the pederastic dreams which disappeared like a fata morgana whenever he attempted to realize them in more or less burlesque adventures, he came home, became melancholy and suffered from an obstinate frontal headache. To gratify his over-running passion, he suddenly decided to substitute a billiard ball for his penis. The first one he tried was too large and injured him. Finally he found one of the desired calibre and went through a procedure which he describes as follows: Squatting low, wearing a pair of pink, silk bloomers which I had bought some time previously, I vaselined the billiard ball and stuck it in my anus. I carefully protected the silk pantalets from becoming soiled by covering them with a linen cloth. Then I would press the billiard ball brusquely against my anus with my left hand, so that it would almost snap in. Meanwhile, I held the bloomers with my right. At that moment I had but half an erection, but the real thrill came when the ball was finally in my rectum. Then while I masturbated with my right hand, I tried to get the billiard ball out of my rectum with the left. When I had done this, I repeated the procedure and often carried it out as many as six to twelve times. My delight was especially great if I was able to snap the ball in with one stroke. I always tried to withhold the ejaculation as long as possible and derived the most gusto from an orgasm when I held the ball firmly between my buttocks after the last expulsion."

His descriptions of the sensations he experienced during this act are very complicated and much less clear than the masturbatory images of former years. His pleasure was a double one: I— Whenever he would introduce the billiard ball into his rectum, he would picture to himself the penis of the last object he had seen which had particularly caught his eye with elegance and patent leather shoes. "They always appeared to me in rows of 4, 5, 6, until I had chosen the most attractive one of the lot and thereby achieved an orgasm." 2—He imagined that while he was going through the pederastic act, one of his favorites was masturbating him.

Nevertheless, he was not completely alleviated by these extraordinary procedures and went so far as to insert stereotyped advertisements in the public print which read about as follows: "I hereby offer my buttocks to handsome men with patent leather shoes." He also didn't hesitate to make the most disgusting promises, and even while writing the words "patent leather shoes" he got an erection. Patent leather shoes was an obsessional idea with him. He stared at the shoes of every man he passed on the street. The trinity: patent leather shoes; fine, young man; elegance led to an immediate erection. He would stand for hours before shoe stores, go blocks out of his way to get to one, and had the greatest difficulty pulling himself out of the state of drunkenness which such sights brought over him. The shinier the shoes were, the more fascinated he became, and at night he dreamed that he had robbed the store of the patent leather shoes. He finally decided to buy a pair of them himself, ones similar to those the young cadets wear. What followed this purchase was a delirious possession which he describes as follows: "In overheated excitement I ran home with them. My heart was nearly beating through my breast, I locked the door in order to enjoy my possession to the full. I placed the new shoes on the silk bloomers. My sexual excitement suddenly achieved a maximum in an instantaneous erection. 'Finally, finally, I have you,' I cried. Before retiring, I placed the shoes on the little night table where they could be brightly lighted up by the lamp. I couldn't take my eyes from the wonderful sight and my sensual animation was expressed in a permanent erection. The following morning, I had to look at them long and hard before I could decide to leave them. From then on I spent some time each day looking at my shoes after I had taken them out of their box."

X. protects his patent leather shoes with the jealous attention of a lover. One day the maid had put the shoes in another place when she had cleaned up the room. This cut him terribly and thereafter he locked them safely in a closet.

His greatest pleasure consists in pulling them out each day and gloating over them. He seeks out everything which will increase their polish. He stands them on the window sill in order thus to enjoy the reflected glint of the sun on them. He marvels at them. He becomes so fascinated that he gets a spontaneous orgasm. He considered for a long time, however, whether or not he should put the shoes on and go out with them. He finally decided to put them on and wear a riding habit. He hoped thereby to create a stir and thus catch the eye and the desire of one of his favorite types. Quite naturally, he did not achieve his purpose. "I returned home," he writes, "powerfully excited and couldn't eat a bite. Of course, plenty of people turned about to look at me on the street, but they didn't give me any thrills since they were not my type. I also noticed a slight crack in one of the shoes and that depressed me as much as if I had seen the first wrinkle in the face of a beloved woman. I have not put them on since then."

But sight alone is not the only portal to his pleasures. The very odor of his shoes can bring about an immediate orgasm. He derives the utmost joy from smelling at them, and touching them is rapture. Upon waking in the morning, he takes them in the bed and places them between his legs, but he feels that he must control himself to some extent as otherwise he might damage them. X. draws the following picture of his relations with the shoes:

"I pull on my pink, silk bloomers and then put on my patent leather shoes. I climb up on two chairs, spread my legs and then admire myself in the mirror. I masturbate, fixating my buttocks, my legs and especially my shoes in the mirror all the while. At such a moment I am in love with myself, I could pet and hug my own body as I look at it in the mirror. This sight can sometimes so excite me that I frequently don't need the billiard ball at all in order to achieve an orgasm. In this position, it is always my purpose to direct the stream of semen that spurts out into the opening of the shoes and if I succeed in doing this I am seized with a paroxysm of lascivious lust. Another time, I will rub my anus, my legs and my buttocks with a shoe just before ejaculation, meanwhile steadily staring at the reflection from the shiny surface of the other. But I most usually place each shoe on a separate chair near the window, turn them until they reflect the light the brightest and then take up a distance which will just permit me to squirt into the opening of the shoe. The moment the semen touches the shoe I feel not only a sensation of fullest gratification, but also one of complete triumph."

Finally, X. attempted the realization of his phantasies. He went walking in his patent leather shoes. He saw a young man on a bicycle who pleased him considerably. The cyclist turned

about and looked at his shoes. That was his ideal! In the throes
of his excitement, he displayed his genitals, but his disillusionment
was great when the other coolly removed himself from the scene.
The result of this episode was his arrest upon the charge of a
passer-by.

The opinion of both specialists directed attention to the
hereditary stigmatisation of the patient, the compulsive character of his conduct, and pleaded for the internment of the
patient in an institution. The court followed the advice of the
specialists.

This remarkable and almost unique case discloses the characteristic signs of true fetishism. In the first place, we note the
steady avoidance of the female. X. tried coitus once or twice,
but it gave him no pleasure. He then elaborated his homosexual components and acts as if he is searching for a partner.
But he never finds one. He has no force, no aggressiveness,
and actually passes up any opportunity which offers itself.
Whenever a young man gives him an opening, he finds that the
gentleman falls short of his ideal. Succinctly, he avoids reality
and lives in a world of phantasy.

The true fetishist expresses himself in masturbation. There
is no fetishism without onanism. X., too, is quite a devotee of
masturbation and reality has lost all value for him. He walks
in a world of dreams.

But this world of dreams reaches all the way back to his
childhood. Like all other cases of fetishism, X. is a typical
case of psycho-sexual infantilism. At the same time, he suffers from impulsive conduct. He actually could have stolen the
shoes in the store windows. He finally did exhibit his genitals
publicly in the Bois de Vincennes. Whoever among my readers has studied Volumes V [11] and VI [12] will easily understand
the complicated procedures of our patient. These shoes are the
representatives of two people (perhaps the parents). They are
for him the symbols of certain persons or experiences. By
means of emotional displacements, mighty affects, having their
origin in earliest childhood, are apparently drawn from their
object of original attachment and transposed to these shoes.
The latter then become idols, real gods, genuine fetishes.

There is in all cases of fetishism a tendency to the formation of series and a sort of harem. The individual seems to be true to his love object. The construction of a series of love objects is exhibited in the person's choice of a partner by first imagining a whole row of possibilities and then, during masturbation, picking out one of them as a favorite. This repetition compulsion of the onanistic act indicates the individual's deficient sexual gratification. His phantasies do not achieve the desired effect, i.e., the original goal has been replaced by a fictitious one. Gratification is therefore possible only by exhaustion. That is why most of these cases go to excess in masturbation and often succumb to onanism as often as twelve times a day.

Their masturbation contains, also, an impulse to exhibitionism, to public masturbation, to a symbolic representation of their secret wishes. This patient X. advertises himself in the papers, he makes himself noticeable, and finally exhibits his genitals in a public place.

All these patients suffer from the irresistible power of a fermenting secret. They hide themselves away in shyness to live in their world of dreams, but there is another force which impels them to betray themselves, to communicate themselves to others, to reveal their secret symbolically or directly to all the world.

In X.'s case, too, we see him roaming about in a sort of twilight state (the hyponoic state of Kretschmer), similar to the conditions we have found in an examination of impulsive acts. We have observed in him an irresistible drive to make-believe and a narcissism which expresses itself in onanism before a mirror. Narcissistic love is present in every case of fetishism and the habit of masturbating before a mirror is very characteristic.

In other words, Louis is a genuine fetish lover. It is not irrelevant at this point to interpret the symbolic meaning of his patent leather shoes and his divers manipulations. The reader will doubtless already have thought that the shoes probably represent his parents, that they are pluralistic phantasies and may be a condensation of birth phantasies and other sexual processes. In some of my analyses later on, I will be able completely to interpret similar cases. X. was not analyzed, but was sent to an asylum. It would have been possible to free him from his morbid leanings by a proper analysis.

Before we define fetishism formally, it will pay us to consider another interesting case. In the Archives internationales de neurologie, Nr. 1, 1922, Viollet reports the following case:

Case 4. Mr. D., twenty-five, is the eldest son of a family of three children. The one sister died at eighteen and the other is sixteen years old. His father suffers from chronic bronchitis "et a des habitudes d'éthylisme." His mother is a moron, brutal and irritable. There are no other hereditary stigmata.

D. was never seriously ill, but he was always somewhat delicate. During the war he was called to the colors three years after his class.

Shortly after being conscripted, he married and now has a four-month-old baby which shows a spina bifida incompleta and an atresia ani.

He states that he masturbated as early as eight years of age and claims that he came by it alone. He says that he has either of two images during onanism: the one is that he masturbates on ("sur") a pillow, a child's feather pillow, the other is a picture of a little girl who lives near by.

These images he has been using while masturbating ever since childhood. If he happens to meet the little girl, who is now twenty-five, on the street, he immediately has an erection, runs home, pulls out his little pillow, hides himself usually in the attic, and masturbates. When he is about to have the orgasm, her image stands almost physically before him and he experiences deepest pleasure.

The reason he hides himself is because his mother always beat him brutally whenever she would catch him masturbating. Once his wife helped his mother beat him fearfully. He has been living, since marriage, together with his wife at his parents' house. He is greatly afraid of his mother. His wife he finds quite pretty, but she is quite agitated over his masturbation.

He has intercourse with his wife every day, but he finds that less enjoyable than when he is alone with his little pillow. One day his wife found him masturbating and invited him to give it up and lie down with her, but when he tried to have intercourse he promptly lost his erection. That has happened often and D. states that whenever he has an erection and has his pillow he can never finish the act by means of normal coitus.

He must always have that special pillow. When he goes to sleep he has a clean pillow slip beneath his head, but when he uses the pillow for masturbating, he pulls a dirty, old, unwashed pillow slip over it. Once his wife hid the pillow under the mattress and he searched for it frantically, but he did not masturbate without it. It was only after he had found it that he masturbated again.

The image of the girl can cause him to have an erection, but he cannot masturbate without the pillow. This girl who plays such a large part in his phantasies has never been the object of D's actual attentions. On the contrary, he once even refused to dance with her and has never so much as thought of having intercourse with her. He invariably pictures her at her present age and dressed in the clothes she wears in the street. It is interesting to learn that he could have married this girl who comes from the same stratum of society as himself, but he never took the opportunity to make her acquaintance. She does not exist for him outside his onanistic phantasies, nor does he love her.

The author of the report was not able to decide just what form of obsessional imagination this case represented. He wrote: "Il m'a été impossible de découvrir décisevement s'il s'agissait là d'une obsession."

D. is an anxious, monosyllabic type, quite good-natured, but he probably did not understand the meaning of the questions which the author put to him.

It is nevertheless important to remember that D. also masturbated without having seen the girl just previously. His one condition was that he had to be alone, undisturbed and with his little pillow. In that state, he did not even need the phantasy of the woman. The pillow and being alone were absolute conditions. But with his mother and his wife around, he was finally unable to find the slightest peace at home; and thus he was one day observed by two women masturbating in a little side street near his home. Upon their charges, he was arrested.

Viollet hastened to remark that it was not D.'s desire to masturbate publicly, as the court had assumed, but that he had simply hoped, at the time he was seen by the two women, to find the quiet in this place that he wanted. If he had been able to masturbate at home, he would not have chosen the alley for the purpose.

D. is of masculine build, is a steady and capable worker and earns a livelihood for himself and his family. He is by no means an asocial individual. Nevertheless he appears to be a man of low grade mentality. He has had a meagre education, is dull mentally, displays abnormal anxiety and possesses a very weak will. In addition to this he is addicted to alcohol. That is, he is like many men in Burgundy. They drink their red wine and crew on bread crusts—usually many bread crusts. He is, in short, not an alcoholic in the strict sense of the word. He neither exhibits symptoms of alcoholism "nor can alcohol be blamed for any part in his case."

In view of the fact that D. did not masturbate during his military service and during the period when his wife had hidden the pillow, Viollet concluded that simply burning the pillow would bring the patient's masturbation to a stop, that D.'s desire would cease. The author further thought that it behooved the two women to become a little more considerate of the patient.

This is doubtless a typical case of fetishism, i.e., a rudimentary form. D. was able to marry and to have regular intercourse, but he was not able to give up his fetish. We are here clearly able to see two forms of displacement of affect: the one towards the girl and the other towards the pillow. In both cases, we are dealing with a regression back to an infantile ideal, very probably the mother. But the formation of series in phantasies is missing. His marriage appears to have precluded the development of a complete fetishism. In this case we also observe that, instead of the formation of series or a harem of fetishes, the patient is quite faithful to his love object: the pillow, or the girl. D. resembles Louis X. in this respect. It is probable, however, that a deep analysis in this case would have been able to discover serial formations. This case also was ended by the "force of fermenting secrets." D. was prompted to carry out an exhibitionistic act and was arrested. The therapy which the author suggests (burning the pillow) seems to me to be laughable and doomed to failure. Were it to be carried out, the patient would probably replace the lost object by a harem of new pillows.

We are now enabled to come to the following conclusions. In a case of true fetishism we can observe:

1. The fetish replaces the sexual partner. This initiates a manifest retreat from active heterosexual activity. The male fetish devotee either flees from or depreciates the female. The female fetishist is either anæsthetic when with a man or she avoids coitus entirely.

2. The fetishist suffers from a form of psycho-sexual infantilism and expresses this infantilism in his onanistic phantasies.

3. There is usually present a tendency to construct a series of fetishes (the harem cult of the fetishist).

4. The individual's tendency to repeat the forbidden infantile pleasure leads him to impulsive acts of all kinds. Fetishists are vagrants, kleptomaniacs, exhibitionists, etc.

5. The fetish itself is determined in its choice by emotional displacements and symbolization. It gradually absorbs the whole sexual activity of the individual.

6. Fetishism is a complicated compulsion neurosis and also serves the purposes of asceticism. Fetishism is repentance and pleasure together.

7. The impulsive acts take place in a kind of twilight state. The fetishist is a day-dreamer to whom the borders between reality and the dream world become hazy.

8. There is also an invariable criminal component present (the sadistic traits of Mr. F.).

9. Fetishism is a kind of religion.

10. The symbolism of fetishism can be interpreted and cleared up only by a deep driving psychoanalysis.

These conclusions will serve for the present. In the following chapters we shall have occasion to make important additions to these ten points.

II

THE ANALYSIS OF AN INDIVIDUAL LOVE
CONDITION

In employing the expression fetishism, as we have, only for
such cases of severe paraphilia in which the fetish totally replaces the sexual object and forms the nucleus of a complicated system, we must necessarily reject a number of other eccentricities which have heretofore been described as fetishistic.
We here arrive at a well-known province, that of the specific
love condition. In reference to this condition, I need only call
the reader's attention to *Frigidity in Woman* (the chapters on
"Love At First Sight" and "The Individual Love Condition")
and *Impotence in the Male* (the chapter on "The Conditions of
Male Potency") of this series.

The field of "partialisms" is practically inexhaustible.
Everybody has his own sexual predilections and points of
preference, the basis of which is partly constitutional and partly
conditional. But the more deeply I delve into my material, the
more surprised I am at the inconceivable wealth of "erogenous
zones" which we possess and the number of individual love
conditions.

It shall not be my purpose to consider the divers forms of
partialism which are scientifically of little interest and can have
value only as curiosities. On the basis of a few analyses, I
shall try to show how complicated the situations sometimes are
and what abstruse determinants often appear for the partialism
in question. The example I choose here is the analysis of a
case of so-called "breast and buttocks fetishism" which, being
coupled with impotence, could easily have misled one to considering it as a case of true fetishism.

Case 5. Mr. I. O., thirty-eight years old, a bank official, consulted me because of absolute impotence. He has been unable to
perform intercourse for the past two years. Not long ago he still

had a weak erection, but it ended in an ejaculatio præcox. Now he is not able to produce even this weak erection.

He states that he masturbated only a year, between the ages of fifteen and sixteen, and that he then gave it up. When asked about his phantasies and his love conditions, he confessed that he remembered a scene which once excited him considerably. This scene he must always picture to himself during intercourse. He was seventeen years old and worked in a tailor's shop. He saw that the tailors often grasped the girls by the breasts or by the buttocks and since then, he says, these memories have been his sexual conditions. He invariably imagines that he is standing behind a girl and grasps her by the breasts. Without this fondling, he was always impotent and now not even this image helps him.

He readily accepted analysis as a means of cure.

He relates the obligatory but unimportant story of his early life. There were seven children. He was the youngest and was pampered. He was never beaten and states that he first was introduced to onanism at fifteen by a schoolmate. He soon gave it up.

He exhibits marked resistance to the analysis.

He is convinced that he cannot be helped. He does not doubt my ability and my good will, but thinks, nevertheless, that his cause is lost. He is told that he is really afraid of what's coming and that that is the real reason why he is considering breaking off the analysis.

He reports that for eight years (between twenty and twenty-eight) he regularly visited a certain blonde prostitute who attracted him considerably, to such an extent, as a matter of fact, that he was never impotent with her. He nevertheless performed a certain special ceremonial whenever he was with her, otherwise he never got an erection. He placed her beside himself in a naked state before a mirror. He then went behind her and gasped her by the breasts. He remained in this position for a while and then grasped her by the buttocks. Finally, intercourse would be effected in the usual position. With other prostitutes it frequently happened that he was impotent, but with his blonde he was always potent.

"Did this prostitute look like anyone who was prominent in your childhood life?"

He said no, but then bethought himself:

"I find that she is remarkably like my sister who is five years older than myself. That is, not so much in appearance as in her movements, expression, lovely character. . . ."

He thus confesses the possibility of a fixation to an older sister (the patient, by the way, has no knowledge of Freud).

He reports further that he has also frequently masturbated in recent years and that he must take up a curious position while doing so. He places his erected penis as far back between his legs as he can and then rubs it at the root until he ejaculates.

Suddenly he remembers that an uncle once forbade him to masturbate and told him all kinds of stories about what diseases he would have if he continued. This uncle died when he was eight years old. In other words, he had masturbated before he was eight and had already been warned of what the results would be if he persisted.

Now we understand why he insists repeatedly that masturbation has made him impotent. His guilty feelings spring from his childhood experiences.

He is a distinct slave of his family and knows nothing but the family. He lives with his mother and an unmarried sister with whom he is constantly quarreling. On the slightest provocation they can make the biggest scenes. He has often thought of marrying her off, but she is very discriminating and turns all wooers down. An older sister is very well married and quite well to do. The one at home will not live below the social status of her married sister. He once thought: when my sister marries, I'll live with her. The thought surprised him very much, since he thought that he would be glad to get rid of her.

He relates hesitatingly that he once dreamed he was having intercourse with his sister and that the memory of the dream was very painful to him. He treats every woman like a sister, femininity is "taboo" for him.

This gives us some understanding of why he must approach the woman from behind. He cannot look her in the face and maintain the fiction that she is, symbolically, his sister.

He once fell in love with a "sister of mercy" in the hospital and the bridge of associations offered by the word sister helped him into this. He kissed her when they were on an outing together and felt nothing but devotion to her. An inexplicable anxiety and the fear of making a fool of himself nevertheless withheld him from trying to have intercourse with her.

Spontaneously he tells of a fondness he once had for a schoolmate. A strong homosexual component thus comes to light. A few days ago he went to a Turkish bath and it is plain that the men he saw there excited him somewhat, for while he was washing himself with soap, he ran his finger into his rectum and said, "That's the way the homos do it." Then a wave of revulsion came over him. Otherwise, however, he has nothing against homosexuals. On the contrary, he feels that he must pity them.

His preferred posterior position is also illuminated by his homosexual instincts. He apparently also thinks of a man when in this position. He often used to place his penis between a prostitute's legs from behind and would thus achieve a greater erection than otherwise. Formerly he was able, by this trick, to achieve intercourse.

The patient remembers that he was always placed on the pot until he was five years old, because his parents were afraid that he might fall into the toilet. He shared this anxiety even during the first years that he went to school and actually defecated in his pants one day in an emergency.

Since his sisters also used the pot at that time, it is understandable that he often observed them in this position. It is probable that this sight—observing his sister from behind—was the origin of his paraphilia.

He presents numerous idiosyncrasies which have persisted since childhood. Thus, for example, he cannot eat bread and butter nor any Swiss cheese, because the odor is unpleasant to him. Closer probing discloses the fact that the odor is unpleasant because it reminds him of the odor given off by the vagina. He remembers a vulgar verse he once heard in school, which made a terrific impression on him: "Old Swiss cheese and girls' holes stink, but just the same they're great I think. . . ."

It is not a great step from such a memory to the phantasy of cunnilingus. He confesses that he has always been filled with such phantasies, but that he has always thought he could do it only on a clean, appetizing girl. Prostitutes were always somewhat disgusting to him and he never had anything to do with any other kind of woman.

He produces a wealth of memories which prove how greatly he loved his sister and how much he leans upon her. He always used to meet her after office hours, divided every tasty morsel with her, used to walk only with her, etc.

He wants information on a rather curious phenomenon. He states that he feels compelled to worry about what would happen if this or that brother-in-law or even his mother should die. He says that he cannot protect himself from these death ideas. The following dream of the patient's gives us a little light on the subject.

I found myself in a house—I don't know whether it was mine or some other house—where I felt very comfortable. The socialistic congressman Domes (whom I don't know at all) also lived there. He, however, was a stranger there, whereas I was quite at home. Domes was relieved of duty as a farm hand. My brother-in-law, Max W., was also relieved of serving because, as a merchant, he had planted a very small part of the large piece of property he had in the Prater (a large park in Vienna—Translator). I thought my brother-in-law was quite clever in getting himself exempted because he had made use of this miserably small piece of land. Suddenly I see my brother-in-law as if he were in Domes's place. He had joined the colors. I called attention to the fact that my brother-in-law was a smart man because, contrary to my brother's luck, he had got himself exempted just because of that little lot.

Just before this dream he had a waking dream:

My brother calls me to the telephone and says: "Guess who's calling you? The Kaiser!" I was quite overjoyed at this and awoke.

The Kaiser in the dream represents the controlling power, the guiding thought here, the person who is loved above all others. We shall soon learn who this person is. The next dream reveals to us that it was his favorite sister who was married to Mr. W.

The house in question in this dream is the house of his sister. There he is at home and his brother-in-law is the real intruder. This congressman Domes died not long ago. He had once heard him speak at a meeting and envied him. His brother-in-law W. has a very large penis and he had heard his sister complain that her husband gave her no peace. It went so far that his family intervened and begged W. to have some consideration for the woman. This evidence of capacity animated him, who was impotent, tremendously. He found his sister quite reduced physically, thought she looked badly and even discussed the possibility of a divorce with her since she was said to feel so badly about her lot.

His brother-in-law had often emphasized the fact to him that he (the brother-in-law) could cohabit whenever he had the desire. He was a fast worker in the "vineyard (Weinberg) of the Lord." His brother's wife had died. But if the husband of his sister were to fall in battle (he was later on the Western front where he was seriously wounded), he would now be at home with her and would have been rid of both his brother-in-law and his jealousy. Wherefore, the death wishes against his brother-in-law who was so potent and a whole he-man, whereas he felt himself inferior and impotent.

The next dream leads us still deeper into the complicated problems of his parapathia:

After dinner I went to the Ungargasse to the riding academy. Before the gate I pulled off my regular shoes, apparently getting ready to go to sleep. I was afraid of a few of the military persons going in and out the gate. After sun-down I picked up my shoes to put them on and noticed that there was also a pair of new "Christian" half shoes, brown, soft, canvas-like material. I wanted to take these, too, and leave, but I couldn't walk away barefoot. So I sat down to put on my shoes with the new, half shoes beside me. It took me about half an hour to pull on the right one, it being already dark. At that moment along came a big, coarse man with a blouse on—I thought he was the color sergeant—and asked gruffly after picking up the half shoes, "Where did you get these shoes?" I was so scared, I said they belonged to me. He turned the shoes over to look for the "Christian" mark which I noticed then for the first time. I was so afraid that I thought that was the end of me and was about to let him know that I had found the shoes lying on the spot, when he said: "Well, if you like them, you can keep them." I was also somewhat familiar with him in order to show him that we were brothers in arms, although I was only a corporal. During this conversation, I began to pull on the left shoe, but the tongue was a little loose and I had to fasten it by pulling the string through about eight or ten eyelets. After I had put the shoe on, I noticed that the tongue, which I had laced inside, was now out, and that it barely hung to the shoe by one eyelet. So I took the shoe off again to begin from the beginning. All this time, the other man stalked up and down, stopping now and again to bore me through with his gaze. I couldn't stand his stare and was altogether very much frightened. I thought to myself that he looked rather intelligent, that he was, perhaps, an officer, a captain, and that he was angry with me for having been so familiar with him. I thought I had better be more formal with him the next time I spoke with him. Then I awoke.

The color-sergeant of the dream reminds him of his father. His father was just as strict with him and minded the morals of the family pretty well. The color-sergeant is here the representative of authority (father—physician—God). His anxiety with this man reminded him of an experience he had had during his military days. He had received the order to buy up some foodstuffs for his company in the neighboring countryside. He then used some of these provisions to supply his family. During one of these buying trips, he was stopped by a policeman, arrested and brought before a military tribunal. He suffered terrific anxiety at the time. He was afraid of every and any kind of official office. In this dream, he is afraid of the men who go and come. That is his anxiety of homosexuality, since riding is a symbol of coitus. He went there to learn how to cohabit. There are two ways of doing it. One is to do it normally (regular store shoes), and the other is to do it the way the roués do it (elegant half shoes). But how can he do it like an old roué if he is impotent? He is always attracted to the wives and sweethearts of his friends and acquaintances. It would tickle him to flirt with them. He has had phantasies of these men dying and the women then falling to him. But how can he tread the moral path without protecting himself with impotence? His emasculation is symbolized distinctly enough by his scene with the shoes. Putting it in is still possible for him, but he evidently has trouble keeping it in. The right and the left shoe are dealt with separately according to the symbolism of left and right in the dream.[1] He can still make it on the right, but on the left, the tongue gives him trouble.

At this point the dream becomes somewhat transparent and reveals some relationship between his tongue and his impotence as well as his "specific phantasies." With considerable resistance, he confesses that he has frequently turned the thoughts of fellatio and cunnilingus over in his mind. He would gladly carry out cunnilingus on a virgin or a "pure girl." He also permitted fellatio on himself once, but desisted from repeating the experience, because he thought that it "must be terribly harmful."

I ventilated a suspicion that some important experience in his life had something to do with this dream, but he denied this. He knew of no color-sergeant and believed that the whole dream was nothing more than a memory of his military days. Only a hazy memory of having once crawled into his sister's bed as a child and being caught by his father. He remembers also having been told to get out of his mother's bed (riding academy). Before the eyes of his father (boring glances) he was always fearful. His father had always demanded of the children that they speak formally with him, whereas in other families he knew that the children were quite familiar with their parents.

A much more important meaning of this dream will become apparent to us only later.

The next night he dreamed:

I came to the office twenty minutes after eight i.e., twenty minutes late. In order not to meet the general manager, I made a short cut through the chief clerk's office. He very courteously wanted to know what I meant by coming late. I mumbled some kind of excuse. . . .

Again we find the old anxiety and fearfulness of the slightest authority, the fear of being caught in transgression.

The analysis progresses. He remembers various infantile wishes and phantasies. Thus, he had often thought of stabbing (raping) his elder sister and then landing in jail. His relatives would visit him there, but he would remain silent and would speak no word. His family would then suffer for shame.

His parents were not happy together. His father was very strict and found much for which to reproach his mother. It appears that the boy very early nurtured ideas of revenge upon his father and these go well with the latent sadism shown in his rape phantasies. The latter even reappeared a few years ago and were repressed again. It is possible that the war helped to reactivate them.

Whenever he returns to his desk from the toilet, he is rather ashamed to meet any of the women in the office, especially if they happen to have provoked his fancy. He then feels as if he had just done something dirty or forbidden.

To-day he had a day-dream of a lost ring and reports a compulsion idea in connection with it which is not at all seldom. I repeat in his words:

"I imagined that whenever I passed by an open window, my *pure* solitaire would fall from my finger and roll in the gutter. Then I want to call my younger sister to watch that no one picks the ring up and runs off with it. In the office, this phantasy is related to a Miss L.

"I trust both these women and consider them both sensible and energetic. At the same time I am afraid that the ring will be lost and will never be found again."

The first association is his pure, white diamond. He manifestly doesn't want to lose his purity. Miss L. is a poor, little girl of thirty summers who has managed to retain her virtue. His sister is also virtuous. He has constructed a condition by which his impotence is determined, viz., "As long as I remain virtuous, my sister will not lose her virginity." Miss L. is but a substitute for his sister.

It is plain that the ring is also a symbolisation of his love. He wants to give it to his sister. At the present time, his incest phantasies are expressed by his feverish desire to find a man for his sister, only because he believes that she needs sexual satisfaction. He has nevertheless never brought any of his friends into his house out of simple jealousy and his sister has always thrown this up to him.

The ring he actually received from his family just before he left for the front. It is a symbol of his family's love for him. He will be able to give himself to another person only when he has lost the ring, i.e., freed himself from his family. But he is quite well protected from love and marriage, for did he not see a misalliance at home and are his sisters not unhappy or the lords in their husbands' homes? He doesn't want to be lorded over. He's afraid of marriage. He claims he could have married long ago. But how can an impotent man marry?

To-day he dreamed:

I had an emission in the dream and saw a moist spot on the ceiling. I knew that my mother would come in my room in the morning and I was afraid that she would see that spot.

When he awakened he found that he had had no emission at all. He then went on to describe the mother's jealousy of her children's love. She even complained to his married sister that she loved her husband more than her own mother.

He often slept in the house of one or another of his sisters and was able to hear at night how one of them rebuffed the amorous attentions of his brother-in-law. This excited him greatly. Once he heard her say: "Will you please take your hands away!" Ever since then he is in the habit of holding his hands on his genitals (a perennial memorial).

He dreamed:

I transposed entries from the pay to the balance side of the books, about half a page. After I had finished about half the job, I suddenly thought to myself: you've probably entered something that's none of your business and you'll have to make it good. I looked the work over carefully and found that there were no mistakes (i.e., that I had not entered such a figure). The book was in order.

The dream discloses the secret of his inner guilt (indebtedness). This is a symbolic representation of the analysis. He looks the credit and debit side of his analytical book over carefully and finds everything in order. We, however, must suspect that he has kept a very important entry (guilt, indebtedness) from us. This is also expressed by the ambiguous termination of the dream. He has made the entries and he has not made the entries.

He is quite as talkative as usual, but his associations are largely unimportant. He reports something about his kleptomaniacal tendencies, slight transgressions and tendencies to little bits of dishonesty. I note the fact that when the analysis is left to him, he wanders off into endless side paths; so I take matters into my own hands and ask him directly about his sexual habits (standing behind the woman—grasping her breasts). I want to know when he first tried this trick. He said he thought the first time was with his prostitute Anna with whom he had had intercourse for 8 years and who looked so much like his sister. Then he first confessed that his brother had first recommended this prostitute to him and that his brother had used her for years before he began.

This information sheds new light on her importance in his erotic life. He uses his brother via this prostitute. The position he takes up—standing behind—rhymes well with his homosexual impulses. Furthermore, such a position permits him to imagine other girls in place of the one he has. When this was mentioned, he confessed that he was quite a subject of this form of imagery. At that time he had frantically loved a girl named "Franzi." He didn't marry her because she was too poor for his grand ideas. But this girl was the only one he had ever really loved. It was a year already that he had completely broken off with her except that he would see her and kiss her. But he didn't dare to go further because she was a decent girl and he was afraid to get so deeply involved that he would have to marry her. One day he caught her in a corner of the room and it was there that he first tried this position and the grasping of the breasts (he was twenty-one). When he went to his prostitute, he repeated the manipulation, but pictured his girl Franzi in his mind.

More and more he begins to talk of the repressed love for Franzi. He always met her on the street after work in the place where he was employed with his brother. They would then go walking together and would stop in dark corners to kiss. Finally she asked him to come to her house because she wished to introduce him to her parents. He became frightened and didn't want to bind himself to anything. She was a frivolous sort and he could easily have had her if he wished, but he was afraid to take what he could have practically for the asking. He loved her too much. He would then feel lost and would have to marry her. Instead, he withdrew, but suffered the tortures of the damned for his weakness. He went to his brother-in-law and begged him for some advice. He said he loved this girl and wanted to know how he could forget her. His brother-in-law said: "Get another."

He then began constantly to think of Franzi whenever he was with Anna the prostitute. His brother, too, tried to win Franzi and got as far as a kiss. Being very jealous, the patient suffered terrible pangs. He would hear his brother talking with her over the telephone, would let his brother tell him how frivolous she was, how she carried on with this one and that one. He would even follow her on the street, observed her every move and couldn't get her out of his mind.

She soon left the business and became a cabaret singer. He met her once or twice, but soon began to avoid the old places where he was likely to run into her, where she sang. She became quite well known and he learned that she had an affair with some composer. That was during the war. The composer was a color-sergeant. And now we understand the dream about the riding academy better. The right word is—mare. He thought: I'd like to ride this mare. He knew that he'd have no peace until he had slept with her. In the dream he sleeps before a riding academy (where one rides mares). The color-sergeant is now her lover. She is symbolized by the Christian shoes. He's a Jew and she is Christian. The ordinary shoes symbolize the prostitute. The Kaiser in the dream is also Franzi, and the false entries of the next dream also refer to her.

And now the long dammed-up love of this patient breaks forth in the analysis. He feels that he can love only Franzi and will never come to rest if he cannot win her. What does any other woman mean to him if he cannot have her? She will always be engraved in his soul. His obstinately persistent love condition is nothing but the expression of his unfulfilled wish to return to her. He cannot pardon himself for not having taken her when he had the opportunity. It would have been easy and he would not have had to marry her either. He loves her to-day after twelve years just as passionately as when he was a youngster. A few months ago he met her on the street and boasted like a youth. She found that he looked quite fresh and well preserved. He said he didn't know what made her say that. He had had numerous women since seeing her last, the prettiest girls and the smartest women. Then they shook hands and parted, each wishing to return to the other. But now he is well protected from seducing her by virtue of his impotence. How can he hope to approach her, the experienced and artful woman who has already tried so many men? And he impotent. His impotence is a means of self-protection against Franzi. If he were not impotent to-day, he would go after her and live with her.

Now we also understand why he became so wrought up when a friend of his married a girl who had been the sweetheart of others before him. He was quite enraged and declared that he would be unable to do such a thing. His protests were nothing but the overtones of his yearning for Franzi.

She is the girl who was to be found by his ring. Miss L. in the office is a representative of Franzi and the ring is a symbol of his love for her. He could give up the ring only to his sister or to Franzi.

For some time he spoke only of his love for Franzi. With her he'd be potent, of that he's sure. With her he'd be able to do without his habit of standing behind and grasping the breasts. He doesn't believe that he used this manipulation before he met her. It only happened that Franzi had been standing so that he could embrace her from behind. He then continued the petting in this position and reached for her breasts. Breasts and buttocks are the only parts of a woman that attract him, and this interest goes back to childhood.

A considerable load of material corroborates the childhood origin of these two erogenous zones. He had once played with a younger sister and observed her buttocks. The form of the nates interested him in every little girl and boy with whom he played.

He was also interested in the business of his sisters washing their breasts. His girl Franzi also bears a great resemblance to his favorite sister. She has the same eyes and he also believes she has the same type of figure, i.e., the same form posteriorly. He always makes observations of women from behind. Although it is possible for him to forget faces, he can never mistake a person if he sees them from behind.

He went again to a prostitute and was this time able to have intercourse without resorting to his usual manipulations. He has made up his mind to marry soon, but he doesn't choose to look up Franzi. He is still afraid of her, but believes that he is finally getting her out of his mind, because he feels that he has disrupted the identification of her with his sister. He has also gained some insight into the fact that his brother's love and affairs with Franzi probably intensified his own feelings for the girl, and that his homosexual impulses towards this brother were connected with this. He knows, too, that Franzi's promiscuity attracted him willy-nilly as a means of satisfying this homosexual lust.

A few more remarks on his kleptomaniacal acts. He recalls the fact that he takes only round or spherical objects. For example, he is tickled whenever he can steal an apple or an orange. In front of the grocery or fruit stores, there are always open crates of fruit and whenever he can steal a large apple out of one of these crates he is overjoyed. The following day, he usually goes back to the same store to buy several things in order, as it were, to repay the grocer, and frequently he has sent the money in anonymously. He once took a round, crystal ball from one of his friends and a spherical vase from another, but afterwards threw these objects away. As a boy, he had been impelled to grasp his sisters by the buttocks, but had been reprimanded by his father and even severely whipped for it. His kleptomaniacal impulse is a transformation of the sexual tendencies which are re-pressed by the incest barrier. These twicking habits, which are so well loved by children, were also exploited whenever he and his brother got together. Once he placed a pencil on his brother's seat in such a way that his brother injured himself slightly when he sat down on it. This symbolic act is certainly transparent.

I know nothing further of his destiny.

This case is very instructive because it shows us the back-ground for the development of a specific love condition after the twentieth year of life. This alleged sexual condition was noth-ing more than a perennial memory of his lost love and meant to say: I would like to have Franzi back again.

His preference for buttocks and breasts is not at all patho-logical. As I have already emphasized, every man and every woman has his or her preferred erogenous zones. They are predilections which determine the lover's choice and represent the individual's sexual taste. Such forms of preference have nothing to do with true fetishism. When the sexual gratification is effected in the specific erogenous zone, then we can consider them as cases of partialism. There are men who prefer to have coitus inter mammas, for whom, indeed, this is the only form of cohabitation which leads to satisfaction. I have also seen men who preferred coitus inter femora mulieris a tergo and who rejected normal intercourse (in vaginam). These are cases of partialism which often disclose an infantile origin. But they may frequently develop only during or even after puberty. I know a girl who was seduced at sixteen by her employer. He had her masturbate him while he kissed, licked and bit her on the back of her neck. To this very day, ten years later, that has remained the most gratifying form of sexual pleasure for her. The teeth of her sexual partner play an important rôle in this manipulation. If her friend has large, broad, spade-like teeth (like her first lover's) she becomes very passionate and pictures his kiss and his bite.

Even the first sexual experience of an adult can become a fixation and form the basis of an individual love condition.

The analysis of the case described in this chapter has taught us that infantile experiences and incestuous tendencies can give the experience of adult life a specific quality and color.

III

EROTIC SYMBOLISM

ON IMPULSIVE ACTS ARISING FROM OBSESSIONAL LOVE OF
DOLLS, CLOTHES, DRESS GOODS, ETC.

We have already seen that kleptomaniacs really are chasing childhood phantasies. They want to revive their past. This impression seems to conflict with the observations of de Clerambault, who has described a special type of kleptomaniacal fetishism under the name of hephephilia.[1] This type is characterized by a preference for certain cloths or goods. De Clerambault emphasizes the fact that his cases exhibited a remarkable indifference to their past (indifférence au passé). Kurt Boas[1] however, has rightfully doubted this supposition and has shown that a careful analysis of the author's cases discloses exactly the opposite. He says: "There can be no talk of an 'indifférence au passé.' On the contrary, what is actually to be found in these patients is a sexual anæsthesia or, rather, a hypæsthesia towards normal coitus." In other words, there is an avoidance of the sexual partner just as we have been able to demonstrate in many of our cases.

The alleged indifference towards the past is only apparent. Actually all these patients are slaves of the past. They have really remained infantile and I could just as well have described them in *Infantile Psycho-Sexuality* of this series as examples of "psycho-sexual infantilism."

Whereas the cases of genuine fetishism, on the one hand, are very complicated in their psychic structure, the cases of partialism are fairly simple in form and may frequently be easy of reduction to some infantile impression. It is invariably possible to show that such patients live in the past, i.e., that they reveal a typical psycho-sexual infantilism. But one case, that of Laquer, may serve as a sample: "Thus in the next few weeks I shall have the opportunity of examining an eighteen-year-old student of music, stigmatized and hereditarily degenerated, who twice stole money from an open cash register for the purpose of buying himself a boy's suit, blouse and knee pants. In this dress, the patient walked around the streets for two hours. Even without it, he gives the impression of being a child. He excused himself with the statement that he 'derives gratification and ecstasy from being a child or at least from being looked upon as a child by elders, talked to familiarly and being kissed by them.' Sexual factors play no part here (?). He also stole in the department store, but threw away the suit he took there once he had worn it. He claims to have succumbed to this perverse habit suddenly when he once visited an institute of minor children and felt the desire to be their equals again."

In this case we have the opportunity of observing the very widespread combination of psycho-sexual infantilism and kleptomania—naturally on a sexual basis. The impulsive conduct of the individual represents a regression into the infantile period of his life. It is noteworthy that this sort of combination is especially to be found in women, and it is characteristic of such females or female-infants that they often show a preference for dolls. Indeed, these dolls can become fetishes, they take on a real value for the woman only when they have been stolen.

The doll can represent either a real doll or be a symbol of a child. It can, however, also be a symbol of the genitals, as I was able to point out years ago in my book on *The Language of Dreams.* Kurt Boas has made the following accurate remarks in a critical discussion of the passion for dolls: [2]

"Vinchon considers the combination of doll fetishism and homosexuality as an especially widespread occurrence. He includes both the Uranian and the Lesbian types. As a matter of fact, his first case does show Lesbian relations with a prostitute. The relationship, however, was not at all circumscribed to the two women themselves, but radiated also to the dolls: the patient's partner gave her a doll which they both called their common child. The doll was dressed in gorgeous pink or blue dresses (the preferred colors of the patients). She was laid upon a small sofa in the corner of the room and carried a small savings bank hung around her neck. This was for the collection of the gratuities of the prostitute's usual visitors. But it must not be supposed that the doll served only the purpose of fleecing the customers. Both women were actually devoted to the object as if it were their living offspring. The patient, especially, spoke of the doll with marked agitation.

"Dolls are to be found with remarkable frequency in the rooms of demimonde women, prostitutes and inmates of bordellos. The last type of woman almost invariably has a doll with her to which she gives either her own name or that of a child of hers. The dolls are always of the female sex and it appears that they have nothing to do with perverse purposes in respect of exciting the men. Neither can they be there purely for decorative purposes. In many cases, the doll serves a simultaneously pleasant and practical purpose, as in the case of Vinchon: the doll with the savings bank. But the dolls are certainly also a conscious representation to the prostitute of certain sexual attributes: they are symbols of chastity and purity. It is also possible that they symbolize the genitals ('my little sister,' as the genital is often termed). But it is not logical, simply because of such traits, to take for granted that every such woman is a Lesbian. I believe that Lesbian habits are to be found in clandestine as well as public prostitutes especially during the early stages of their careers and particularly during a period of compulsory internment in a hospital department for venereal disease. The older prostitutes have overcome this stage and finally become quite indifferent sexually. There are, however, also prostitutes who are not outand-out Lesbians but who are nevertheless devoted doll fetishists. Contrary to the case of Vinchon, such cases do not represent the presence of both the father and mother in the picture, with the child, the doll, as the offspring of the relationship. Instead, the father or the mother is dropped from the relationship and it is a case of only father or mother with the patient and the doll: a trinity. The doll is then the child which is pampered, fastidiously cared for and spoiled in all directions. At night the doll sleeps with the fetishist.

"These discussions lead us to ask ourselves: what gives us the right to talk of doll fetishism in such cases? We see clearly that it is quite inaccurate to speak of doll fetishism here."

Boas is perfectly right. These are cases of psycho-sexual infantilism with an impulse to collect (harem cult). In the analysis of infantilism, we saw that the patients saved books from childhood, infantile mementos, playthings, etc., and used them to amuse themselves. Why shouldn't the doll serve similar purposes, especially since it can so well serve to revive infantile memories symbolically?

The following is a case of my own observation:

Case 6. Mrs. G. J., a woman in her forties, has the impulse always to be playing the child. She talks baby talk, prefers to wear children's or very short dresses, and is considerably aided in these habits by the trend of fashion. When she is home alone, she jumps about the room like an active little girl and piles all her old playthings out of the drawer onto the floor. Among other things, she has several old dolls with which she used to play years ago. She begins to pet the doll and then imagines that she herself is the doll. She would give anything not to be a day older.

The woman was raised by an aunt who spoiled her to an unusual degree. The aunt died when the patient was thirteen and ever since then the girl has been fighting the passing of the years. In the beginning of their marriage, her husband was very tender towards her, but lately he has been more and more indifferent. She still has, however, a tremendous need for being pampered and can still this desire only in her activity with the dolls.

At first she satisfied herself by playing with the dolls behind the locked doors of her room. The hours passed in sheer delight and she felt herself transported back to the days of her childhood. At the time, her husband had no notion of her habits.[8] One day he came home unexpectedly and found his wife in the midst of her practices, a doll in her hand and surrounded by all kinds of dolls and playthings. He became furious at this scene of childishness. With the lightning accuracy of the lover he had realized that these dolls were his rivals. Blind with rage and jealousy, he tore the dolls out of her hands, ripped them to pieces, destroyed the other playthings and threw the lamentable remains into the great fire in the fireplace.

The poor woman looked upon the sack, helpless and dumb. Then she fell in a faint. Or was it an hysterical fit? She awakened in bed, a doctor was sitting beside her and her husband was crying bitterly and begging her for forgiveness. She was unable to speak. The doctor found that she had a high temperature. She was seriously ill. The temperature persisted for a month. The diagnosis was vague and uncertain. Typhoid fever was thought of, some consultants suggested the possibility of an occult tuberculosis and one of them thought it might be hysterical fever. Finally the fever gradually subsided, she recuperated visibly, but her character had manifestly changed. Whereas she had formerly been quite happy and alert, she became morbid and seemed to be dreamy. She was no longer able to read through a book, nor did she display her old interest in the theatre or the arts.

Formerly she had frequently had an orgasm during coitus and was easily provoked to orgasm by irritation of the clitoris. Now she became anaesthetic. She could not forgive her husband the murder of her dolls. She ceased to be a child. She felt old and often said that she had nothing more to live for. What is the use of living? she would always ask.

It was at this time that her kleptomaniacal impulses set in. She began to steal large and small dolls in all the department stores and would lock them in her closet. One day she was caught and her husband discovered her doll harem. She, however, appeared to have no memory of having stolen them and declared she had bought them. The fact was that she had actually bought a doll now and then when she found no opportunity to steal one. When asked about the collection, she stated that she would suddenly find herself impelled by an unknown force to go searching for a doll. She seemed as if drunk and trembled all over as if she had just committed a crime. She would tell the sales-persons that she was looking for a fine plaything for her child and was fearful and ashamed lest they should suspect that she was buying the dolls for herself.

At this stage of her difficulty she came to consult me. The analysis showed that as a child she had suffered a curious series of traumata such as a girl of a better class family seldom experiences. When she was seven, her nine-year-old brother played with her and carried out cunnilingus on her. Then, one day, he brought three of his friends who also played with her. Later, she slept with her aunt in the same bed and was always petted and stroked over the whole body. Her aunt called her "my dolly" and said that she was as pretty as a doll. The next trauma was suffered at the hands of her brother's tutor who always caught her in a quiet corner of the house, kissed her furiously and would feel her parts. She confesses that she was quite a coquette as a child and practically enticed the men to play with her. At thirteen she became the mistress of her piano teacher. She had no intercourse with him, but he would put his penis in her hand and play with her parts. At fifteen she was deflorated by a physician whom she practically seduced. Then followed a few more affairs before she met her husband, who was very naïve, engaged himself to her and always played with her without having intercourse, although she was never resistive to his blandishments. The first few weeks of their marriage he was impotent, and when he was finally able to cohabit with her, he was so excited that he did not notice that she was not a virgin.

She vowed she would be true to her husband and also kept her promise. Her faithlessness was expressed only in her play with the dolls. Each of the dolls represented a separate experience from life. They each had a name which was taken from her own past. Her aunt's name had been Rosa and one doll (the favorite of the harem) was called Rosalinde. The doll which represented her brother Carl was called Charlotte, the piano teacher was revived in Franzi, etc.

Following the scene with her husband, her hate awakened and she swore revenge. Although she had felt herself to be a child and, like all infantile women, actually looked young, she claimed that she now felt very old and displayed the contrariness of the parapathics which contrasts with their fictions in life. She claimed she was an old woman whom no one liked. But she was driven to revive her past and revenge herself on her husband, nevertheless. She wanted to look up all the old lovers of her past, but where could they be found? The piano teacher was an old man by this time. Her brother was in America and the other men seemed unapproachable and had long since forgotten their former playmate. She therefore had to reach these men in her phantasy. She enjoyed her forbidden fruit in her dreams and became a kleptomaniac.

A protracted analysis was followed by complete cure.

In this case we meet with an impulse to revenge. The dominating idea is: You must do something to revenge yourself. You must revenge yourself on your husband. You must revive the old pleasures which he has destroyed. The most clear of all the pictures of her youth were those of her aunt and the piano teacher. She desired again to be the dolly of her auntie and to play with the piano teacher's penis. In this wise she fulfilled Gross's formula: she took the forbidden fruit into her hands.

Curiously enough, she had always refused to gratify her husband in this manner and it was certainly the painful memory of her childhood which kept her from doing so. This manipulation belonged, as it were, to a fictitious world and dared not be dragged into the world of realities. These patients always remain true to their phantasies and refuse to have them profaned by reality. One can frequently observe how such patients feel that reality depreciates their fictions and tends to make them superfluous. It is not true that parapathics always desire to see their phantasies realized. Many flee from reality and reserve the specific scene for their phantastic life and their onanistic manipulations.

And now let us turn to some other observations. We have the case of Duboisson and several cases from Vinchon which I have taken from the paper of Kurt Boas. Unfortunately, all these cases lack the very necessary psychological analysis and yet they offer such interesting points of approach that we shall understand them better when we have added our own analysis of them. I begin with the case of Duboisson:

Case 7. Mrs. C. is a large, strong woman of thirty-three who shows no special physical signs except, perhaps, that slightly jaundiced and pale complexion of persons suffering from diseases of the liver.

She had the various diseases of children, such as measles, scarlet fever, small pox, etc., but none of them were serious. She never had typhoid fever or convulsions, but with the incidence of puberty, she began to show signs of nervousness and irritability.

Even as a little girl she used to become quite excited upon the slightest provocation, could not sit still, would laugh or cry almost for the asking, but usually for no reason at all. Occasionally she would have a fit of laughter which she could not control. Her father died of pneumonia and her mother, who had been an irritable woman all her life, died of a heart disease. Upon the slightest irritation, the mother used to fall in a faint.

Between her thirteenth and fourteenth year, Mrs. C. suffered more attacks. She developed slowly and the beginning of menstruation was attended by great pain and a noticeable deterioration of her personality. She would throw herself to the floor, have fits which looked for all the world like true convulsions. At that time she first experienced the curious drawing feeling in her throat and breast which is so characteristic of hysteria.

Since adolescence, these symptoms have become aggravated rather than improved. Mrs. C. is constantly in need of movement and activity. Even her sleep is restless and characterized by muscle twitchings and various other convulsive phenomena. She is incomparably irritable, moody, and ready either to burst into tears or laughter. At the slightest excitement or irritation, she also has the feeling as if a ball is rising in her throat. This feeling she holds as a secret, since she has never told it either to her husband or her physician. It is understandable that at certain times all these symptoms would become worse, e.g., they would reach their high-water mark each month at the time she would menstruate and also during each of the three times she was pregnant. To complete the picture, I must also add that she suffers from gall stones which cause her more or less periodic attacks. These attacks are not at all irrelevant to the psychic and mental condition of the patient.

From the mental point of view, we find that Mrs. C. is doubtless below the average in intelligence. She went to elementary school, but no further. She writes orthographically correct, knows how to add and subtract and even to divide, but has never been able to do the most simple multiplication. Between the ages of twelve and fifteen, she was brought to Germany, where she easily and quickly learned to speak German and spoke it even after she returned to France. To-day she has forgotten every word and states that she feels that she has even lost her memory. The real fact is that, like many patients of her kind, she has lost her ability to pay attention. She is unable to pin her mind down to anything. That is also the reason why she is completely incompetent for any serious business. Her husband, who is a leading author, wanted to interest her in his works, but the best he could get out of her were a few examples of copy work and these were so bad that he had to give up making use of her.

Before entering upon a discussion of the acts for which the woman was indicted, I must add a few more remarks on her family life. The C. family suffers from but one disturbance and that is one of the children. Mrs. C. has two children, a boy and a girl. The girl is now five and one-half and has, since birth, been the one and only worry the mother has had. After an especially difficult birth, the child began to have convulsions at three months of age which made the doctors think it had a tuberculous meningitis. Thanks, however, to the unusually devoted care which the child enjoyed, it remained alive and has reached its sixth year. Its health is nevertheless not all that could be desired and much caution and attention is necessary. From the day the child first became ill, Mrs. C. forgot everything else and began to live only for this child. She became the little girl's slave and devoted both her days and her nights to her daughter. For the daughter's sake she gives up every form of amusement and distraction and if she does go out sometimes without the child, it is only to buy something which the child wants or needs. This, of course, is per se nothing unusual. Many mothers sacrifice their lives for the children they love. But the mother love of Mrs. C. is marked by something more, something pathological. We all know how the majority of hysterical persons suffer from obsessional ideas, although such ideas are usually varied. Mrs. C.'s obsession is perennial. Her desire to please and gratify the child has gone so far as to endanger the health and even the life of the girl. It is useless for the doctor, with the aid of the husband, to tell the woman that nothing is more dangerous than to fuss with a child in this manner when it needs quiet and not constant excitement in each of its moods and phantasies. Everything was in vain against such mother love, and all that the doctor accomplished was to bring the mother's hate down upon his head.

And now we come to the criminal act. At the suggestion of the physician, the husband, who had become more and more irritated by the extravagant spending of money for the littlest things, forbade his wife to buy the child playthings almost every day. He felt that about forty dolls with all the trappings that go with them ought to be sufficient distraction for the child. She conceived this rather righteous opposition as animosity and knew no other way to satisfy her desire than to take what she was forbidden to buy, feeling that once the things were in the house, her husband would have to pay for them if it were demanded.

It does not seem as if she operated under a well-thought-out plan. If one is to believe her, this seems to have been her attitude when, one November day, she stood before an object in the magasin de Printemps which seemed suitable as a plaything for

her child (a sheep). She succumbed to her feelings and carried
out her intention. Two weeks later she appeared again in the
store and in the course of time had carried off more than sixty articles of various kinds: playthings, dolls, clothes for dolls, etc., all
of a value of about three hundred francs. Arriving at home without accident, she hid the objects in a closet and awaited the coming of Christmas in order to surprise the child with this wealth of
presents and simultaneously confess her action to her husband.

Mrs. C. stated that she knew she had stolen, but that she felt
the theft to be very innocuous if not entirely pardoned by the fact
that her husband would pay for them sooner or later. She seemed
to feel that she had floated a loan rather than committed a theft.
With a truly wonderful naïveté, she declared that this one quiet-
ing thought was the reason why she was able to go through with
her criminal actions with the greatest of composure, absolutely sure
of her conscience, without a trace of excitement, she, who had always been so excitable, and without any sign of subsequent pangs.
Even when she was caught in the act and led away to the police
commissioner, she was composed and so indifferent that a witness
who happened by suspected the soundness of her mind and rushed
to inform her husband. It was only when the whole muddle
came before a judge and she was impressed with the fact that
her acts were not to be taken so lightly that she became somewhat
animated. Even to-day she is not completely convinced of the
state of affairs at that time and cannot believe that such acts as
hers are, to say the least, inexcusable. Mrs. C. can be described
in a word: she is a child, but this thirty-three-year-old child is hysterical and that includes all the cerebral deficiencies which such
a condition entails.

Here we have a characteristic case which is really very little
different from the case I described. As in most of these cases,
we find a married woman with marked signs of psycho-sexual
infantilism. But, in all these cases, we must not forget one
motive: the marriage and the duty to be faithful are conceived
as compulsions. The kleptomania expresses one phase of the
struggle of the sexes. This woman also has the tendency to
trouble her husband, to hurt him, to irritate him, to test his love
for her. There can be no question that this woman loves her
child more than she does her husband. The formula in her
case would read: I want to please my child even at the expense

of hurting my husband. The fact that she told her husband about her deeds Christmas Eve is a sufficient proof of how deeply her desire for revenge pervaded her. Manifestly she was to a great extent guided in this action by memories of her childhood when she herself was bountifully heaped with presents. Her husband had had enough at forty dolls, but she showed him that she was capable of transgressing his orders (that's what you get if you don't do as I want you to do). This case shows clearly her tendency to humiliate her husband and come out triumphant over him.

The following will be a case of Vinchon's [4] which I have taken from Kurt Boas:

Case 8. Jeanne C., called Carmen, was first seen in June 1908, when the diagnosis of general paralysis was made with a statement that she was mentally deteriorated, euphoric, childish and lacking in insight. It appeared that the onset of the illness occurred about January of the same year and is said to have been provoked by a sudden moral shock. There followed the opinions of three specialists and the first findings in the psychiatric clinic corroborated the above conclusions.

In January, 1903, it actually appeared as if Carmen, who is now forty-five (1904), had lost her memory following an accident with a wagon. Her whole character seemed to become entirely childish and her former tendencies and habits seemed to revive and become intensified. She laid hands on everything which she found loose about her, stole the papers from under the very arms of passers-by, etc. She was interned because of these acts.

Carmen left the asylum in October, 1903, considerably improved. Her acts and manner of speech, however, are still childish in character. She remained fairly well watched and cared for until 1906, at which time she tried an unsuccessful theft. Her arrest was confirmed because a collection of things was found in her possession which provoked the astonishment of the police. Following a forensic opinion handed down by psychiatrists, she was provisionally turned over to her friend for safe keeping. She soon after appeared at the gates of the "infirmerie speciale," however, talked in a bizarre manner and was again arrested. This time the physician thought she was simulating, although he agreed that she was diseased. After a few days of excitement, she became quiet again and was able to be discharged from the clinic.

During the next six years, i.e., until 1912, she displayed nothing pathological except a short and hardly clear state of excitement, which occurred in the summer of 1910. But she was always more nervous in the summer and rather susceptible to attacks of this nature. March, 1912, she was again interned, this time in the asylum of Sainte Clotilde. She was picked up at a funeral. The doctor again looked upon her as a malingerer. During her sojourn in Saint Lazare she again had an attack of excitement and was transferred to Magnan's clinic where she received the diagnosis of low grade mentality with maniacal excitement. In the beginning, Carmen was not at all willing to share her secrets with us. Whenever we spoke with her about her thefts, she said she remembered nothing. She nevertheless told us with her well-known verve about a lot of details from her past life, e.g., the story (which surprises one in a woman of her age) about the dolls which she cannot leave for a moment and has never left except for the one time of a few weeks when she had to busy herself with a little boy.

She has two blonde dolls. The one is large like a baby, and always lies in bed behind her. The other one is small and can be taken with her wherever she goes. In an endless collection of boxes, she keeps silk remnants, pieces of lace, divers ribbons, etc. It is her greatest pleasure to make use of these articles in making a dress for one of her dolls. She likes to sew the silk, to use heavy linen materials, and is especially fond of working with the laces. Learning of these predilections, we got the idea of giving her a doll, especially since, in the hospital, she complained that she missed them. Hardly had she seen the thing, when she grabbed it out of our hands, pressed it lovingly to her bosom and then hid it under her dress. She became considerably excited, could hardly speak, mumbled huskily something like "thank you" and tried to embrace us. At the same time, she looked as if she were experiencing the heights of passion.

An hour later we had her brought to the examining room. Her answers are still confused and her facial expression sufficiently portrays her shame and distraction. She finally brought herself to communicate the following to us:

She had formerly cultivated many intimate affairs, but no longer has any interest in normal sexual appetites. She is supposed to have been syphilitic at one time and, although she was treated at the time, she feels that it is the same old disease which keeps returning and provokes her attacks of excitement. As a child she used to masturbate by rubbing herself against the backs of chairs and the legs of tables, especially because her parents, having noticed her habits, had commanded her to keep her hands behind her back. She was quite a fiery little girl who identified even the possession of a plaything with sexual gratification. This habit of mind disappeared during puberty, but returned with the onset of her menopause about ten years ago (she was forty-four in 1903). It was at this time that she executed her first thefts.

Carmen has never resisted. It comes upon her with great sud-denness, although she is somewhat upset for a few days before. She goes to a church she usually makes use of, Sainte Clotilde, in a rich parish. She first senses an indefinable unpleasantness in the stomach, after which her desires take on form and then she wishes to have one of those vanity cases which the women of the world generally carry, particularly a small box of rice powder.

In trying to get such an object, her misfortune usually causes her failure and she is arrested. In that moment her face becomes congested, beads of perspiration stand out upon her forehead, her genitals become wet, and the possession of the object, if only for a moment, consummates an actual sexual thrill which she describes as "making my thing." For a time the stolen object takes on the value of a fetish and she adds it to her collection which she always carries on her person. The very sight of this harem of hers is a source of rapture for her, but it can also become an object of disgust. In such a case, she will break an object and throw it away.

Sometimes she buys what she wants instead of stealing it. The result is that she is then less affected by the object than if she had stolen it, but this does not spoil her pleasure completely for she recalls the joy she experienced in paying out the money and having a heap of bands, remnants, laces, etc., sent home. Her friend usually has the articles exchanged later on, but if he lets her keep them, she uses them to dress her dolls.

This "impulse to steal," as she expresses it, causes her much unhappiness and she would like best to commit suicide in order to be rid of it all. These words, nevertheless, cause her an ambiguous feeling which derives from the memory of both the pleasurable and the disgusting sensation she experienced when she once stole something.

Hardly had Carmen bared her secret when she felt sorry for having done so. She took it ill of us that we had wheedled it out of her. Her first reaction was to fall into a terrible anger which was manifestly not simulated. Finally she quieted herself and begged us to tell nothing to her lover. She is ashamed of it all and would rather be taken for an ordinary thief. "And above all, it's not so bad in Saint Lazare. The nurses are very nice to me."

On the ward we were able to observe an action similar to the ones she had described to us. Following a short period of excitement, she tried one morning in October, 1912, to take a ribbon which was bound about the hair of another patient. She produced the same symptoms she had described to us, but this time it was sufficient only to touch the object of her desires. Soon after, she grabbed the ribbon and demanded that it be destroyed.

As regards the doll, Carmen surrounded it with nothing short of a cult. She is so fearful that we shall take the doll away from her that she hides it by day under her skirts and by night in her bed. She ordered remnants to be sent to the ward and made up some clothes for the doll, among other things a coat of blue linen against which she often rubs her cheek in dreamy raptures. The doll reminds her very much of the small child she once tended to so willingly.

She tells us that this doll is the best protection against her thieving tendencies. She has never been in the least cowed by the punishment society deals out to thieves, and professional thieves among the women command her affection, although she despises them, too. It is possible, she says, to get along with such women as one like, i.e., badly more often than otherwise. This questionable friendship once went so far as to cause her to start up a Lesbian affair with a woman who—strangely enough—counted most neurologists as her friends. Another companion who was also interned because of thievery, made her the proposition to live together "and also to work together" when she was discharged.

It appears that Carmen is affectionate with her lover, but the slightest irritation can precipitate her into a fit of anger. She is incapable of protracted attention and is subject to constant changes of mood. She is especially touchy about her age and her physically deteriorated condition.

Carmen was subject to all the children's diseases in infancy. Her bringing-up was lamentable and her mother pampered her beyond endurance. She could not stand the school to which she was sent and had to be reared at home. A private teacher taught her how to read and also a little music. Ever since twenty years of age she has lived in Paris and has been everything between a demi-

monde and a model, making her living as best she could. She frequently drank champagne and other forms of alcohol to excess
and fared poorly in these bouts.

I must call attention to the pointed epicritical remarks which
Kurt Boas has appended to the report of this case and I desire
to point out here only the fact that the relationship between this
woman's love for dolls and her homosexuality seems pretty
clear. She was very much spoiled by her mother and yearns to
be back in her mother's lap again. She plays her own past when
she plays with her dolls. She also confessed to Lesbian relationships.

She is frequently the subject of fits of anger against her
lover. I have analyzed such cases many times. Such women
are usually habituated to some form of Lesbian gratification
(mutual cunnilingus is very widespread among prostitutes).
They are generally frigid when with a man and the slightest
provocation can engender outbursts of temper because of their
deficient satisfaction. They nevertheless protest their great
love, portray the virtues of their husbands or their lovers, fling
the dirtiest vulgarities in his face when they are mad, and re-
pent afterwards, saying that they didn't mean it, their words
were only senseless epithets, pathological products of an irritated fancy. One of my patients used to accuse her husband
of homosexual relations with his friends whenever she would
become angry, and thus revealed the root of her own hatred.
The above case is further marked as homosexual by the desire
to steal a powder box and by the attempt to steal the ribbon
of another female patient.

Now we turn to another case of doll fetishism which was
published by Vinchon in the *Journal de Médicine* in 1914 under
the title "Le Fétichisme de la Poupée et le Vol aux Étalages." [5]

Case 9. This deals with a girl by the name of Louise who
came of a silk weaver's family in Lyons (this detail is of importance in the development of her sexual perversion). She soon
came to Paris from the provinces and there became a member of
a gang of department store thieves to which not only she, but also
her daughters, daughters-in-law and her sons belonged. The following information from the anamnesis is of importance.

Her father and one of her brothers were epileptics. A maternal uncle is an idiot. One of her sisters committed suicide and the patient herself was retarded in school. She began to speak with difficulty at the age of five and at seven she suffered from "nervous fever" due to anxiety. She claimed that someone ran after her in the street and accused her of having stolen a little dog. She did poorly in school and preferred manual work.

She was a depressed and anxious sort, suffered frequently from headaches and liked to be alone. At times, also, she would get attacks of pathological irritability of an hysterical type.

At fifteen she began to work and then passed through all the stages of tailoring, finally interesting herself especially in the making of silk corsets. Her taste for this type of cloth appeared as early as her seventh year. An uncle surprised her once at that time while she was in the act of rubbing silk with which she was working. She described her feelings as a kind of shivers (frisson).

At seventeen she first began to menstruate and also fell ill with chorea minor subsequent to an attack of typhoid fever. She was choreatic for three years before the illness disappeared, thanks to isolation. When she had recovered, she went to work for three hundred francs per month as a seamstress for a ladies' tailor.

She was also supported in part by a lover, a writer with whom she lived from the time she was twenty-one and by whom she had a child. Two other children died in infancy, there were three miscarriages and the last was a daughter who was delicate. During her pregnancies, she was always ravenous for certain foods, but had never succumbed to the desire so far as to steal.

Her lover died after ten years of common law marriage. Louise, who was then thirty-one, began to masturbate with silk, but she had not yet begun to steal silks. Whenever she experiences the impulse to steal, she usually has alternate attacks of vicious anger and hysteria, but she can withstand other temptations.

At thirty-six she had a second attack of typhoid fever and she claims that she stole for the first time during her convalescence. She cannot give the details. Since then she has lived in Paris, where she has been a devoted silk fetichist.

Her first thefts provoked in her an exceeding sensual gusto such as she had not known when only masturbating with silk. The very contact with the silk, especially if it were red, and its rustling were sufficient to bring on the sexual paroxysm. She would become so excited in the act, that she took no care to protect herself and was caught every time.

As soon as she has stolen the goods, she is either disgusted and ashamed, tries to throw the stuff away, or she feels spent and tired. Like all patients of her kind, she is very bashful about answering questions on this subject.

It does not take long before she must leave her position. She is thrown out of every department store as soon as they learn that she is the cause of the disappearance of so much silk. She became a professional thief and sought in this way to earn a livelihood.

The impulse to steal appears especially when she is in the throes of certain states of depression, after her second typhoid attack, during her climacteric, etc. During such times, she felt little incentive to work and harbored ideas of suicide. She even attempted suicide on several occasions and in many different ways, e.g., by cutting open her veins at the wrists, choking herself, throwing herself down the stairs or out the window and once she tried to throw herself under a train.

Altogether, Louise was arrested twenty times, was convicted eleven times, received eighteen months in prison each time she was convicted and was interned for nine months in the insane asylum, all since 1911 (she was then forty-five). Each time, she had the same story to tell. Each time she was interned, she suffered hysterical attacks and also exhibited all the signs and symptoms of this neurosis.

Four times she broke away from the asylum, thanks to the aid of her children and probably also the aid of those who were financially interested in her thefts. They always faded from view as soon as she was arrested again.

As a child, Louise had loved passionately to play with dolls. It was one of her greatest pleasures to make silk clothes for them and she continued this habit up to the present day. She states that, in order not to appear foolish because of this habit, she always excuses herself by saying that she is working for her children, and now that she has grandchildren, she says she is working for them.

The doll itself is not a fetish for her. It must first be dressed in silks and red is her favorite color. Her pleasures in these operations were quite active and used to be distinctly sexual in nature. Now they are but pleasant memories of former enjoyment.

This is a typical case of psycho-sexual infantilism which finds an animated expression in playing with dolls. Here, too, we find the attacks of vicious anger against the lover, just as we were able to see them in the former case. Kurt Boas is right when he says that the regression to the level of the old memories of silk fetishism appeared after the death of her lover. "They had up to that time remained just below the threshold of consciousness." Another cause of the regression is to be looked for in the second attack of typhoid fever. As I have already pointed out in *Infantile Psycho-sexuality* of this series, a regression frequently begins after a long and exhausting illness. The menopause may also have played a part here (Cf. *Frigidity in Woman*, the chapter on the critical age of woman, 2 ed.). It is the critical age of woman, the battle against the years. Boas also takes this stand and adds the following epicritical remarks to the case:

"I would like to take a stand on some of Vinchon's conclusions. He first points to the fact that the doll cult is frequently to be found coupled with homosexuality, especially in the case of Lesbians.

"As a proof of this, Vinchon makes use of some cases from Krafft-Ebing. Some Miss Marie writes in a letter to her Lesbian friend Sandor: "I no longer love the children of others, I love only my own little baby from Sandi, a darling little doll. Oh, how happy I am with my little Sandi."

"Male homosexuals also are sometimes devoted to dolls. I mentioned a case of Laquer's above.[6] Krafft-Ebing reports the case of an Uranian type who confessed that he liked to play with girls who played with dolls. He would also make up clothing for the dolls. At thirty he was still greatly interested in dolls of all kinds. The cases 122, 124 and 129 from Krafft-Ebing's casuistic collection also reported a preference for dolls as against girls, and they also tailored for their playthings."

"Vinchon himself emphasizes the fact that this cannot be called true doll fetishism. There is no evidence of any of the criteria laid down by Stekel and myself.

"When Vinchon states further that there is the possibility of border-line cases and gradual transition between marked and indistinct cases, he is doubtless right. This is probably the reason why dolls are so preferred in the Christmas and other holiday presents in insane asylums. They can never be too numerous.

"In the metropolitan cities, one finds the usual doll cult in the accepted sense of the word (according to Vinchon) quite widespread. This is particularly apparent in certain trades, such as tailoring, costuming, hat making, etc. In cabarets they sell dolls filled with bon bons or smoking articles. They are also sold in boxes which also include cocaine, but this is not general. Every woman has her favorite type of doll. The more grotesque a doll is, the more readily will it find a buyer.

"Vinchon then gives us examples of doll cults from other cultural eras, the old Greeks, the Romans, Japanese and Chinese. The last-named people have special artists for the manufacture of valuable silk clothing and all kinds of decorations and enhancements for the dolls.

"One must be careful not to place all these cases under the pathological magnifying glass and summarily dispose of them as cases of fetishism. Vinchon recommends that we hold ourselves to Garnier's definition,[7] but I believe that the criteria advanced by Stekel and myself are superior to his."

I must add a few explanations to these pointed remarks of Kurt Boas'. The last case we described displayed an extraordinary love for certain goods, a sexual symbolism (I am careful in the use of the much misused title of fetishism) which is very widespread. We know also of a passion for furs which can even lead to kleptomaniacal episodes. We can understand the addiction, as it were, to furs by our understanding of the passion for hair. The furs are the symbols of the hairy body, especially of the beard, the axillary hair, the hairy vulva.[8] The love for satin is also common and the sexual object is frequently attractive only when wearing satin. I have also found a passion for very ordinary goods in patients and in the discussion of genuine fetishism later on we shall have an opportunity of becoming acquainted with such a case. These habits can, however, also have a negative value, e.g., women in silk can be unattractive to one who displays a passion for woollens.

In addition to Clerambault, such cases have also been described by Langlois.[9] The first of these authors avoids the false term fetishism, but the second always speaks of cloth or goods fetishism, which is summarily criticized by Boas[10] in his exhaustive paper on this subject. The following cases from these authors have been taken from Boas' paper.

Case 10. The first patient of de Clerambault, a forty-year-old woman, gave the following information about her vita sexualis: She came home from school at fifteen and was married at sixteen and one-half years. She never cared for sexual intercourse with her husband and latterly became even disgusted and pained by it. She preferred to satisfy herself in onanism, a habit with her even before she was married.

She found out about it spontaneously. When she was alone in the room one day, she felt a curious kind of thrill when her genitals touched a chair. She describes it as follows: "I wasn't sitting as one usually sits on a chair, but like on a horse. The chair was upholstered in satin. Since I liked the feelings I got, I continued to try the practise over again. I also heard them speak about such things then, too, but I did not begin to use my finger until later."

She was pregnant seventeen times altogether, among them being four abortions. She had a lover whom she liked very much, but sexual intercourse with him was far less gratifying than masturbation. Every morning, after he left, she would masturbate. She also had frequent erotic dreams in which she would have intercourse with a dog or with men who "did all kinds of things to her" ("qui lui faisaient des choses épouvantables").

The cause of her psychiatric examination was found in repeated silk thefts. She had already been punished four times previously for persistent stealing of silk coupons and was under arrest for recurrence of theft at the time of the examination. Her first theft was committed when she was thirty-two years old. She had no objective grounds for the act, since she had plenty of silk at home, but she sensed a certain lustful feeling during the commitment of the theft. This thrill she got only when she would steal, whereas the buying of the goods leaves her cold. Following the theft, she always rubs the silk against her genitals.

This patient also discloses some signs of homosexual tendencies in that she masturbates, she imagines to herself a completely naked girl of about sixteen.

When asked whether she could not give up the onanism, she replied that she felt too weak to do so. She said that she tried to rid herself of the habit by getting herself a lover.

The chief points about this case are : first of all, an anæsthesia when with her husband. Later she even became resistive to intercourse. With her lover she was relatively anæsthetic. As far as she can remember, her first enjoyment came with her early onanism on the satin chair. It is probable that this was a recrudescence of a repressed infantile impression. Finally, there is here the almost invariable homosexual determinant of the kleptomania. This may be a fixation of some person out of her childhood who wore silks. This symbolism can also represent a fine (silky) skin.

Case 11. The second patient dates her passion for satin and linen as far back as her sixth year. Later she passed to using silk and cloths for rubbing herself, using the remnants of her tailoring sister. Whenever she did this, she felt quite miserable, and stopped it only when she began normal sexual intercourse. She can no longer wear silks, although there is nothing more enjoyable for her than the rustle of fine silk and the feel of it next to her body. Satin no longer has any attraction for her. Because of her passion for silks, she has frequently stolen the goods. The last attempt was the theft, together with her daughter, of a silk corset from the window of a corsetier's. She cannot resist the temptation to steal silks. She is particularly attracted to silk ribbons, bands, caps, skirts and corsets. Whenever she feels the rustle of the silk, there is a peculiar tickling sensation in her finger tips. Then the temptation becomes too great, and if she does fight it off, she becomes exhausted and falls into a fit of tearfulness. If she does take the silk, she experiences a curious pleasantness in the region of the stomach and feels a rapture pass through her which makes her hold her breath. She then immediately searches for a lonesome corner in order to carry out all kinds of manipulations with the silk. When the sensual flight has passed, she feels herself exhausted, all her limbs are dead.

There are many points of similarity between this case and the one described before. In both, the "fetishism" appeared rather early and was altogether the first form of sexual activity. The transition to normal sexual intercourse took place only afterwards.

Case 12. De Clerambault's third case concerns a widow of forty-five who had always lived happily with her husband, despite the fact that she had no taste for cohabitation. Between 1881 and '89, the patient was convicted three times for theft, falsification and once because of unknown reasons. Cessatio mensium began at thirty-eight with her, and she began to use ether, morphine, cocaine, rum, and either rum or Cologne water mixed with ether. Ever since she began to use ether (at thirty-nine), she has the impulse to steal silks. She achieves thereby a sensation of lustfulness which she describes in characteristic terms. Taffeta excites her most of all, since it is of finest silk. She has less of a passion for satin than for silk. She did not, however, go in for heavy silk things, because she felt that these would excite her too greatly. She would like to sleep in silks, but thinks that this is not nice for a decent woman. She says she would be unable to sleep if she ever put such goods on. She would be so fired with passion that she would have to get up constantly and cool herself off with water. Whenever she is about to steal some silk, she is overcome by a great trepidation, but this soon is replaced by a feeling of pleasure.

Epicritical remarks of Dr. Boas: "In these cases, too, we will have to dispense with the diagnosis of fetishism. We don't have to discuss the reasons. In this case, kleptomania has occurred in a woman in climacterium. The cessatio mensium, per se, can hardly be the cause of the thefts, but the cause is doubtless the chronic use of toxic substances, especially ether, which provoke in the patient a general and chronic excitement in which she is not conscious of her acts."

Case 13. This is Case IV of de Clerambault. It resembles the last case described almost to a hair. It concerns a forty-nine-year-old widow who possessed a questionable past, especially as regards her sexual history. She is heavily stigmatized by heredty. Her father and mother both committed suicide and her brother is in an asylum.

As early as seven or eight, she began to masturbate, either alone or in company with another little girl with whom she played father and mother. She began to menstruate at twelve and married at twenty-six, although she was never satisfied during coitus. She stated that she early had a passion for silks (there are, unfortunately, no definite data), and states that her sole motive in marrying was to become the possessor of a black silk robe. Her words are understandable and characteristic even in the original: "La soie

a un frou-frou, un cri-cri, qui me fait jouir." The very mention
of the word silk or even the thought of the goods, provokes sexual
ecstasy in her. She also senses an "érection des parties sexuelles."
She experiences a tremendous orgasm if she then rubs the silk
against her parts. In addition to this, she is excessive in matters
of alcohol and ether and masturbates daily. She has repeatedly
stolen in department stores; three times in 1914. One of these
thefts was a black silk robe worth one hundred and sixty francs.
When she took it, she rolled it up and went off with it between
her legs. One day of the same year, she says, she went into a
department store at the behest of a vision. She had previously
taken ether. In the department for silks, she saw a blue and
white dress which created a spasm of joy in her. She passed it
into a large bag beneath her skirts and then masturbated publicly
in the store.

Masturbation, per se, does not afford her complete satisfaction.
She must always think of the rustling of silk in order to bring
about an orgasm. Sometimes men do play a part in her onanistic
phantasies, but they have no real attraction for her sexually.

Case 14. The fifth case of hephephilia (Langlois) concerns a
twenty-five-year-old woman who has been married for five years
and is the mother of three small children. The following was
taken on her vita sexualis.

She dates the awakening of her sexual life from her eighteenth
year at which time she first menstruated, i.e., rather late. Soon
thereafter she began to masturbate and first used her finger. She
states that she never suffered any somatic detriment thereby. One
day she accidentally discovered her peculiar love for satins. She
states that she experienced great happiness and felt deeply tempted
when handling satin. She was partly sorry and partly happy that
she was not working in the silk department of the store where she
was employed. She thought that if she were employed in that department, she would be impelled to steal the silks and that would
reveal her perversion.

Women who came to buy from her and wore silk dresses were
subjected by her to variously guarded stroking and petting,
whereby she felt rapturous sensations. One day she suddenly got
the idea that it must be a great feeling to masturbate with satin.
She then said that she was unwell a few days before she actually
began to menstruate, laid herself on her bed at home and masturbated with the aid of pieces of silk. She said that this gave

her "une sensation indéfinissable qui la transportait et la faisait jouir."

All these experiences happened in her eighteenth year and since then they have grown upon her. She is especially overcome with this impulse about the time she gets her period and has been able to deceive her family. She has a constant sensation of itching and tickling in the genital region which drives her to masturbate again and again. She states that she is quite indifferent to normal coitus, but (just like the previous patient) she conceives marriage as a good means of achieving her particular sexual objects, i.e., satins, clothes, etc.

At the request of her parents she married. She was not satisfied by normal intercourse, but always acceded to her husband's desires. When they furnished their home, she managed to have the bedroom done entirely in satin and even the bed clothing was made of this goods. No one thought further of this matter, but simply gratified the wishes of the young wife. For her it was the highest of pleasures to hide herself away in the room alone and masturbate at will. She was, however, afraid to make use of the satin decorations or the satin bed clothing in her onanistic acts because they might be soiled. She soon began to wear satin constantly. One day she had a voluptuous dream in which she saw her naked body clothed entirely in satin, but such a dream has not recurred in her thoughts. She also confessed to her examiner that her husband would attract her much more sexually if he would wear satins sometimes, even if it were only a servant's garment. Upon further questioning, she stated that any man who wore satin could excite her. She also declares that when she pictures her husband in satins during cohabitation, she is animated more than usual, and feels that this would give her greater pleasure than masturbating with satins. She answers negatively when asked whether she has homosexual feelings and also denies that her masturbation reminds her of a man. She added, however, that she would feel an especial lust if the satins with which she masturbated had previously touched her husband's genitals. The husband had no inkling of these perverse habits and thought that his wife's pruritus vulvæ was due to excessive intercourse instead of to excessive masturbation.

The patient usually masturbated by day when her husband was at work. If she happened to be caught in bed, she declared she suffered from migraine. She displayed her passion only for satins and was not animated by silks, furs or other goods. The color of the goods also played a certain rôle, black being her favorite color. She usually burns the satin cloths which she at first is afraid to soil with her sexual secretions.

These are all cases which Eulenburg has termed sexual picacism. It is a characteristic of this woman that she is frigid in normal sexual intercourse. Her impulses are what we have seen to be a regression into the past. It is unfortunate that these cases were treated in a purely descriptive manner and not psychoanalyzed.

This case, however, doubtless approaches that which we call true fetishism. She is anæsthetic to coitus, a condition which is similar to male impotence. She gratifies her sexuality in onanistic acts, whereby the specifically determining phantasy seems to be inaccessible to her consciousness. She shows the same kleptomaniacal impulses as the preceding patient.

Kersten reports a case of "Fetishistic Theft Complicated by Alcoholism" in Gross' Archiv, Vol. XXIII, p. 365.

Case 15. One May day, 1905, the fifty-three-year-old lamp-polisher F. stole a doll's pillow from a child's doll carriage on the street of a small town. He confessed to the theft and added that he had no clear notion of what he was going to do with the pillow. He was drunk. He had been convicted of thefts before and the cases had always been concerned with the stealing of bed clothing from children's beds or cradles. He was divorced from his wife, but exhibited nothing further of note and was also a desirable worker in the factory where he was employed. All these factors pointed to a fetishism in the patient.

According to the forensic opinion of the specialist, his sexual appetite was activated by the sight of beds and their appurtenances. The slightest taste of alcohol so intensified F.'s impulses that he was unable to withstand them, especially since he was already so much of an alcoholic that he was looked upon as an alcoholic psychotic. The court action was therefore dropped. (Records of the Royal Barrister, Dresden, St. A. VIII/94/05.)

Here we have the same results that we have seen in all cases of impulsive acts. The alcohol destroys whatever inhibitions are present and makes room for the expression of the infantile impulse.

The following is a highly interesting case of clothes fetishism reported by Pappenheim:

Case 16. On the evening of the first of June, 1919, the thirty-five-year-old pastry baker's helper, K. L., was arrested at the terminal of one of Vienna's most congested car lines for having taken a folded velour hat out of the pocket of a stranger. When arrested, L. was found to have in his possession another velour hat and four men's belts which he had stolen shortly before at the same place. When his rooms were searched, eight hats and thirty-nine belts were found and L. confessed that he had acquired these in the same way.

L. had already been convicted for petty larceny before, in 1913, 1915 and 1916. The last of the three had been because of an analogous theft. When arrested for the theft of a velour hat in 1913, L. had at home nine velour hats, a camera, three pairs of opera glasses and a cigarette case, all of which he had stolen. In 1915, while substituting in the cloak room of the opera, he stole an overcoat.

L. denies ever having been seriously ill. He had an inflammation on his penis when he was nine or ten years old because, as he claimed, he played with himself too much. He can remember that his father often beat him for doing this and also clipped his finger nails.

He claims always to have been a good boy, but adds with a smile, that even as a boy he was peculiar. He always liked to play with dolls and even carried them to school with him in his knapsack. His father beat him for it until he gave up the habit. At home he liked best to model cribs and houses out of his box of blocks, and was always at home around the kitchen stove where he liked to cook, scrub the floor, etc. He never had any friends and was always alone. In the summer he would walk in the wood near by, catch butterflies, etc. He was always a quiet person, took life seriously. As a child he read fairy tales and later drew only romances from the library.

He offers the following information on his sexual life: He never had any erotic relationships with schoolmates. Many years ago, when he was about eighteen, he tried to masturbate, having heard about the practise, but was unable to gain an erection. At nineteen, after having withstood the jibes of his companions about his virginity and because he suffered from an acne (which the laity usually blames upon sexual chastity), he visited a prostitute, but was unable to get an erection. A second visit which lasted throughout the night failed as miserably, and he never tried again. He nevertheless picked up a gonorrhœa during these trials, but this soon healed. At about the same time, he was once grasped by the penis by a man in the Turkish bath, but he was not especially enlivened by the experience. His first notion of abnormal sexual feelings occurred at about twenty-five, soon after he had returned from Germany. He noticed that whenever he would brush past men in a well-filled street, he would have "peculiar feelings." Now and again he would also have an erection. He then began to prefer second-hand suits, especially such as were fitted for a belt, although he was not financially forced to wear such clothing. It was at about this time that he began to steal belts in motion picture houses. His first arrest occurred some years after he had already been practising these habits. Latterly he had been in the habit of taking only velour hats and belts. Upon direct questioning, he replied that any other objects which he had stolen, he had also taken from men. He remembered that the man whose overcoat he had stolen was also dressed in sports clothing.

L. describes how, when he sees a hat peeping from a man's pocket—he can hardly make it clear—he becomes excited, feels a sort of knocking within his breast, and frequently gets an erection. If the theft of the hat or the withdrawal of the belt from the trousers is difficult, he has an orgasm which follows a pain in the penis as if he suffered urgency. Then he is weak and spent. If the theft is easy, he is not particularly pleased. When questioned about it, L. agreed that he was always fearful of being caught, but that could not prevent him from succumbing to his impulses. He states that he is not at all sexually provoked when conversing with men, nor does he have that sensation he once used to have whenever he would brush by men in the street. He becomes animated only when he sees a man with a velour hat or a belt, but not every man with a velour hat or belt will catch his eye. He prefers men with curly hair. At home he has the hats covered with a white cloth and the belts all folded away. He handles them occasionally, feels them, and now and again has an erection. His own hat never gives him the same feeling, only stolen ones.

The especial point about this case which makes its publication appear indicated—I have found no similar case in the course of a superficial search through the literature—is that L.'s fetishism is marked by a homosexual component which is expressed in his desire to steal male clothing from men. ("Ueber einen Fall von

Kleidungsfetischismus homosexueller Art." Ztschr. f. Sexualwissenschaft, Vol. VII, Nr. 19, Dec., 1920.)

This is a case of genuine fetishism. The patient is homosexual only in his phantasies. It seems plain that the hat,
sticking in a pocket, symbolizes for him the phallus protruding
into a vagina. We have here the factors of impulsive conduct,
the expression of an infantile phantasy and the harem cult.
The hat, and perhaps also the belt, have a phallic meaning for
this patient.

There is no piece of clothing that cannot be made the center
of a fetishistic habit. The specific form and type of clothing
also plays a part. Garnier described a case in which a wedding
gown was the specific love condition.

Kersten reported the following case of fetishistic theft in
Gross' Archiv, Vol. XXV.

Case 17. One evening in February, 1906, the village of L. was
astounded by the theft of a ball dress from a garden which had
been entered clandestinely. A forty-year-old stone cutter, who had
been living a hitherto blameless life, had been married for fifteen
years but was without children, was arrested as the thief and confessed the crime. When, upon search, his home was found filled
with a suspicious number of evening gowns, dresses and petticoats, he confessed further that, to gratify his sexual appetite, he
had for two years been clandestinely stealing women's apparel
from gardens where they had been hung out to dry or air. He
usually stole at dusk or night and either climbed over the fences
or broke into the places.

The forensic opinion on S. was that he was a fetish lover whose
free will and responsibility had been sufficiently circumscribed at
the time of the deed by a pathologically disturbed mind as to absolve him from punishable blame. S's. over-weaning instinct is
doubtless based in great part upon his low mental status, although
his hereditary rating appears negative. Whenever he sees a petticoat hanging on a line, he becomes involuntarily provoked sexually,
especially if the wind lends the petticoat some form. He is then
an impulsive automaton, driven willy-nilly to become possessor of
that piece of apparel. He takes the skirt and presses it close to
his bosom, which is in itself a kind of sexual gratification for him.
When he gets home, he puts the petticoat on in the fashion of a

woman, and, dressed in this manner, he has intercourse with his wife. Allegedly, S. has not cohabited with his wife during the past two years without wearing a petticoat or skirt, and it is his desire always to have a new one on, i.e., one that he has but recently stolen. Only in an emergency would he use an old one, but then the pleasure was not the same. The case was dropped. (Records of the Royal Barrister, Dresden, St. A. VII, 103/06.)

In all the above cases we have been able to observe a combination of erotic symbolism with impulsive acts of a kleptomanical type. The fetishist is a collector and every monomaniacal collector is, in certain circumstances, a thief. Whoever has read the previous volumes of this series will understand that this kleptomaniacal impulse is an irresistible one. The tremendous displacement of affect, the transference of emotions, makes an emotional debauchery possible which circumscribes consciousness and thus intensifies the erotic ecstasy.

The impulse derives from childhood and attempts a revival of the past. Stealing dolls is a palpably infantile trait. It is as if these parapathics had recovered their infantile past with one dash. In the days before psychoanalysis, it was possible to talk in such cases of degeneration and impulsive acts on a constitutionally degenerative basis. Psychoanalysis, however, first discovered to the world the power of infantile experiences and childhood attitudes. But the interpretation of infantile phantasies alone is not enough. Whoever tries to solve the riddle of fetishism with the key of the infantile trauma will soon learn otherwise by his failure.

The true fetish lover is an actor who, like the erotic symbolist, possesses the power to annul reality and feel and think his way into his rôle. There is not a single object which he is not capable of drawing into the charmed circle of his system and creating it a bearer of emotion and affect. If the object—let us say a doll—appears suitable to represent the past, if it can take on the symbolic meaning of the genitals, or a sexual act, then it will all the more easily become the foundation of a complicated structure which I have chosen to call a "fixed castle in the air."

But the patient does not satisfy himself with thinking and

phantasies alone. The call of the past, an unfulfilled childhood wish, the desire to revive an old scene, impel the fetishist to the execution of compulsive acts which bring him into conflict with the law. He often achieves a secret goal thereby: he makes himself interesting and also plays the martyr, suffers, and enjoys his suffering.

IV

THE HIEROGLYPHICS OF FETISHISM

Most so-called fetish lovers harbor a complicated system and also display a peculiarly individual taste. They try to surprise the physician with a wealth of details the importance of which they specially emphasize, and then add: "You have doubtless never heard of such abstruseness in your life." They plainly reveal what they think is a secret pride in their neurotic fictions, their sexual neoplasms, their illness; a pride which can be compared only with that found in marked and typical hypochondriacs. The latter may be called narcissistic fetishists. Fetish lovers often shown signs of hypochondria and hypochondriacs, on the other hand, make a fetish out of their symptoms and their diseases. They are downright in love with their troubles.

The fetishist usually expresses his true tendencies and the causes of his sexual symbolism in a kind of secret code. In the course of an analysis, he will strive more and more to cover up the meaning of this code. He becomes unhappy when he sees that the physician is beginning seriously to unravel his secrets, and then generally takes flight. I can therefore give all analysts the advice not to disclose their knowledge and understanding to the fetishist too early, nor to let him feel that he and his system have been discovered for what they really are.

We meet with the most curious displacements. Thus, for example, a hand which is the object of a most passionate partialism is not at all representative of itself, but symbolizes an action which was once carried out with a hand. The more complicated the patient's system is, the more suspicious must we be of it.

All these patients cry miserably for cure and promise one eternal thankfulness if they are freed from the bonds of their sexual symbolism. But they must not be believed. They only

82

act as if they really wanted freedom, whereas actually they live by their fictions, embrace their symbolism and want to have nothing to do with cures.

As we have already seen, sexual symbolism has the tendency to free an individual from the necessity of a sexual partner. The love conditions become more and more circumscribed until the fetishism becomes equivalent to asceticism. Finally, this trend drives the person away from the partner and towards a symbol, a part of the body, even a part which has little or nothing to do with sexuality or perhaps altogether a foreign and inanimate object. But always, the person strives to preserve his secret code and to prevent anyone from deciphering it. The following is an instructive example of this tendency.

Case 18. Fritz K., a twenty-nine-year-old chemist, suffers from a complete incapacity for work. Originally he was to be trained as a business man according to his father's wishes. At seventeen he suddenly became ambitious, began to study hard, passed the college examinations with good marks and went in for the university studies with an industry which finally enabled him to achieve the doctorate after the conquest of all his inner troubles. But now he seems unable to do anything. He seems interested enough in a lot of things, but is always at the surface of whatever he does. He is a good musician, can compose at the piano, but lacks any foundation. He cannot decide upon a profession. He doesn't like chemistry any more and is bored by it. He would like to become a musician or a philosopher. He believes that his pathological sexuality is the cause of all his troubles and his weak will. He states that he has been masturbating since earliest youth and always with one and the same picture in his mind:

He imagines two women struggling with each other. The one is slender and has a graceful leg. She wears white, sheer, silk stockings. The other is strong, robust and stocky, and wears black stockings. The struggle between them is bitter and it always seems as if the slender one will win. But always at the last moment, the black legs win and at that very moment he has an ejaculation. He frequently must masturbate as many as five times in one night.

He is always restless and unable to concentrate. After he has masturbated, however, he becomes somewhat more composed and attentive to things. It is as if a motor were being driven ceaselessly through space. He visited many cities, looked up many physicians, but left them all after a short time. In Vienna he is restless, cannot remain in his rooms, runs to the cafés, from the cafés to the theatre, and there he is bored. He would like to read books, begins with great interest and attention, but throws the work away after a quarter of an hour.

He is constantly searching, searching for the proper sexual object in all the streets and alleys. He is interested in nothing but the stockinged ankle, and women with sheer silk stockings are the chief attraction.

He can run after them for hours. Then he will run home and masturbate with the above-mentioned mental picture, the woman he has just seen taking the place of one of the amazons.

He has also tried normal coitus. He found his potency good, but the orgasm was rather weak in comparison with that provoked by masturbation. He has read very many analytical books, but this is a detriment rather than an aid to treatment.

Second visit: He came a quarter of an hour too late and excused himself by saying that he had to wait at the barber's (he was reminded of the fact that this only corroborated the prophecy that he would be resistive to treatment).

Sometimes the masturbation was an expression of his despair. He wanted to ruin himself in this pleasurable manner. Following every onanistic act, he experienced a moral and physical depression, but the physical or hygienic dejection has disappeared since he has read my book on onanism. He still gets a moral hangover, however, after every act.

Wrestling has always interested him, and in school he often wrestled, naturally picking on the smaller boys so that he would come out a winner. Only once did he see two women wrestling, and that excited him greatly. That was three years ago and some time after the compulsion idea had been formed. He also struggled with his masturbatory tendencies (here he was reminded of the fact that he was a wrestler with all things in life. He was also asked about his parents' lives). His parents, he said, fought like cats and dogs. There were always arguments and he cannot remember ever having heard a tender word pass between them. His father was a drunkard and committed suicide (one of his brothers, too). He was then nineteen and the father fifty-six.

His mother was more intelligent than his father and often trumped up illness in order to have her way. The patient blames his mother as the cause of his illness, claiming that she pampered him and reared him as a very introspective type. Even as a child, he was always alone and played with his building set. At ten he was sent away and the letters he received from his mother were full of imperatives. Do this and don't do that. Honor thy parents that thou mayest prosper on earth. She also inculcated too much religion into him. He states that between five and fourteen he was very pious. He recalls a very strict teacher of religion who tried his mightiest to fill his soul with the fear of God. He was therefore always afraid of the wrath of God, and suffers from an oppressive guilt feeling of which he has been unable to divest himself to this day. He was still confessing at eighteen, but "finally overcame the whole mess." Nevertheless, there were always substitutes for the religion afterwards. He became an evangelical protestant, then raved about Johannes Müller (the biologist), Lhotzky, Mulford, etc.

He sought God's aid against his onanistic impulses, and when yet a child he struggled with this "depravity." He remembers that he came by masturbation himself. He was leaning out the window when he felt a curious tickling sensation in the region of the prostate. He pressed his hand unconsciously against his penis and that was the beginning of his unhappiness. From the very first, his onanistic phantasies consisted of lovely legs. His first objects of lust were girls he had seen on the street wearing yellow stockings. The wrestling phantasies were developed only during the past three years.

His onanistic phantasies are not always as simple as he has described them. The chief point is that both these women wrestle for him just as two knights would be struggling for the possession of a castle beauty. He is always interested in the question of which one he will possess. When the legs of the two women are intertwined during the match, he is especially tickled. He often imagines that there may be a gladiator's school for women in every land. Every country chooses its best amazon and then an international championship is staged (cf. the modern international beauty contests—trans.). The best wrestler then becomes his mistress. The audience at these wrestling matches consists only of men. There are three rooms; the match begins in the first room and then the stronger woman drags the weaker one through the second into the third, where she wrestles some more with the latter and finally conquers her.

"In my mind, I often measure their leg sizes. For example, ankle 18 and calf 32. The other one has a smaller ankle, 16, but a larger calf, let's say 34. She's the winner. The wrestlers are always contrasts. A brunette usually wins over a blonde." When he was twenty-three, a ten-year-old girl he saw on the street provoked his fancy. He had to contain himself in order not to attack her on the street. He would like to rape a little girl. Being the stronger would excite him. For example, he is greatly animated when women let him carry them. Once when he carried a girl across a stream, he was almost beside himself with passion.

Yesterday he didn't masturbate. Why? (He was told that he knew that he would observe himself in order to be able to tell me the phantasies.) What he told me with such seeming exhaustiveness did not in the least complete the list of his onanistic phantasies.

At the beginning of the war he was so excited that he practically forgot to masturbate (wrestling match between Germany and France). This state persisted for a few months. He was wounded and ended in a hospital. There he naturally fell into his old phantasies and habits. He protests, however, that onanism is not always pleasure and vows he will take his life to punish himself. Whenever he had an opportunity to command in the war, he felt much better and masturbated less.

He describes the story of his life and explains how he has always been led by chance. He was always lucky, always found someone who was interested in him and produced the means whereby he educated himself.

Again he produces an appendix to and elaboration of his wrestling phantasies. The time factor plays a large rôle. The women first wrestle for a period of five minutes and during this phase it is possible that the weaker one may forge ahead. Then there is a pause of several minutes, after which they begin to wrestle again for ten minutes. During this second period, it is possible that the weaker one may win once, but the stronger woman will win at least six times. The winner is then entitled to have intercourse. She falls upon the loser and copies the movements of sexual intercourse until the weaker one is exhausted and declares herself beaten. The stronger woman then places her knee upon the breast of the loser, and in this moment he has an orgasm.

As a child, he had seen a picture in a magazine called *Modern Art* which was entitled "Rivals." Two women were struggling with each other. One was lying on the ground, her hair flowing in the breeze, while the other braced one knee on her breast. He was then eight years old and now believes that he has been using a similar mental picture because that one made such a deep erotic impression upon him.

He has already tried to remember whether or not he ever spied on his parents during intercourse. His father often came home drunk and he knows that his mother no longer loved his father. Perhaps there was a kind of wrestling match between his parents which ended in his mother's conquest. Perhaps he was a witness to such bouts, but his memory fails him. He considers this supposition to be a theoretical construction.

He manifests a great yearning for a fine woman, an ideal love. A few years ago he made the acquaintance of a very dear girl and thought that he loved her. At that time, he had no wrestling phantasies whatever, but he also did not love this girl really. He believes that a true affection for a noble, sensitive soul could save him from himself. He even wonders that he has no leg phantasies in the company of fine, chaste girls. He is inflamed only by sensuous-looking, provoking women.

"Can you explain this to me?" he asks.

"I think so. I also understand your wrestling phantasies now. Two tendencies are wrestling within your breast for the upper hand. You desire to love spiritually, to belong to a single woman, to woo and wed her according to the laws of the Catholic religion (the sacrament of marriage). That could be called heavenly love. You know Titian's painting of heavenly and earthly love, don't you?"

"Certainly. I like it very much."

"You can masturbate and love only when earthly love conquers. Your difficulty is the expression of a battle between eros and sexuality, instinct and sublimation, brain and spinal cord. You want to kill God within you, conquer the need for a spiritual love by crass sensuality. The devil wrestles with God. (Think of Job and of Faust.) You have projected this struggle to the outside world. You have a picture of it before your mind's eye."

The patient thought these conclusions over and corroborated their validity. We now also understand the meaning of the three rooms. They represent his three decades of life in which sensuality has always won over spirituality. His Satanism has always conquered his Catholicism. The minutes he mentions can also be explained in this way. For five years he was very devout, then came a recess period of some time, after which he entered a ten-year period of Satanism. The black stocking symbolizes the branded, sinful woman. The white stocking is a symbol of purity.

He then relates something of the terrible religious impressions he received in childhood. He comes of a family in which there were always fights between the liberals and the zealots. His mother engraved piety into his brain with the strongest imperatives, and now he takes pleasure in proselyting his relatives to a more modern form of devotion. Three of his mother's brothers became freethinkers and tried to draw his mother away from the church. They were, of course, only partially successful. He believes that she became hysterical only when her religious beliefs were shaken.

"Didn't you want to become a priest?" I asked.

He hesitates to answer, but then confesses that when he was a child they gave him a small altar. He played the preacher, read masses and acted the high priest. His ideal was to become a pastor. His piety was nothing short of fanatical.

"At bottom you have remained devout. To believe is a feeling, an emotion. Your disbelief is the product of your intellect and the intellect can never conquer one's feelings. It is a struggle between a whale and an elephant. They can never come together. Your belief has withdrawn into your unconscious and is protected by your parapathia. Your wrestling phantasies insure your chastity, for, in reality, you approach woman only very seldom."

He agrees that he is still devout and that during the war he occasionally prayed, especially when he was at the front. He would like to drive out this "foolish belief," but has been unsuccessful to this day.

And now he knows why he is dissatisfied with all professions. At bottom he sticks to his ideal and would prefer to become a priest. Studying chemistry was an accident and music is but a substitute for religion with him. He prays while he plays. Wild military melodies pass into chorals to the glory of God.

His resistances increase. He comes late and his associations are halting. His one new addition is that he now states having had phantasies in which he himself wrestles with a woman, but the woman is always of the coarse and sensual type, not the spiritual kind which he adores and would like to love. He avoids connecting the latter type with his phantasies about legs and ankles. Only occasionally will he create a combination between a coarse and graceful female. It is much more difficult to phantasy such a woman than the usual kind.

He is always vacillating between wish and counter-wish. He has now become quite conscious of this trend. Last night he had a dream and a voice said to him: "You will tell this dream to Dr. Stekel." "But, no!" said another voice, "you will tell him nothing." And he forgot the dream. This keeps up the whole day long. Two forces are struggling within him—among others, the female and the male principles. He wants to be a man and yet remains a woman.

More and more he is beginning to realize that the cause of his "fetishism" is his repressed religious feeling. He conceives the wrestling phantasies with the two women as a symbolization of a struggle between sensuality and belief.

Last night he had two dreams:

I went on a mountain-climbing trip. It seems as if my brother fell.

My father had a large business. A large theft was discovered and there was an unpleasant scene. . . .

To the first dream he associates a memory that he once went on a mountain-climbing trip with a girl. They were caught in a thick fog and lost their way. Finally they came to a point where further passage was impossible. He tried to pass and slid down about thirty yards. He received slight injuries, but was able to find a way to a mountain shelter. There a rescue crew was formed and the girl was freed from her rather uncomfortable position. It was already dark and cold and the girl was in danger of freezing.

To the second dream he recalls that his father suffered business reversals and hung himself in despair. He believes, however, that his father's unhappy marriage was partly the cause of his father's bitterness.

It becomes increasingly plainer that the patient is afraid of woman and marriage. His parent's unhappy marriage had the effect of an "eternal warning" even in childhood. He then proposed never to succumb to a woman. For that reason, he constructed a fetishistic system which enabled him to avoid women and celebrate triumphs in his phantasies. In his mind, every marriage was a wrestling match in which the stronger one wins. The weaker must then die, as his father did.

Now we understand the first dream. His brother is in the Alps, climbing mountains. Since childhood he has had the desire to see his brother die so that he might become the sole heir to his mother's small fortune. The dream has, however, also another meaning. This brother is the symbol of his other self, his parapathia, the pious man yearning for love and marriage. He tried to reach the heights with a woman, but was caught in a fog, lost his way, and fell. The second dream has a religious import. The father is God the Father. He wanted to become a wandering preacher and offer mankind the evangelism of love. He wanted to speak the word of God. But he thwarted God, deprived himself of his belief in Him. Therefore the stir (the scene) in his soul.

He has a singular conception of religion. It is for him a kind of altruism. Whenever he does something for the good of another and not for his own advantage, he feels pious. Whenever he loves something for its own sake (and not for the sake of possession), he feels that this is true love. Religion is thus love without possession. The egoist and the altruist struggle for his soul.

He dreams: The chief postal inspector comes to inspect a post-office of which his brother is the postmaster. There was quite a scandal because the books were not in order.

I am the inspector who is dissatisfied with the analysis. He himself is dissatisfied with his past life.

Here he produced an important memory. When he was 3 years old, his fourteen-year-old brother came into his bed and placed his (brother's) erected penis in his hand. When he was eight, he was bathing with another brother and they played with their parts.

His sexuality was awakened early. He clearly remembers having had thrills as a child of two to three when he played with other children and laid himself upon them. They played they were dogs, ran about on all fours and barked "bow wow." Then he would be the stronger dog and would hop up on the others. He would experience quite a pleasurable sensation. Later he gained the same thrills from wrestling with his playmates, especially at the moment when he bent their backs, i.e., just before they fell to the ground. His earliest wrestling phantasies were purely homosexual, and the first time he was fired by the image of male, not female, legs. Even to-day he is animated by youths. Only the other day he was at an open-air bathing pool where he lay next to a boy in cotton stockings. He got an immediate erection.

He is somewhat disturbed by his fierce sadistic impulses. On the streets he can follow girls between seventeen and twenty for blocks and has to fight off the impulse to fall upon them and rape them. He calls this a fit. Once a woman provokes one of these fits, he feels through with her (self-protection). Recently he had adored a woman in a purely Platonic fashion. But she provoked one of these attacks in him (desire to rape), and since then she has passed out of his mind.

He is very vain and wants always to make a good impression. He invariably becomes confused and embarrassed in the presence of those whose respect he cherishes. He lacks the capacity to enjoy things harmlessly. He is always observing himself. He had periods in which he was always impelled to provoke another's attention and wanted always to be looked at.

He is especially delighted by a marked contrast between the calf and the ankle in his wrestling phantasies. The calf reminds him of a penis. It appears that this is a bisexual symbol.

The homosexual factor forges more and more to the fore. Girls in short skirts remind him of boys and the wrestling women in his phantasies are pages. This is the reason why he is never satisfied by coitus, but must masturbate afterwards. Only once did he ever experience an exception to this. That was with a prostitute in Vienna who had a boyish bob and was built like a boy. He does not like to have intercourse in the usual position, but prefers it with closely intertwined legs. When he masturbates, he also crosses his legs. The pressure provokes a kind of ecstasy in him and when he is about to have an ejaculation, he presses the right leg close upon the left. (The right leg plays the male and the left the female.) He can never find the vagina when with a woman and always permits her to pass his penis into the introitus (he seeks the anus and desires to avoid any sign of activity or guilt. He is the seduced, not the seducer). This is a contrast to his rape phantasies. His maleness was originally sadistic, but is now masochistic. He is not impassioned by a woman lying still, but only by the movements of the female. There must be a play of the muscles, especially of the calves. If a woman wears shoes, stockings and a skirt of different colors, he is animated, whereas solid or ensemble colors leave him cold.

He achieved his most gratifying orgasm while wrestling with boys and at the moment when his energy was almost spent and he was barely able to bend the other down.

Suddenly he remembers that his mother made much of his legs. She often slapped him on the legs and sometimes on the buttocks.

He has an older brother who is feeble-minded. When the

patient was eight, the seventeen-year-old brother attempted a pederastic assault upon him which failed because the patient cried out loudly.

Sometimes when he looks at women he looks cross-eyed. One eye is exophoric. He knows that this is a parapathic strabismus. It first appeared in youth and recurs only occasionally. He had all kinds of compulsion habits, e.g., he would jump up and down in the room like a frog and developed a kind of ecstasy. Again he would imagine that he were some important personage and would then execute all kinds of ceremonials (e.g., a general reviewing the army, etc.). His phantasies are so active that the figures almost live. If he imagines that he sees a corpse on the floor, he actually sees it and could touch it. It is often difficult for him to differentiate between his phantasies and reality. He believes himself to be the emperor of Japan and can walk about for hours under the influence of this phantasy.

The most terrible feeling comes over him when he comes out of such trances. Especially after masturbation, he has the feeling that he's going insane.

Every ankle he sees on the street is a new trauma for him, for it is the beginning of another series of innumerable phantasies. He feels himself to be the unhappiest of men and life is one grand disappointment. A loving couple on the street makes him sad, for he has never known the happiness of love. He would like to be completely bound up in some woman, but has to satisfy himself with his phantasies for his disillusionment. He masturbates after every touch of depression and becomes dejected after every onanistic act. At the same time he has the feeling as if his phantasies are running away with him and disappearing in a fog.

Yesterday he had a characteristic experience. He saw a young woman standing in front of a theatre. She had pretty ankles, well-formed legs, and wore elegant, sheer stockings. He accosted her and, although she hesitated at first, she permitted herself to be taken to a café. There she prevailed upon him to buy drinks and even asked him for money, which he gave her, unresisting, again and again. He became frightfully excited, his whole body trembled. Finally, he accompanied her home, where she bade him good-night in front of the door, although she had promised to sleep with him. He hadn't the nerve to demand the money back or to force himself upon her.

His first association was the memory of an apache dance which had once inflamed him sexually. In this dance, the apache apparently killed his female partner after he had gratified his lust.

This is evidence that he is struggling against the phantasy of a love murder. Whenever he is with prostitutes, he is bashful and exhibits tics, which makes them afraid of him. One of them once told him he was too sinister-looking.

He has manifestly repressed his original stock of sadism. He can't bear to look at blood, is full of sympathy, and could hardly hurt a fly. He nevertheless knows that he hates women and could kill them.

He comes to the hour loaded with a bushel of notes, associations which he has collected throughout the day. I want to warn all my analytic colleagues against falling into this sort of trap. Such a wealth of apparent material only disguises the resistances present and makes it possible for the patient to dispense with the necessity of getting down to work in free associations. I therefore refused to listen to all his "associations."

He then refuses to associate. He says he can think of nothing. He then begins to produce a lot of faults he finds with me. Naturally, only after I had called his attention to the fact that he is doubtless dissatisfied with me to-day. He said he expected more complacency. He had hoped we would become friends, take walks together, etc. He is told that such intimacies would disturb the progress of the analysis. In such a circumstance we have great need of the effect of personal distance. Finally he brings forth the declaration that he does not believe in his sadism unconditionally. He believes and yet he doesn't believe. The next association is:

"I once saw a picture which stimulated me unbearably. A girl was tied hand and foot and bound to the railway tracks. In the distance was the speeding train which was soon to run over her and kill her."

He experienced a most powerful impression once when he saw a steer hop a cow. The animal violence of the act made him thrill. Yesterday he masturbated with the phantasy that he were injured in one arm and carried it in a sling. In another phantasy, he wrestles with a woman and conquers her with one arm.

Onanism has the meaning of castration for him. For a time he has emasculated himself. He is also subject to the phantasy that his penis is a woman and his right hand a man. He thus overcomes woman.

He remembers an old house which he knew in his youth. The place was filthy and full of rats. It was a sinister spot and he never dared go in. It was said that the place was connected with a castle by means of an underground passage. He would have given anything to crawl through this underground tunnel, but he was too fearful.

He is here told that he has just represented his resistance to the analysis in a pictorial fashion. The old house symbolizes his parapathia, his past. He is afraid to get down to the underground passage of his repressed ego. (In addition to this the association is also a plain phantasy of the mother's womb.) He corroborates the interpretation by saying that he hasn't the nerve to look his own unconscious in the face. He would rather run away from himself.

He had a perturbing experience. He was in the postoffice and had to wait in line. There he saw a woman standing at one of the tables and writing something. He was behind her and she animated him greatly because she had "the most wonderful calves." He sped home and wanted to write his mother a letter, but couldn't. He had to masturbate with the phantasy of those ankles. Then he was able to write the letter, and afterwards he fell off into a deep sleep. When he awoke, he felt like a new-born child. "He could have torn up a tree."

The language of the patient is especially important. His simile is a psychic revelation. I hope later to show just what he meant by it. At any rate, it seems plain that his colossal excitement was somehow connected with incestuous phantasies (mother?).

He associates the name Marie to the girl (the mother of God?). But he says he can't remember any Marie in his life.

He continues to describe his parapathic symptoms. He is afraid of high mountains and looking out the window. He feels drawn into the depths. He feels himself weak and small and helpless like a child.

It also occurs that the weaker of the two women in his wrestling phantasies wins. Indeed, in the wrestling matches he had with other boys, he would often let the weaker one conquer him and would then experience an enormous pleasure (a phantasy of wrestling with his father? Being a boy, he identifies himself with his father. This explanation is not communicated to him). He often has the woman conquer the man in these phantasies. This is contrary to his feelings of propriety in sexual matters, but affords him a paroxysmal orgasm nevertheless. He also is

sensually thrilled when the woman kills the man in his imaginations. (The female in him overcomes the male, and he then
submits to the father who is the representative of manhood.)

The following day he brought a dream. Last evening he had
to masturbate three times and it was after the third time that he
fell asleep and had the dream. Just before the second time he
masturbated, he had a waking dream which he noted as follows:

Two persons are wrestling with each other. One is a woman
and the other is either a woman or perhaps a man. The first
female is slender, delicate, lovely (but) quick and muscular.
Ankle circumference, 12.3 cm.; calf, 23.8 cm.; weight, 112 lbs.;
difference between calf and ankle, 11.5 cm., i.e., about 100 per cent.

The second woman possesses a manifestly heavier build, and
is naturally stronger and superior as regards her muscular energy.
She is, however, plumper and less agile. Ankle, 19.4 cm.; calf,
25.1 cm.; weight, 135 lbs.; difference between calf and ankle,
5.7 cm., or only about 30 per cent.

During the match, the coarse strength of the second woman is
easily superior to the effort of the other. The delicate one wins,
however, because of her greater agility and especially because of
her finer display of muscular control and the greater difference between ankle and calf circumference.

Symbol of the delicate ankle: weakness. Symbol of the well-
developed calf, i.e., the greater difference between the two:
strength.

The deep dream following the third onanistic act took place
about 1.30 to 2.30 in the morning.

An old man leads me into a garden (home) and shows me
about. This garden (?) lies within the midst of someone's else
property (I don't recall what we did in that garden). Suddenly
I notice that I have forgotten the key to my house. The old man
looks at a watch and says, "A quarter to ten." And I replied,
"Then I can get home just in time to get in before they lock the
door at ten o'clock." To my astonishment I discover that I am
minus some of my clothing (the trousers?).

A young man is added to our dinner table. He says at table
(apparently to the woman of the house, the wife of the old man),
"If you eat as late (9.45) as this again, I'll give notice and leave!"
The old man looked up at him in surprise and pointed to me as if
to say, "You're not alone here." I acted (wrote) as if I hadn't
heard anything.

First of all, it is not infrequent that patients tell us they had to masturbate several times in one night. That reveals an irresistible sexual impulse which cannot, evidently, be stilled by onanism. The reason for this is that the specifically determining phantasy is not accessible to consciousness and only mitigated by substitutes. The patient states that he is busied only with the wrestling phantasies and that he has no idea what could have been the prototype for these pictures. We know, on the other hand, that he first began to indulge in these phantasies long after he had actually seen a wrestling match. The above waking phantasy is characterized by a curious precision which reckons to a decimal. Such precision cannot be a haphazard occurrence. There must be some connection between these figures and his paraphilia or his specific onanistic phantasies. We can go on the assumption that a closer analysis of these figures will lead us to a deeper understanding of his parapathia, i.e., if the patient willingly delivers up his material. I nevertheless reckon with bitter resistance for I cannot expect that he will willingly disclose the secret hidden behind these figures.

I say, "I am especially surprised by the precision of your figures in these wrestling phantasies. What can you associate to these figures? What is the meaning of that difference of 11.5 cm. and 5.7 cm.? Have these particular figures any relationship with occurrences in your family history?"

He is quiet and thinks long. Then he says, "Such numbers fall into my mind in droves. They are the product of my playful fancy. I can't find any kind of special sense in them."

I am not the less convinced that these numbers have a special determination and turn to the analysis of the dream. I think that perhaps the dream will forge a path back to the numbers.

The first thing is the episode with the elderly gentleman who leads him through his garden. His first association is myself and the functional interpretation of the dream becomes clear.

I lead him through the garden of my science which lies in the midst of foreign property (religion—parapathia). He is supposed to help me find the solution to his parapathia, but he has forgotten the key. I remind him of the fact that it is high time he were getting well and on the way home, i.e., becoming pure and able to work. It is already a quarter to ten and the hour when all the houses lock their outer doors is drawing near. He is willing to dispense with the key and run for it (this time for his mother to whom he is greatly attached). But he discovers that he has undressed before me, he is missing several articles of apparel. In-

deed, he has revealed a considerable portion of himself to me. He
is dissatisfied with the analysis. Before one gets to the material
benefits of life, it's too late. He will give notice on the analysis
and leave. He is conscious of these tendencies of his neurotic
ego and, being sensitive, puts on as if he would continue the
treatment and not have noticed the conduct of his enraged inner
person, his brother.

He has, however, a rather recent experience to relate in reference to the numbers 9.45 and 10 o'clock. He believes that this
experience has something to do with the cause of his onanistic
acts. Yesterday, after the analytic hour, he felt quite perturbed
and was impelled to run about and look for a woman, any woman,
a girl, a sexual object that wore sheer stockings and had a narrow
ankle. For the first time, he felt curious about how far up he
could see, whether he would be able to see as far as the garter
and how the stocking was held up (ankle and garter as symbols
of pressure and impression). He accosted a girl who seemed
quite plainly dressed. He noticed immediately that she was a
Jewess, and, although he is a full-blooded Nordic and a German
nationalist, too, his weak spot is a Jewess. He feels they have
more class, more . . . Well, he asked her to go walking with
him and she surprised him by accepting the invitation. Then she
began telling him her troubles, how her parents were dead and
she had to live with relatives, etc., etc. Although he appeared to
be very touched by the story, he never forgot his purpose. He
wanted to take her to a hotel. He tried to kiss her, but she
slapped him and said, "What do you think I am, anyhow? I
want you to know that I'm a decent girl and even if I'm not
dressed up in finery, I'll have you understand I'm no prostitute."
Suddenly she looked at her watch and said, "Oh, I must be home
by 9.45 or 10 at the latest." He escorted her home and then asked
her if he could see her again. She said that she would leave that
to chance.

This episode was a deep humiliation for him. He felt as if
slapped in the face by this answer. He had been used to conquer
whomever he had set out to overcome. But this little Jewess,
who looked like nobody at all, showed him so much resistance.
Isn't he fine and stimulating enough for anyone to want to be
with him?

Then he began to think of me. He considers it even more of a
humiliation to be analyzed by me without enjoying the pleasure
of making the analyst's acquaintance. I don't permit him the

intimacy of the house. But in the dream, he has revenged himself. He has made himself a part of my family, goes through all the intimate and hateful little family scenes, but he acts discreetly, as if he hadn't heard or seen a thing.

The coarsely material interpretation is even more clear. He is now reminded of the narrow crevice between the buttocks. This is provoked by the narrow piece of property between two other properties in the dream. The garden is the anus, his trousers are down, but he acts like that little Jewess: he doesn't want to give me his penis (he left his key at home). He says he must run home and thus wants to revenge himself upon me by refusing me (identification with the girl he met). He is the young gent and gives me, the elderly gentleman, notice that he will quit the analysis.

While he is developing the sexual side of the interpretation, I call his attention to the approaching termination of the analysis. He laughs and says he would be tickled, finally, to have someone who seemed to understand his difficulties. He believes the young man could also be someone else.

"Have you ever heard anyone say that if dinner were ever served so late again, they would give notice and leave?"

"Sure," he called out, jumping up, "that's what my brother once threatened."

"Which brother?"

"My older brother, who committed suicide."

"How much older was he?"

"About five years."

"Exactly?"

"Well, let's see. Why, it's exactly five years and seven months (5.7) and the other brother who's alive is just eleven years and five months older than myself (11.5)."

The figures are completely cleared up when we understand that when he was nineteen years and four months old, his brother was twenty-five years exactly. His weight is one hundred and thirty-five pounds. The figures for the first wrestling match refer manifestly to an older brother. In other words we have here the curious fact that the figures have nothing to do with the female ankles and calves, but that they simply express in a roundabout way the age and weight differences between himself and his brothers.

The whole business about the ankles and calves is thus seen to be a blind, a hoax. He is not at all interested in women's legs.

He is provoked by his relationships with his brothers. We know from the data he has given us that he was the object of homosexual attention on the part of his brothers. One of his brothers led him through the forbidden garden of homosexuality, but now that brother is cool towards him, has married, and is no longer a sexual object.

He was always insanely jealous of his brothers. Jealous when they were intimate and confidential with each other while he was left out of it. He was jealous of his father, too, and especially of his mother whose little playmate he wanted to be. He wished all his rivals dead and then later suffered pangs of guilt over the suicide of his father and brother because he had harbored death wishes against them.

The wrestling matches of the weaker woman with the stronger one represent his struggle with his older (stronger) brother. But the younger, more agile, one wins despite his lighter weight. The winner then gains the highest prize, the mother, whose life he shares. The eleven and one-half-year older brother now lives with his mother and that is what drove him out of the house. He wants to possess either the brother or the mother, but only for himself alone.

He harbors murder in his breast. He became a chemist in order to be able to get rid of people. In the dream, too, he sees a meal served in which he takes no part, but acts only as an onlooker to whom the meal means nothing.

The effect of this explanation of the figures as symbols of the age differences between himself and his brothers was dumbfounding. I have never seen such an expression of surprise. He was not happily excited, but stood there as if he were a criminal caught in the act. He became red as a beet, searched for something to say, but had no answer for the facts.

I felt that I had made a mistake and reckoned with the fact that the "satisfied" patient would never return. The following day he told my maid that his mother was ill and that he would have to go home. He bade her good-bye, but left me not even a line.

For months I didn't hear from him but then a repenting letter came. I had been the only one who had ever understood him and he would like to continue the treatment at all costs. Could I pardon his flight? His mother had died meanwhile, his feelings had not betrayed him. Now he has but one goal in life and that is to overcome his leg phantasies and become well again.

I answered him in the affirmative, since I was interested in the further possibilities of the analysis, but neither the horse nor the rider ever returned.

In this case we have observed the signs of genuine fetishism:

1. The system. The fetish lover builds himself a complicated system with all kinds of abstruse and eccentric love conditions. This system contains pointers to the origin of the parapathia and the patient's family history.

2. The fetishism is a means to the avoidance of the sexual partner. Our patient never had an orgasm with women, nor does he have intercourse frequently although he finds it easy to win them. He never sticks to one woman for any length of time. He gives her up and remains faithful to his masturbatory tendencies. In the past year, he tried to have intercourse but twice and both times he failed.

3. The harem cult. He collected innumerable photos of many favorites. Photographs of the legs, of course, which he used alternately during his onanistic practices.

4. The fetishism disguises the obsessional neurosis. He exhibits the well-known impulse to search, to hunt; an impulse which we have already disclosed as the call of the past.

5. He is pious and makes of this piety a fetish. Inwardly he is devout, but outwardly he is a freethinker who tries to proselyte the various members of his family to newer religious forms. His fetishism enables him to turn from the female, but he complicates the condition to such an extent that he finally has altogether depreciated reality. We must ask ourselves: When will our patient ever have the opportunity to witness such a wrestling match as he dreams of? It is also interesting to note that he avoids these wrestling matches. Although at the time he was being analyzed, female wrestling matches were being held in Vienna, he never went to a one, feigning an anxiety to become completely overcome by his illness.

We, however, know better. The amazons didn't interest him per se. The match which provokes him is the struggle with his brothers, the struggle for a better position in life, the struggle for his mother's love and for the love of one of his brothers. This is what shadows him and makes him incapable of any work.

V

FETISHISM AND INCEST

An especially important case of fetishism came under the observation of Dr. Sigg. The author, who had reported on the case at the annual meeting of the Swiss Psychiatric Society in 1914, offered me his still unpublished material for this book. Because of the war, my book was not published at that time, although the material was prepared. I took the opportunity to expand the material and to search for new cases. At my request, Dr. Sigg's paper was published in the *Zeitscrift für Sexualwissenschaft* in 1915 under the title "Zur Casuistik des Fetischismus," and I added epicritical remarks ("Ergänzende Bemerkungen zum Fall von Dr. Sigg"). With Dr. Sigg's authorization, I herewith present the case because of its interest and instructiveness.

Case 19—At four years of age, the healthy, intelligent and now thirty-year-old patient used to crawl into his parents' bed. They played with him. He imagined his mother to have a penis until the observation of his little sister taught him better. He preferred his mother to his father because she was more tender and soft. Up to seven he used to sleep in the room next to his parents. He would kiss his mother on the neck or on the breast; and he liked to play with his penis, but always was slapped if he were caught. They used to tell him that if he did that any more, he wouldn't grow. When his little sister came in his fourth year, he still believed the fable of the stork, but at eleven he was already sexually enlightened enough to know just where the latest addition came from. He cannot remember having seen his parents naked nor can he recall ever having heard anything special while eavesdropping about their room. It was thus that the second pregnancy of his mother (when he was ten) quite surprised him.

As a boy he was rather untidy, afraid of water and being washed, dependent and spendthrifty. He was very much afraid of one of his uncles because of the latter's strictness and whippings. At about four he used to like playing with his penis and pushing it all the way back into the scrotum. At six he followed a little girl and wanted to "marry" her. In his seventh year, he played a good deal with a somewhat younger cousin, practised mutual masturbation with him, pressed his erected penis between the thighs of his cousin and played "father and mother" with him. In addition to these onanistic manipulations, he already had another sexual object at this time which, however, he always kept a secret from everyone for "fear that it would get about."

At nine years of age he succumbed to a desire for the possession of his mother's brown leather gloves, took them to bed with him, pressed them against his perineum between the anus and the scrotum, and then put them on and masturbated. He claims that it made no difference to him that they belonged to his mother. He put them on "because of the feeling it gave" him, because he "had a thrill," "simply feeling the leather gives me pleasure." That certainly meant something sensual, he thought. In the same box with the gloves, he also found some rubber tubes for irrigators and these he either carried around with him, like the gloves, in his bag, or he would press them also to his bottom and wind them around his penis whenever he were alone and felt himself unwatched. In doing so, he always felt a "pleasant pain." At about this time, too, he began to develop an interest in women's gloves, and in the dancing class, he would dance only with the girls who wore kid gloves. He liked gray gloves pretty well, but the woollen ones the dancing teacher wore left him cold. His daily masturbation was more regular than the dancing lesson.

He was twelve years old before he had his first ejaculation, and soon thereafter the glove, too, took on an increased sexual importance. Whenever he would feel the leather of the glove, he would get an erection and would begin to think of girls who could wear them. He denies having had coitus phantasies at the time. In his walks, he would count the number of pairs of gloves he had seen and said: "My eyes were spellbound." The brown or black gloves on the street were his chief source of interest, whereas silk gloves or white ones made no impression upon him. At about the same time he began to get erections whenever he would fight with other boys, and the same would take place in climbing. He liked to brace himself again the trunk of the tree.

He found some rubber probes at home and used them to sound his urethra as far up as the bladder. He said the pain was a pleasant one. He would give himself enemas and, as with his urine, he would withhold the water as long as possible. In addition to gaining pleasure from touching leather or rubber goods, he also liked to smell them, but denies ever having had an interest in the odor of his excrements. His chief intentions were to come in contact with leather and rubber goods as much and as frequently as possible (he never cultivated any love affairs and was quite proud to be a boy). Whenever he had to defecate, he remained in the toilet as long as he could.

At sixteen, the horizon of his autoerotic activities was advanced. He would tie rubber bands together and then bind his penis and his scrotum with the elastic, or he would push his penis far back into his scrotum. Rubber tubes were also made use of in this manner and finally he came to tie the elastic about his penis or his scrotum or both in certain definite ways. He was thereby especially concerned that his perineum should be pressed down tight. At that point below the scrotum he would tie big, elastic knots in order to create constant pressure. "Of course, it always pained me somewhat, but I liked it."

With his entrance into a boys' school, all these manipulations as well as the daily masturbation found a temporary end. He nevertheless continued to take gloves to bed with him until he was caught. On the other hand, he finally retained his urine so long that the doctor had to be called. He was in bed for six weeks, but claims that he suffered from appendicitis. The doctor, he said, told him it "all came from masturbation."

Just before he left for school, he visited a prostitute with some of his friends, and had intercourse with a woman for the first time. Since then he often has phantasies of normal coitus when masturbating. He has also paid attention to the girls, but has never gone further than petting and kissing. Away from home, he felt a little more free in the exploitation of his interests in gloves, made the acquaintance of women who wore brown or black new gloves, made them gifts of gloves, but later demanded them back again. When walking with a girl, it was always a special pleasure to hold her gloved hand. This excited and gratified him sexually. He would stand before the window of a rubber goods store and derive great enjoyment from the sight. He bought considerable quantities of rubber tubing, such as is used for douches, and bound the tubing, as in earlier days, several times about his penis or scrotum and also took the tubing to bed with him, or carried it about in his bag. He became acquainted with an elderly gentleman with whom he practised mutual masturbation. This man still plays a part in his phantasies.

When he returned home, he took active part in some clubs, sat on committees, exercised, acted in a dramatic society where he played female rôles, played some music, but could not banish a certain persistent moodiness. At bottom he was reticent, never satisfied with himself and frequently the subject of suicidal ideas. At home he was usually depressed. Whereas, in youth, he had been an impassioned reader of Indian stories, he now became interested in the singular sadism of the Middle Ages with their torturous and inquisitory instruments. He bought numbers of books about these practices, but also continued to buy more and more rubber goods. With long rubber tubing he would wind spirals about his loins and scrotum, hang condoms on the tubing, roll a rubber bed-flask about his penis and scrotum, insert tubes into his rectum and give himself copious enemas or shove sounds into his ears and his nose. To satisfy his sadistic trends, he would visit divers museums where he would become almost glued to the collections of instruments of torture, and afterwards he would dream about them all over again in his phantasies with himself as the tortured subject. Strangely enough, he cultivated the intimacy of a woman at the same time and cohabited with her several times a week in normal fashion. This, of course, tended to inhibit his onanistic habits, and he even gave up carrying his rubber goods collection about with him. He also served in the army without taking his rubber tubing with him. But as soon as his clandestine love affair was at an end, he withdrew again to the cultivation of his former eccentricities, bought up more rubber goods, masturbated with a rubber bottle, and even tied the bottle to his penis and scrotum in order that he might walk about during the day in constant satisfaction. He was very much afraid of venereal infections, read a great deal about syphilis, and claims that this was the reason he circumscribed his heterosexual relations.

From year to year, his onanistic indulgence increased in scope. It is of note that he was not especially interested in the consummation of sexual satisfaction by means of the ejaculation, he was rather more attached to the phantasies he had, how he would become rich, have a fine future, etc. Or he would fancy tortures which would be demonstrated to him. He claims to have masturbated whole nights, simultaneously reading masochistic literature (see his bibliography attached at the end of the case history).

Finally, he became engaged, although the chief purpose of the engagement was the acquisition of further capital for his business. During the two years that he was engaged, he continued his rubber and glove fetishism unabated because "he wanted to get in all that he could while there was yet time." He went to extreme pains to hide his collection of fetishes from his fiancée, but soon after they were married, his wife discovered the bag filled with rubber goods and even noticed that her husband was not so clean and tidy as she had believed him to be. She abruptly refused to comply with his request that she wear gloves whenever they went out together. After four years of married life, they began to consult specialists, but these all gave them an unfavorable prognosis. The wife naturally also suffered from her husband's moodiness, depressions and from the constant quarreling, which was provoked by his being caught at his old habits. He began to feign business trips, but would use his time away from home gratifying his fetishistic tendencies to the full or having intercourse with other women. His wife gave birth to three children, the youngest of which was generally considered as oversexed. He played constantly with his penis and had frequent erections at two years of age.

His hopes of ridding himself of his perversions by marriage were not fulfilled, and soon his wife afforded him no satisfaction at all. But his interest in gloves continued to increase. In the street car, he always tried to gain a seat from which he could see all the women and at the theatre or during a concert he would look about him towards the women who were wearing gloves. Whenever he catches sight of women's new brown or black gloves, he is promptly seized by the desire to grasp the hand that wears them in his own, to touch the leather. He stated that he would not have gone with other women had his wife worn the gloves he always prepared for her before a walk. He even threatened her whenever she would refuse, by saying that he would leave her for others who, he claimed, would gladly comply with his wishes. Gloves had such an effect upon him that he would first have to rub his eyes before he could look away from them. He also had the desire to masturbate with such gloves or to cohabit with the women who wore them. To suit him they must be tight-fitting, without a single crease, and absolutely clean. He cannot tolerate any defects in them. Nor does he evince the slightest interest in the usual or coarse glove such as those of suède. The gloves he has once given as a gift and then demanded back in return for new ones he prefers to carry in his pockets. He would first grasp them firmly in his hand, press and rub them a little, and feel relieved. It was not uncommon for him to follow women wearing new black gloves about the streets and thus forget his

own business. On such escapades he was always oppressed by
the fear of being seen by his friends. This was also the cause of
his anxiety whenever he would look for gloves in a theatre. At
home, he would often pull on a pair of gloves and masturbate, but
only if he felt that he were surely alone, or only in bed where he
was able to satisfy himself and deceive his wife. Before he could
shake hands with anyone, he would first have to rub his hands,
wipe them off, and then look to see if they were dry. He made
repeated promises to his wife to stop his practises, but was not able
to desist from them. His wife, by the way, played no part in his
onanistic phantasies. On the contrary, he preferred to indulge
himself in dreams of being a wealthy merchant, in phantasies about
the rapid rise of his business, etc.

It was not long before he began to interest himself in sadistic
literature, bought a considerable number of the desired books and
also added to his collection of fetishes. He had a mistress, too,
but she would not comply with his perverse desires. More and
more his sexual satisfaction with his wife depended upon what
was contained in his phantasies. In short, he gratified her, but
never himself. He also wet the bed a few times. His clandestine
affairs originated, he claims, through the agency of his glove
escapades. The longer he was married, the more he felt himself
to be nothing but his wife's slave, and yet he did not wish to
give in to her. In one respect, he derived pleasure even from the
little quarrels with his wife and from the scenes in which she
would catch him at his practises. He preferred to see her in her
underthings, would love to pet and kiss her then, and often experienced a sudden desire to have intercourse with her immediately after a meal. Many times, his onanistic phantasies consisted
of images in which he saw himself beaten and punished by her.
Nevertheless, he did suffer greatly from the continual quarreling
with his wife and was also very jealous of her. He was always
afraid that she was on the lookout for a substitute, especially since
she always boasted to him of her many admirers. In his suicidal
depressions, he never thought of the act without first thinking of
taking her into death with him so that she should not be able to
marry again. For his clandestine affairs he preferred thin and
slender figures, apart from those who attracted him because of
perversities, but he did not care for women of the male type.

Whenever he went on a trip, he invariably sent his collection of
fetishes secretly before him and would happily anticipate the
night when he could live alone. His collection was contained in a

large cardboard box and consisted of stomach tubes, enema tubes, rubber bottles, long, black stockings, rubber bathing caps, ice bags, condoms and a few dozen adapters for hypodermic syringes. In addition: leather aprons, a leather-lined corset (which he made himself), leather puttees, a leather headgear and mask with holes in front for the eyes, nose and mouth; leather sleeves which reached from the shoulders to the fingers, black, leather gloves as well as a pile of old, collected gloves and divers small rubber articles, the last of which he would stuff under his pillow. The patient himself stated that he had always desired the closest contact with leather goods and always had to have the leather fit his body or an organ as tightly as possible. The patient was a confirmed smoker, but was not a heavy drinker. He considered his perineum as his most sensitively erogenous zone. Before he would indulge himself in the pleasures of dressing himself in his leather clothing (which he had made with his own hands of the finest glove leather), he would first press a bundle of gloves, which had been rolled together with rubber tubing, tightly against his perineum. He would then also wind tubing about his hips and genitals. He preferred to use the rubber goods between his legs because these articles were washable. Altogether he was a great lover of change in his divers utensils, but would then promptly achieve sexual gratification on the new article. Another of his favorite practises was to fill a rubber bag with warm water, press it against his anus and then bind his feet together. In order to have everything fit closely to the body he had to make use of a great number of straps. The final stage of indulgence consisted in a masturbatory period of several hours without ejaculation. This excess, he feared, was very injurious to his health. Meanwhile, he would read such trash as *Les Gants de l'Idole* or similar books. If it were at all possible, he always tried to stand a mirror opposite his bed, so that he could look at himself whenever he wanted. He differentiates the value of the two fetish types by saying that the rubber had a more tactile, the leather a more optical, effect on him. It was a fact that the sight of leather and skin gave him the greatest thrill.

Some days he would introduce rubber tubes into his rectum and walk about the house in this fashion with a part of the tube hanging out. He liked to cover his penis with condoms and withheld his urine for as long a time as possible. Simple urethral douches he would follow with complete filling of the bladder by means of syringes to which needles with olive tips were attached. He also liked to press his penis against hard objects or clamp it between things. He said that he was able to preserve an erection during matrimonial cohabitation only as long as he was twicked in the perineum. He denies ever having had a premature ejaculation.

His passive and also somewhat active algolagnia was gratified by occasional visits to a similarly perverse prostitute. He nevertheless retained more of a passivity than an activity in these acts. He would permit himself to be whipped until the blood nearly ran, would delight in the "warm feeling" which he compared with the simile of a pair of warm trousers. He permitted himself to be strapped prone to the bed in a crucifixion position. The whipping would not provoke an erection. "I let myself be whipped and beaten because I like it." After his turn, he would then do the same to the prostitute and would also derive enjoyment from this. They would then stick each other with pins and needles about twenty times in the back, buttocks and legs and were tickled if the blood spurted. When alone, sometimes, he would even tie himself down and would then concoct all kinds of procedures in his phantasies, such as cold-water douches, etc. He would beat himself over the back and buttocks with his stomach tubes until he were bruised. His lust was always intensified by simultaneous onanism. The mirror had always to be in readiness for him after such self-inflicted punishment. His female partner he would often nearly choke to death.

He became more and more estranged from his wife and, though he was finally impotent with her, he simulated orgasm until his failure to get an erection betrayed him. The erection then became impossible except during fetishistic onanism. In addition, his wife's strict observation forced him to drop his illegitimate relations with women, too, and this bound him all the more to his rubber and leather goods. He felt that he could no longer exist without them, became almost encapsulated and finally began to forget even his business duties for the sake of his perversions.

The persistent snooping of his wife forced him to transfer his collection of tools to his country place near by and it was there that he indulged himself extravagantly for a few days when his wife forbade him to enter the house in town. His impotence continued to give him more and more food for thought, however. He considered whether or not his wife wouldn't begin divorce proceedings which would let the cat out of the bag. It is noteworthy that he was easily able to forego during his military service all those things which attracted him irresistibly in his private life. Nevertheless, he was always able to make plenty of female acquaintances which he excused with the aid of his glove fetishism. He also liked to watch the slaughtering of animals. Although he was a great smoker, he did not like cigarettes with tips, and often liked to chew his cigars thoroughly. If he were at any time not in a position to make use of his rubber things during the day he would resort to the trick of using a handkerchief or the tail of his shirt to press against his perineum until he could feel it. His onanistic phantasies grew greater in importance and the chief characteristic now was that they became increasingly masochistic. He would see himself the subject of the cruelest attacks, the slave of the brutal hangings by the feet. He displayed no verbal masochism and reacted sensitively when abused, but he liked to be caught by his wife. This "letting himself be caught" played a leading rôle in his dreams. He was frequently dejected, sought less and less social contact, suffered greatly from his constant moodiness. Following his onanistic excesses, he was an especially irritable creature and could be plunged into long fits of silence by the slightest business details. He denies having had the slightest leanings towards men after his childhood days.

With a few exceptions, this completely healthy and very intelli-gent man was able to desist from his masturbatory habits with the aid of the sedative cure with Sedobrol. He was, however, never able to keep his hands quiet during a conversation; they were always reaching for his genitals. In the beginning, he paid no attention to his external appearance, but soon became an excellent social being with his musical inclinations, his dancing and his refreshing effect on others. He ceased carrying things in his pockets, but was able to take his mind off gloves only with difficulty. His chief diversion was the weaving of baskets. It was never noticed in the place that he displayed any schizophrenic signs, but he was doubtless an introverted individual. His very free disposition of affect was remarked by his observers and he was able to entertain others for long periods of time. He desired very much to be freed from his suffering, but his business soon called him away. At that time, his fetish collection was withheld from him as well as his library of about fifty perverse books.

Once returned home, he was not immediately able to cohabit with his wife and there was a resumption of the furious scenes as a result of his moodiness. I feared that I might hear he had had a relapse of his old trouble, but one day he called on me, gave me permission to make scientific use of his case and told me that he was living on the best of terms with his wife, has intercourse with her which satisfies him and is able to work steadily and industriously in his business. It is seldom that he succumbs to onanism, but he still must carry a glove in his pocket. He has not collected any more fetishes than that, however.

We have here a man who has masturbated since earliest youth. His whole perverse construction has been built upon this onanism. It is to the greater effect of this masturbation that he indulged himself in his fetishistic, masochistic and sadistic impulses, and the longer he lived the more truly did this habit take over his entire sexuality. Stekel is doubtless right when he says that we should not take too much stock of the earliest infantile memories. These so-called memories may be later products. An important factor in this case is his great interest in his mother's gloves at nine years of age. He promptly made a fetish of them, pressed them against his genitals and either masturbated with them or carried them about with him. It was not possible, however, to elicit the original provocation of this first perverse expression. We cannot say whether or not the fact that the mother's gloves were brown also decided the color of later glove fetishes. This is a possibility, but cannot be proved. It is of interest to us to learn that this glove provoked sexual excitement when pressed to the perineum as well as to the penis and that the autoerotic former habit continued throughout the patient's life to possess an undiminished force. In the course of time he began to use rubber in this region instead of leather, the reasons doubtless being the greater cleanliness and the cheaper cost. The earlier indulgences in simple glove bundles gave place to more and more complicated applications to the perineum which all had the common purpose of provoking a "pleasurable pressure" (his coitus phantasies). He yearned for his "pleasurable pain" and was gratified by it. Beginning with simple circles about the penis and scrotum, he advanced to double circles and was finally executing figures of eight about the hips and genitals. This indicates a considerable extension of his erogenous zone upwards in the course of time. We may also note a special tendency to bring the leather as close to the skin as possible and this attitude applies to every conceivable mucous membrane in the apertures of the body. He went in for probings of the urethra, bladder douches, large enemas, the introduction of objects into the rectum, nasal and gastric soundings and the occlusion of the ears with rubber. Finally, his whole skin was made to feel the fetish. He practically encased himself in corsets, puttees and bandages and found such a strait-jacket condition pleas-

urable or at least the pleasurable preface to a gratifying masturbation. This skin fetish also was of the same material as his
most original fetishistic object, the glove. This man who paid
so little attention to his own appearance demanded the extreme of
cleanliness in gloves and rubber goods. The enjoyment he derived in a fetish became greater when that fetish was compressed,
a trait which characterized his early relations with gloves, the
objects which directed the course of all his later sexual life. Compulsion, grasping, pressing, all these traits run throughout the
course of his perversity. The compulsion evidently increased the
fetishistic delight. It was only in moments of external coercion,
at times when he was unable to adhere to his fetishistic practises,
that he satisfied himself by simply carrying the object in his
pockets or under his coat.

Parallel with this fetishistic habit, his normal sexuality appears
to have developed also. At seventeen he already had his first sex
relations and continued from then on more and more prolifically.
Despite the patient's claim that his engagement, which took place
at a ball, was in large measure controlled by the effect of gloves,
we know that the essential motivation lay in the fact that this marriage meant a considerable increase in his business strength, that
this increased business stability, further, meant that he would
have to pay less attention to business and would consequently have
more time for his perversities. And although his eccentricities
were noticed even during the engagement period, they were married nevertheless, i.e., the business deal went through. There can
be no doubt that the patient knew himself well enough to mean
that statement about wanting to get in as much of his masturbation as possible before marriage only as a bit of humor. His
extra-marital relations continued even after marriage and were
actually made the substitute of marital duties whenever possible
because his wife made any addition of fetishistic habits, even of
normal ones, impossible. The more he became involved in masochistic and sadistic phantasies and practises, the more he withdrew from his wife. His business incapacity had been sufficiently
covered by his wife's dowry. We have, as a matter of fact,
already seen how his wife had enabled him to indulge himself
more than ever. His relationship with a perverse prostitute constituted, as he said, the high-water mark of his perverse existence.
The strict and persistent threats of his wife as well as his own
fear of public revelations, finally drove the man back to autoerotic
habits, and it was then that he became impotent. He was lastly

in a curiously autistic and perverse state of autoerotism such as can hardly be described adequately. His jealousy of his wife increased in direct proportion to the advance of his impotence. Following his estrangement from his wife, a perverse female companion served him for a while, until even this was dropped and he landed at a level where it appears that the fetish had completely supplanted the female.

In summarizing the gradual development of this abnormal sexuality, its proliferation over the bounds of normal instinct, we must say that this man was suffering from a compulsion neurosis in the full sense of the word. As Stekel so accurately puts it, this is a case of flight from woman. It is also rather certain that, even had his wife gratified his perverse designs upon her, she would not have satisfied him to the end.

This case offers numerous analogies to the case of corset fetishism published by Abraham. "As with a magic attraction my eyes were always directed to women's shoes . . . an inelegant shoe invariably repulses me and fills me with abhorrence," says Abraham's patient. We have only to exchange the word shoes for gloves and the quotation could fit the words of our own patient. In this patient's glove fetishism, the thought of how the hand contained in the glove would be pressed also played a major part. At the age of about sixteen to eighteen the patient also developed an interest for his mother's corset, tried it on several times and felt well in it. He always preserved his perverse tendencies as a deep secret. It was not possible to elicit any psychic traumata in infancy, but we see that the perversion was already present in his early interest in his mother's gloves. The one difference between this case and that of Abraham is to be found in the fact that our patient early developed normal sexual contact, and the regression to autoerotic habits took place comparatively late. For some time his sexual goal consisted of gloves and his desire did not go beyond looking at or feeling them. His visual pleasure in this was incomparably great. A common feature of these two cases is found in the "affective rejection" of the fetish if it possessed unsatisfactory form or color or, conversely, a very imperative and demanding attachment to the fetish. In contrast to Abraham's patient, further, our patient displayed no koprophilic pleasure in smelling, but he did have castration phantasies. He enjoyed his penis tremendously, dreamed frequently of its size and how it was marvelled at by others. We must also emphasize his habit of retaining his excrements and the enemas he gave himself. It was not possible to elicit from the patient any information as to whether the same tendency dominated his masochistic punishing and binding habits. He did, however, like to lie motionless for hours at a time and create phantasies of all kinds of methods by which he would be showered with cold water at the slightest motion of his body. I am nevertheless chary about connecting this phantasy with his pleasurable habits of withholding his excrements. An important feature of these habits, however, was also the clamping of his genitals, the great emphasis of the anal zone. Water was also a constantly recurring element of his dreams.

At the time the gloves began to play such a rôle in his life, our patient must already have been specially constituted from a psychic point of view. We see that many other children have similar experiences without falling into the same habits. It is simply that others conceive gloves to be something quite different from what they mean to this patient. He made use of this first fetish in sexual practises on a very definite erogenous zone, but in addition to this perverse tendency he developed his normal sexuality, too. It was only after the period of marital and extra-marital sexuality that we saw a rapid increase in his perversions and a corresponding reduction of his normal libido. He regressed to his earlier autoerotic activities, but transformed them to approximate the level of his adult intelligence. His normal sexuality itself had never actually been purely normal. He had brought the habit of masturbation with him from childhood and had not been able to divest himself of it as the normal individual is.

Jung writes: "The concept of normal sexuality contains the clause that all infantile tendencies be removed as far as possible, including even those which are not per se sexual in nature. The less this is the case, the greater is there a danger that the sexuality will become perverse. The basic condition of perversion is an infantile and poorly developed condition of sexuality." He considers perversion to be due to a disintegration of fully developed sexuality and not, as Freud, a rudimentary phase of normal sexuality. I consider our case to be a proof of Jung's position. Normal sexuality was present, but finally disintegrated again to form as a product a perversion which was recharged with libido. And the chief receptacle of this libido was our patient's hyperbolic phantasy, provoked by and at once attached to the perverse habits. Almost the entire reserve of libido was poured into these phantasies instead of being used for objects in the real world. It was at the point of being stuck fast in these phantasies that the patient came for treatment.

The success of my treatment is to be seen in the fact that this man, who was completely impotent and estranged from his wife, now lives a normal sexual life with her again, is able to work with his full powers and discloses no more perverse tendencies. The analytically cathartic probing of the perversions themselves and the consequent transference were alone sufficient to achieve a satisfactory goal, although the analysis of the unconscious was not effected. Whether, for this reason, the case will successfully withstand the test of time is a question I cannot answer, but a number of specialists gave him such a bad prognosis several years ago that the patient didn't dare to undertake any treatment until dire necessity finally drove him to it. The exhaustive discussions about his perversions dragged the patient out of that dark seclusion which had hitherto been so pleasant to him that asceticism which, to him as to every other pervert, was so valuable. He transferred his phantasies to me and disclosed to me the dark secret which had held him spellbound ever since his thirteenth year. This aided in taking the joy out of perversions which derived a major portion of their effect from the fact that they were practised in seclusion. In addition, he proceeded to transfer a part of his libido to his wife and to his work, i.e., to real objects instead of to phantasies. His libido was re-channelled from perversities back to normal desire and if this is not a permanent effect, it is only because the patient never learned the nature of his unconscious. Nor would this knowledge have been susceptible of constructive integration in his future.

The interesting development of this case of perversion was the sufficient cause of my exhaustive report.

THE PATIENT'S LIBRARY

1—Die Macht der Rute und die Macht der Frauen. 2—Qualvolle Stunden. 3—Die Peitsche als letztes Erziehungsmittel. 4—Der Sklave seiner Sklavin. 5—Die Prügelzucht in der Pension. 6—Die Selbstbewahrung (84 ed.). 7—Die

Zuchtrute von Tante Anna, by Else Romberg. 8—Sexuelle Irrwege, by Steingiesser. 9—Die Folter in der deutschen Rechtspflege sonst und jetzt. 10—Die Liebes-und Lebensstrafen. 11—Venus im Pelz, by L. von Sacher-Masoch. 12— Im Rausche der Sinne. 13—Unter strenger Hand. 14— Klostersitten und Nonnendisziplin. 15—Grausame Frauen, von Sacher-Masoch. 16—Aerztliche Untersuchungen und Scham-und Sittlichkeitsgefühl des weiblichen Geschlechtes. 17 —En 1592 : Le tour d'Europe d'un flagellant. 18—La ceinture de chasteté de Casanova. 19—Le Château de fouet. 20—En Luoisiane. 21—Les grands marchés d'esclaves. 22—Contes paillards. 23—Le journal d'une flagellée. 24—L'esclave gantée. 25—Souvenirs cuisants. 26—Les mille et une nuits. 27—Le jardin des supplices. 28—La divine Marquise. 29— Les déséquilibrées de l'amour : L'Abbe Ecornifleur. 30—L'inceste perverse. 31—Le fouet au moyen age. 32—Mémoires d'une fouetée. 33—Le trimophe de fouet. 34—Nos belles flagellantes. 35—La philosophie du fouet. 36—La terreur du fouet. 37—L'ecole du fouet. 38—Vierges fouettées. 39— La revanche du marmon. 40—Le pensionat du fouet. 41— Les humiliations de Miss Magde, etc., etc. . . .

The following are my "Epicritical Remarks on the Case of Dr. Sigg."

"To him who knows cases of genuine fetishism well, the above case will not be surprising. They are not at all so seldom as their discoverers or the patients believe, but they are seen so seldom by physicians because the secret of eccentricity is one of the psychic factors which give the disease its value and charm.

"One of the chief characteristics of these fetishists is that they feel themselves to be the only one who is suffering from such a perversion. The result of such a feeling of isolation is a 'pride of illness' which is also quite typical of every hypochondriac and every obsessional neurotic.

"The reason I take the liberty here to add a few remarks to the case of Dr. Sigg is because this case forms an extraordinarily clear and emphatic corroboration of the thesis which I laid down in my paper on 'The Psychology and Therapy of Fetishism.' [1]

"We find here first of all the harem cult which is present in every case of fetishism. Every one of them has a large collection of fetishes which continues to grow in size and serves the phantasy of the possessor in the same fashion as a harem of wives serves a pasha. There are always certain favorites among these fetishes and they alternate in being the favorites.

"Quite frequently we are told that the very first fetish was taken from among the mother's possessions (but even the father's or the sister's personal objects can be fixed upon). Such a statement gives us a lead to the problem of incest, the details of which have not yet been worked out analytically in respect of the question of fetishism. I am nevertheless not afraid to declare that the nucleus of the fetishistic neurosis can be the forbidden love of the patient for a close relative. Such a love is then subjected to repression and the result is that the repression is subsequently directed at the whole sex. In the case of Dr. Sigg it could be explained about as follows: His first leanings were towards his mother, the gloves being the symbolical representation of that woman. This could be one of the roots of the case and would also explain why he finds himself in flight from the female. Every woman becomes for him the incarnation of his mother and thus reflects his sinful thoughts. In the end, his love for his mother is transferred to leather and rubber goods. He clothed himself in his love, it pressed him, bound him; it was the obsession which he could not dodge.

"This case also displays the sign of 'auto-symbolic representation of the compulsion,' a factor which I have stressed so much. The fetish must symbolize the obsession. Thus: tight-fitting trousers, tight shoes, tightly-tied aprons, etc. Bandages, corsets, suspenders, abdominal compresses are preferred. Among my patients, there is one who makes a fetish of abdominal compresses and ties the compresses of others so tightly about his body that he feels a slight pain. The patient of Dr. Sigg laces himself in a leather suit and thus surrounds himself with his chosen neurosis, although it is really an indication that he has removed himself from a female partner and directed his attention to a secondary object. It is this displacement of libido from the living flesh to an inanimate object which quite typifies the fetishist. The fetish is not only a neutral thing which can serve either one of the bisexual intentions, but it is also something which has no relationship with living nature, it is the lifeless representative of a phantasy, helplessly serving the will of the fetish lover. The same tendency appears in a negative form in the masochistic phantasies and practises of this patient (law of bipolarity). He permits himself to be bound, beaten, tortured, and likes it because he has involuntarily merged the concepts of 'guilt and atonement' in one act. These tendencies of his disappear during the days of his military service because the strict compulsions of the service make every other form of obsession or compulsion, the fetishism included, quite superfluous. We must remember that the meaning of this neurosis is: I want to be compelled to something in order that I may not be guilty of it (pleasure without guilt).

"It is remarkable, also, how infantile the perversions are which the patient described. He wets the bed, is a little child again, and plays with dolls. His 'letting himself be caught' also rhymes with this characteristic. It is a typically infantile feeling which is derived from the well-known games of children.

"But what, let us ask, is the deeper motivation of this eccentric illness? What is the driving force which always keeps him on edge? I will answer these questions by quoting the conclusions of my remarks on the above-mentioned paper:

"Fetishism is a substitute for religion. In the form of a perversion it offers the possessor a new religion in which he can find his satisfactions according to his beliefs. This religion is derived from a compromise between an almost insurmountable sexuality and a strict piety. It offers the individual the opportunity of a more or less complete asceticism. Behind the façade of Satanism and libertinism there hides a devoutness whose aims lie far beyond the horizon of this world. The fetishist is embroiled in an open battle with every form of authority, but especially with God whom he secretly honors and believes to be serving in his own way by divers forms of abstinence."

"In other words: every true fetishist copies Christ. He suffers from a 'Christ neurosis.' Inwardly he is excessively proud of his suffering and hopes that the special nature of his pains will gain him something in the beyond.

"Many may think this declaration rather bold, but only a far-reaching analysis will disclose these hidden religious tendencies in any case. At bottom, every fetishist is chaste. He is a lamb in a wolf's skin.

"These Christ-like characteristics are also manifest in Dr. Sigg's case. Did we not hear the patient say that he liked to have himself tied to the bed in a crucifixion position and whipped. It is not improbable that the Saviour there appeared before his mind's eye."

I would like to add to these epicritical remarks by saying that this case contains many more corroborations of my theses. We see, first of all, quite an extraordinary harem cult and also a gradual retreat from woman. But we also see the patient's infantile attitude and the masked incest phantasies. Just as a sister's sewing pillow became a symbol of the sister in one case, so in this case does the mother's glove, which was the first object to fulfill a wealth of fetishistic conditions, become a symbol of the mother. It is probable that the inevitable stroking of the perineum during the care of the baby provoked libidinous sensations which led to the fixation of the perineum as a highly erogenous zone. But we must also not forget that the importance of tying, binding and pressing in this case points to the original situation of the child in diapers. This patient often pressed his shirt-tail between his legs, just as the diapers are drawn between babies' legs (psycho-sexual infantilism). In all cases of fetishism we come across a great pleasure in looking in at store windows which display goods of fetishistic value to them.

Such staring at a window display is a manifest recrudescence of childhood and possesses a certain symbolical meaning. It is looking backward at the display of memory, just as roaming reflects a tendency towards the past. Once before such a window display, the patient comes under the influence of a dreamy state, a sort of mental absence, in which the regression takes place. The patient's impulsive acts also take place in such a state, which permits of a complete regression to earlier levels and perhaps even to the mother's womb. The act of pressing against the perineum is a symbolization of the act of birth, which, for this patient, doubtless means a re-birth. It thus displays a sort of anagogic tendency.

The rubber goods are also to be taken symbolically. It stands for the phallus. What he really wants is a phallus so big that he can wind it about his body, large enough to put it into his own anus. He thus manifests a desire to create all his pleasures within his own body. He intensifies his autoerotism. It is for this reason that he is in love with his own penis, admires himself and his parts in the mirror. He wants to be a man and a woman simultaneously. This typically infantile attitude is also displayed by his bed-wetting habits, his urine retention (urine sexuality) [2] and his letting himself be caught, a well-known infantile habit perhaps best portrayed by the children's game of hide-and-go-seek. His wife must always play the bugbear which catches him.

The Christ tendency in his neurosis is indicated by his need for symbolical washing and the circumstance we have already mentioned of his being tied to the bed in crucifixion position and then whipped.

The criminal tendencies break through in his sadistic impulses. He nearly choked his fetishistic partner to death. It is very probable that his hate is directed against women as the representatives of sin. This is also the conception defended by the Christian religion and by the Bible—the female as the incarnation of sin, as the holy fathers described her. We will soon have an opportunity of seeing how a dream well appears to corroborate this approach to the problem (the two following dreams were kindly put at my disposal by Dr. Sigg of Zürich).

The dream which will give us so much insight into the psychology of the fetishist reads as follows:

"I find myself in one of the outlying districts of a metropolitan city (Paris?). On the sidewalk at the corner of the street, there is a table covered with fowl and passers-by take what they want without paying for it. As soon as I reached for a piece, however, they all looked at me out of the corners of their eyes. I immediately thought of apaches and quickly faded from the scene, but a pack of people with drawn knives sprang after me. I ran faster and faster. Suddenly some streetwalker ran towards me and cried, 'I'll grab him, I'll stab him.' She stabbed me through the tongue and yelled, 'Now I've poisoned him.' I felt a sharp pain in the tongue, was seized with a fear of blood poisoning and bit a piece of my tongue right off. Then I suddenly found myself at home in my parents' room. Other family relatives were also there. Even the chippy from the former scene was there, although better dressed. She offered me some powder with which to rub my hands. This was supposed to make my hands soft and smooth. I took the powder from her and rubbed my hands with it. But immediately I sensed some unpleasant tickling, my hands began to burn and I wanted to wash them. As soon as I touched the water, however, they burned even more because an acid was formed. My hands became quite bloody and I began to think of sulphuric acid. I called to my relatives under no circumstances to touch my wounded hands nor even the powder that that wench had. I saw thick scabs form on my hands and awakened with a terrific feeling of anxiety."

(The other dream of which the patient spoke is summarized as follows: He found himself to have an unnaturally large penis in his dreams. People congratulated him on the size of it and marvelled at him everywhere. The dream also had him on the water frequently, on small boats which were either half submerged or even flew through the air. He himself frequently walked through the air in his dreams, about a yard above the earth. Thus, e.g., from his home to the office or vice versa. Those who wondered at him tried to ape him, but were unsuccessful.)

The analysis of this dream brings a wealth of important points of view to light. It is, first of all, rather striking that his dream contains nothing of his fetishes, but that is a phenomenon which we can quite often observe. The dreams of the fetishist occur on another planet. By day they sin, but by night they act the holiest of the holies. They fight terrible battles with depravity and temptation and finally come out of the struggle as conquerors. Either that or they conceive themselves as saints and triumph over mere mortals. We see, in other words, that the background of every fetishism is a religious one. The basic tendency of the patient is to dream a pure life, to begin all over again and make it as chaste as possible. It is for this reason that the contrasts of white and black, vile and pure, etc., play such an important rôle in fetishistic lives. But to return to the analysis of the dream.

"I find myself in an outlying district of a metropolitan city (Paris?). On the sidewalk at a street corner there is a table covered with fowl." This scene is laid in Paris, the Babel of sin, i.e., the world is filled with depravity and temptation. Temptation is found even on the street (fowl as phallic symbols and the "board" instead of the "bed").

"The passers-by take what they want without paying for it, but as soon as I reach for a piece they all look at me out of the corners of their eyes." Everybody else may sin and doesn't have to pay the wages of sin, but for every little misstep I must expiate. "I hardly dare to taste of the joys of life which delight everybody, and immediately I am reprimanded." The apaches are the symbols of his conscience. They are the same figures as the fates. They run after him and stab him. He wants to fly from them. He is also fleeing from the homosexuality within him (the fowl as phallic symbols).

Then comes the prostitute who stabs and infects him. He tries to rid himself of the sin and bites off the infected part of his tongue (castration complex and death of his sexuality). His mouth is probably his most sensitive erogenous zone and the relationships between this symbol and the infantile pleasures of suckling are clear. The syphilis takes on the character of impurity altogether, of depravity, of incest. He is infected by sinful thoughts. Then he begins the great exodus from Paris back to his early childhood (Quo vadis?). The correct conclusion is that he should finally land at home in the room of his parents. The dream here also develops the relationship between the prostitute and the mother, the contrasts appear to fade and the streetwalker appears to take on the symbolization of sensual lust in all its meanings. Sexuality is thus the sin which is contrasted with the apparently desexualized mother. The powder which he used appears to me to be the sin of masturbation: first pleasurable, then burning. He wants to wash his hands of these sins. But the wounds burn in water. He becomes more and more widely infected, he is covered with

putrid wounds, he is a Lazarus. These bloody wounds indicate
the martyrdom he has embraced, his fetishism. The fear of
expiation, the anxiety that his wounds might infect his mother,
awaken him.

The trips he takes on small boats and his flying through space
are also interesting factors of the second dream. They are
nothing but spermatozoon dreams and mean to say: "I want to
begin life anew. I want to be pure and go through life as a
clean man. I want to be above all other men. I desire to be
something extraordinary." As it is, he is an exception because
of his parapathia, his fetishism.

The unnaturally large penis of his dreams quite corroborates
my statement that he desires such a large organ only in order
that he may be able to put it in his mouth or his anus. The
rubber tubing is but the symbolization of the long penis. What
a rubber bust does in one place, these tubes do in another: they
replace what he doesn't possess. He realizes an age-old children's dream to possess the longest penis in the world, or at
least the largest one that he has ever seen.

Dr. Sigg was good enough to put other dreams of this patient
at my disposal and, although it is a difficult matter to judge
dreams outside the bounds of an analysis, they might nevertheless permit us to come to some conclusions.

"1. I fitted the Czar with shoes and had to make them wider.
. . . Accompanied by a cousin (girl) of mine, I looked for a
carriage. A workingman was also with us. I found no carriage
and wandered about.

"2. I felt injured while at dinner and went off into another
room where a man was lying in bed drinking wine out of a bottle.
The wine ran over his lips and onto the bed and that greatly incensed me. Unpleasant awakening (the wine was some red, sticky
fluid and 'there was a dirty time in the bed. I was afraid that I
would be driven out, felt restless and cried because I felt so
pained.').

"3. I am a recruit in the army (is a captain as a matter of fact)
and had to go through training in the street. I had to get my rifle
which lay on the pavement and, in doing so, I had to crawl over
two upturned boats which lay there. There were several rooms in
a row on that pavement and I went into one of them to change my

clothes. But people were passing back and forth in front of the rooms and I felt somewhat ashamed. I lost time. Going back again, I was the forager and had to find a camping site for our kitchen. The place was filled with troops. A comrade in arms demanded wine of me, but I had none and gave him syrup to drink. He cursed and swore that it was water and I was quite upset to find that the bottle actually contained only watery lees.

"4. I find myself in the company of men, all of whom have their trousers down as far as the knees. We were in some reading room and there were no women present (this dream repeated itself many time).

"5. I am among schoolmates. I walk dejectedly about because it was said that I had to leave. Something was said about a venereal disease. The doctor says that the disease is not venereal. I was disconsolate because it was thought I had a venereal disease.

"6. I am walking with a friend named B. We walk into a hotel and are told that someone has been murdered. Bank notes have been stolen. B. and I are supposed to have committed the murder. The police commissioner comes in and we are questioned. A bunch of bank notes are found on B. (he is penniless in fact). The police commissioner holds a revolver against my neck, so that I can feel the coldness of its barrel. He threatens to shoot me. Then he turns to B., who confesses. They shoot him in the head and he drops as if dead, but he soon comes to and says that the bullet is still in his head. We see blood on the sofa and the bank notes are also there."

The first dream displays the frequent use of the Czar as a symbol. The Czar, the monarch, is the symbol of omnipotence, autocracy, i.e., in this case the fetishism (picture of compulsion). He finds his shoes too narrow. His parapathia oppresses him. He wants to make the shoes wider, and this expresses his prospective tendency to loosen the bonds of his parapathia. He then looks for a carriage which is supposed to take him further (his cousin as an incest compromise, a mitigated incestuous figure), but he doesn't find one, and has to wander about. This wandering about, searching for the right way out of his dilemma, is a feature we will find in the dreams of all these cases. Even by day they play this lost condition, can't find the way to the doctor, have suddenly lost the sense of direction or position. The reason is because they are being driven towards an unknown, an unconscious, goal while in a dreamy state.

The second dream seems to me to exhibit relationships with urine sexuality (wine instead of urine). Perhaps an indication of urolagnia and cannibalism. Every bit of emotion is important in the dream. His feelings in this dream are indicative of his realization that the man in bed, his alter ego, is a pig. He is afraid of his own impulses.

The third dream provokes the following remarks: Most fetishists dream about military service and find themselves in the most menial positions. They are recruits and the compulsions of fetishism are expressed by the compulsions of military service. He, a captain, is again a recruit, i.e., a common soldier (later on we shall have an opportunity of exhaustively analyzing a similar military dream of a fetishist). He further symbolizes his humiliation by his having to crawl. He needs a new philosophy of life and expresses it here by having to change his clothing. Again we see the drinking scene, but this time the wine has been replaced by syrup which, in turn, is not even syrup, but water, so that his comrade curses. This appears to be a religious symbol: holy communion. The body and the blood of Christ. But his piety is just as false as his fetishism.

The fourth dream is important because it is of a stereotyped nature and is often repeated. It is plainly a case of homosexual exhibitionism.

The fifth dream expresses his sorrow at being infected with paraphilic thoughts, i.e., that he is impure.

The origins of his guilt feelings come to the surface in his sixth dream. B. is his other ego, the murderer and thief. The sexual symbolism of the dream is quite transparent and permits us to leap to some experience in childhood, the memories of which may still be traced in his unconscious (the bullet is still in his head). The police commissioner is probably the doctor (in the fifth dream he said, "The doctor said that the illness did not come from intercourse") to whom he has effected a transference. His other ego, B., must die.

As far as we are able to make any conclusions on the basis of these dreams, I should say that the patient is marked by an hypertrophic urine sexuality. This rhymes well with the retentive tricks he used to enjoy. I would like to emphasize the fact, also, that fetishists generally disclose the tendency to withhold their urine or their feces. Their goal is the conquest of their sexual impulses by a roundabout means, i.e., by means of a paraphilia. But the other instincts also provoke these persons to a playful sort of struggle with themselves. They want to see whether they can overcome such impulses or not. One not infrequently finds the patients to be ascetic in type, they don't drink or smoke, have given up meat and are vegetarians. Whenever they do withhold their excrements, they try it until it hurts. Defecation and micturition are then highly delightful for them—incidentally, a habit which is characteristic of many children. Perhaps this obsessional tendency to try to overcome an organic compulsion, the struggle between the compulsions of the will and the compulsions of instinct, contains the infantile roots of the fetishism.

What is, after all, a saint? A man who has been able to overcome the pressure of his deepest instincts by means of the compulsions of religion. Freud very accurately described religion as a compulsion neurosis. Fetishism is analogous to religion in that they are both motivated by prohibitions, but beyond that they both disclose the same tendency, viz., the exclusion of the sexual instinct. Religion, however, goes after sexuality directly, whereas fetishism sidetracks it.

Feelings of guilt are the motive for the fetish lover's religious fervor. In reality he is not avoiding intercourse, but sin, and the reason intercourse becomes sinful in his mind is because during the act he is plagued by incestuous phantasies and tends to transform the real sexual partner into an imaginary one. The imaginary female is, at bottom, his mother. This explanation is certainly quite plain.

There are, however, cases which speak an even more clear and understandable language. The incestuous difficulties of fetishists are, after all, also found to be the plague of other parapathics, too. We must conceive the fetishist as a man with an abnormally strong sexual drive, as a sort of sexual atavist. This runs counter to Freud's [3] opinion. He writes: "A certain reduction in the striving for normal sexual gratification seems to be the prerequisite for all cases (weak sexual execution)."

And in a note he says, "This weakness would reflect the constitutional condition of the individual." He nevertheless weakens these statements when he adds, "Psychoanalysis has discovered in these cases an early sexual intimidation as an accidental factor in the development of the disease, an intimidation which drives the individual from the normal sexual object to the acceptance of a substitute." The constitutional weakness of the sexual apparatus is, nevertheless, a conditio sine qua non for Freud. An opinion which is quite invalidated by my own experience.

The fetishist is a person with an unusually strong sexual instinct. It is for this reason that he becomes attached to the divers members of the family perhaps even earlier than other children and is marked by a characteristic emphasis of all paraphilic activity. This is the reason he looks for protective mechanisms and finds them—in religion. But it is perhaps this early infantile interest in the family which may have moved Sadger [4] to write: "The final and genuine fetish, however, the fetish which is always looked for and desired, no matter in what disguise or symbolization, is the naked genital of the mother or the mother image."

How does that rhyme with a case of foot fetishism whose mother died at his birth? Is his wet-nurse or his governess to be classed among his forbidden and tabooed mother images? We shall see that it was his father who served as the point of fixation. One thing is certain: the fetishist discloses a pathological fixation on his family.

The next case shows us the relationships between a fetishist and his mother rather clearly.

Case 20. Max Rudolf Senf described a case of petticoat fetishism in Gross' Archiv, Vol. LX. The strong, thirty-year-old farmer had never had intercourse with a woman despite frequent opportunities. Thirteen years ago he first began to put his mother's or his sister's petticoats between his legs and masturbate with them. Even before that he had masturbated with a quilt. He said that the coverlet and, later, the petticoats were, for him, the same as a woman. Senf also found a letter on the man's person, after he had been arrested for the theft of petticoats, which was addressed to his mother. It was characterized by "an extravagantly sentimental tone." This peasant wrote his mother that he would soon come home and that then they would all "experience a freshet of spring love such as the poets sing about."

This case of Dr. Senf's exhibits one factor which is so frequently observed in fetishism that we must consider it as typical. This peasant stated that he had first begun to masturbate with the aid of his mother's and his sister's petticoats. If we remember what his mother seems to have meant to him, we cannot but see that his fetishes very frequently were symbols of his mother, and thus represented incest.

It is stated that this fetishism began in the patient's sixteenth year, a fact which shows us that we must not always look for the sources of fetishism in earliest childhood. The relations of fetishism to infantile family contacts are nevertheless so close that only the blind or the arbitrary could overlook them. The patient always used the mother's clothing as a symbolic representation of the whole mother during his onanistic acts, and this explains us his asceticism. The psychogenesis of fetishism has many points in common with that of homosexuality. The fetishist also has a distaste for women and retreats into an asexual, homosexual, or autoerotic life.

The road to woman is closed to the male fetishist, for before her stands the threatening figure of the mother or the sister. Every coitus thus becomes the rashest depravity, but not only because the female is the symbol of evil, but because his sexual libido really belongs to his mother or her younger substitute, the sister. This makes intercourse a tenfold sin and asceticism becomes imperative. The impossibility of achieving his desire makes the fetishist reject all women, and his continual searching only masks the real goal. The fetishist acts like a real Don Juan. They both have the same type of harem cult. They both act as if they were looking for a definite object and yet they cannot see their real sexual objects. Adults often play with children by looking feverishly for some object which they themselves have hidden. The fetishist likewise always seeks his satisfaction in symbols. But these symbols are analogous to spiritual nourishment. They cannot still the physical hunger of the individual and the result is a tremendous damming up of

energy because an ungratified wish is indestructible. Like un-
touched capital, it increases in value by the constant addition of
the interest of associated emotions. The desire grows upon
the individual and soon makes a caricature of the symbolism.
The infantile incestuous fixations are often repressed and the
sexual symbolist hasn't the slightest notion of how he arrived
at his manifestly eccentric tastes.

A patient who, in her youth, had long ministered to her
father and often had to give him the urine bottle, the bed-pan
and an air cushion, confessed to me that whenever she saw this
trinity of articles in the windows of surgical shops, she would
experience an involuntary flurry of excitement and get an immediate orgasm. Often only a urine bottle or a bed-pan, or
also the odor of rubber, which reminds her of the air cushion,
are sufficient to bring on the orgasm. It is understandable that
this woman became a nurse during the war. She had made her
confessions to me before the war. But when I took charge of
a hospital unit in which she was a nurse, she·was considerably
embarrassed.

Such experiences as these give us greater insight into a case
like the following one. This is an excellent complement to the
case of the irrigator attachment we saw before. Hirschfeld described this case as rubber cushion fetishism in *Sexual Pathologie*, Vol. III.

Case 21. B. Z., a twenty-one-year-old student of political economy, displays a peculiar form of fetishism, viz., a remarkable
sexual reactivity to rubber air cushions. Mr. Z., whose feminine
traits had long been known to his family without their having understood the true nature of his character, noticed that at about
fourteen years of age he suddenly experienced the curious desire to
collect air cushions, blow them up and press them to his body. At
first he was unable to relate any sort of imagery to these secret
habits, and they remained quite inexplicable to him because he had,
as yet, no knowledge of sexual matters. The purely instinctual
drive to hide away with such cushions, keep them always close to
his body, increased in power and soon led to rather serious depressions on his part until, about four weeks after the first experiences,
he gained his first relief in an ejaculation. On that evening, he

had, as usual, blown the bag up tightly and then laid himself upon it in bed in such a manner that his genitals and the lower part of his abdomen just covered it. The singular irritative quality of the fetish was primarily of a tactile nature, although later he experienced an associated erotic thrill by the odor of the rubber, too. The visual effects of the fetish were quite negligible and the acoustic avenue of excitement was, of course, entirely absent.

For the six years following he masturbated with the aid of this fetish every day and the images which he had from the very beginning and throughout this infrequently interrupted period were characterized by the same general motive: He phantasied a large, strong, fat man who was diversely placed in various masochistic positions. The pleasurable images of fat legs and thick body were provoked by touching and rubbing the smooth surface of the tightly blown-up air cushion. It is noteworthy that in the course of time this symbolization gradually became a substitute as the patient gave way to the impulse to possess the living partner. Since, however, the living partner was not readily obtainable, he arranged a situation which at first appears to be highly narcissistic, but is doubtless of heterogeneous derivation. He would dress himself in a large-sized suit which would be stuffed out with his air cushion, and then he would look at himself in the mirror. But, seeing a virtual, fat, sexual partner in the mirror instead of his real self, he would become sexually titillated and experience final gratification and relief. He never used anything but a rubber cushion to stuff the suit, since other materials, such as pillows, had no sexual effect upon him whatever. As already mentioned, his first sexual experiences of this kind occurred when he was fourteen, but it was possible to elicit a memory from his eighth year which had some relationship with this complex. In that year of his life he saw an air cushion for the first time, and a few days after that he was taken to the circus where he saw a clown dressed up as if he were a balloon. He seems to have been deeply affected by both these experiences, but they were nevertheless soon forgotten, to become reactivated by sexual maturation as adequate sexual motives.

There was no analysis in this case; so that we can depend only on our own conclusions in the matter. The exhaustive analyses of later chapters will show us, however, how complicated the psychogenesis of such a case can be. For the present, we can consider this case as simply a continuation of the case of Dr. Sigg. Analysts with any degree of experience will be able to draw their own conclusions.

Frequently, we observe that the objects which become fetishes are useful or staple articles. That makes the erotic and symbolic use of nursing articles more understandable. Everything which achieves any contact with the human body is especially subject to become a fetish. Thus, also, the preference for shirts, trousers, underwear, trusses, pads, etc. All that is necessary is that someone in the family wore them. The shirt is a highly prized object, the specific body odor of the wearer being an important secondary item. The earlier volumes of this series contain many relevant examples, but the following case from my own experience will serve to illustrate.

Case 22. Mr. Adolf N. is a healthy, thirty-five-year-old traveling salesman who comes of a healthy family. He suffers from a pathological mania for women's chemises. At home he has a large collection of such underthings and he can spend hours before the windows of the various women's shops in town. Sometimes he will spend days going from one shop to another until he has finally acquired a chemise. But the new article must first acquire a specific odor of urine by being urinated on before it possesses any sexual effect upon him. He would like to collect old, worn, sweaty chemises from women, ones that also had the odor of urine, and he would be glad to pay any price for them. He has also stolen these goods on two occasions in hotels. He pretends that he has made a mistake in the room number and, after stealing the chemise he's looking for, he disappears, leaving a new and better one in its stead. When he has donned such a chemise he will stand before a mirror and masturbate. He claims that he was subject to this peculiar habit as early as 7 years of age. At that time he would smell his mother's night gown and experience cascades of sexual ecstasy at the odor of perspiration and urine. He even tried once to take one of these night gowns and hide it in his bed at night. His mother discovered the absence of the piece, however, and he had a hard time lying his way out of the situation when it was found among his things.

He tried normal intercourse a few times, but was never able to have an orgasm. Only once did he ever have an ejaculation with a woman and that was when he was having intercourse with a prostitute who wore a dirty old shirt which smelled of sweat and urine. He agreed with the incestuous interpretation of his condition and said that he often had dreams in which he saw himself having intercourse with his mother.

It is easy to see the connection between fetishism and incest in this and similar cases. The same is true of the following case by Garnier.

Case 23. Louis I., a young butcher, was brought to the hospital in the following dress: 1. A corset of black cloth under a large-sized coat. 2. A second corset underneath the first. 3. A third corset. 4. A camisole. 5. A woman's collar. 6. A thin woven shirt, and 7. A chemise. He wore fine, women's stockings and women's garters. When he was 10 years old he had had the burning desire to put on the chemise of his sister who was four years older than himself, and during puberty he actually would sneak into his sister's room at times and put one of her under-things on. As soon as the chemise had enveloped his body, his sexual excitement was tremendous and he would have an immediate ejaculation. Afterwards, he would sorrowfully put his own clothing on again and go back to his father's butcher shop. In the course of time, he began to buy himself chemises and later acquired the other articles which were found on his person (l. c., pp. 62-63).

Armand Silvestre says of the chemise that it is not so much the woman as that object of hers which best portrays her "spirit." In the days of the Directorate, the character of female dress became entirely shirt-like and the female was thus more properly displayed as such. Modern fashions have achieved the highest possible refinement in the manufacture of silk and silken chemises and it is thus no wonder that, especially in France, this piquant transformation of what was formerly quite a simple piece of clothing has produced a great number of so-called chemise fetishists who hunt feverishly for women's underthings and find their sole sexual satisfaction in the possession and handling of these objects. In one of the poems of that decadent poet Rollinat, a girl gives her lover her chemise with the following words:

> Conserve la toujours! Qu'elle soit pour ton âme
> La chair mystérieuse et vague de la femme
> Qu'elle soit l'oreiller de tes regrets moroses.

Qu'elle soit l'oreiller de tes regrets moroses
Quand tu la baiseras, songes aux nudités roses
    Qui furent ton festin charnel!
Que les parfums ambrés de ma peau qui l'imprégnent,
Pour l'odorat subtil de tes rêves y règnent,
    Candides et luxurieux!
Qu'elle garde à jamais l'empreinte de mes formes!
J'ai dit à mon amour: "J'exige que tu dormes
    Entre ses plis mystérieux,"

and her lover replies in true fetishistic style:

"Adieu!"—J'ai conservé la mignonne chemise,
Je l'exhume parfois du coffre où je l'ai mise,
    Et jé la baise avec ferveur;
Et mon rêve est si chaud, qu'en elle il fait revivre
Ce corps si capiteux dont je suis encore ivre,
    Car il m'en reste la saveur.[5]

The chemise represents the woman who wears it. By virtue
of the transposition of certain specific qualities and the displacement of affect, it becomes the woman herself. In the course of
time, the fetish then becomes the symbolical representative of
the person who was the source of the original provocation.
This person is usually some member of the family.

I have never yet analyzed a case of fetishism in which this
root was not to be found. The original object can be either
homosexual or heterosexual in nature. The homosexual types
of fetishism can be reduced to such a fixation on the father or
a brother. But not in all cases. The fixation can sometimes
be the mother, a sister, an aunt or grandmother; so that the
sources of the fetishism become intimately interwoven with the
homosexual components.

Every one of these cases shows a marked psycho-sexual infantilism, however, and a tendency to impulsive conduct. Our
further material will reveal to us that despite the importance
of these factors, the riddle of fetishism is not at all completely
solved by means of the incestuous fixations involved. We shall
have an opportunity of considering the above-mentioned preference for chemises in another light in the next chapter.

VI

CALF PARTIALISM, SADISM AND KLEPTOMANIA

In the course of an analysis of a case of partialism, it is always possible to show that the so-called partialism is but one symptom of a complicated parapathia and cannot be explained or resolved except in connection with all the other symptoms. The cases are frequently complicated by sadism, masochism or other paraphilias, and there is almost invariably a sign of psycho-sexual infantilism. In the following case, the partialism was but one symptom in a rather severe compulsion neurosis which considerably hindered the patient in the execution of his profession. I once called an obsessional neurosis the imperative of atonement, but the repentance is often only a façade behind which the patient can wallow in the pleasurable memories of the past.

Such patients as these often consult the physician because of impotence, i.e., their sexual potency is conditioned by certain situational qualities. When their sexual conditions are not fulfilled, they look like the clinical picture of a case of actual impotence. Now, the striving for what is normal is a natural and instinctive drive in humans. It is an immanent imperative, so to speak. Whereas, the formula of the parapathia would read: be different from the other, the tendency to be cured is expressed in the desire to be normal, i.e., like the others.

There is a bitter struggle between both these tendencies and the result depends upon the intervention of the psycho-therapeutist. Every parapathia discloses the strictest reactionism. The patient refuses to change. He refuses to give up his infantile springs of pleasure. He would like to get well, but not at the price of his phantasies or the infantile sources of those phantasies.

The following case clearly shows us the psychogenesis of a compulsion neurosis, the cause of the partialism and the sexual

root of the patient's kleptomania. This is also a contribution
to the psychogenesis of relative impotence.

Case 24. Mr. G. T., a thirty-eight-year-old actor, consulted me
because of impotence. Although married for the past two years, he
is not capable of coitus with his exquisitely beautiful wife. At the
beginning of marriage, he made his matrimonial début by ejaculatio
præcox, but for the past six months he is not even able to get an
erection when with his wife, although, under certain circumstances,
he is able to have intercourse with other women.

I was able to gain the following information about these conditions or circumstances: G. belongs to that group of men who fall
only for ankles and calves. He is lost if he sees a woman on the
street who has a well-shaped leg and sheer stockings on. He often
gets an erection at the sight of such a leg or even if he imagines
himself whipping it. As long as he can remember—and his memory is excellent as far back as his earliest babyhood—he has always
been attracted by ankles and calves. In youth, it was only the
calf of a girl or boy, but now it is the calves of young women, girls
and children.

The physical examination showed him to have a small penis,
gynecomastia, a female pelvis, and everything else negative. There
were no hereditary stigmata. He agreed upon an analysis.

His preference for young girls and boys with lovely calves makes
every walk he takes a highly erotic experience. He even goes
out with the intention of "finding something," and in these searches
he has developed considerable psychological acumen; so that he is
very seldom suspected. Later on we will see what he does with
these girls. In the first hour or two, he says: "Only little games
that were perhaps somewhat sadistic, and also the normal thing."
Once or twice a week he becomes quite restless and is often beside
himself with passion. He can't sit still at home, can't remain in
a café, runs about town and searches for something. Under such
circumstances he is as if confused and becomes an easy mark.
It is then that he can fall for some streetwalker, whereas he otherwise never goes to them. This restless wandering about is an
irresistible compulsion, but he becomes somewhat quieter as soon
as he gets into a hotel with a girl. That is, for only a short while,
for soon he becomes restless again, wants to begin all over again,
to look for something, find something to do in order to quiet
himself.

In such moments, he has also stolen things. Thus, for example, he will visit a friend and there put something in his pocket. Usually some worthless object which he either throws away or soon returns. He has also developed the trick of pulling handkerchiefs out of the pockets of his friends and then giving them back. He likes to keep them in his own pocket for a while first, however.

Then he also has another passion which he has not indulged especially. He would like to steal the underthings of women who appeal to him and take the goods to bed with him. He carried out his desire only once and then said it was a mistake. It was the chemise of a cousin of his who attracted him, but she was married to an old gentleman. He was staying with them a few days and there found the opportunity to hide the chemise among his own linens and then put it on at night.

During such periods, he seems to smell the odor of old underwear or of toilets (feces), but he cannot explain these hallucinations to himself.

He relates the following of his earliest childhood: "I can recall all the experiences of my childhood with great clarity. My first sexual excitement took place in my fifth year. I was standing between my mother's legs and brushed or, rather, stroked her calf. My mother was a very lovely and rather well-built woman, and I sensed a very strong feeling of pleasure. My penis became stiff.

"This impression was quite definitive for the rest of my life. I continued to desire my mother's leg and wanted to stroke it again. For a while, my mother permitted me to do so, but she soon noticed the sexual ecstasy I derived from this play and forbade me the pleasure. I found a way nevertheless. Whenever she would lie down to sleep, I would wait until she were asleep and then lay myself next to her on the sofa in such a position that I could stroke her leg and even rub my penis against her calf. I derived the keenest delight from this, but it soon became insufficient for my desires. I then began to masturbate without being near my mother. I would pick out one of her old petticoats, put it between my legs and then masturbate or rub on it until that fine feeling came. Frequently I would be surprised in the act by my four-year-old sister who would ask me what I was doing. I would mumble something badly articulate, but she kept quiet and never told a soul. She seemed to understand. I also had a younger sister, but neither the elder nor the younger sister were objects of my sexual desire. I always hated them and felt not the slightest sexual attraction for them. At the age of five, however, I was quite infatuated in a small cousin of mine and always wanted to be taken to see her.

"At six I went to public school and even masturbated there. But I recall distinctly that my onanistic acts there were accompanied by outspoken sadistic phantasies, viz., the desire to beat girls, especially to whip their naked legs. When I was fourteen, I was one day leaning out the window when a cousin of mine whacked me on the buttocks and thereby somehow touched my anus. That was the beginning of a serious illness from which I have been suffering to this day. I believed that he had injured my spine and began to suffer from a host of obsessions of which I shall speak at length later on. I was especially plagued by the fear that a rat might bite me in the behind. I must state that we were living on the third floor and it was impossible for the rats to come up from the cellar that high. In addition to that, we had a modern, closed toilet, not one of the old, open ones."

Such an anxiety is especially common among homosexuals and, particularly, among unconscious homosexuals. I therefore asked him whether or not he had produced homosexual phantasies during his onanistic procedures. He became quite upset and assured me that he had never had the slightest homosexual thoughts. No man ever caused him the least animation. On the contrary, such notions disgusted him. He confesses, however, that as a boy he often thought of whipping boys, too. He then continued his story:

"At fifteen, I wanted to put an end to masturbation and my sadistic phantasies. I therefore went to a prostitute and had intercourse, but without any gratification. The whole thing took me a couple of seconds and I must add that such a weakness has remained with me to this day. I have never been able to keep up intercourse for more than a very short time and I never derive the pleasure from it which masturbation affords me.

"I also remember having stroked my aunt's calf when I was about six years old. I was just like a little puppy. I went for every leg I saw. Even to-day, the calf of some woman's leg plays a most important part in my life. I know definitely that at six years of age, I always masturbated with phantasies of some calf in my mind. After my aunt visited us, I imagined her leg to myself and masturbated. I stuck a pillow between my legs and thought it would be a good substitute for her calf.

"Once my father caught me and forbade me strictly to masturbate. But I would wait until my parents were asleep and then, feigning that I was sleeping, too, I would be able to enjoy myself as I wanted. My conscience was troubled nevertheless for I thought to myself that God sees everything and that father had said it was a great sin. I was also beaten once for continuing despite my father's warning.

"I was quite a vain little boy. Until I was four, I had long locks and also wore dresses. Everybody thought I was a girl and would say, 'Oh! What a pretty little girlie!' I mutinied against having to wear pants and always wanted to have the dresses back again.

"Often I would put on some of my mother's clothes and that would invariably incite me to masturbation. Sometimes I would crawl into bed, pull one of mother's petticoats over my head in order to be able to enjoy the odor, and would then play with myself. (These habits later turned out to be phantasies of the mother's womb).

"My parents quarrelled a lot and I always took my mother's side. I also remember lying in bed between them, but I don't recall ever having heard or seen them having intercourse. But I later had plenty of opportunity to eavesdrop while my mother was having intercourse. My father had become quite poor, having lost his money in a bankruptcy. We were all on rather short rations. It was then that my mother made some money out of men. When I was eleven, she would take me along, find herself a man, and bring him along home. We children then had to leave the room and would have lots of fun. 'Uncle' often promised me presents and gave me money, but my mother would take it away and then say she lost it. Some time later, my sister also had many affairs, my mother having played the go-between.

"My first masochistic thoughts came to me at about six while I was struggling to overcome my onanism to please God. I imagined myself being beaten. The sadistic phantasies developed only later, although I am not very sure whether or not I may have had such sadistic thoughts even earlier.

"Two girls were living in our house, piano teachers. I was hardly six and yet I was in love with them. I was terribly jealous, too, especially when they were more friendly with my sisters than with me. I was altogether quite jealous of my sisters, anyway.

"By seventeen I felt an aversion to the whole family, although my sisters were beauties and my mother was still quite a chic woman. But I couldn't stand any of them, always growled and was thoroughly dissatisfied with everything.

"You have told me that what I was looking for was freedom and some distance from my ties. I now understand my attitude. It was then that my sadistic phantasies and conduct began."

I asked about these sadistic procedures and learned the following:

He always seeks his prey on the streets and prefers young girls of a childlike type. He accosts them in a very friendly and casual manner, beams upon them, and asks them if they are not interested in learning how to dance. He tells them that he can fix them up with an excellent position in a high class dancing troupe. The one condition being that they have to be willing to undergo a rather strenuous bit of training. He then takes the girl to a hotel where he is already well known and where his splendid tips make him a welcome guest.

The girl must undress to her shoes and stockings. Soon after the first few steps, he manages to find some mistake or other and begins to smack the girl lightly on the calf. He uses a belt. When he notices that the girl is frightened or cowardly and rather subdued, his lashes become stronger and he sometimes also whips her across the buttocks. He binds the girls to the window sash so that they must stand on their tip-toes. Their discomfort and pains afford him pleasure and he gloats. Finally, he uses the girls for intercourse which, however, is quite weak in potency and lasts but a couple of seconds.

Many girls seem to like these procedures and act as if fascinated. Most of them become frightened, however, and cry. If the girls revolt and begin to yell, he stops immediately and tries to make a joke of the whole thing. He repeats this game about twice a week, each time with a different girl. He is also impelled by the desire to rape girls and to whip them across the calves, but he has never succumbed to such a desire yet out of fear for the law.

He dreams:

I went walking with my colleague Otto. He was quite friendly to me. Then I saw that both his hands were nailed to a board.

Otto is a vaudeville artist whom he likes very much. He would like to play with Otto and have Otto caress him. In the dream, Otto's hands are nailed down, which is an expression for the fact that Otto is married. Otto's wife is rather distasteful to him and this antipathy is at once also an expression of his antipathy towards his own sisters, i.e., the inversion of a definite attraction (self-protective tendency).

Otto is his second self, his parapathia. He has nailed his inner self down. It is apparent that his actions are only a small part of his programme. On the other hand, this can also be understood as his parapathia having nailed him down. His hands are tied and he cannot do anything evil. In other words, he must have done something sinful with his hands.

He is also overcome by the unconscious desire to have Otto play with his penis, but this cannot be done if Otto's hands are nailed to the board. Boards represent flesh. Otto is married, he is not a free agent. G. is jealous and would like to have Otto for himself.

G. feels himself likewise bound by his own marriage. He once loved his wife, but now he is impotent with her. His love appears to have died. It is only the spiritual ghost of its former self. There is also an indication of the Christ neurosis here (Christ nailed to the cross). Like the Saviour, he is also nailed to the board. Despite his paraphilic tendencies, G. is pious and daily chastises himself by means of his suceptibilities and humiliations.

The following night he dreams:

I kissed Otto's wife on the arm, sucked her arm, and derived intense pleasure.

He recalls that lovely arms have also occasionally interested him, and that Otto's wife does have lovely arms and hands. No other associations. Resistances. Otto's wife seems to stand for some other person. A third dream:

A very obese and dirty man who seemed to be some vaudeville artist engaged in our show wanted to appear on the stage. I cursed. "How can you dare to come into our fine establishment looking like that? I won't let you appear. Such swine don't belong in this place."

In order to understand this dream, we will have to spend some time with his obsessional ideas. He is constantly obsessed with compulsions which have to do with his stage appearance. If he doesn't do this or that, he will be a failure. He presents all kinds of ceremonials which I shall consider later on. The most important point is that he won't permit himself any great success. He ruins his own successes. He always says to himself (after some sadistic scene): "Now you won't have any success. You don't deserve to have any." Thus he spoils his own hopes.

Now we can see through the third dream. He is the man who is supposed to appear in such a dirty condition. He robs himself of the possibility of success. He is the swine. He is a manifest masochist and went through a markedly masochistic period during childhood.

He later recalls that his masochistic period lasted but a week. Before that he had indulged considerably in sadistic phantasies. In order, however, to rid himself ot these sadistic ideas, he imagined himself to be a very pretty girl whom the whole world admired, but whose lover beat her. His sadism is the reaction to his feminine tendencies. He wants to be a man and show women that he is a man.

A maid who was with the family during his childhood played quite an important rôle in his life. She was in the house for many years and shared the family's happiness and troubles. She was the confidante and friend of his mother. But for him she was an equivalent of his sisters: taboo and lacking in any sexual attractiveness.

When he was six, his first obsessional stewing began. He would ask himself: "What is happiness? I dare not experience happiness."

He recalls how his father beat him because he had been fresh. He acted as if he were going to faint, and ever since then he has used illness as a means of avoiding all unpleasant responsibilities. After being whipped (his mother had saved him by calling out to his father that he had done enough), he hated his father and wished him dead. But he immediately began to punish himself by mulling over the same compulsion ideas again. He ruined every bit of pleasure for himself. What good is happiness? Does it help at all? When he was seven, a schoolmate dared him to show his penis. He wanted to play together, but G. felt disgusted and didn't want to have anything to do with him (screen memory?).

Shortly after, i.e., in his seventh year, he received the slap on the behind from his cousin (he had first placed this memory in his fourteenth year). For a long time thereafter he was sure he was going to suffer from some spinal cord disease. He listened to his elders talking about pains and illness and thought he had all of them. He was especially fearful that his veins would burst (initial hypochondria as a result of guilt feeling).

At about this time, while playing blind man's buff, he fell on his head, cut his temple, and was in a faint for some time. His mother told him that that was the punishment of God, and ever since then he has firmly believed that he will die of some terrible disease whenever he has an evil thought.

At three years of age, he underwent an operation on the penis. He remembers what happened after the operation, the nurses, the physician, even their cutting off his locks just before the operation and his crying when they bandaged him. But he cannot recall why he was operated upon. He was quite a fresh little boy and said to the nurse: "You can kiss my ———."

He claims never to have suffered from castration anxiety. Only later did he become disconsolate at having such a small penis, and he believed that that was the result of masturbation. He was afraid that his penis would not grow, and felt overjoyed when he would see it swell and grow larger on erection.

He became rather devout at eleven years, prayed regularly, and believed that God would help him and deliver him from masturbation. He nevertheless made use of onanism to make himself ill. At thirteen he was apprenticed in a business house where he was somewhat mistreated. At that time, he masturbated six times in one night in order to make himself sick, and the following day he suffered from fainting spells. But he also had such dreamy states and sweet fainting spells on the street. He would suddenly feel giddy and light-headed and say to himself: "I'm no longer here."

At about this same time, he would dampen any joy by telling himself that he didn't deserve it. He joined some society as a comic, and enjoyed quite a success. But he soon began to ruin his success. He would have to look at his hands (the memory of masturbation) and would tell himself before every appearance over and over again not to look at his hands. Of course, he would then spend most of the evening thinking of his hands. He didn't know what to do with them. They embarrassed him. They were the hands with which he had sinned. His onanistic phantasies weren't clear in his mind. He thought it had something to do with his sadistic notions.

He brought two rather curious dreams:

Mrs. L. held a thresher in her hand and it looked like an arm or a leg. I wanted it as such. Added weight. . . . Then in the background she shows me something that looks like a bone. I felt that I shouldn't be seeing these things.

I had had a terrible scene with my mother, ran away in the heat of anger and found myself naked on the street. Two persons walked towards me and made some comment. I pulled my night-shirt on and then found myself in some sort of family store-room. My mother said: "Now I've torn it," and tore a red-cheeked, fleshy face to pieces. It looked like a fleshy mask of some kind.

I was quite angry and cried, "Is that so? Well, now *you* can make the speech. I need the mask for my speech." I also heard that she had torn up this mask because she had done something bad.

The analysis of the first dream proved that the missing bone represented the penis. His family used to get some added weight whenever they bought meat at the butcher's. That was always bone. He is quite attracted to Mrs. L. and looks for some added weight in her, the penis. He had always believed as a child that women also have a penis. The calf was for him a substitute for that organ.

In the second dream, his mother tears up his mask. Even as a child he had had quarrels with his mother and had told her she could kiss his little ——. But when his mother would shed tears at such language, he would show shame and regret. His indifference to his mother in later years was only a mask. If he would only show himself as he really is, in his naked state as on the street in the dream, or if he would but take the mask of hypocrisy from his face, one could see how much he really loves and cherishes his mother. Two years ago his mother died. He is quite conscious of his incestuous thoughts. But the fourth commandment, "Honor thy father and thy mother," gave him the shivers and he always tried to repress the desires. As a child he did look like that mask: red-cheeked and fleshy. His mother tore up the picture of his childhood. He hated his mother whenever she had anything to do with strange men. Now his hate breaks through in the dream. He tears the mask from his mother's face. She was a whore and is to blame for his illness. That's why he hates all women. In every woman he tortures his own mother.

The sentence about his not supposing to see those things in the first dream is rather revealing. He recalls that his mother showed not the slightest reticence before her children and not only dressed or undressed before them, but also satisfied her daily physical needs with them about. Under such circumstances, he was able to see her legs and even more. But did he really want to see her genitals as a boy? He seems to have no recollection ever of having seen either his mother's or his sisters' genitals in childhood. He was a fresh and forward youngster and yet he cannot understand how it was that his sisters and the maid, then as now, left him cold. He protests this with such emphasis that he makes himself liable to suspicion. We must suspect a fixation on the sisters here, but we do not share this suspicion with him.

Whenever he becomes frightened, he feels a tickling sensation around the testicles. Any creepy impression provokes the same sensations. He lays that to the operation he had when he was three years old. It was an operation on the testicles after a testis had been injured. That's what his older sister told him when he had asked her about it. He returns to the boy who had made a homosexual advance to him. It was in the first grade and he had enjoyed such things only in his phantasies up to that time. But this was a real partner. He was nevertheless repelled when he was to touch his schoolmate's penis. It seems that his father had portrayed the handling of the genitals as something especially disgusting. As a child he always tried to avoid touching any part of his bottom, and it was only when masturbating or urinating that this taboo was breached. He masturbated several times a week.

It was only when he was fourteen that a physician forbade him to masturbate and he promptly stopped. But his parapathia became increasingly worse.

The chief characteristic of this patient is obsinacy. He resists himself and ruins his own successes. Yesterday was the best day he has had in years. He feels that the analysis has relieved him greatly.

I continue the analysis of the last dream because I expect that it will offer me important disclosures. I ask him for associations on the mask which his mother tore up in the dream. He says:

"The mask was red and round. It had a beard and looked like a hot water bag. There was a tear at the top. Mother said: 'That's why I'll burn it. . . .'"

"Burn? Didn't you say tear at first?"

"Burn or tear . . . Because it had a tear and was therefore no good any more."

"What did the beard look like?"

"A beard and a face like a butcher's. A coarse, ordinary bird. Perhaps it was Anton's face." (That was the cousin who had slapped him on the buttocks. Screen memory?)

"Did your father have a beard like this?"

"Oh! No! My father had a Vandyke and a fine face. But this was a tough face. I don't know. I ought to be able to remember how it looked. [He thought awhile and then suddenly called out.] I've got it! It was the man we used to laugh about. A great story, but silly stuff. No importance."

"Tell me about it."

"Well, mother got herself a man on the street who looked coarse and rather ordinary, like a butcher. Then she brought him home, took him into her room and locked the door. My sister and I wanted to peek through the keyhole, but we couldn't see anything. Then we heard some groaning, muffled giggling and all kinds of suspicious noises. Then they both came out of the room and the man looked red-faced and wiped the perspiration from his face. He looked like that mask."

"Were you jealous or angry with your mother?"

"Not at all. We laughed and had a good time out of it." He is quiet for a while and then continues. "I haven't the slightest notion why I'm impotent with my wife. She has the prettiest leg you can imagine. And what's more, whenever I see a woman with similar legs, I'm also impotent with her. Children interest me most of all. I would like to play with every child and torture it. Even as a boy I would imagine girls during masturbation and the ejaculation would make me feel as if I were sailing in heaven. A great gusto, that was. The acme of delight and rapture. I often had a similar feeling later during my attacks. I could even produce them at will right on the street."

"Did you always masturbate with the phantasy that you were beating a girl?"

"No. As I have already mentioned, I often used to put a chemise or a petticoat of my mother's or sister's between my legs. Or I would cover myself with it, smell it and think that mother should be punished—because she stinks."

"Who would beat her? Your father?"

"No. Never my father. That always disturbed my onanism. That would spoil all my fun. It was always a different person. Father always quarreled with mother. I can recall that whenever they spoke quietly with each other, I felt very happy. I was in paradise." He is quiet again.

"What's on your mind?"

"I'm thinking of that dream again. In the dream I was quite angry with mother. That reminds me of the scene with the veloci-pede. There was an 'uncle' who came to see us rather frequently, a Mr. S. He came twice a week. 'A season ticket' was what my mother called him. We were quite happy about his visits, because whenever he came mother got money and that meant that we had a warm meal. Once he gave mother twenty crowns to buy me a velocipede. When he left, mother refused to think of buying me the bicycle. I became angry, yelled and cried, swore at mother, called her a whore and cut up until she made ready to go out and buy the plaything. On the way she suddenly told me she had lost the money. I believed her and was miserable. She bought me some small toy as heart-balm. To-day, of course, I realize that she used the money to keep us fed. I remember well that one day, instead of Mr. S., a porter came with his card which said that he had to excuse himself. That night we didn't have a warm meal, but only dry bread. Mother showed me the card. It said, 'I deeply regret not being able to come to-day.' I was seven and was already able to read that. How do you like that for education?"

"You certainly must have hated or despised your mother."

"Hated? Only because she didn't buy me that bicycle. I usually sided with mother whenever there was a quarrel in the family. I can remember that father always threw it up to mother what a fine past she had. There seems to have been something like that early in their married life."

"And you heard all that?"

"Yes. My parents didn't care a hoot whether I was in the room or not. That's why I learned so fast."

He continues talking about the scenes with his mother. He remembers how happy they all were whenever Mr. S., their sub-scriber, came. They often had only bread crusts to eat and perhaps a piece of cold sausage, but S. meant a fine, warm meal for them. He nevertheless has a shadowy recollection that something in him revolted against S. and that he was jealous of the man. He appears to have repressed his jealousy completely. He also seems not to recall whether or not he also played with his little sister while all this was going on. No, that he is sure he never did. His younger sister was never a sexual object for him. They only made a lot of fun whenever S. would come out of mother's room, red-faced and excited.

"Did you look through the keyhole?"

He does not answer. He can't recall. It is possible, he thinks.

He dreamed:

I held a lecture on air. Then it was something about the mark and the crown. I talked with a German about the matter. Some-how he was able to quiet me. Then I sat on the toilet. It was all wet with urine. Someone said: "It's certainly a good thing that the Germans come in here and clean the place up." Suddenly I feel a tickling sensation behind and turn around to see a small rat which had just crawled out of a hole above me and was tickling me. Curiously enough, I was not at all frightened or disgusted as I am in reality.

Then we were riding in an omnibus. The conductor was rather fresh. My wife came aboard only later and sat down next to me. When the conductor saw that she was paying no fare, he said, "Ah ha! you're talking with the woman, eh?"—as if we were making up to cheat him out of the fare. That got me into an argument with him. In front of St. Stephen's I called him some name or other. He said, "I'll have you locked up!" I wanted to climb over the window sill and fight it out with him.

I was at the stage door of a theatre. Suddenly I missed a package which I had had in my hand. "Don't fool me now. I know that some bird has hidden it." I growled at a small, ugly man who was stronger than I. I couldn't get the best of him. Then I had the package again. It contained a heavy and dirty table cloth and some other things. I then went home with the package and cursed my wife because she wasn't with me at the time. When I opened the package, the red table cloth was missing. I went back to the theatre and they had found it.

I went home. It was like K—— street in my youth, dark and dreary. It made me afraid and I thought of burglars. In the third room of the apartment there was a figure, a slender, skinny, old, hunch-backed woman. She had a cloth about her and said she had nothing to wear. I gave her something, but it wasn't enough for her. She looked about and wanted books. She looked through a pile of books.

Then the scene changed. I was looking for a coach on the street. Suddenly I see my father, but he looked strange to me. I was nevertheless happy to be able to invite him to ride in the carriage with me. But I never found one.

Again a wagon. Three of us were riding down a hill. One was fat, and at one place where it was rather steep, the fat man got out in order to go to the toilet on another hill. The coachman said that he could have driven closer to the toilet.

I will now turn to the analysis of this important long dream. When I asked him to associate on the word air, he said: "Thoughts are as thin as air." Then he wonders how the change from air to marks and crowns came about. From there he begins to speak about the inflation of the mark and the crown and says that money is now as thin as air in Germany and Austria (this shows us the connections between air-feces-money-anal complex). Yesterday his wife let wind without shaming herself. He said to her: "You're a fine woman, you are. Any ordinary person would be ashamed of such a thing and would certainly feel that it's not

right." Then he begins to speak about his mother. She had no
shame at all. She displayed all kinds of disgusting little habits.
For instance, she would rub her fingers through her toes and then
put them in her mouth. She often had her fingers in her vagina,
so that her hand always smelled strongly. That was the reason
they all felt so disgusted at table sometimes. Whenever she went
to the toilet, it always stunk terribly. He never wanted to go to
the toilet after his mother had been there. His father, however,
was a meticulously clean person.

Suddenly he recalls a lot of important details from childhood.
He liked to smell his own wind. He would pull the covers over
his head and thus create a cavern in which he could retain the odor
of his wind for a long time. As he put it, defecation was always
a fête. It was a source of great pleasure to him. Following the
whack he got from his cousin, he was always afraid to be bitten
by a rat in the toilet. From then on his pleasures in the toilet were
spoilt. He would stand on the seat instead of sitting and even
turned himself about in order to be able to see the rat if it appeared. Later, he would defecate on a piece of paper and throw
the feces into the toilet. It was only after he was seventeen that
he gave up the rat phobia after a consultation with a physician.
But his pleasures in defecation have also disappeared since then.

This demonstrates clearly to us how he himself was the cause
of his loss of pleasure. In the dream there is a clear-cut pleasure,
a gratifying tickle, accompanying the appearance of the rat, and
no disgust.

We continue the analysis of the dream. A short dream of last
night landed him in the care of another analyst. There he found
me, saw that I was also a parapathic and also had to be analyzed.
This is the typical revenge of the patient who sees that he must
bend himself to the authority of the physician.

His further associations on air: There is thick and thin air.
Then he comes to his statement that several Germans were there.

"What does that make you think of? Several Germans."

"Germans like to keep order. They are clean and neat. Father
was also clean. Germans are homosexuals. I hate homosexuality.
. . . You once told me that the rat means a man, means homosexuality. That rat came out of a pipe."

Further analysis showed that this dealt with a womb phantasy.
Many lovers come to visit her (the dirty closet). Father won't
stand for that (the Germans come and clean up the place). Out
of the pipe (the vagina) comes the father's penis (the rat). He

goes into detail about his disgust for homosexuals and how he could never enter into a homosexual act.

We continue with the second part of the dream about the bus. To the conductor he associates: "A coarse, heavy fellow. Like a beer brewer. A very strict man. . . ."

"Who does he make you think of?"

"I can think only of father. He was very strict and we all were afraid of him."

Here the bipolar attitude towards his father breaks through (love and hate). Whenever father had a quarrel with mother, he always sided with mother. If he had been larger and stronger, he would have beaten his father. In the dream, he reënacts the scene as he would have liked to do it in childhood. Father would sometimes go for weeks without exchanging a word with mother. That is indicated by the exclamation in the dream: "Ah ha! You're talking with the woman!" The woman is the representative of his mother. Further analysis showed that he had also transposed emotions from his sisters to the woman. It is for this reason that he is impotent. His relations with the woman (his wife) are those of brother and sister.

That brings us to the point where he is to be locked up. Being locked up or locked in was always an abhorrent and fearful situation for him. As a child, he was frequently locked in. We also know that whenever he would have his parties with girls in the hotel, he would be afraid to have his will because he was afraid of the law. Recently he also received a threatening letter from an attorney. His anxiety about being locked up has sufficient basis in fact and manifestly breaks through in the dream. He is afraid to come into conflict with the police because of the things he has done. On the other hand, the bus is also a symbol of woman. He recalls the well-worn joke: If my grandmother had wheels, she'd be an omnibus. He had the phantasy that he and his sister were locked in his mother's womb and that there he would whip her.

The association after whipping is raping. As a child he had heard a great deal about raping and wondered what it meant. When his father caught him masturbating, he said that he was committing sin. He always imagined that a man beat a woman in intercourse and raped her. He saw a rooster topping a hen and said that the rooster was raping the hen. He understood that this was animal intercourse.

At first when his mother began to have strange men in the

house, he believed that the men would beat his mother, and sympathized with her. The phantasy that he wants to beat a girl means, really, that he wants to have intercourse with a girl. He is still a big boy and depends very much upon all his infantile habits. He has not yet developed to full manhood. He is still mama's little boy. He talks baby talk with his wife, calls her Maupi, Kraupi, Mutzi, Shnuzzi, Shutzi and is called the same kind of names by her.

When, at six years of age, he wanted to kill all his joy and fun in life, he really wanted also to kill his fun and pleasure in masturbation. But that was impossible; so that he had to say to himself that he did get some fun out of it all. At this age, too, he would stand before the mirror and doubt his identity (this phenomenon is frequently observed in womb phantasies). He would ask himself: "Is that I? No, that can't be myself!" He felt strange to himself. He would become suddenly anxious standing before the mirror, because he thought the face he saw was strange. He would call out: "Who's that?"

Womb phantasies have the curious appearance of "déja vu" or the contrary, i.e., that something, a street, looks strange and new. At least once every year he experiences the feeling that he has been in or seen this or that situation sometime before, has been in the same neighborhood, the same mood, etc.

When he was nine, a maid showed him her genitals. She told him to look at a black spot. Later she went to the hospital with syphilis and even then he understood that that was a serious venereal disease. But the chief factor about sexuality as far as he was concerned was its punishing character (raping).

During masturbation, he would picture to himself that a roomer in their house, who was serving in the army, was being punished. This roomer would tell them about the various punishments they received for divers transgressions: binding, chaining, solitary confinement, etc. He would then enlarge upon these sentences in his phantasies. Then he would have his schoolmates whipped across the legs, a favorite phantasy of his.

He speaks of all these associations during the analysis of the dream. They are all a part of the latent dream thoughts and are related to his guilt feelings. That leads us to the analysis of that part of the dream which had to do with the burglars and the old woman. His first association is his grandmother. She was a respectable and righteous person, the very opposite of his mother. He has a fear of the ideas of atonement which persist in penetrating to consciousness. These ideas consolidate to form the person of his respectable grandmother who runs the books of his soul, as it were. How have you spent your life? Why haven't you become a decent man? He now wants to finish his life in the manner of his father.

The last portion of the dream discloses to us his repentance at having deceived his wife. He is the fat man who goes looking for a toilet on another hill, though it costs him great effort and despite the presence of one in his vicinity (association: "Woman is a receptacle," a quotation from the famous trial of Eulenburg). The dream really says: "Be true to your wife and leave all these escapades. Be a decent man." The dream is the voice of his conscience which plays such a dominant rôle in the symptom-formation of his parapathia.

Also, the dirty table cloth must be replaced by a clean one. He takes it ill of his wife that she cannot prevent him from cheating her. That small, ugly fellow is his alter ego. He struggles with his inner self. . . .

The red table cloth points to his blood complex. It is as if he were blaming his wife for something which is connected with his own glory phantasies. He produces many associations which touch on the theme of love murders. (Is it because he wants to murder his wife that he is impotent?)

He dreamed:

Dr. Stekel had a little girl who had some sexual relationship with a maid.

His first association is that last evening he had a tickling or itching sensation in his rectum which felt rather pleasant. It was connected with the phantasy that he were a woman. That was his deepest wish as a child and we will recall that he was miserable when they cut off his beautiful locks at three years of age. He believes that it was their maid who had cut off his hair, and he also associates their maid to the one I have. He also remembers having lain in bed with her frequently as a child, but he believes that nothing happened. Whenever he was washed he would scream lamentably and yell: "Oh! I'm sick." That was especially true after the experience with his cousin and his mother often took him to the doctor, although there was nothing to be found.

As a child he had a typical dream which often repeated itself:

There was a round arena on the roof of the school, round like a ball, and I wondered how it was possible for me to remain so high up. There was often snow in this arena, but always in the form of large balls. It was necessary for him to crawl through all kinds of dark passages and narrow holes in order to get up there. This is a stereotyped dream which retains his memory of the large breasts of his mother in symbolical form (she was a noticeably luxurious-looking woman). After he is born, he achieves the breast.

He often thought of birth and death and even as a child he had frequently wondered why people must die, hoping, of course, that he would remain immortal. Whenever he liked other children, he was impelled to embrace them so hard that they would cry out (memories of his mother's embraces).

When he was seven, they spent some months in the country and there he would see white figures passing through the garden. This made him terribly afraid.

I will pass over some dream analyses in this case, because they only repeat old and well-worn motives: unpleasant affairs with girls, whom he had beaten, repentance because of his faithlessness, homosexual phantasies, etc.

An important dream:
The street car stopped twice before it reached the station. I thought to myself: it is certainly difficult, dangerous, even impossible to reach one's goal.

The meaning of this dream is simply that it is dangerous to reach any goal. What is his goal, after all? He thinks of his sadistic scenes and we learn that at bottom he would like to choke or stab these women to death, but his mortal fear of the law stops him just short of his sexual goal. It is also important as an indication that twice during the analysis he was about to divulge deciding material, but caught himself just in time.

He associates to his calf fetishism: it first occurred to him when he was not quite three years old. His Aunt Rosa had a baby and he was told that the stork had bitten her in the leg.

"Where?" he asked.

"In the calf!" was the answer. He then believed that children came from the calf. He is always on the lookout for women with quite fleshy calves, but small genitals.

He dreamed:
In the dream, I felt a heavy hand on my head. I looked lasciviously at an old woman and she stabbed me in the head.

I was at the race track. On a slight elevation, there was a small house in which my wife was sitting. One of the horses became wild and ran away. The crowd scattered and some of them yelled to me to catch the horse. Then the horse changed to a crazy man. I turned and ran, but a small whip almost tripped me. Then I was in a small room and locked the door, but I noticed with sudden fright that a second door was still open. I awoke with anxiety.

This dream is rather easy to interpret. He, the patient, is the wild horse, the insane man (one of his great fears is that he will go crazy). He is afraid of his own sadism. He is supposed to do something to inhibit his own passions (catch the horse), but his impulse to use the whip trips him up and prevents him from managing his paraphilia. He has locked the main entrance, but his sadism can still come in through the other door.

He says he is interested in the beheading of women. He would like to be the executioner.

Another determinant for his misogyny: he would like to kill the woman within him.

The woman who provoked his lust in the dream reminds him of his mother, whom he manifestly still loved with considerable passion, even when she had become old and had lost her charms. His mother used to lay her hand on his head whenever he had a fever. Often he complained to her that his head felt as if it were being stabbed and then she would be specially sweet to him, would put cold packs on his brow and sit by his bed. Only later will we be able to understand the passage about the heavy hand.

Fables and fairy tales always made a deep impression upon him. He was once able to see a children's play in which they presented that part of Snow White where the hunter cuts out the child's heart. Later, he reproduced the scene in his onanistic phantasies. He likes to take trips into the country, but he is afraid to go with his wife alone. They invariably have a friend come along. As the analysis of this showed, he needs the friend as a protection against himself and his murderous tendencies.

When he was thirteen, he played with a little six-year-old cousin of his. He would win her with presents of candy and then she would permit him to put his penis between her legs and imitate the movements of coitus. He was already having orgasms with ejaculation at this time, although he later wanted to correct himself and say that he had his first ejaculation when he was fourteen or fifteen. These little meetings with his cousin continued for several years.

At thirteen he also fell in love with a boy who was a most beautiful schoolmate of his. The patient tried at all costs to be like him, imitated his dress, and jealously sought his friendship. He was very vain and always wanted to be the most handsome of men. At fifteen he went to a prostitute because he had heard that masturbation makes one ugly, while coitus is better than the best cosmetic.

They had a roomer who, he thought, didn't think much of him. Later this roomer became one of his teachers in grammar school. This roomer also cultivated homosexual relations with another teacher and they would exchange handsome boys with each other and play with them. The teacher would beat the boys over their naked calves and this excited our patient considerably.

We will recall that he always plays the teacher in his sadistic hotel scenes and it appears that the above experience was the determining factor in this habit. Indeed, although he claims to have experienced his teacher's habits in earliest childhood, it is possible that his memory betrays him. He desired to become a teacher at any price because he wanted to be able to beat the little boys across the calves. The earliest objects of his sadistic phantasies were little boys.

The analysis proceeds, but with the greatest difficulties. He remembers divers acts he perpetrated upon little children, but his memory is halting and fraught with resistance. To this day, the child is his chief object of sexual desire. He even looks upon his wife only as a child.

The story of his marriage is quite characteristic of his psychic make-up. He made the acquaintance of his wife when she was sixteen and after a short time she became his sweetheart. He often wondered how it was possible for him to remain potent with her although he never had any sadistic phantasies in regard to her. He soon became a little tired of her, but snapped up with jealousy as soon as he noticed that she began to lean towards other men. He again won her affections and again tired of her. This game then repeated itself about a dozen times, and he always became deeply dejected whenever he would try to leave her. When they lived together, however, they were always at each other's throats, so to speak, until he finally made up his mind to marry her because he saw that he couldn't live without her and thought that it would end his troubles. He hadn't been married two weeks before he became impotent with his wife and has remained so to the present day. I noticed that he had completed an identification here with his sister and asked him to produce all that he could remember about his sister from his childhood.

It was here that a most curious fact appeared, viz., that, although he had even boasted of his enviable memory for every detail of his childhood, he could remember nothing about his games or his relations with his sister. Whenever he would try to recall anything about her, he would always think of something or other relating to a cousin. He dimly remembers having played papa and mama with this cousin out in a garden veranda. The cousin's name was Elizabeth, and that is also his wife's name. The further analysis shows definitely that Elizabeth was only a screen memory behind which was hidden the person of his sister, and we see that he actually has been treating his wife as a sister. She is taboo for him, noli me tangere.

During one of the first few grades of school, one of his schoolmates said to him: "Nobody plays with a sister. That's no fun." He now recalls that he often played with his sister. It was a game in which they played the parts of two women, she was the rich one and he the poor one. They would meet as if at the market place, complain of the hard times and scarcity of money. But he denies that they ever had anything sexual to do with each other. He could swear to it. His memory never fails him.

Now we want to look into his compulsions a little more. The obsessional ideas are specially connected with his appearance as an actor. Whenever he is in trouble on the stage, he feels his gaze drawn to his left hand as if he were hypnotized. It is then he fears that he will be a failure, God will punish him. Lately, however, he has been doing very well and he has been saying to himself: "You don't have to give yourself so much trouble. What must be will be." He nevertheless fears that just then an evil thought will enter his mind. It seems as if he were punishing himself for some experience of childhood in which his hand played an important part. He had repeatedly dreamed that his left hand lay heavily on his head. One of his most obsessive ideas is the torturing thought that he will never forget his evil phantasies (he has repressed something and these evil thoughts are the symbols of it).

He sometimes feels that there is a colossal difference between his right and left hands. Just as if they were two strange hands that didn't know each other (the right hand shall not know what the left hand doeth). I call his attention to the fact that left means incest and homosexuality and that right stands for normal. It has been his desire to be normal, but he has not been able to achieve his wish.

He then begins to speak about homosexuality and I call his attention to the conflicting data he has offered. He had first dated the story about his cousin whacking him on the behind with his fourteenth year and later he changed it to his seventh year. This uncertainty reveals to us that we must be dealing with two different experiences. He is asked to repeat the story about his cousin and relates the following:

"I was seven years old and was leaning out the window. My cousin came up behind me and gave me a whack on my buttocks. I was so frightened that I thought he had injured something. I always held my hand over my behind. After a while I began to be anxious about the rat, about a rat biting me in the behind."

I tell him that the whole story has an untrue ring and that he is probably relating what might be called a screen memory. We know that he is given to dreamy states and such persons are liable to experience things during such a state which they later forget. He should remember the roomer who certainly has something to do with his parapathia.

This roomer must certainly have been a perverse individual. He had relations with the patient's mother and probably also with the maid. Once both these women spent some time in the teacher's room together. He first heard laughing and crying and then it turned out to be quite an excited and hilarious time.

"Weren't you ever in this roomer's quarters?"

"No. Never."

After a while, he says: "Well, perhaps . . . it seems to me that he must have given me some tutoring. He called me into the room and had me learn something. Oh, yes, now I can see it again. He whipped me across the calves and the naked buttocks with a switch."

"Did he do anything else with you?"

"Impossible!"

He then relates something about the homosexual phantasies of his childhood and the experiences he had with homosexuals who made him all kinds of tempting offers. He claims to have rejected all such offers with disgust and astonishment.

During this tale, he suddenly excuses himself and asks to be permitted to leave the room because he has an imperative urge.

When he returned, he said: "I know it is not nice, but I must tell you. I felt as if a hard piece of feces were sticking in my rectum. But when I got there, I found that it was nothing. How we can err."

I realize that this is a homosexual phantasy and call his attention to the fact. I tell him that he is apparently not clear on one definite experience of his childhood. But he says he can't see anything in it. He agrees that he feels a positive transference to me, but he has never considered love of other men as anything but low and inconceivable. He denies ever having had homosexual phantasies.

The analysis halts and sputters. There are innumerable resistances. He is struggling against his better judgement. But some dreams carry us along.

He dreamed:

It was a small room. I am with my mother and sister and ring for the maid. A lovely, blonde girl appeared. I ring ten times.

He associates the fact that his sister had almost the same face as the maid. The number ten has been worrying him for some time. Recently he awoke and heard someone call out the number ten.

The second dream had him in his small home. Several aristocrats also slept there, but there was a porter there, too, who took care of everything. This porter was an important personage (a busy body). It seemed like a sort of competition. I was supposed to ride from the bed to the hall. I won and got six points. Then the aristocrats rode into the Prater with the porter, and without paying any attention to me. I then rode backwards towards the sulky park.

Then I saw a horrid, large bird carrying my wife on its beak. I also saw my father and several other persons riding off—further and further away until I didn't see them any more.

He was especially attracted by his wife on the beak of that bird. He recalls having dozed off a little last night and his wife awakening him. When he opened his eyes he seemed not to see her, but some old, wrinkled woman. His association to the bird is that the bird is a stork which brings the babies.

The bird is thus the phallic symbol of his father. His wife represents his sister (stork and spermatozoa dream). The old, ugly face reminds him of his grandmother and now he remembers that it was she and not the maid who had cut off his hair (Samson complex—impotence. He continues to be impotent with his wife). He recalls the riding from the bed into the hall. His sister once slept in the hall, but he can't remember clearly whether or not he ever rode up to her. He can only remember that he had a hobby horse which for some strange reason was taken from him. It is probable that he used to masturbate on it. He would often play horse with his sister; also coachmen and horse. The lost hobby horse appears to be a screen memory for his sister.

It seems that he directed his earliest sadistic impulses at the hobby horse. It was taken from him and put into the store room in the attic. They always promised him that if he would be a good boy, he would get his hobby horse back again. But he never saw it again. The rest of the dream cannot be interpreted at this time.

Thus far, we can readily see his "weaning complex," called the castration complex by Freud. The castration character may be indicated by his having torn out the hobby horse's tail.

Another dream continues the theme about the horse:

I was in Lawrence Hill Avenue and wanted to climb into a one-horse carriage with my wife. The coachman fell forwards over the horse from off the box. I jumped out and ran away with my wife, leaving my new suit in the carriage. I was in my shirt, but I had a suit in my hands. In the Brandstaette (a city street), a man and a woman came out of a door.

It was in Lawrence Hill Avenue that he had had his next to last unpleasant experience just prior to marriage. He had run into a shop to buy a whip. He had found a girl who was willing to go to a hotel with him, but she turned out to be a whore who demanded plenty of money. He had also had his last unpleasant meeting just before marriage in the Brandstaette. It was then that he decided to marry in order to protect himself against his paraphilia.

We thus see that his marriage has a distinct relationship with his paraphilia. He is afraid to become well and give up his illness. That is the reason he is impotent with his wife. If he were not, he would be in danger of losing his delight in the whipping scenes, which represent a cherished treasure of his childhood and are apparently connected with his sister. The new suit symbolizes his new attitude towards life, but the coachman (his conscious) succumbs to the power of his instincts.

He recalls having beaten an inanimate ball because it did not roll after him. He was four years old. Then he took a funnel and stuck a big hole in the ball. He cried bitterly afterwards because he had spoiled his plaything. The deeper relationships of this memory with his paraphilia are not yet clear, but the sadistic element (ball-woman) appears to be clear.

Various dreams which he brings appear to point to the fact

that his first experiences occurred with his sister. Dimly he recalls that he used to crawl into her bed at night. He also used to sleep beside his mother, whose warm body made him feel comfortable.

At this point he stopped the analysis.

After about a month, he returns to the analysis in order to gain some light on the following dream:

I did something to some little girl (Mizzi?) and some woman caught me in the act (Mizzi's mother?). Afterwards I saw the child lying in bed and holding two sticks in the air, they were thin sticks. She invited me to do something to her again. I purposely said: "No. I won't do it," in order that the woman who had forbidden me to do it might hear.

As I awoke from the dream, I had the feeling that I was poking a stick into my ribs on either side.

He spontaneously associates his sister's legs to the sticks.

It was not possible to gain any further information on this dream. He comes late to the hour, talks about banal actualities and manifests the greatest resistances. I decided upon another method and hypnotized him. He fell asleep easily. I then gave him the suggestion to think about the dream and to reproduce some scene from his childhood which might enter his mind as an explanation for the dream.

What he said was as follows:

"I see my sister. I see her lovely blonde head. She wears a blue bow. It is evening. My parents have gone to the theatre and the maid has left us alone. We play school and my sister is the teacher. We sit in the first row and she teaches me. Then we play dog. I'm the dog and begin to bite her. I bite her softly in the arms and cheeks. Then she falls on the floor and lies quite still as if dead or asleep. I fall upon her and she spreads her legs, but she doesn't move. Then I lick her. She twitches her legs, but holds them tightly about me. Then I jump up and she scolds me with her finger, saying: "You disgusting little brat, you!" But we play again and I repeated it several times. Then the maid came into the room and threatened to tell mama. She spanked me rather lightly on the behind. Then we were quiet and I ate a piece of bread and butter. After that we went into the hall and the maid left us again. As soon as she was gone, my sister sat herself on the window sill and I licked at her again and bit her in the calf."

He is awakened from the hypnosis and doesn't remember what

he said. He was told about the scene he had described and immediately began to feel nauseated.

In the next hour, he repeated the scene and added a few details. It appears that this cunnilingus was repeated frequently. We then hear of another disclosure. Without my asking him anything, he begins to tell me the following:

"I see before me a large, white—immense—belly. I have my fingers beneath it. I smell my fingers and put them in my mouth. I am lying between my parents in bed. I raise myself a little. Both parents are fast asleep. I crawl over to my mother, who doesn't mind. I crawl down to her feet and embrace her calves. I lick her feet and then her calves. Gradually I crawled up higher—no—it's not possible—yet—I can see it quite clearly. I licked my mother. She closed her legs tightly about me so that her knees touched me. She tousled my hair" (cf. the first part of the dream about the heavy hand on his head)."

He adds a lot of details and repetitions which I can pass over here. As I was able to learn by chance, the mother was a lewd person who had a bad name. Her sensuality was pathological and even as an old woman she continued her profession, partly for pleasure and partly for money.

He is asked what he has to say about his rat phobia. When he was eight, he saw two giant rats in the Prater. They had tremendous bellies and long tails. In childhood, he saw a terrible picture: "Hatto in the Mouse Tower" was the name. Hatto sitting beside some bread and water. The mice ran hither and thither— the Pied Piper of Hamelin—tadpoles also have wiggly tails—rats have wiggly tails—I see snakes that turn and twist—I see a noodle in my mouth which is fat and smooth and shiny and moist and slippery. It is slowly sliding down my throat (noodle is a Viennese vulgar term for penis)—I'm biting on a penis and won't let go—just like a dog that has something in his mouth and won't let go—I see a small penis without hairs—just like fountain—city park—Danube Girl (a half-naked fountain figure in Vienna)— children are playing in the sand—they are playing with a switch which is being swung hither and thither in the sand—swaying like a snake—someone scares us with a dead rat's tail—nauseating— fear and disgust—two tails which entwine, one hangs on the other —two men embrace, entwine—they go off hand in hand, their penises entwined—a rat climbs up a man's leg (sickening)—the noodle in my mouth—a canary bird.

"When I was five I saw my father's penis. Whenever I masturbated and wanted to spoil my fun, I thought of my father's penis and it was all over. Now I am sick and disgusted with every penis as if it were a rat. I think of that teacher, that homosexual, who was a roomer in our house. He was a handsome man. I was in his room once." What happened in that room? . . . His memory fails him.

His sister had told him that when he was thirteen he had masturbated against the leg of his sleeping mother. She was quite used to that in him. His mother pervaded a repelling odor, but this odor did not at all disturb his onanistic habits. On the contrary, it activated them.

He dreamed:

It is the room in R—— street. I am sitting at the secretary. I have a little girl on my lap and am licking her eyes out. They are full of tears. The door to the next room is open and there is a round table in there round which the family sits. One of them was a man with a pince-nez. Emission.

I have a quarrel with Mr. Pfeiffer. He punched me on the jaw, but I was a coward and only appeared to return him a slap on the face. It was more of a joke; so that he could boast that he had really punched me.

I received an invitation to a sanatorium. The sanatorium was on one of Vienna's hills and yet out in the country. We came up to the place from behind. It was a narrow little house and as we went in we saw peasant's children at play. I said: "It's lovely in the country when the sun is shining." A man and his wife who had just come up thought the same. In the hall of the place there was quite a crowd but the hallman knew us (we had already been there once). Inside, it looked like some sort of play. I had a seat down front and there were two others with me, among them an ugly Jew with a round, bent back, but larger than me. I took a piece of paper and stuck it in his behind so that everybody laughed at him. He took my place.

He adds to the first dream that his sister was also along. This dream manifestly contains a repetition and corroboration of the cunnilingus scene. The eye represents the vagina and the man with the *pince-nez* is his father, the father who chased him out of his mother's bed once and also caught him masturbating.

The second dream represents his inner struggle with himself.

The third portion of the dream finds its explanation through the medium of the hallman who reminds him of his deceased brother-in-law. His sister was quite as light-headed as his mother (great crowd in the hall; the sanatorium represents a bordello). The big, ugly Jew is paying amorous attention to his wife. He takes his place. He is afraid to be cheated just as his father was betrayed. The children, playing in the sun, are symbols of the genitals.

I recall the fact that in that uninterpreted dream about the aristocrats, G. rode backwards to the sulky track. In this one, he sticks the paper into the Jew's behind and everybody laughs.

He asks me for a hypnosis and is soon asleep. He is asked to produce his associations to the dream about the aristocrats and to pay especial attention to the porter. He delivered the following explanation:

"The aristocrats are the adults and the other people are the children. The aristocrats ride into the Prater, which means that the parents have gone to the park. The porter, who is supposed to take care of everything, is the roomer at home. He also had a pince-nez. He was the man with the glasses. He was the lover of my mother and the maid. I played with my sister in the hall. The porter, the big bird, are both the penis of that roomer. He had a very large penis."

"How do you know that?"

"I told you that already."

"Tell me about it again." (As a matter of fact, he had never said a word about it. He had probably intended speaking about it, and the intention is retained in memory as a matter of fact. This frequently occurs during an analysis.)

"Well—the teacher gave me lessons. We were often alone in his room. He would put his penis in my left hand and I would rub it until a white juice would run out."

"How often did he do that?"

"Ten times, he did it."

"You're sure?"

"Yes. Ten times." (See the dream with the number ten.)

"What does that mean in the dream where you say 'we came up to the place from behind'? Why did you stick that piece of paper into the Jew's behind?"

"The teacher used to undress me and then switch me lightly on the legs. Later on he used to do that in school, too. He also tried to put his penis in my rectum, but it hurt me and I cried out. He then put his finger in and I liked it. I was quite under

his spell. He was the teacher and said that I had to do everything he told me to do. If I were to speak of this, however, I'd
feel like dying."

"Do you remember what his name was?"

"Certainly. Sonnenthal. ('It's lovely in the country when the
sun is shining.') He is also the man with the *pince-nez*. He used
to pinch my whole body, but especially my calves and buttocks.
He also commanded me to put my penis into his rectum. He
would bend his back and bend over. He was really nothing but
a dirty Jew ('it was like a play inside; an ugly Jew was with me')."

"Do you remember all these things clearly?"

"Certainly."

"Then why haven't you said anything about them?"

"I don't know, doctor. May I open my eyes? I'm not sleeping. I'm awake. I'm not even sure whether I was asleep the
first time I was hypnotized. I'm sure I've always remembered
this thing about Sonnenthal, but I didn't want to know it, as you
so accurately wrote. I understand now why I'm always running
about so much. I'm really running after all these experiences I
had in childhood."

We still had to explain his impotence, but this, too, found an unexpected interpretation. It appears that he has staged the impotence for his own benefit. We know that ever since his childhood
he has been fighting to destroy all his joys. He feels that he
doesn't deserve any happiness in life and even as a boy he would
ask himself what good happiness would do him. He would imagine that he had had his pleasures and everything was the same as
before. He always had a good erection when with his wife. But
whenever he was about to have intercourse, the very philosophic
thought would enter his mind: "Imagine that it's half an hour
later. What did you get out of your delights?" That would then
be the end of his erection.

The explanation of this staging of a defeat is to be found in
his childhood. He had a burning desire for the possession of his
sisters. But he would spoil his yearning by asking himself: What
have you left of your pleasure after half an hour? On the mor-
row? When you're dead? In short, he was so completely able to
depreciate the value of his sisters and push them into the background of his life, that even at the beginning of the analysis he
was able to wonder that they played no part in his sexual life,
that he had no memories of sexual relations of any kind with
them. But we have learned that he had good reason for his bad

conscience. He fears God and wants to expiate by spoiling his every joy. He is impotent with his wife because he really desires her but feels he doesn't deserve her. Even as a child he believed that everyone was in league with God against him, and he has preserved this feeling to this very day. He's an unlucky bird because he doesn't want to give himself any luck. He possesses the loveliest of women and can't have her. As soon as he wants to have intercourse he spoils his fun by starting to philosophize. That is not a fate. It is a self-willed and personally staged defeat.

The analysis was at an end. G. was no longer troubled by his obsessions, he was able to appear without hindering his own progress and spoiling his own successes. He lost his desire to run after girls and entice them into sadistic scenes. Three weeks after the analysis, he had resumed sexual relations with his wife. She was no longer his sister or his mother image, but his wife.

From many points of view, this case is an exceptional picture. First of all, we see here the power of infantile experiences and the influence of the environment. A sullied mother who used her child as a badge of respectability to catch men (a married woman with a child—a trick of many prostitutes who even borrow children in order to use them for this purpose. Also a speculation in pedophilic possibilities). Contrasted with this, a strict and respectable father who, along with the pious grandmother, was a representative of morality. The ambivalence in his soul was undoubtedly caused by this anomalous environment of his childhood.

His marriage was a trial to free himself from the bonds of his infantile habits. But identifying his wife with his sister, as he did, made her taboo and the road to his paraphilia was again open.

We observe a massive impulse to achieve a repetition of the experiences of early childhood. The scenes he enacts in the hotel with the girls is really a composite of several early memories (mother, sister and teacher). His steady battle against his homosexuality leads to the repression of these instincts and their consequent absorption in the symptomatology of the specific scene. He becomes the teacher and the girls play the little boy who is switched across the legs. We also have here an explanation of why he was always so weak and uncertain during the coitus which would follow these scenes with the girls. He could hardly find the vagina because he was really looking for the teacher's anus.

His kleptomania was really secondary. It becomes interesting only through its connection with the linens and underthings he took. This habit is reducible to a very primitive instinct, the olfactory impulse. He began to use his mother's underthings for his onanistic purposes when yet a little boy. Rudiments of this impulse are still within him and he would still like to steal women's underthings if it were not such a dangerous business. Not all such cases show clear connections with incestuous tendencies as this one has.

Wagner-Jauregg described a case of a maid who used to steal her master's shirts and put them on at night. I know of a maid who used the cast-off chemises of her mistress as nightgowns. She was surprised in one by the mistress and suffered an hysterical attack as a result of which she was brought to me for an opinion. It was easy to judge that this maid was in love with her mistress and liked to titillate herself with the mistress's odor.

There are kleptomaniacs who steal corsets, handkerchiefs, underwear, stockings, etc., and use them as a means of sexual excitement. They are usually called fetishists. If our patient had been interested only in these underthings, had collected a harem of such articles, had completely rejected the female in their favor, then we could call him a fetishist. His calf partialism is determined by many factors. Sadger's declaration, which is supposed to represent Freud's opinion, too, viz., that every fetish represents the female genital to the fetish lover, does not exhaust the problem. Their proofs are supposed to be found in the fact that such cases improve after analysis. A bust fetishist (Sadger's terminology) loses his monopolizing interest in breasts after the treatment and begins to have intercourse, i.e., he interests himself in the female genitals. That is, of course, no proof at all that the breasts are supposed to represent the female genital. We know that any erogenous zone can be genitalized, as it were, and take over the rôle of the genitals. As soon as the infantile fixations are lifted, the patient turns his interest again to the central theme of normal sexual relations.

In Chapter II, we were able to observe how it is possible that in a case of bust partialism special circumstances can fixate an interest in a certain erogenous zone after puberty without the basis of an incestuous determinant. In the above-mentioned case, the bust was the memory of an unforgotten sweetheart.

Partialism is such a widespread and common characteristic among humans that we can hardly look upon it as anything but normal. It is naturally individualized in each case. One would have to cite many, many cases to illustrate and explain all types of partial preference psychologically and analytically. We may be satisfied with the above cases. Such a work as this is not supposed to be a cabinet of curiosities, but a scientific treatise. Now that we have fulfilled our duties in analyzing some of these curious conditions, we may turn again to the complicated problems of true fetishism.

To return to our case again, we must say that G. is always staging one scene—always the same. He has not been able to overcome the tyranny of infantile symbolisms and to fix himself to a single object of reality. He is subject to the compulsion of serial formation, nor is he capable of concentrating his attention for any length of time on one person. Not even the acme of masochism, the woman who serves his every sadistic will, can hold him. He may try a few repetitions, but is fleeting in his tastes. He flies out on the street, seeks another object. But he does not search for the girl, he looks for the resistance to his wishes, the barrier to overcome.

Chance had it that soon after I had finished with this case, a colleague came to me with a girl who, he declared, must be suffering from a paralogia because the story she has constructed about her defloration sounded so improbable. I had the girl tell me her story and immediately realized that she must have been one of G.'s girls.[1] Her description corresponded in detail with everything which I knew only too well. I was, of course, able to reassure my colleague that the girl was not suffering from a paralogia, but that her story consisted of sad facts. I was, however, able to learn that G. had described his sadistic acts much more harmlessly to me than they actually were. This girl

had been recommended to him by another gentleman to learn
dancing. G. led her onto a half-darkened stage and had her do
some steps for him. Elise—as we may call the girl—was a
twenty-one-year-old, nervous, hysterical person whose one desire it was to become a famous dancer. She had, however,
never learned to dance before and was able to do only a few
simple steps and some graceful bows. G. told her that she
would have to go through some strenuous training in order to
become famous. He locked her in a dark chamber for half an
hour, pulled her by the hair and finally took her to a hotel.
There he had her take everything but her chemise off and when
she made a false step, he would switch her over the calves with
a girdle (he was not able to get a whip). He commanded her
to hold her hands behind her back. Elise complied because she
was fascinated by the thought of becoming a famous dancer.
As soon as she had her hands behind her back, he tied them
and continued to become more and more strict and cruel. She
began to protect herself. She yelled and cried for help, but no
one came. He became even more vicious and finally threw her
across the bed, so that her legs were pressed close to his body.
She implored him to spare her, cried that she was yet a virgin,
but he laughed sarcastically and said that they didn't need virgins in the theatre. She finally weakened and he deflorated her
in a coitus that lasted but a few seconds, but was painful to her
nevertheless. He then unbound her and gave her some money
which she took hesitatingly. We are not here interested in
Elise's further destiny, except to say that she tried to gain
redress through the courts. She consulted an attorney, but was
unsuccessful. G. had arranged things so well that no one was
able to catch him.[2]

We see clearly that his special scenes are a composite of four
separate experiences. (1) His father's beatings; (2) Love and
hate of the mother; (3) The scene with the teacher; (4) The
scene with his sister.

I was immediately struck by the similarity which Elise bore
to G. She looked as if she were his sister and might have
been his younger sister, especially. I had known his younger
sister and had treated her for a parapathia.

If we analyze this scene of his, we can observe the fact that the chief factor in it is ascribable to the influence of his teacher.

1. He is the teacher. He is punished and allegedly must study in that little room. Instead, he is forced to suffer a homosexual act. His restlessness is due to his eternal reactivation of this one scene.

2. He is the father. The sadistic part of the scene is derived from his father, who was his first teacher. This man had chastised him and had also punished him by locking him in a dark room.

3. He beats his mother—the whore. The whipping across the calves is a sadistic transformation of his original love scenes with his mother (we know, on the other hand, that he had also been highly interested in the calves of boys, especially between the ages of seven and fourteen).

4. He repeats the old scenes with his sister. The coitus is violently executed on the bed in such a manner that the girl's legs are pressed close about his body (see the dream about his sister and his mother). Instead of cunnilingus, he has intercourse. He also confessed that he sometimes practised cunnilingus instead of coitus.

5. He pays the girl just as the men used to pay his mother. He identifies himself with the innumerable lovers his mother had and perhaps also with one his sister had.

We have not been able to corroborate Sadger and Freud's statement that the fetish (the calf) represents the female genital. In this case, the calf is determined by the calves of his mother, his sister and the maid who always went about the house with naked legs and bare feet. In addition to this determinant, the calves represent the calves of boys and also the phallus to which he is homosexually fixated. Like many sadists, he has a small phallus, and that is one of the bases of their desire to revenge themselves on human kind. His hatred of women is derived from his hatred of his mother, who was a prostitute. It follows that he married a woman with a more than questionable past, i.e., he has recreated his mother in her (also his sister, who began her life along the lines of her mother. She later saved herself by marriage, but paid for her life with a serious parapathia).

The calf is thus a complex symbol in this case, just as in the case I described in Chapter IV, where it represented the brother's phallus and many other complexes. It is a dangerous thing to try to solve paraphilias with a single formula. They are usually of a very complicated structure. We shall have sufficient opportunity to dwell upon this point in our analyses of true fetishism.

In this case, we can see how the up-bringing started an otherwise well-fitted, highly talented, fine and well-liked man on the road to criminality. The blame rests finally with his mother.

VII

PARTIALISM AND THE HAREM CULT

Variatio delectat! How innumerable are the variations which Eros creates in order to make the monotonous simplicity of the natural sex organ interesting to the sexologist. The most widespread form of partialism is the preference for feet. I have always wondered at the fact that there are many more foot fetishists than hand lovers. I must admit of some bias in view of the fact that I paid especial attention to the sexual importance of the hand when I made a study of autoerotism and both male and female impotence. The previous volumes of this series contain sufficient material to corroborate the importance of the hand in human sexual life. Nevertheless, the number of those who seek only the hand, seek only to kiss, stroke, pet or suck on it, is rather circumscribed. A far greater number of men emphasize the importance of the beautiful hand only as a means to the attractive female herself. I know many æsthetes who could never kiss a woman whose hands repelled them. I know of cases, on the other hand, where the one partner has fallen in love at first sight primarily through the effective agency of well-shaped hands which happened to fulfill his particular love conditions. They were, in such cases, the short-circuit between love preparedness and infatuation.[1]

In the two following cases, the hand is the central theme of interest. Both cases, however, show flight from the female. The chief point is really not whether a patient has been able to have coitus one time more or less. The deciding factor is rather that behind the partialism, there lurks an anti-feminine tendency, even an anti-sexual and ascetic striving.

Moll reports the first case as follows:

Case 25. P. L., a twenty-eight-year-old Westfalian business man, revealed no hereditary stigmatization. Upon questioning, he gave the following information about his sexual life. As far as he can remember, his first sexual experience came when he was seven years old. Si pueri eiusdem fere ætatis mingentis membrum adspexit, valde libidinibus excitatus est. L. claims with great certainty that he had an erection during this excitement. He stated that he was taught to masturbate by another boy when he was about seven or eight. "Being a very easily excitable nature," says L., "I masturbated frequently until I was eighteen without in the least feeling any deleterious results or being at all conscious of the real nature of the act." He liked especially cum nonullis com-militonibus mutuam masturbationem tractare, but he was not at all indifferent to who the other boy was. On the contrary, not every schoolmate satisfied him in this respect. When questioned about the possible conditions he sought in another boy, he an-swered that it was particularly a pale, well-formed hand which attracted him to mutual masturbation. L. also recalls that during the time when he took exercises, he would often find himself alone on the bars at one end of the gymnasium. He did this with the view ut quam maxime excitaretur idque tantopere assectus est, ut membro manu non tacto, sine ejaculatione—puerili ætate erat—voluptatem clare senserit. Still another procedure in his child-hood commands our interest. One of L.'s favorite schoolmates, N., with whom he mutually masturbated once made him the fol-lowing proposition: ut L. membrum N.—i apprehendere conaretur, he, N., would struggle as much as possible and try to prevent L. from doing it. L. agreed and the masturbation was thus directly connected with a sort of fight between the two, L. always being the winner and N. the conquered (in other words, a sort of rudi-mentary sadism in L. and masochism in N.—St.).

The struggle always ended regularly ut N. tandem coatus sit membrum masturbari. L. assured me that this type of masturba-tion afforded not only himself but also N. a particularly height-ened sense of gratification. It was in this fashion that L. con-tinued to masturbate until he was eighteen, but once he was told about the nature of masturbation by his friend, he tried with all his might to desist. He was also able to execute his will more and more as time went on until, as soon as he had experienced his first coitus, he was able to stop masturbation entirely. By that time, however, he was over twenty-one. To-day he says he can hardly understand how he was able to masturbate with other boys and he feels nauseated at the thought. No power in the world could make him touch another man's organ now, and even the sight of another's penis is disgusting to him. He claims that the last vestige of his attraction to other men has faded and that he feels himself wholly attracted to women. We must mention, however, that although he feels himself dedicated sexually to women, this attraction is marked by a rather abnormal characteristic. The chief source of his sexual excitement in a woman is the sight of a lovely hand. He is far more deeply affected by the sight or touch of a graceful, feminine hand quam si candam feminam plane nudatam adspiceret. Just how completely he is held spellbound by a woman's hand may be seen from the following incident.

L. was acquainted with a young woman who possessed almost all of the feminine virtues, but her hands were fairly large and not well shaped. They were perhaps also not always very clean, as he would wish. It was therefore not only impossible for L. to cultivate a very intimate friendship with the woman, he was not even capable of touching her. L. feels that there can hardly be a more disgusting sight for him than dirty finger nails, and unclean nails alone would make it impossible for him to have anything to do with the most beautiful of women. L. frequently used to substitute for coitus in earlier years by ut puellam usque ad ejaculationem effectam membrum suum manu tractare iusserit.

He was asked just what it might be in a woman's hand that provoked him, whether it might be the symbol of strength and whether he would like to be directly humiliated by a woman. He answered that it was simply the form of the hand which attracted him and that he would derive no pleasure whatever in being humiliated by a woman, furthermore, that he had never thought of the hand as the symbol of female strength. His preference for a woman's hand is even to-day so great ut majore voluptat afficiatur si manus feminæ membrum tractat quam coitu in vaginam. He nevertheless likes to perform the latter instead, because intercourse appeals to him as something more normal whereas his other leaning makes him feel pathological. Whenever a lovely female hand touches him, his erection is instantaneous. He states that kisses and other forms of petting or adulation haven't nearly the same effect on him.

The patient performed intercourse only during the last few years, but even so, the determination to do so was not easy. He also found far less gratification in coitus than otherwise. If, however, he finds himself in the immediate vicinity of a woman to whom he is attracted, the very sight of her alone is often so effective that his excitement can rise until he ejaculates. L. assures me that under such circumstances he never so much as touches his penis, but the orgasm gives him a much deeper satisfaction than if he were having intercourse.

L.'s dreams are never concerned with intercourse, and whenever he has an emission during the night, it occurs in connection with quite different thoughts from those prevailing in the minds of most men. The dreams L. has are recapitulations of his experiences during his school days. At that time he also would have an orgasm whenever he was greatly frightened or anxious. When, e.g., the teacher would read a passage for the boys to translate and he was not able to follow, he would frequently have an ejaculation. His present nocturnal emissions are always accompanied by dreams which reënact some such scene as the one described. The patient feels that because of his abnormal feelings and desires he will never be able to love one woman for any length of time.

This case reveals a marked bisexual tendency and also a retreat from the female. His dreams betray some secret sexual desire which is inaccessible to the patient's conscious. All such dreams about not getting through or not achieving something show, according to my own experience in the matter, that the patient has some goal in mind which cannot be achieved or reached. It is quite false to believe that the anxiety about not getting finished in time can provoke an orgasm. The psychic mechanism is rather that the duty he must apparently perform is only a mask behind which a much more important or difficult duty is hidden. The manifest problem is only a symbol of a hidden sexual life. You won't achieve your sexual objective! (Unfortunately, Moll's case was not analyzed.) The present duty of the individual is thus a sort of oracle, i.e., if you can perform this duty well then you will have solved the other, more difficult, one, too. The problem, however, is a forbidden fruit (usually incest or some serious paraphilia) and that is the reason the impulse is inhibited by anxiety. The development of anxiety then accompanies the orgasm.

The next case gives us even deeper insight into the structure of hand fetishism.

Case 26. G. L. is a twenty-three-year-old student of medicine and would like to be freed from a passion which now so takes up his energies that he can hardly think properly. The livelong day he thinks and dreams of lovely women's hands, to such an extent, as a matter of fact, that he can no longer do the slightest bit of work. We note the characteristically complete immolation of the fetishist. Like weeds, the fetishistic thoughts and phantasies overgrow the entire field of the patient's life. Even the most gratifying transient relief does not satisfy for long nor give him peace. That is precisely the difference between normal sexual gratification and compulsive satisfaction. When a normal man is tortured by the pressure of great libidinal desire, there is for him one act of relief, after which he falls into a more or less long period of relative peace and sexual indifference. In fetishistic paraphilias, however, which are nothing but obsessional neuroses, the gratification and surcease is only short lived and soon the old, implacable impulses are at it again.

G. L. portrays his fetishism as follows:

Ever since I can remember, I have had a pathological preference for hands and have taken every possible oppportunity to kiss the hands of every girl and woman I can get hold of. My pleasures are not connected directly with the kissing of the hands, however, but rather when I soar off into phantasies about doing it. I suppose, therefore, that my raptures are not provoked by the actual contact of "hand and lip," but probably by the associated feeling of humiliation. I can recall that even when I was five years old, I used to kiss my governess' hands and—when no one else was about—used to call her "gracious lady." That tickled me. Between the ages of eight and seventeen, I masturbated almost daily and invariably excited myself by imagining all kinds of the basest humiliations. I now remember a most pleasing phantasy I had: I would dream that I was a plantation owner and that I had my female slaves whip and tread me under their feet. I came to masturbate in the following manner. I went to public school for but half a year and while there I recall having to do some arithmetic problem which was too difficult for me. I felt a great anxiety come over me which soon turned to distinct rapture. I did something involuntarily with my hand and this noticeably increased my pleasure. While in high school, I was quite proud of my dangerous secret, but I soon began to suffer from a nervous breakdown. During the later years of high school, I had a distinct homosexual leaning. I was downright in love with one of my schoolmates, but nothing serious ever came of it except harmless tenderness and a deep mutual trust. The fact that he was anti-Semitic and suffered my attraction to him rather than invited it, increased my pleasure in the relationship if anything. Even to-day, his type of person gives me a thrill of delight whenever I see an example. I nevertheless feel towards him now as if he were the cause of my present nature (although he is not), a bitter hate it is, and I have often had phantasies of murdering him in cold blood.

I first began to notice girls when, in the dancing school, etc., I had to be a little gallant towards them. As soon as a girl becomes at all friendly towards me, I like her immensely, but she immediately loses all sexual charms for me. I am always looking out for plenty of variety in my abasement. I am already a little jaded by the thrill I used to get out of hand-kissing and bending on my knee, but these extravagant forms of mine have had the effect on one girl of causing her spontaneously to raise her hand for me to kiss whenever she sees me. At such a moment I have often had a prompt ejaculation which depleted me tremendously. Whenever I offer my seat in the street car to a woman, I feel that my voice trembles with emotion. If I feel impelled to kiss a woman's hand in front of many other people, my lips twitch. You see, I like to talk about my illness. As a matter of fact, one of my bad points is that I have very little sense of shame. I haven't yet gone in for masochistic literature, but I like to commit social errors and then regret them with pleasure afterwards. Every morning, I awaken with great anxiety which disappears only after I have reached the street. I am very stingy with my time and if I feel that I have wasted even a quarter of an hour, I reproach myself mercilessly. I once had the habit of looking stealthily at the clock every few minutes, but even so my nervousness makes me completely incapable of any work. I have a fervent desire for independence in everything, dislike to have books recommended to me, react indifferently or antipathetically to persons with whom I am brought together, and usually listen to advice courteously only to forget it immediately afterwards. I seem to derive pleasure from lying and I have probably never spoken a true word to even my best friends. Sometimes I am cowardly and yet again I can be foolhardy, but always I am moody. I am sometimes subject to outbursts of niggardliness which can be downright grotesque. Thus, for example, I cannot see any line of a piece of paper unused without feeling disturbed about it, and I often consider spending money for a street car ride very carefully, although I have, on the other hand, given out a good deal of money for superfluous articles. I also lose money frequently. Names and the sense of direction drop from my mind immediately and I find myself quite distracted. I cannot pay attention to lectures for more than a very short time and whereas I formerly went to the theatre frequently, I can now hardly bring myself to look at the stage. It is a habit with me to procrastinate and leave important things to the last minute. I also come late for appointments and keep people waiting. There have been Sundays when I have made three or four appointments for the same time and I seem to get a feeling of triumph from the knowledge that someone is waiting for me in vain. Philosophy and literature interest me especially, but I have a distaste for the special sciences. For the past twelve years I have had the determination to become a writer and although I frequently change my plans abruptly, I have never been shaken in this one purpose. It has practically become a fixed idea with me. I have the courage of my convictions, believe in my own talent and am rather insensitive to both the teasing of my colleagues or their objective criticisms. Well-meant advice, however, especially if it is given by anyone upon whom I look as an authority, can provoke me to actual fits of frothy anger (e.g., "lyrics aren't being read, it's better to go into business"). Frequently I have played with the idea of committing suicide. For the past ten years I have been keeping a rather exhaustive and detailed diary which, as far as I know, no person has ever read. I have never been able to accomplish normal intercourse, but I feel that I am becoming more and more sensually excited every day. In this very personal diary of mine, by the way, I have the tendency (perhaps unconscious) to falsify everything in such a manner that it makes me appear in a more favorable light. My dreams are frequently masochistic in character.

This patient reveals a number of compulsive actions which are quite transparent if one remembers that his mother died on the 5th of November (5/11) and that he reproached himself bitterly for death wishes he harbored against her.

He continues:

Ever since the death of my sister, I close every notation in my diary with the words: "Regards to my dead!" I have never yet left a single space unwritten in that diary, and if any page happens to have a line unfilled, I scribble a few irrelevant words in it as a filler. On important occasions I pray for my deceased relatives in the following order (strict routine): mother, sister, grandparents, grandfather (paternal). During the first wave of sorrow that overcame me after the death of a great artist, I thought of including him in my prayer also, but that soon appeared to be a sacrilege against my mother. I am also subject to the habit of repeating the word mother five or eleven times in my mind before every important decision. The numbers five and eleven have altogether monopolized my mind. My explanation is as follows: Whenever I climb stairs, for example, I feel that I must begin and finish with the right foot. While climbing the stairs, I propose various obsessional problems to myself, e.g., to climb three stairs before anyone meets me coming down ("three of a kind"). But even more. I feel that I must have passed this end point (i.e., the third step) completely and to this end I feel that I must go beyond it by at least one step with each foot. In short, my life seems to have no absolute resting point. The same is true of the numbers nine (three times three) and two in my mind. I count from one to eleven and then from eleven to one backwards and finally repeat to myself the word zero eleven times. When I am telephoning, I feel impelled to stand first on one foot, then on the other and finally on both feet long enough for me to have counted quickly to five or eleven. I cannot comfortably begin the conversation until I have done this. I become unbearably embarrassed whenever I have to converse with anyone in my father's presence. Without actually wishing to do so, I find that I invariably make use of the same figures and manners of speech in the presence of the same persons. Thus, e.g., there is one colleague whom I always greet with the stereotyped statement that I consider his phlegmatic make-up as an indication of hidden power. A girl once told me that she was not in the least interested in conversation about travel or philosophy and as often as I meet her I serve her nothing but these dishes as food for her ears. I almost laugh in the face of one of my acquaintances whenever I meet him, but not because he is so funny, only because he once told me that I had "such a nervous laugh." As long as I liked any friend, I would find myself involuntarily passing his house or the place where he lived several times a day, and while I was under the spell of the great artist I mentioned before, I would find myself unconsciously wandering into the opera house even in the morning, although I may have left the house in quite the opposite direction. On the street, I invariably endeavor to pass as many people as I can, loving couples being of special interest in this game. In passing them up, I get the feeling as if I were getting further in life (and love) than they or their posterity. During the past winter I became subject to the fixed notion that I had to kiss the hand of at least one girl per day. I would disconsolately consider that day as lost and wasted on which I had been unable to carry out my project. As a matter of fact, I am continuously plagued by the obsession of "losing time." I feel in the most comfortable spirits if I can hold some shakeable or handy object in my hand (such as a blade of grass or a stalk of wheat or oats). There are many persons whom I like a great deal, but I have never been able to say a sweet or kind word to them yet. I am obsessed with the habit of drinking to the bottom every glass of water which stands on the table before me, even though I may not be thirsty. I have often drunk up pitchers full in this fashion.

This list of compulsive acts demands our careful analysis. In the first place, we see here a totem cult which reminds one very much of the habits of primitive peoples who fear the revenge of the deceased and especially the killed.[2] Our patient has every reason for fearing the revenge of the dead, for he feels nothing but malicious joy at the death of another: What luck that it's not I! What advantage would I have? In short, he reacts to the situation with the most direct and primitive of feelings, but these in turn provoke a moral backwash which is the expression of highly cultivated sensitivity. Even the death of mother and sister were a source of satisfaction to him, for from then on his father was dependent upon him. Father was then entirely his own. The fact that he says prayers for all the dead (despite his boasting of his being a freethinker and atheist) shows that he wants to over-compensate for his sinful thoughts. Now that they're dead, he feels, I hope they're all right. What he was unable to wish the living, he wishes the the dead: bliss. But when a great artist died, he did not pray for him. He had no reason for doing so, for the death of this artist had actually shaken him. He had really lost a dear person in the artist, a person who had afforded him pleasure and against whom he had never had any death wishes.

He can't stand the presence of an unused line in his diary, nor can he suffer any free time during his day. He reveals the well-known horror vacui of parapathics who dare not think certain thoughts which might express their guilt consciousness. He speaks the word mother before making any important decision. He needs her protection, the woman he had loved so deeply and had nevertheless wished dead because of his jealous desire to have her for himself alone.

The obsessional use of the numbers 5 and 11 is easily explained on the basis of his mother's date of death as the fifth day of the eleventh month. All his other explanations are simply rationalizations. His eleven-fold repetition of zero is only the annulment of an unpleasant past experience. The stereotyped manners he discloses have the apparent purpose of covering his embarrassment. He is even embarrassed in the presence of his father when he has to speak with other persons, the reason being that he fears they might guess his real attitude. There is always the danger that he might betray himself in a slip of the tongue, but the stereotypes and platitudes form a mechanism which insure his security. Still other habits reveal the cruelty of the man and the sense of superiority which constantly alternates in his breast with inferiority feelings and envy. He is indescribably ambitious and wants to be the leader. That is the hidden meaning of his walking tests in the street. He looks upon them as indicative.[8]

Like all obsessional neurotics he is superstitious and believes himself surrounded by mystic wonders and miracles. He believes in the omnipotence of his thoughts and that is the basis for his belief of himself as the murderer of his relatives and all the other dead whom he once envied in life.

Every day he feels impelled to kiss another girl's hand. This illustrates again the serial formations of fetishists. They can never satisfy themselves with one sexual object. This patient has his own harem of lovely hands, but although he has a large variety to choose from, he cannot be true to any one. That is a characteristic which makes these cases typical. Even should he find the loveliest hands in the world one day, he would not be faithful to their possessor. He would soon be driven to another.

In turning our attention to the closer analysis of the case, I find the most important communication to be the circumstance that even as a child he was already kissing everybody's hands.

In childhood, this was a courteous form of play for which he was always praised. Everyone would say: "Oh! What a courteous and well-behaved little fellow he is." But even then he revealed disturbing signs which have stuck to him to this day. Thus, for instance, he cannot suffer the knowledge that anyone is indifferent to him. He feels that he must mean something to everyone, the world must love him and marvel at him. Whenever this is not the case, he feels frustrated and reacts by being unpleasant and disaffected. He can even become terribly vicious, especially when he is concerned about a girl who appears to be paying him no attention. He poses as a gallant person, but this attitude is only affected. At bottom he is filled with but two feelings about women: anxiety and scorn. Anxiety because he cannot suffer any superiority which is permanent, and scorn because he considers their powers as limited and looks upon them all as essentially nothing but seducers and sexual creatures ("A uterus with some lady hung on"). He also claims that he could make every woman love him. His affectation of obsequiousness, his humble hand kiss, is but a method of assuring his final triumph over all women. But the phantasy of the kiss is more important to him than the kiss itself, a circumstance which discloses to us that his hand kissing but hides some process which is inaccessible to his own consciousness. His humility and obsequiousness are only apparent, he likes himself in this pose of the woman's friend and the masochist. The basis of his conduct, however, is sadistic, a relationship which we will discuss more thoroughly when we consider the question of masochism. Masochists are sadists who have turned their cruelty in upon themselves. In his childhood, G. L. also had a period of sadism during which he lived only in purely cruel phantasies. Since, however, he wanted to be loved by everybody, he considered every questionable expression of affection as an injury and hated all the persons who stood in the way of his achieving such love. His sister was his chief rival. He wished her dead, but when she did die, he had to suffer all the tortures of repentance. We see that his character strives to revamp all his original sadistic and egoistic desires on an altruistic mould. He suffers from a hypersensitive morality which has become strict to the extreme of piety. He

may protest his atheism, but inwardly he is devout and constrained by innumerable prayers and devotions.

Thus, for example, he is bound by the resolution: "You will
never really possess a woman, because you must punish yourself deeply." Following the death of his dearest kin, he made
the resolution which he could keep only by the aid of his hand
fetishism. The intention as such was not conscious and appeared only during the analysis.

He repeatedly had the opportunity to have intercourse with
girls. Some even came to his room with him and practically
offered themselves to him. But, despite the worst kind of an
erection, he remained always within the bounds of harmless
petting and playing. The important thing in his mind was to
make his father believe that he was a regular Don Juan, to make
his father jealous. His father was really his greatest love and
also the final cause of his illness. After his mother died, he
took her place in bed and slept next to his father. The latter,
for his part, gave up most of the joys of life for the sake of
his son and thus, in time, a sort of marriage relationship was
built up between the two. The son, however, was shut-in and
reticent with respect to his father. He wanted the father to
feel that perhaps the son didn't love him so much as he thought.
This apparent coolness was, however, only a repression of a
great love. In the last analysis, this man really loved men and
not women, whereas in life he played the opposite rôle.

He can recall only one really deep love in his life. This was
a colleague in school who probably reminded him of his sister
or mother. The patient also believes that the other even resem-
bled him somewhat; so that we have, in addition, a narcissistic
basis for the relationship. At present, however, his entire life
turns about the person of his father although he makes it appear
as if he were furiously cultivating the memory of his mother.
He has a picture of her on his desk, carries another with him
and also wears a ring which she gave him. Such piety has but
the purpose of pouring oil on the fire of his father's jealousy,
to cause him pain because he does not love the patient according
to the latter's wishes.

The infantile nature of his conduct is well enough demonstrated in his preservation of the childish game of kissing hands

and playing with time. He treats time as one might treat a
mistress, now he loves her, now he doesn't. He doesn't want to
become old, he wants to remain a child because he is afraid of
the time when he might fall in love with a woman and thus lose
his father. All the hands he kisses are, after all, his father's.

He firmly believes in his becoming a godsend in his own
historical mission. Christ is always on his mind. He feels
himself as Christ and harbors all kinds of savior ideas. The
kissing of hands also has some connection with this Christ
neurosis of his. There is a scene described in the Bible which
always excites him whenever he reads it. It is the scene where
Mary Magdalene wets the Lord's toes with her tears and kisses
his feet. "She hath been forgiven many sins, for she hath loved
much; but whosoever hath been forgiven little, he hath loved
little." He thinks of this scene from the Bible whenever he has
occasion to kiss a woman's hand. He is the repenter, the re-
gretful sinner whom God hath forgiven. He awaits salvation
from a woman. He is Mary Magdalene. He plays and lives
himself so deeply into the part that at times he doubts his maleness. He then trims his sexuality to fit his feelings. Gradually, however, his ideas of Christ and being an apostle are transformed into the notion that he may as a poet give the world a
new kind of religion. He considers his life to be one grand
preparation for this profession. Women are disturbing elements in such plans, fame is more important than love.

His obsessional ideas are nothing but deeds of penance ad
majorem gloriam Dei. These acts of penance are calculated to
soften God's wrath so that he might look more mildly upon his
own final triumph. He wants to get ahead of everybody. He
is beside himself with envy at the slightest success of another
and only in the most infrequent cases will he confess his envy
even to himself. Sometimes he actually transforms his envy
abruptly to uncritical and limitless wonderment. But even in
this he has a chance to feel himself superior to all others and
particularly superior to the girls whose hands he kisses. He
wants to possess everything in some way or other, he must
drink from all the fountains of knowledge and understanding,
drink to the last drop. What he cannot accomplish in life

(empty the cup of happiness), he achieves by means of innumerable compulsive acts.

The hand is also a protective measure for him against all the temptations of this mortal world. He had sinned with the hand, masturbated, hit others with it, and it is on the hand that he must atone. Everywhere he sees hands, they reach out from heaven to him, the giant hands of God whom he feels over his head at all times. He is one of the chosen and must therefore not succumb to the lamentable weaknesses of the mortal children of the earth.

He looks upon the eccentricity of his sexual make-up as something superior. One should never believe such patients when they come to the physician and beg for cure. Inwardly they are proud of their singularity, delight in the illness which divides them from others. What troubles another suffers to achieve a woman! Our patient has only to kiss her hand and presto! he has an orgasm and ejaculation. He is not alone in this kind of gratification. I know many men who satisfy themselves in this manner. One can frequently recognize the fetishist in the hand kisser. They smell the hand, suck on it hard, and soon one can see that peculiar glint in their eyes which betrays sexual ecstasy. I once knew a renowned artist who gratified himself only in this manner. He also was filled with ideas of salvation, founded religious movements, and wanted to start a sect of his own. He became a wandering preacher and an ascetic. With the aid of the hand, he was able to do without woman and thus successfully preserved his chastity which, furthermore, triumped in his old age when he became a missionary. He had strong ascetic tendencies, wanted to become a hermit, build himself a house on the top of a lonely hill, and all sorts of other phantasies.

Havelock Ellis excellently describes these attributes of the fetishist in the following passage from his book on perverted sexual feelings:

"The cause of the pathological and dangerous isolation of the fetishist is to be looked for in the extreme individualism which the development of his erotic symbolism presupposes. The lover who lets himself be guided by the elements of sexual selection will always find the right way through the communal feeling which binds him to the society of other human beings. He is controlled by the feeling of his descent, by the sense of his people, at least by that of fashion and habit. Even the pervert can usually find himself an environment in the course of time whose ideals coincide with his own. But the erotic symbolist is different. He almost invariably remains alone. He is doomed to loneliness from the very beginning because it appears that erotic symbolism develops best upon the basis of abnormal reticence and anxiety. Whenever the symbolist tries to achieve his desires (he often feels them to be something new) and finds how different they are from the goals of other men, his original anxiety and inaccessibility are increased. He is a lonely person. What are the highest ideals to him are either childish prattle or disgusting banalities to others, and sometimes even subject to police force. We have forgotten that all these impulses which appear to us to be so unnatural, making an apotheosis of the foot, and other parts of the body, the retention of urine and feces, the desire to have intercourse with animals, emphatic exhibition—all these are expressions ethically of what were concepts of the highest forms of living and deeply mystical feeling to our ancestors.

"Without some abnormal constitutional background no one can diverge very greatly from the instinctual life of the rest of human kind. An individual would at least possess a neuropathic impressionableness for abnormal irritations. Not infrequently the person discloses still other abnormal signs: stigmata, occasionally a certain degree of congenital imbecility or some disposition to mental disease.

"Quite apart from the frequency with which the manifestations of erotic symbolism point to congenital abnormalities, they are altogether of the greatest interest to the careful and unbiassed psychologist. They may appear absurd or even repulsive at times, but of all the manifestations of normal or abnormal sexual psychology they are the most specifically human. More than all the other forms of expression, they reveal the colossal plastic power of the imagination. They disclose to us the extreme individualist who lives not only in no accord with the others of the world, but even diametrically opposed to them.

He creates his own paradise on earth. They are the acme of human idealistic capacity."

It is certainly true that one may frequently observe rudiments of fetishism among the biologically degenerate and the mentally diseased. The marked infantilism of such persons may be the cause for the development. But fetishism is *per se* certainly no sign of biological degeneration. We must not forget that a paralogia is a regression to an infantile level and shows the same mechanisms as a parapathia. The circumstance that a person possesses a fetishistic leaning is not yet a sign that he is hereditarily stigmatized. It is especially among the fetishists that I have been unable to find even a trace of hereditary deviation in the family history. The patients themselves were decidedly of the intellectual class. Two of these cases will concern us in the next chapter. In many cases, this abnormality is the only pathological streak in the individual. But beyond the hereditary principle, we can always find the repressed psychic conflict between sexual desire and sexual anxiety, the fear of the sexual partner, the inner piety of the man and the tendency to fix one's infantile experiences for all time.

It is at this point that I wish to discuss that curious phenomenon of fetishists: series formation, harem cult. The fetish lover recompenses himself for his loneliness by means of a host of phantasies which become incarnate in one symbol. This plurality of figures is really a substitute for one single figure as the case of our pillow fetishist showed. In my experience such cases are not at all so seldom.

One of the most curious cases on record, and one which is of importance for our purpose, is that of Dr. R. Hahn (Ein merkwürdiger Fall von Diebstahl aus Gegenstandsfetishismus. H. Gross' Archiv, Vol. LX, 1914).

Case 27. This is the case of a cabinet-maker, T., who was caught in the act of stealing children's and infants' bed clothing and thereupon arrested. In the course of the investigation against him, it came to light that, although he was an otherwise blameless individual, he had already been punished several times before for very similar thefts and that he had never committed the thefts for personal gain (he always stole only infants' bed clothing), but apparently because of an abnormal sexual impulse. This was the reason for his psychiatric examination.

The story of his life is negative. He states that he began to masturbate at twelve years of age, having come upon the habit by chance or, rather, as a result of the sinister effects of a significant experience. He got hold of a book at that time which revealed to him all the details of matrimonial and sexual life, and reading it excited him to a terrific sexual pitch. It was precisely at this time, too, that his greatly pregnant sister came home and began to get the crib, the linens and all the baby's things ready for the coming child. He claims that the combination of the book, his pregnant sister and the infant's things made an unforgettable impression upon him. So much so that he suffered from painful erections and felt impelled to find relief in masturbation, but, in some way which he is unable to explain, he seized upon the unborn child's bed clothes for his purpose. From then on he masturbated almost daily, using his sister's quilts because he soon learned that they afforded him an even greater gratification. In the course of time, his sexual excitement became more and more intimately bound up with the thought and the sight of infant's bed clothing.

After his confirmation he was apprenticed and learned cabinetmaking. His statements to the effect that he had always done satisfactory work and led a quiet and respectable life were confirmed by the certificates he bore with him. He was not given to drink, showed no pathological intolerance for the drug, nor effected any crime or theft while under the influence of the same. He continued to masturbate excessively even while apprenticed, although, as he claims, he tried vainly to overcome the habit for a few weeks, the result being that his lust became even more deeply affected by the thought or sight of children's bed linens and he masturbated twice as much as before. He was invariably attached to the use of baby quilts or infant's clothing while satisfying himself and often bought himself the desired objects for his purposes. Since, however, he liked to change his fetishes frequently, and he neither earned nor had access to sufficient money to acquire them as often as he wanted; since, also, he was not nearly so provoked by ones he bought as by ones which may have been used already, he found himself driven to the acquisition of these goods in a criminal manner, i.e., he stole them whenever and wherever it was possible for him to find access to them.

November 5, 1898, he tried to shoot himself in the heart with a revolver because he felt that his abnormal sexual feelings had brought him to distraction.

He had never had anything to do with a girl and since he never felt any special desire to cultivate the acquaintance of women, he also never frequented places where he might meet them, e.g., a dance hall. He did have intercourse when he was nineteen; he was taken in by a prostitute. After 1903, he frequently visited houses of prostitution. He had coitus several times, but always found it difficult to produce an erection or achieve ejaculation unless he imagined babies' quilts or stared steadily at the corner of his prostitute's pillow (it seems always to have been the same one). In most cases, he had to complete his satisfaction after intercourse by masturbating, and at any rate, these trials of normal sexual contact did not in the least aid him in ridding himself of his fetishistic tendencies. His passionate impulse to find gratification only in infant's things was not at all diminished. It was for this reason that he soon chose to give up normal intercourse altogether. Even after he had been severely punished several times by heavy prison sentences for his thefts of infant's bed goods, he always returned to his old habit with irresistible alacrity. Wherever he would see little quilts and babies' goods, he felt goaded by the impulse to acquire them, to steal them. He would force himself to walk past the place, turn back once, twice, three times; go on again; but finally he could not resist and would have to return. He has often take the greatest pains, overcome the greatest difficulties, has even exposed himself to the most threatening dangers in order to achieve his purpose. Thus, for example, he would collect babies' blankets and quilts from the windows of each story in a house, without thinking, apparently, that he could be seen (these statements were corroborated by sworn witnesses and incorporated in the records). He would even drag up ladders or climb over fences and shrubbery, break into private grounds and property, only to gain possession of the bed clothing. He would be plunged into an almost feverish animation which would pass only with the acquisition of the desired object. His impulse to steal, however, never concerned any other type of object. He never tried to enrich himself through stealing nor had he ever been subject to police punishment for any other reason. He invariably took the stolen goods home with him, but the very achievement or possession of the things was sufficient gratification for him, although he usually felt the desire to use them during masturbation. He usually kept them at home for a while and used them in this wise, but finally he would destroy the goods, especially because no one object was ever able to hold his attention for long. Altogether he committed about eighty or ninety such dangerous and difficulty thefts.

There was only one type of quilt which was able to provoke immediate erection in him and make him desire prompt gratification on the object and that was any red or red and white striped blanket with a flowered coverlet and lace trimming. He states that this preference doubtless derives from the fact that his sister, as he can still remember very well, had just such little coverlets when he was a boy. The greater the similarity between coverlets he sees and the ones his sister had, the greater is his sexual lust, and he feels himself impelled to acquire the piece at any price. He claims never to have been excited about blue, brown or other colored goods, but the sight of the right colored quilt will create a sudden and irresistible wave of feeling in him. He cannot wait until he goes home for money or borrows it. He must gain possession of the article forthwith. But even though he recognizes the serious mistakes he commits, he feels that he is hopelessly delivered into the hands of an unhappy habit. He fears that he shall never be otherwise. He assures one that he has often tried to repress his abnormal impulse to theft and sexual gratification, to forget, control or fight an instinct which makes him so unhappy; but even though he may have been able to accomplish this purpose for a week or two with the aid of all his reserve energy, the first sight of the proper fetish plunged him again into his habits. His unhappy passion shadows him even in his dreams and in them he has often experienced sexual situations which he repeatedly knew in life, whereas he cannot remember having had any other kind of sexual dream. He would usually awaken from such dreams with a great erection or just after an emission. He declares that the best thing would have been the successful termination of his attempt at suicide, especially since he does not feel sure that he would now have the nerve to take up the revolver again. As it is, he finds no more use in living.

Since the findings of the experts, with which the court agreed, were to the effect that the prisoner's soundness of mind and responsibility at the time of the theft could not be absolutely denied, he was again sentenced to a new and increased term in prison. He was found repeatedly masturbating while in jail, but had nothing further to add to his above statements. He himself seemed to meet his fate with inner composure. He never revealed any sign of marked psychic disturbance. Nothing further is known of him.

It is seldom that one can find such an open approach to the psychogenesis of an uncomplicated case as this. It must be apparent even to the analytically lay person, that this man has displaced his emotional attachments in sexual phantasies about his sister to the bed things. The quilts are nothing but a mental bridge over which he reaches his pregnant sister again, the sister who will soon have a child. This eternally unfulfilled desire for his sister creates an impulse in him and the forbidden or taboo character of the process is transposed to the kleptomania according to a manner which we have already explained in detail. In this case, the harem cult is particularly striking (80-90 quilts), and it is also subject to analysis.

We see a plurality of fetishes appear whenever a certain, definite object is not obtainable. The endless series of objects then has the purpose of removing the original point of departure to a greater distance, making it seem further away. In my discussion of Don Juan,[4] I called attention to this serial formation as a substitute for something else. Unfulfilled wishes create symbolic acts, the constant and frequent repetition of which symbolically represents the individual seeking and never finding his ideal.

The infantile character of the kleptomania and the pleasure in this case is strikingly portrayed by the choice of the sexual object. Coitus itself does not satisfy him and must be helped along by phantasies of babies' bed clothing. After intercourse, he continues with masturbation because onanism as an adequate method of gratification ends in orgasm, too. His incestuous phantasies are manifestly smuggled into his onanistic phantasies.

It is inconceivable that they still have judges who could sentence this poor patient to a "protracted term in prison." The character of this insurmountable obsession is so marked, the reduced state of his mental vision at the time of the act so clear, that only a deficient education in sexual abnormalities can excuse such a severe sentence.

The harem cult is a trait which gives us more psychological

understanding of all kinds of collectors. They are concerned with the formation of a series, i.e., with substitutes. Originally, the impulse was directed at quite another object, e.g., in this last case it was the sister of the patient. The real motive here was the wish to be her child, to be cared for and nursed by her. He identifies himself with his sister and is really the child in the crib. Actually, he plays both rôles, but since his wish is never fulfilled and cannot be gratified, he can never rest. He is in a state of psychic perpetual motion. We see what it is that makes these persons so restless. They are subject to the repetition compulsion which, according to Freud, is a striving to improve on a former situation, to transform an unpleasant situation into a pleasurable one. "If I had only gone after my sister then I should have possessed her!" But he is left to repeat the play with substitutes. Sobriety follows upon a transient period of emotional drunkenness and the perpetual motion continues. The forbidden or taboo nature of his desires is expressed in the forbidden or anti-social character of his acts (kleptomania). Having repressed his wish to possess his sister, having subjected his own activity, he now releases himself symbolically in the repetition compulsion. It is the categorical imperative of repentance over an omitted aggression which drives him to new symbolical aggressions.

In the following, I have brought together a few more examples of harem cult in fetishists without taking the trouble to add a pyschological explanation. On the basis of what I have said above, however, it is clear that there must necessarily be such an interpretation in every case. Only a psychoanalysis will divulge the proper answer.

Case 28. Kurt Boas reported the case of a wig fetishist in H. Gross' Archiv (Vol. 39, Nos. 1 and 2, criminalistic review). The patient, a clear case of transvestitism, is always trying to get hold of large and modern women's wigs. He then admires himself vainly in a mirror, but his delight is distinctly increased and provoked to heights of desired gratification (ejaculation) if he can then top the wig with a woman's hat of pot, bell or stork's nest form. Having learned from dream analyses that the hat is a symbolical representative of the genitals, we can understand the relations of the patient's animation and the fetishism. For him the act of setting the hat on top of the wig is symbolical of the act of sexual union. Many forms of fetish attachment are based upon a "super-valuation of the symbol" which has deposed reality in the patient's mind.

Keferstein reported the following case in the Zeitschrift f. Med.-Beamte, p. 771, 1914.

Case 29. A married but childless man of about forty-five, impotent and separated from his wife, had for some time been collecting all kinds of colored hats and student's and fraternity caps. He gave the impression of being somewhat mentally abnormal, was inaccessible and shut-in, but otherwise not a social. By virtue of some swindleing deal, he had been able to enrich himself to the extent of six new caps, but this led to his being indicted for fraud. Since, however, he aroused suspicions as to the soundness of his mind, he was remanded for psychiatric examination. The result was the discovery of a case of fetishism. It was after his separation from his wife (which was due to his impotence) that he had begun to collect the caps. Whenever he would see such colored head gear, he would be overpowered by the desire to possess it, and whenever he would look over his collection of caps, he became sexually provoked, would get an erection and immediate orgasm.

But erotic collectors of fetishes commit not only theft but robbery, too. Thus, for example, I was asked to hand in an opinion on a case in America which had given even the judges considerable trouble. The man had fallen upon a woman in a park at night and had commanded her to hand over her shoes and stockings. He took no notice of her money or her jewels.

A similar case was also reported by Ludwig Hoffmann in his *Fräulein von Scuderi* (The Girl of Scuderi). A goldsmith was so deeply in love with his own shop and works that he murdered the buyers of his goods only to regain possession of the golden jewels (the case was dramatically adapted by Otto Ludwig).

Hammond reported a similar case of criminal impulses in the service of an erotic collecting instinct.

Case 30. Among the communicated cases of unquestionably perverted sexual feeling, there is an especially interesting one which, however, was not at first recognized. The details were reported by Beck.[5] It concerned a man named Sprague who was arrested for robbery in a Brooklyn street in 1849. The robbery was executed in the following manner: The defendant, who was a printer by trade, had attacked a young woman one morning while he was on the way to work, threw her to the pavement and ran away as soon as he had quickly taken off one of her shoes. Although she wore a chain and a gold watch and had a few other valuables on her person, he did not touch these, nor did he mistreat the woman in any other manner. At the trial, his attorneys declared that he was not responsible for his acts.

The chief witness was the defendant's father, a highly honorable and respected minister whose testimony was corroborated in every detail by several other witnesses. Charles Sprague, the patient's paternal great-grandfather, his grandmother, his great-grand uncle, three grand aunts and a cousin are or were mentally unbalanced. He himself had suffered several violent clouts on the head in his youth and had also fallen on his head. A year after his last fall, he began to complain of headaches and his friends noticed that his eyes bulged curiously. At about the same time, it was noticed that he began to steal the shoes away from the female members of his family and would hide them. Usually only one shoe of a pair would be missing, but it would sooner or later be found somewhere about the house, water soaked, turned and twisted like a piece of rope and then stuck away in a feather bed, a sack of straw, a box in the attic or among the clothes of some closet in the house.

The family's suspicions first turned to the servants, whereas the real miscreant remained shrouded in silence whenever he was questioned. It was only during the past six years that he confessed to the deeds. When they began to dispute with him about these eccentric acts, he would admit the possibility of his having taken the shoes, but he claimed neither to remember whether or when he did it nor to know for what purpose he may have taken them. The intervals between his thefts never lasted more than three or four months. When the family finally realized that it was he who was carrying off the shoes, they naturally began to lock these articles away, but this did not prevent the occasional discovery of a water-soaked, wrung and twisted shoe. At one time it was rumored about that Sprague had tried to take a shoe from a foot of one of the maids in the house, and on another occasion one of his sisters surprised him in the act of taking a shoe out of one of her locked drawers. In the same spring in which the trial took place, two girls had complained of having lost shoes which they had taken off on a warm evening in the park. They did not find the thief. (*Sexual Impotence in Men and Women.* By William H. Hammond, M.D., Surgeon General of the Union Army, Prof. of Psychiatry and Neurology in the New York Post Graduate Medical School.)

This case clearly reveals the impulse in question as the consequence of an omitted aggression and its relationships with incestuous phantasies. We must remember that the first shoes he stole were those of the female members of his family and in this case the shoe is a manifest symbol of the female genital. The shoe is genitalized, as it were.

In most cases, too, the traumatic infantile scene may be reconstructed with a certain degree of accuracy. Thus, in the following case.

Case 31. A case of underwear fetishism in a railroad man was found to be rather difficult. He had been caught just as he was breaking into the home of a high police official with the intent of stealing women's underthings. It was learned that he would often prowl about the streets of his town at night, looking for some opening or crack in window shades through which he might catch a glimpse of a woman disrobing herself. It would be here that he would later that night break in and steal some underthings and thereafter wear them on his own person. He differed from a partial transvestitist in the fact that he never would wear unused things. At his trial, I defended the point of view that in the case of this hereditarily stigmatized individual, it was not possible to affirm his mental responsibility to the degree that the law demanded. The opposing specialist, a university professor, explained to the court that it was quite irrelevant to the law of the case whether this man wished by his thefts to enrich himself or simply to gratify a sexual desire. In both cases, he was seeking his own advantage. The court agreed with the latter opinion and sentenced the man without mitigation on a charge of burglary. A few days later he was found dead in his cell. He had hanged himself. (Hirschfeld, *Sexualpathologie,* Vol. III.)

The reader who has given some attention to the foregoing chapters and has remembered my discussion of shirt fetishism will readily understand the psychology of this case. It is possible that the patient had once observed the disrobement of one of his family relatives.

The fanatical collecting of these patients often reaches an inconceivable intensity as the following cases demonstrate.

Case 32. K., a forty-five-year-old shoemaker with an allegedly clear inheritance, of peculiar character, possessed of low intelligence and a male habitus without biological stigmata, was caught on the evening of July 13, 1876, as he was in the process of taking stolen female underthings from a hiding place. About three hundred articles of women's apparel were found in his possession, among them chemises, drawers, night caps, garters and even a female doll. He had on one of these women's chemises at the time of his arrest. He had been indulging his passion to steal women's underthings for the past thirteen years and, although chastened by being caught and punished the first time, he had developed considerable dexterity in his happy hunt. When the impulse came over him, he felt that his head became heavier and he could not resist, whatever the dangers were. He was quite indifferent to who might be the victim.

He would then don the stolen articles at night in bed, imagine lovely women and experience lustful passions as well as a satisfying orgasm. This was also the apparent motive for his thefts, since he never disposed of the things he stole, but rather hid them in divers places.

He stated that he had formerly had normal intercourse with women, but denied ever having practised onanism, pederasty or any other sexual habits. He claims to have been engaged at twenty-five and stated that the engagement was broken by the girl for no good cause. He had no insight into the pathological nature of his condition or the criminal character of his acts. (Passow, Vierteljahrsschrift f. ger. Medizin, N. F. XXVIII, p. 61 ; Kraus, Psychologie des Verbrechens, 1884, p. 190.)

Case 33. A hitherto blameless baker's helper, thirty-two years old and single, was caught in the act of stealing a handkerchief from a woman. He confessed with forthright repentance that he had already stolen eighty or ninety handkerchiefs in this manner. He liked to collect his articles only in this way and was impelled to attack only young and attractive women.

He disclosed nothing striking in his external appearance, was

rather carefully dressed and revealed a peculiar character and conduct which was partly anxious and depressed and partly feminine
and complacent. At times he was even whining and lachrymose.
He also manifested a marked awkwardness, weak understanding
and dulness of orientation and abstraction. One of his sisters is
epileptic. He lives in comfortable circumstances, was never seriously ill and has developed well. He manifests some weakness of
memory and confusion in telling his life story, and even arithmetic is difficult for him, although he had learned well in school
and absorbed his material rapidly. His anxious and vacillating
character raises the suspicion of masturbation and he confessed
that he had indulged in this habit excessively ever since his nine-
teenth year.

Because of this vice, he had for some years been suffering from
weakness, lassitude, trembling of the legs, back pains and a distaste for work. He was also subject to periods of anxious
depressiveness and would then avoid all people. He had extravagant and hyperbolic notions of the consequences of sexual intercourse with women and was therefore unable to effect such intercourse. He had nevertheless been thinking of marriage recently.

In a rather imbecilic way and overcome with repentance, X.
confessed that about a half year previously he had sensed an irresistible sexual attraction to a young woman in a crowd and had
pushed his way sufficiently close to her so that he could snatch
her handkerchief as a token of a deeply gratifying, though vi-
carious, sexual pleasure. Subsequently, whenever he laid eyes on
a woman of his type, he would fall before a wave of sensual lust,
his heart would palpitate, he would get a prompt erection and be
overcome with an impetus cœundi. In this state he would approach the woman and—*faute de mieux*—steal her handkerchief.
Although he was not for a moment under the influence of illu-
sions as to the criminality of his acts, he felt that he had to obey
his impulses. He was also subject to considerable anxiety in the
act, partly because of the importunity of the sexual pressure and
partly also because of his fear of being caught.

The specialist's opinion rightfully laid stress on the patient's
congenital imbecility and the detrimental effect of masturbation.
His abnormal appetites were laid to a perverse sexual instinct,
an interesting and well-known physiological relationship between
the olfactory senses and the sexual instincts being recognizable.
X. was set free. (Zippe, Wiener med. Wochenschrift, 1879,
Nr. 23.)

Handkerchiefs are greatly desired objects of fetish lovers and harem collectors because they are easily acquired, stolen and hidden. The same is true of garters and neck-kerchiefs ("Get me a kerchief from her breast—a garter feeds my passion best!" cries Faust). I may also recall Case 5 in Chapter II. Many patients will tell the physician that they first masturbated with the aid of a handkerchief, and often it was the property of some member of the family, a circumstance which lends the object a special significance.

The importance of handkerchiefs in this respect is well illustrated by a patient of Sadger's:[6]

"Yes, and something more about handkerchiefs. The girl I mean must have cried into the handkerchief at least once, and I like to have it smell a little of perfume. I am then able to visualize the girl's face in the cloth, a kind of photograph which I can then kiss. Of course, she has pressed the handkerchief to her face if she cried in it. I received my first handkerchief from my sweetheart when I was sixteen, and thereafter demanded one from every girl I became acquainted with, with the added condition, of course, that she first must have cried in it."—"And who was the very first woman of your childhood days who had any connection with such a tear-stained handkerchief?"—"My mother. When I was about three or four years old, we received news of the death of my grandmother, and my mother cried bitterly. I wanted to cry, too, but I was unable to bring up the tears. Mother went about the house all day long with a handkerchief to her face and cried continuously. It was then that I wanted to boss her as she used to me, when she would say that I went about like a bumpkin with a handkerchief. I took the handkerchief away from her and hid it. She looked everywhere for it, but I wouldn't tell her where it was and called her a bumpkin, too. Of course, I did have a bad conscience about it all and found no peace, but I forgot about it in a little while and the handkerchief was found only later in some drawer when we were moving. Then I told mother everything. She washed the handkerchief and gave it to me with the words: 'If you took it from me then you can keep it, but I shall keep the pretty handkerchiefs which I bought for you.' That, naturally, was more than I'd bargain for, and I disputed with her. I insisted on giving her back her own handkerchief and getting my own new ones, went to bed deeply injured and cried all night. I even continued the whole scene in my dreams, but the next day mother gave me my handkerchiefs back. Her own handkerchief was exquisitely perfumed, as were also all her underthings for which I had a terrific attachment.

"Then I continue my examination by asking him why he were always seeking the girl's face in the handkerchief. 'Were you,' I asked him, 'rebuffed by your mother when trying to kiss her?' 'Yes, she would often do that to me when she was mad at me. She wouldn't let herself be petted or stroked or kissed. It was then that I would quickly take something of hers that I might nevertheless have something of her. I would take a needle, a brooch, a handkerchief or anything that was at hand and make off with it. I collected hair ribbons in order to add them to the guitar bands I had hanging up. They are a kind of spoils of war, as it were, after having achieved a girl. In addition to that, the guitar itself symbolizes the female in its form. You play on both of them, so to speak.'—'How did you get the hair ribbons?'

I got my first guitar when I was eleven after I had noticed that a friend of mine increased his popularity with the girls by playing and singing on it. I got mother to buy me one, learned to play it from him, and then actually found that it brought me a lot of popularity, too. I had also seen girls' hair ribbons in my friend's house and I wanted them, also. My first one I got from mother and then begged them of every woman I knew and considered them as a kind of trophy. I now have fifty-four such ribbons in my collection and the name of the girl is written on each one. Furthermore, I always carried my sweetheart's handkerchief in my pocket, even at the front, and now, too, although I have long since broken off with her. I felt that it was a part of her with me, that I had, as it were, taken her face with me. When I left for the front, she cried, I comforted her, embraced her, and took the handkerchief away on parting."

In this case, the handkerchief appears to be a substitute for the face of the love object. It is an example of symbolic displacement of affect.

Wullfen described some interesting details relevant to kleptomaniacal collectors which were partly his own and partly others' experience.

"A forty-five-year-old shoemaker, without physical signs of degenerative constitution, has been stealing women's underthings since his thirteenth year. At night he would don them himself, imagine female bodies and have an ejaculation. Several different articles were found in his possession. Another patient had had the impulse to put on his sister's chemise ever since he was eleven years old. In his later years, he would have an orgasm every time he did it. As an adult he always bought women's chemises and put them on with a great deal of sensual satisfaction. Still another man would get an ejaculation while tearing up women's underwear, and a fourth masturbated in his fifteenth year while looking at an apron that had been hung out to dry. As an adult, he always became sexually animated whenever he would see an apron, regardless of whether it were being worn by a man or woman. Manifestly, the erogenous zone hidden by the apron had some sexual relationship with the apron itself. A clothes fetishist would steal white linen petticoats from dry goods houses, try them on (a procedure which in itself gave him a thrill) and even wore them when having intercourse with his wife. He alleged not to have had intercourse even once during the past thirteen years without first donning one of the petticoats. He always strove to use a new one which he had just recently stolen. The use of an old petticoat would not afford him the same gratification (Kersten). Another fetishist would erect a circle of poles in an open field and then hang his stolen petticoats on the sticks. He would walk around the circle, stroking and petting the dolls, and would suddenly fall upon one of the figures, press it closely to his bosom and masturbate. Thus, in addition to theft, he also committed a public nuisance or disorder by his immoral act in public. He claimed that his impulse was almost invariably irresistible, that he would sometimes spring out of bed at night, run out into the open, find some petticoat and gratify himself. He stated that at such times he felt so wild that he neither knew where he was or what he was doing. He would find himself in a wood or in a field when he would come to."

Such an erotic collecting impulse can acquire the most grotesque forms. Sometimes our Don Juan will collect trophies of his victories, thus revealing the fact that the trophy rather than the victory or the woman means more to him. An elderly gentleman once showed me a large book into which he had carefully pasted nice visiting cards. They were all from prostitutes of whom he had demanded them either before or after every coitus. He never visited the same prostitute twice and always had the date marked on the card. On some of the cards, he had made a note of some paraphilia or infection. I knew of another who collected ball souvenirs which he would take violently from the women at an affair. A third one was a collector of locks of hair (not infrequent) and the collection of pubic hairs is well known.

Sadger (l. c.) also reports on such a partialist.

Case 34. "I began to desire the pubic hairs of a woman rather than her genitals as early as thirteen years of age. At that time I asked our maid to give me some of her hair and begged her not to take it from her head, but to cut some off from between her legs. These hairs then gave me a great gusto, colossal delight. I have since developed a real museum of such hairs, have cut off a nice, little bunch from the genitals of every mistress and packed it neatly away tied with a string. I would also write the girl's name on the little band." Another patient related the following from as early as his ninth or even eighth year: "At that time, i.e., when I myself had no pubic hairs as yet, I would make for the hairs in my sister's comb and wind them about my penis. Now, whenever I see a hair in my girl's comb, I become speechless with emotion and the same is true when I run my hands through a woman's hair or see her axillary hairs. When I used to lie in bed with my mother as a child and she were asleep I would love to play with her pubic hair and pull on them. I also like to smell pubic hairs and become very excited sexually when doing so. It all reminds me of the odor mother had."

In all these cases we must remember to differentiate whether the fetishist is directed towards the object itself or whether the object serves simply as a representative of the process of conquest. We have already pointed out this difference when discussing the cases of underwear fetishism. In this class also belong those who collect toilet paper or any other object pervaded with body odor. Two typical cases will suffice to illustrate the subject.

Case 35 is a patient of mine, Mrs. W. H., who declares that she becomes sexually excited only when the man in question wears shoes made of Russian leather. The very odor of such leather alone excites her to the pitch of orgasm. She states that she was frequently provoked by a stable boy when she was seven years of age. He would put her up on a horse whenever she would come into the stables, but later he began to play with her parts. Such a memory is pretty well engraved in her mind and demands constant and continuous repetition. She possesses quite a collection of leather pieces which she cut out of old shoes and boots.

Magnus Hirschfeld (*Sexualpathologie*, Part III) reports a similar case.

Case 36. A woman once showed me a small piece of Russian or Muscovy hide which she carried under her dress on a string hung close to her bosom. Using the strongest superlatives, she described to me the significance of this leather's odor for her sexual life. Her erotic attachment to her husband, who is said to have been rather ugly (she was widowed early), consisted solely of a bunch of odors, chief among them being a "male odor well mixed with tobacco and Russian leather." She still enraptures herself in the stale odors of her husband's clothing, claiming that there is yet "a good deal of that sweet aroma" in them. She would have to summon all her reserve resistance in order to keep from succumbing to a man who would make use of these odors. In a case which became known to me, the woman would have her husband send his shirts home from the front during the war, in order that she might become drunk on the odor of them and thus achieve an orgasm.[7]

In *Impotence in the Male* in this series, I have exhaustively described the psychology of the erotic collector, but I should like to add a few remarks at this point. Every special sense can be exploited by the collector, the chief one among them being the sense of sight, and then the olfactory and the sense of touch, but I know of cases in which the sense of hearing or that of taste plays the dominant rôle. In the case of the shirt and chemise fetishists, for example, we made the acquaintance of erotic collectors for whom the odor of perspiration and urine first made the object valuable and desirable. Our cloth fetishist delighted herself with the soft, lovely touch of silk and satin. The eccentricities of the urge to collect are to be understood and cleared up only by the psychoanalytical approach. Through the courtesy of Mr. O. B., I am able to conclude with two more cases.

Case 37. Mr. N. K. collects slices of sausage from every part of the world, and already has a veritable museum of such sausages. He preserves them in formalin, each slice in a glass jar of its own which bears the label of the time and the place of acquisition as well as the kind of wurst. He takes long trips in order to enrich his collection.

What sort of eccentric experiences can have brought this man to such an abnormal habit? What can be his sexual make-up? Can the wurst be a phallus substitute or does it signify castration? Our informant could give us no enlightening information on this point.

He was, however, able to afford us more light on the next case, making good use of his psychoanalytical knowledge. In the words of Mr. O. B.:

Case 38. "During the war I was obliged to share my quarters with Captain E. He was a very considerate, but shut-in, person who had become so accustomed to me that he manifestly preferred me for his room-mate. I had already been struck by the fact that, in addition to his regular luggage, E. packed a large box about with him wherever we moved, and this box he watched carefully, permitting no one to have even a peak into it. It was only after several months together that he disclosed the nature of the case's contents to me. It contained a mass of keys which E. had stolen, not bought. He confessed to an irresistible impulse to steal these things. Each one of them had a label through the handle which designated the time and the place it had been stolen. The collection consisted of fine ones, coarse ones, large and small, artful and artless. When I asked him about this mania, he could give me no information as to what the source of it could be. But one day we were talking about the sense of shame. We were observing a pair of dogs copulating and I remarked how strongly the sense of shame had been developed in our day. 'Nonsense,' said E., 'we're no better to-day than we ever were. I was able to observe my parents many times when a little child, and even later when I was seven years or so.'

" 'How did you manage that?'

" 'Well, when I was quite small, my parents used to copulate in my presence without any inhibitions, but as I began to grow, they would send me out of the room. I, however, would close the door and promptly begin to look through the key-hole and see just as much. Only once did my father catch me at it, and then he locked the door and turned the key in the lock, so that I couldn't see anything.'

"Then I heard that E., who avoided all women and was looked upon as a peculiar bachelor, wanted to steal that key which had blocked his view of his parents' paradise in order that he might enjoy the scene of the intercourse again. E. thus betrayed the real root of his kleptomania to me."

This is an exemplary case of the repetition compulsion in the service of erotic symbolism. E. continues to conduct himself as if he were about to experience that same old scene. Father cannot, however, deprive him of his view now for he has the evil key in his own possession. In Freud's sense, the repetition signifies the correction of an infantile situation, but it all means a repetition in which the key as a phallic symbol gratifies the homosexual component of the patient. His thefts have displaced aggressions against the phallus of his comrade. His entire sexuality has been shifted to a side track and this was possible only because of a colossal displacement of affect.

All such cases disclose a marked tendency to day-dreaming. The patients live in a world of dreams and even their acts are effected in a sort of hypnoic state.

Nevertheless, not all cases are as transparent and easily solved as that of Captain E. Fetishism is usually a quite complicated condition, as our further discussion will show. Our solution of simple and uncomplicated cases, however, will give us increasing insight into the more difficult cases to follow.

VIII

THE BIBLE OF THE FETISHIST

The fetish lover's harem cult can also express itself in books full of drawings, sketches or confessions which the fetishist may keep. These contents then express the fetishism. Merzbach described the case of a man who collected the pubic hairs of his sweethearts in a book and finally had quite a collection of these trophies.[1] The man was not a true fetishist, but simply a man with partial preferences who had an impulse to collect the objects of his love.

I know fetishists, however, who make themselves a sort of fetishistic bible. They open this book whenever they want to indulge in their fetishism, in their own religion. They hide the book with a deal of apprehension and it is not easy to gain access to such a volume. They never permit their bible out of their hands and if they do then it is because they have decided to give up the paraphilia. The normal person cannot possibly appreciate the greatness, the significance of such a sacrifice.

In order to demonstrate a comprehensive picture of such a fetishistic bible, I will describe a case of corset fetishism in detail which came under my treatment about four years ago. The very manner in which he began treatment was peculiar enough. Months before he appeared, he inquired about the method of treatment, the price, the length of time it would take, and then considered the matter at great length only to come—not to cure his fetishism, but his impotence.

This case concerns a very seriously handicapped person who yearns to save himself from the hell of satanic phantasies and live the pure and regular life of marriage. His account is a veritable and valuable *"document humain,"* despite its almost incoherent style.

Case 39. The thirty-six-year-old policeman, W. G.—we shall call him William—has been impotent all his life. He blames excessive onanism for this impotence. He was married two years ago, but, despite a good erection, he was unable to effect a normal coitus. He claims that this failure was due to his wife's awkwardness, but he confesses that he has also failed miserably with prostitutes. He is quite normally built, shows no degenerative stigmata, and derives from a healthy family. He relates that he is interested only in corsets and tightly laced, heavy women, and that his wife does not correspond to this type. She is thin and never wears a corset, whereas he is animated only by quite heavy or even obese women who are well corseted; those who are so tied in that they give the impression of being hardly able to breathe. This tight lacing is an unconditional love prerequisite for him, but he has never yet possessed such a woman.

He himself derives his interest for corsets from a pubertal impression. He was fourteen years of age when his attention was attracted to a luxurious and buxom blonde who lived next door. She was tightly corseted and was allegedly the first object of his onanistic phantasies.

He is subject to the well-known impulsive restlessness of fetish lovers, runs about the streets for hours at a time until he has caught sight of a desirable object and then returns home to pull on a corset and masturbate before a mirror with the phantasy that he is the woman he saw. Before I go into the results of his analysis, I want here to reproduce some parts of his bible. I must mention that about a week after we had met, he handed me a very elegantly bound, but thumbed, volume and asked me to study it. He would return in a fortnight.

The major part of the book was written in shorthand, but some of it was in longhand. At the beginning there are several rather long, well-meant, but naïve, poems which express the nature of his phantasies. He is, however, a poor poet, despite the vividness of his phantasy life. Then come a few confessions and, finally, a whole series of pictures, most of them clippings from newspapers and magazines. We shall reproduce some of these also later on. Most of these pictures, however, have been changed and transformed by his having sketched or drawn obscene figures into them; genitals are introduced; extravagant breasts added to corsets, etc. . . .

I shall begin with some of his writings.

And now to-day on the 18-3-1905 unhesitating end of all spiritual onanistic comments and notes! Reason: self-realization, because thereby cause and course of the disease sufficiently defined, cure would be impossible, spirit would be on the royal road to insanity (softening of the brain, sexual dementia). Rather, if it cannot be otherwise, lewdness with some woman, whether virgin, wife or widow, but especially with some public prostitute, in reality as a useless, constantly changeable degeneration and deviation in respect of the female intercourse as I put it down on paper. In future I shall make note only of serious comments or pictures concerning the sexual sphere, e.g., results and course of relevant medical examinations and tables of measurements on the female (prostitute's) body, and also "love-letter" remarks. That, with respect to my immanent cure from spiritual and physical masturbation, so help me God!

Last evening about 7:30-8 o'clock the first and perhaps not last visit with my well-known father confessor who has been my confessor since about 1896, formerly preacher, pater Erhardus. Place: large, comfortable room with an adjoining cabinet on the left. Lovely and clean, electric light (the priesthood is quite well maintained).

Went there to confess after I had spoken with him down in the church on the 2-3-1903. Naturally stressed masturbation, my unhappiness. He knows my suffering, the chain of sorrowful circumstances, he knows my material state rather well.

Concise contents of his statements because I earnestly asked him whether extra-marital intercourse were absolutely sinful and punishable before God or whether this might be permitted the mature man who could no longer contain himself. Answer:

"Every extra-marital cohabitation, quite irrespective of whether it be carried out in maturity or later, is sinful! Only marriage gives one the religious right which then becomes a duty."

Were every man and every woman so pervaded with the holy command of God to be chaste and remain so until the ties of marriage did bind them, irrespective of whether the marriage took place early or perhaps late because of economic conditions, then surely the majority of cares and evils would disappear, perhaps even ninety-nine percent of unhappiness. Then life would not be so miserable as it is to-day or as many take it to be, just because, having become infected or having lost their chastity, they have not been capable of protecting themselves from more mistakes. In answer to my declaration that it is unjust to have to bear such suffering and marry only when thirty-five or forty, while a luckier man with sufficient funds may marry at twenty, he trustfully expressed the view that it were foreordained and perhaps even good for some that they were not able to marry early. He said further:

"Matrimonial love, which soon blows over, must contain mutual respect and the firm resolve to remain true to the other partner for life even should sexual incapacity of either one occur."

"The path which leads to the loss of chastity is doubtless easier to tread and calls forth the impulse to continue unholy intercourse indefinitely and thus descend ever deeper and deeper until finally virgin, girl and wife have been seduced simply because one has been unable to withstand and has let one's self go. It is easier, I say, than the return to moderation and the rejection of such unholy indulgence." Aids against inchastity: continuous vigilance in moderation, prayer, trust in God, work, shame, industry, hard bed, etc., etc.

Before he would absolve me, he demanded my promise "to desist with all my strength from any unholy intercourse."

"Yes, if I can," I said.

"I do not ask whether you can or not, for there is no dispute with the word of God. It must be followed, may the fulfillment be ever so impossible and difficult in your mind. Fulfilled in so far as you are willing and will give me your promise to remain chaste."

A few seconds of deep silence.

Tensely he waits in his cabinet, sitting on a stool next to me while I kneel on the hassock.

"No, I cannot promise you that," I say, oppressed at heart but forthright. This moment in which my heart and soul broke so decidedly with the word of God was frightful, but I couldn't help it. Mistrust of the truths and commands of the Catholic church, repugnance against the "dead hand," against the power of the clergy, the wish to avoid the general mental debauchery of the people and wait patiently, seek cure, seek medical assistance, even err humanly if need be, with the consciousness that it was done, not out of sacrilegious and spiteful desire to insult God, but only in order to live on in this world, not out of humility before the pillars of the church who then use it as a means of repressing human ambition and progress, but rather as an acceptance of the principle of enlightenment. Perhaps, then (because I can no longer contain my swelling passions), I shall marry and never be able to enjoy life because I shall be a hard pressed father of a family. Others may laugh at me, gratify their instincts pleasurably and not in an emergency, finally marrying when they are in a good financial position and therefore getting a better wife, whereas I would age rapidly and early with my unstilled desires. "Celibacy" is, after all, official chastity, and yet also the unofficial cause of all the trouble because, many getting off easy, the good name of the Catholic church is smirched, whereas, once removed, the power would weaken the strength of the church with all its nimbus of holiness. Only then would I look upon a priest with respect because, as a man, one would expect only humanity from him and not too sacrificial and hyperbolic an attitude. I understand why so many people become Protestants or want to, at least, like my schoolmate Josef B. With them the clergy can marry, too.

"Then," said the father, "I can say no more," and shook his head. "I can give you only my blessings, but not my absolution."

He blessed me, I crossed myself, thanked him, felt inwardly quieted and happy at my enlightenment, even mentioned the decision the physician had made and bade him not be angry with me.

"No," he said, "I can see that you are honest," and left coldly. He opened the door for me, locked it behind me and probably left for the dining hall as it seemed to be ringing for dinner. Nevertheless, to tell the truth, ashamed and excited as I was, I walked quickly away and was glad when he stopped to talk with the servant who was ringing the dinner bell on the next floor. As I closed the door of the entrance and stepped into the great court, the watch tower struck eight o'clock.

I came home excited. Bargaining with God and the world, yearning to marry, conscious of my desires, excited even yet for fear of God's judgment should I destroy my virginity before marriage. For the present I stop thinking and ask Dr. F. to decide for me as quickly as possible, but I continue to hope for a quick marriage with some pretty girl who will either bring me some money or help earn with me. If that doesn't succeed, then I feel I must seduce some fifteen- to eighteen-year-old girl, keep her company for about ten years and then marry her as some small salaried clerk or other. Or, if I can bring myself to it, whores (why say hypocritically "unholy intercourse"?). But I do sincerely hope that now when I need God's help most in my great emergency, everything will proceed towards a happy end just as He would wish it.

With approval and insight I say that pater E. spoke "golden words" yesterday. He is right. I would be happy if I could live such an ideal life. The world, however, we mortals, are different:

not so good and not so ideal. And just because much that is ideal in life becomes real and prosaic, so must the highest and most idealistic coitus make room for a more natural and mortal attitude introduced by the experience of an unholy and emergency intercourse. I believe that nothing else can work and take place in this vale of tears called world, except in unusual cases. There may be abstemious and passionless people in the world, but I'm not one of them.

He took quite a sensible attitude towards intercourse when he said that it is not a pleasure but a happy duty. For if this act were not filled with so much delight then there would be an end to making children. There would be nothing but care in the business.

True enough, he also was right when he asked what I would do if a naturally diseased body would prevent me from effecting any intercourse whatever. He said that he had had enough to do with all kinds of people, had heard confessions from the healthy and the sick, from insane people, too, had tasted enough of human woe—brought on by themselves.

Insanity may arise from a mistrust in the power of good, from a susceptibility to passion, but never from chastity. They too, the insane, had declared that they could no longer continue, but they fell because of their own weakness, because of their disbelief in God's unimpeachable and chaste laws of morality. Frequently married women complained to him that they could no longer live with or love their husbands, but this was—as he had otherwise learned—after they had committed adultery.

Pater N. could well say: "The greater your defection, your cries against God and his church, the greater is the guilt which accumulates in thy heart; the more you are conscious of your guilt and therefore seek peace in enmity; but this peace of heart thou canst not find, for thou feelest the emptiness of thy heart."

That is also the reason why Pater N. is an enemy of the Society for the re-marriage of divorced Catholics. I didn't want to dispute with him on the last matter because the argument would have led into infinity. After all, how many men are there who actually crush their women as if they were animals? And should she nevertheless give such a man love, perhaps even support him and wait patiently until he dies instead of leaving him to find her happiness at the side of another? He generalizes his horror of this society, perhaps in a Jesuitical and clerical manner. There is, of course, a grain of truth in what he says. Two people should first learn to know each other pretty well and not after it is too late. Indeed, he didn't say just this, but I suppose that would have been his answer.

Concluding comments: How right I was to decide to give up the perversions deriving from spiritual onanism once and for all, especially after I had indulged myself sufficiently in the foregoing comments, is demonstrated by the article on "Insanity and Phantasy" from the *Neues Wiener Tageblatt* of March 27, 1905, which I found in my brief case. If my book were passionately continued in this wise, the article mentioned would define my complete destiny. The end: insanity resulting from spiritual and physical onanism, over-heated phantasy, a pathologically developed imagination which might otherwise have been creative. As it is, however, the basic tendency and course of my sexually phantastic excitement has always been and still is about as follows:

The women who have provoked my passions, quite regardless of their age, class, confession, or education, become, in my mind, my "victims" and my "vassals."

1. I titillate my senses Platonically, as it were, first through their sensuous possibilities and then on their clothed and beautiful bodies. Then I make them lascivious, wanton and lewd; myself, by means of their surrounding charms, my kisses, embraces, touch, talk, in fact with every possible means. Torture them by disregarding their own unsatisfied Platonic or sexual desires, make them wild and giddy through conversation, dress or luxury.

2. More or less gradually, quickly, coolly or violently (depending on the figure), I subject them to the most divers and exciting, painful, but harmless, tortures, such as massage in the prone or hanging position, on the rack, in bonds, by tickling or whipping; or the tortures of baiting, the rope, ducking, and the specially delightful form of corset torture. This period of inquisition, which follows my first phase of wantonness, is diversely repeated and varied with my female figures. Thus, for example, the child, girl, flapper, virgin, wife, mother, matron, all of them are frequently dressed several times, repeatedly tortured, progressively denuded, either by me alone or even with the aid of the victim's "maids" (whores; those women already seduced and debauched), again subjected to different barbarities, but always more and more provoked and tired by means of the unusual bindings and rope tortures; most devilishly photographed in highly irritating positions; clothed again, laced, punched, tickled, petted, pinched, massaged,

etc., etc. Faintings. Awakening in luxurious quarters, resting, amusement and laziness in these "playlands." Their comrades are meanwhile further mistreated and caused to suffer and to sigh.

3. According to the strength of the victim, the beauty and passion of the prey, as well as the character of the man torturing her, the decent woman then arrives at the third and last stage of suffering and (perhaps) secret delight. Extreme abasement and extreme pleasure, alternating, endlessly offered, and not only by one man, but by men, even women. Now comes the coitus, the rape and ravishment, the best and most pleasant period, but also the most exciting even for the strongest woman. Greatest of raptures for the man thus "treating" the woman, happiest wantonness for her companions (the whores; always only five at a time). And then combined, refined and nerve-racking methods of ravishing the female body.

How many attacks on girls over ten, pupils of schools, flappers! How many budding young women and girls have been raped, what numbers of brides, wives, widows have not been ravished and mothers and divorcees desecrated, regardless of the number of their children! And what a delicacy were pregnant women!

There is no use of shame or pain, resistance or despair in any of these three stages. The flapper, the virgin, the young bride, the wilted wife, the mother, they are all downed by the raw strength of the male. And if his strength is not sufficient, or if he does not wish to exert himself, there are the five young and lovely wantons there, ready for any and all of the most repulsive orgies. One at the right and one at the left, each takes one of the victim's arms while one of her legs is lifted up by a third and a fourth pulls the other leg aside. The poor creature raves, but the man is thrilled at the sight of these lovely limbs and peeks up into her open dresses, higher and higher, tickles her on the ——,[2] while the five damsels smilingly stifle the cackling cries, curses and damnations of the hoarse and half-unconscious subject. Now her lover's fingers creep over her full and heaving breasts; embraces; she is pulled into a bed, the gasping victim fights in vain, her blouse is opened, the corset slit at the front, the silks crumpled and often torn, her lovely panties ripped at the very most ticklish point of her belly and in the wild tussle which ensues, both man and whores help to subdue the candidate for violation and reveal her nakedness. Unconsciousness. Ejaculations. Finally, the man undresses before the trembling beauty and violently seduces her.

The cries and echoes die away, her resistance is broken; absorbed in frenzies of passion, she is left alone in bed. Either hopelessly crushed, despairing, or lighter of heart, thankful and infatuated, the lovely victim finds herself bathed in her own blood and secretions, alone in a luxurious love bed with a naked and passionate man in a palatial room. Recess. Remuneration through the selfsame servants who previously violated her so. They tend her and bring her clothing, amuse her and surround her with every luxury. Then renewed and always more impassioned love scenes.

That is, so to speak, only a typical example of the innumerable desecrations of men against women. How many orgies, for example, did I not stage in my mind with all the beautiful girls and women I saw at the V. international automobile exposition in 1905! How I provoked, tortured, denuded the elegant princess H. in my phantasies, and even ——.[3] How quickly did I love that charming Mrs. W., at first Platonically and then under torture. She was finally undressed and violated by a man in each arm pit, another ad vaginam, and another in the mouth.[4] In short, only her own beauty had been able to call forth such an excess of passion. Sick, nearly crazy with shame, shuddering disgust and lustfulness, she was dragged to her resting bed.

How the duchess Y. cried out when her latest corset with a straight front was closely laced about her in her own boudoir by August! Catching her breath, she dropped sitting on the soft couch as August tugged the strings from forty-five inches to twenty inches about her middle. She wore a deeply cut-out negligee (a low-cut, perfumed chemise), silk stockings and bloomers and fine garters. August's eyes sunk themselves through the negligee, embraced her lovely body while he kissed her neck, face, hair and rosy shoulders. Trembling and half beaten she was, tor August spent an hour detailing to her the extent of her subjected position; how she would have to accept his love in any form, have to conduct herself like his own woman, otherwise her five maids and the cruelest of tortures would certainly force her to submission. How she yells when he clasps her so tightly that her buxom breast is pressed forth closely against his chest, covered only by a fine, thin shirt. Her arms push him from her, but he rains kisses upon her breasts and arms. She shrieks. He coddles her, pulls her luxurious breasts out of her chemise. Crack! She whacks him on the face. Bang! He rips the silk from her shoulders to her corset. Simultaneously she tries to run out the door, but he grabs her by her extruded hips and begs her for forgiveness.

Gasping with pain at the closely laced corset, she drops in his arms. Then he calmly —— her between the breasts, —— and belly, carried the almost unconscious duchess before a mirror and tried ——,[5] her thighs and belly. Hardly had she felt the sacrilegious hands of the man upon her genitals, when she quickly pulled herself together for further struggle, the corset groaned as if it would burst, in vain she caught herself in the mirror, hurriedly closed her bloomers, pushed his hand away from her parts and, opening the door, yelled furiously into the hall: "Help! Help! He's raping me!" August, however, caught her and began to feel her up, meanwhile calling to all the girls gathering in the hall. (There were five of them as well as a few others who were just in the process of accompanying a delectable Jewish flapper, a Protestant virgin and another harmless Christian wife for a walk.) Quickly the five wantons gathered about. The other three victims had certainly understood the cries of the duchess, especially when they had heard her yelling so frantically, and had seen her in a costume such as only the most trusted maid is permitted to sight, in addition to which they found her wildly warding off the greedy advances of a totally strange man. They immediately wanted to help, too, but the companions drew them, shuddering, off down the corridor. In answer to their clamorous questions about the scene, they were told something innocuous and advised that they would soon enough find out. As a matter of fact, the fourteen-year-old flapper (Ida!) was raped that very evening, the virgin Elsa the following day during a comfortable moment in her amusements, while the other woman, having arrived and passed her "tests," was brought back to her room and two hours later knew exactly what had been awaiting the duchess.

The duchess breathed anew, but she soon shrank back as strange hands grabbed her, pushed her down, tied her pretty, little feet and held her mouth shut. Terrorized, she felt August in a renewed onrush, but as she was pressed down on the couch and her beautifully made panties again opened, so that her parts became visible, she fell into a fit of tears. When she had become quieter, she learned that the maidens obeyed August implicitly and had gathered the instruments of iniquity to crush her resistance. She begged August for consideration, but he was deaf to her plea. She prayed, she beseeched. The prostitutes threatened her with terrible barbarities, pains, whippings, tweezings, even branding her completely naked body by August while they would be racking her. The duchess was horribly afraid of even the word torture, especially of the drawing, hanging and rack types. Her fear was also heightened by the carefully couched threats and descriptions which the prostitutes and August whispered in her ear. She said that she would rather be laced to death than otherwise tortured to death. She saw August's love for her and also the preparation of the instruments. Passively resistive now, she permitted herself to be mauled and fingered by August and even looked lovingly at him as he kissed her breasts and played with her belly and bottom. The girls, meanwhile, created quite a noise in fixing the torture boards, the straps, the ropes and rods. "Thérèse, throw me another strap or otherwise this one'll bust when he ties this big one in." Or: "Steffi, bring me another corset as strong as the one she's got now or she's liable to croak when the laces pull her too tight." "Empty that bucket, Olga, or she'll drown everything when the fireworks begin." "Don't you think, Mizzi, that August should do her up brown before he takes her off the board? Just because she wouldn't mind him before. Yet she's so spoiled she can hardly stand much." "Just wait, Annie, the duchess'll decide quick when she's on the rack. Then she'll give him anything he wants, but it'll be too late because she'll be sick in bed for a fortnight before those pains are gone."

The duchess heard it all and naturally began to fear the torture more than August's love. She fell in a faint, but was awakened by a quarrel. It was all a hoax! August grabbed one of the maidens who was at fault, tortured her himself and had her also attacked by her colleagues, got her dressed, whipped her, bound her tightly and pressed her in an iron corset. The whore bawled and begged for pardon, fell in a faint and, apparently suffering the most terrible pains, kissed the feet of the duchess and beseeched her for a good word with August. The duchess had become pale with fear and terror as she was being held by August and two of the girls while the other two were punishing their colleague. She became quite submissive and when she was again threatened with the same treatment as the prostitute had suffered if she did not obey, she lay herself close to August on the sofa, did not even whimper when he surreptitiously shoved his finger in vaginam; rather she cuddled closer to him in a lewdly inviting fashion and begged for the pardon of the poor creature whom the two handmaidens had dragged blubbering into a corner. "Set Steffi free! I forgive her." The four girls picked up their colleague and ran to the feet of the duchess to thank her. She, on the other hand, seemed rapidly giving way to adultery. "Tell me that now I won't be tortured either." August remained adamant and the duchess again became excited. The prostitutes begged for her. August embraced the body of the woman who was kissing him for joy and dragged her—not into the bed as she had hoped but to the instruments of barbarism. Oh, what a fate! At a sign from him, she was tied down, hung up and placed on the rack. Unconscious, the duchess was taken down, untied and put in bed, but when she awakened, August racked her still more tightly. As she was again being taken to the torture board with August holding her by the buttocks, she threw her arms about his neck, kissed him ardently and said, as she offered him her breasts:

"Take me, take me, my lover, I love you, be mine."

"Many thanks, lovely sweetheart, I love you, too, and will not torture you any more, but, just as a little warning, I think I'll have to bend you somewhat more to my will." The astonished duchess again began to tussle with the maidens who pulled her hither and thither in the room, baited her, kneaded her belly and her bosom, bent her like a wheel on the sofa until the seams of her corset began to give and they themselves were so exhausted that they drooped their heads and said: "Oh, stop it, August, you two have had enough." Beside himself with passion, August fell upon the sinking woman and laid her in his love bed.

The prostitutes had withdrawn, the duchess saw no more instruments of torture and in August only her dear lover. Voluntarily she became an adulteress and, while August slowly undressed her, she begged with importunate lewdness for union which was freely and frequently granted her. That is how the duchess and August satiated themselves. The duchess was sufficiently fixed and when he had finished admiring her violated form, August again laced her body down to twenty inches and praised her beautiful figure. Flattered, the duchess permitted herself again to be topped while in this corset, vainly she stroked herself over the buttocks, across the iron clad corset, turned her wasp-like waist, her white abdomen and her well-formed pelvis. She was happy to have won the first prize the evening before as the woman who laced herself the tightest of all. The second lacing prize went to an eighteen-year-old Jewish ballet dancer and to a twenty-year-old Christian dressmaker, primarily because of too much racking of their bodies. Seen from behind, this thirty-two-year-old duchess had a waist breadth which was but a quarter of her pelvic breadth, whereas most of the others had a ratio of at least one third the pelvic circumference. That was the reason for the duchess's winning.

And these are the procedures that I varied endlessly in my mind. All with girls, women and "whores." For these last were also treated in the same fashion occasionally along with their mistresses. Often hundreds of them are lying in an immense hall of orgies, bound, naked, in all possible positions, and the women, egged on by lashes of the whip, sprang upon the —— of their men or, like prostitutes, invited them to copulate. One was able to see all kinds of feminine figures there, for it had been arranged to have the women jump down from a balcony on to feather beds and when they would jump, their skirts and dresses would fly in the air (their maids had not permitted them to put on bloomers) and the men standing below would be able to look all the way up their lovely white legs to their sweet ——. Hardly landed, they would be seized by the men and promptly seduced, all their parts, breasts and arm pits being used, etc., etc., ad infinitum!

I repeat: Living an apparently ascetic and chaste existence, I am inwardly given to a pathological development of my instincts, a criminal against woman in my mind, and belong in an asylum. In my own mind, however, there are no laws, there is no protection for children, for girls, no chivalrous respect of womanhood. As often as I practise masturbation, three elements are present: 1. I excite myself and the women in my phantasies, clothed and naked. 2. Then I torture them with all manner of apparatus and machines, cords, ropes, etc., but especially with a tightly fitting and high-class corset. 3. Finally, I force the female to have intercourse, although without torture, and give it to her whether she likes it or not until both she and I have enough.

During the first part of my phantasies, I am being dragged unwillingly, as it were, into my spiritual filth, but my acquiescence grows upon me with the second stage until I am ready for physical masturbation. At the third phase, while the unhappy victim is writhing in the pains preparatory to the highest raptures, my spiritual onanism reaches its acme and provokes physical masturbation. As soon as I have an ejaculation, and my phallus sinks, the phantasies fade away and the dreams of feminine lust and tortures interest me no longer. Moreover, I am unhappier than ever, for I realize that I have unnaturally desecrated both my body and my mind.

I feel crushed and beg God earnestly for forgiveness of my weakness, my oft-repeated sins. I can be saved only by:

1. Will power and trust in God through prayer, vigilance and acceptance of the sacrament.

2. Unexpected material enhancement such as a good gamble, promotion or a paying bit of extra work.

3. I ardently yearn for a true, Platonic love such as my youthful attachment to a charming young neighbor, a chaste and blooming girl.

4. Best of all would be actual intercourse with my own wife, but that is also my greatest despair because I have not yet been able to marry on account of my financial circumstances. Were I to get a girl with some money, I should be relieved of the financial worries in which I now find myself.

5. Intercourse effected with any kind of woman acceptable.

Comments on the above five points:

1. Unfortunately it has rarely been the case. My will is too weak.

2. Tried definitely in 1908 and my salary is larger. But it is not enough, for I must be rich.

3. My list of virgins: Anna B. Rosa L. Marie Z.

4. Woman is false and cheats her man. 18 Nov., 1901. Hansi F., wife of a typesetter, thirty years old. Only kisses and embraces. Nearly seduced her the evening of the 10th of November, 1902, if the presence of her twelve-year-old sister had not frustrated the attempt.

5. I am following my clamorous but, unfortunately, only Platonic devotion to Mrs. F., as of 18 November, 1901. Visited a prostitute of thirty-two living in the Franciscan Square who looks very much like her. My lasciviousness had her undress, but I saw only body and limbs—not F. I nevertheless grasped her, laced her, kissed her, embraced, etc. But I didn't undress myself, didn't lose my virginity. To the devil! Why not? Couldn't I have deflorated myself, as it were, right there and then? But I considered it a success if I even tried to copulate. I have noted this experience down as an exemplary piece in my "love note" collection, my satanic bible.

Once my final fall took place and a visit with a prostitute had transformed me from a boy to a man, I had to preserve my first mistress by measuring her off seventy-five different times. This gave me a basis for choosing a future wife. The seventy-five measurements I took of her were height and breadth and circumferences. Fourteen times with her clothes on, fourteen times naked, twenty-seven limb measurements, twenty special measurements on her naked or laced body, etc. Total: seventy-five measurements with a tailor's tape.

First I try out the measurements in my "book"; pure calculation; and when I have had intercourse, I note the measurements here, having first laid them aside for a while. This concerns only the first visit to a prostitute. After the second copulation with the beauty, the "love notes" are added as an aid to the memory of her personal charms and ten measurements appended.

These ten measurements give me a tangible feeling of the dimensions of the woman's body; so that I pretty well know just what sort of figure of a mistress would satisfy my sensual and æsthetic needs. These few naked statements end an almost too luxuriously grown treatise, and purpose (no infection being presupposed) to cure me from the profligacy and disease of every kind of onanism. Naturally, a love marriage with its holy intercourse would be an unmentionable happiness. Oh, Almighty God! I beseech you for my own true wife and all her charms and pleasures.

Ended this 28th day of April, 1907. Twenty-four years of age.

At this point, the diary ends. William has not continued this satanic bible since that date, nor has he entered any more pictures nor communicated any more phantasies. He struggled with all his might against his paraphilia, tried to save himself first by normal intercourse, sought out divers prostitutes and had them put on corsets he had brought with him, but he was never able to achieve erection or effect coitus. He would begin, but terrific palpitation of the heart would set in and he would flee.

He consulted a physician who diagnosed a cardiac neurosis and forbade him any activity in sports. Hitherto his chief diversion had consisted of mountain climbing, but now that he was advised against such strenuous activity, he was in danger of reverting to his former phantasies. The sadistic imaginations gradually receded, but he continued to indulge in his ideas of the torturing corset until even that didn't give him much gratification either.

Meanwhile, his piety became manifestly more overt, he went

to church more frequently and reduced the practice of masturbation. His salary had increased, but it was insufficient for his
needs. There were certain things which he wanted absolutely:
1. A small house of his own, or a villa if possible. 2. A large
garden of his own. 3. An automobile. He couldn't imagine
himself living without a car.

He searched perseveringly and finally found a girl who had
a little business of her own. She was a designer of hats who
made quite a nice living. Indeed, she was not very young, being
thirty-six, but she appealed to him, especially since he learned
that she was domestically inclined and economical. She was a
Jewess, however, and that meant only a civil marriage. At first
his religious training rose up in him against such a union, but
he said to himself: Jewesses taste better. They are more passionate and certainly better housewives. They are faithful.
You won't be cheated. She's also not so attractive that other
men will be looking at her greedily.

He decided to marry her. The outcome was described at the
beginning of this case history. His wife was deeply frustrated
because she had expected the joys of love and found a man who
talked in big words but couldn't effect intercourse. He was impotent. There came quarrels. He wanted her to be examined
by a gynecologist, claiming that there must be something wrong
with her, that her hymen must be too strongly developed, etc.
The gynecologist examined her and found that her hymen was
but rudimentarily developed and that there was thus no obstacle
to her copulating.

Both of them had some money saved; so that the hope of a
small home of his own was no longer an utopia. Indeed, they
were even in a position to buy a small car and he began to work
on his wife to let him buy the car and other things, protesting
that he would then surely be potent. But the war came and that
was the end of all their savings. He still had his wife, although
the bubbles of his hopes and wishes had burst. It was then that
he came to me with the hope of curing his impotence and gave
me his "satanic bible."

It contained pictures which showed how all his thoughts and
ideas revolved around corsets. He would cut out any and every
advertisement that had to do with them.

Some of the drawings are memories of women he has seen on the street. They indicate what the special features of these women were that provoked his fancy: tightly laced bodies.

His corset phantasies are variously prefaced and illustrated by an accompanying advertisement or picture. It is understandable what sort of an interested public they would attract. Beside the pictures of these advertisements, he would make the following marginal notes:

"Very low cut lady (also serves), elegantly dressed and laced. Awaits male company. Ha! what a thrill to disrobe such an insanely corseted woman and then rape her (first her corset would split in the struggle)."

But soon he begins to transform the pictures himself, and in in his mind and sketches disrobes the women in the pictures He also uses pictorial advertisements of furniture as a background for sketches of his tortured and racked women. He collects these corset pictures from all kinds of advertisements and the collection reveals a manifest interest in the erotic effect.

He also gathers every little newspaper clipping which might have the slightest erotic thread. Sometimes he also adds pictures, drawings and comments to the news articles as illustrations. The following is an example:

(A Nuisance in the Theatre.) Our Berlin correspondent wires the 30th inst., reporting that during the performance in the new royal opera yesterday, a dentist visiting the city was arrested by detectives for having obscenely molested young women and girls who were standing with him in the parquet. The hitherto blameless man confessed to having been the cause of several acts of disorderly conduct recently in which female members of theatre audiences had suffered (31-Jan.-1905).

"I lewdly imagine the scene to myself about as follows: I'm in the National People's Theatre, standing room, and squeeze a buxom Jewess Olga P. on one arm with my right while I pass my left about her soft waist from behind, embrace her bosom and her belly, lock my legs about her dress and limbs. Too bad, that date in the Adlergasse fell through (October, 1902). She was good petting, that luxurious, black Jewess, Olga."

That shall end the excerpts from the patient's "satanic bible." It is readily understandable how such persons find repeated

provocation for their onanistic acts in the perusal of such literature. But his decision to part with the book is in itself an
indication of a strong will to be cured. It derives from his religious, anagogic tendencies. The example of this case clearly
reveals to us the two powers that struggled for supremacy
within his breast: religion and Satanism. Apparently he submitted to the Satanic urge, but in reality he remained chaste.
He has not masturbated since he was twenty-four. He parted
with his bible and gave up his phantasies. But even more. He
remained chaste and virginal even in marriage.

In the analysis, it appeared that he regarded coitus as the
original sin. It is from this sin that he withholds himself and
ever and again reverts to asceticism. He was well on the way
towards achieving his former ideal and becoming a saint.

The analysis of such a fetishist is endlessly difficult and succeeds best, perhaps, when the patient is quite naïve about psychoanalytical matters. These persons are, however, usually
quite complicated individuals, well educated and trained in
philosophical questions. They know well how to cover up infantile motives. This patient came with an apparent desire to
be cured, but he insisted on sticking to his own program and
first confessing his life's sins. He continued this for six weeks,
disregarding all my protests. Whenever I would interrupt the
stream of talk, he would not associate and all my efforts were
in vain. All my analytical tricks were fruitless. What I did
learn was that his mother was a heavy woman who laced herself tightly into a corset, and that even as a child he was greatly
interested in this piece of his mother's apparel. Ever since he
was eleven he always used his mother's corset in masturbation.
He would put it on and claimed that it fitted him well. In
addition to this, he blamed the then prevalent fashion for corsets and several other childhood impressions for his fetishism.

He feigned a necessary trip to the country and did not return
to the analysis for two years. He inquired whether he could
come back, desired an appointment, promised by telephone to
return at a certain time, but never kept his appointment. I see
him about once a year at the most inopportune times, inquiring
whether he cannot return to the analysis. I know that he is
still impotent and is considering getting a divorce and becoming

a monk. His piety has grown, he gets along well with his confessor and has given up his opposition to the church.[6]

The case permits us to glance into the horrible phantasy
world of an ascetic fetishist. I have dared to publish this material because it is of paramount scientific interest and affords
us a greater understanding of the psychology of the erotic collector. The core of his existence is the corseted female. Anything that has to do with corsets is an object of his irritated
interest. We can observe several symptoms of the genuine
fetish lover: 1. The strict asceticism disregarding even marriage. 2. Pathological phantasies which express themselves in
masturbation. 3. The cult of the harem which is here represented by his "Satanic bible." 4. The novel factor of a sadistic
attitude towards the woman. 5. The fetishistic symbol (the
corset) expressing the compulsion.

Externally, this man is a mild, fine and complacent gentleman. Never has he so lost control of himself as to speak an
indelicate word to his wife, let alone physically to insult or torture her. He strives towards a higher, ethical form of life, he
is deeply pious and yet, in his phantasies, a libertine whose cruel
practices could surpass those of a Marquis de Sade. Shuddering, one must recoil from the abortions of his hellish phantasies.
One would take him for a criminal, were it not for the impass-
able crevasse between his real conduct and the world of his
phantasies. But it is precisely this contrast which is typical of
the fetishist. Every attempt to transform his phantasies into
realities fails. All the other fetish lovers whom I have observed
also never dared more than a very bashful attempt which usually
failed and fell far behind the demands of reality.

Sadism is present in every case of genuine fetishism. It appears to be the deepest cause of this illness as well as of every
compulsion neurosis.

The reaction to this sadism is the self-protective buttressing
of the religious urge. As an atonement for the sadistic phantasies, the patient constructs the sexual ideal of asceticism which
is more or less strictly observed.

The primary sadism then becomes transformed to masochism
as a result of the pious ideas of expiation. The fetishist begins
to execute his tortures on himself.

William also laced himself into the corset and tried to torture himself. He would lay himself down on the bed in crucifixion position, tied in a corset, and try to bind himself. That conduct approximated in his mind his ideal of Christ, brought him nearer the fiction of being a martyr (the Christ neurosis). Visiting his father confessor is an expression of his anagogic-religious tendency.

He is, on the other hand, a satan, too. He is the prophet of a new religion the sign of which is the corset. In one of his dreams, Christ and Satan struggle for possession of the world. Christ touches the devil, who wears a corset, with the cross and the devil disappears in a cloud of smoke and dust.

Unfortunately, it was not possible to unearth the infantile roots of his paraphilia, but the incestuous attitude towards his mother explains the early incidence and the stubbornness of his illness. In order to understand his paraphilia accurately, we must unravel the endo-psychic representation of his illness. He himself is the female whom he wishes to conquer. The man in his paraphilia is Satan, the devil who wishes to desecrate the woman in him. Symbolically, the female is the sign of chastity, whereas in life she is the incarnation of sin.

It is this divergence of conscious and unconscious striving which makes the patient incapable of love and affection. The corset is at once the symbol of an ascetic compulsion and the sign of his deepest raptures. It is thus that desire and abstinence become unified in one symbol. In his struggle against the ascetic ideal, he commands five prostitutes, i.e., his five senses, his passionate desires. He strives towards love of life and joy of the senses, but his infantile guiding principle (Adler) leads him on to God and eternal bliss. He is simultaneously devout and agnostic, a libertine and an ascetic, a true Faust without Faust's mental qualities. He desires and rejects the analysis. He wants to be cured and yet fears that the analysis might destroy his ascetic life and rob him of his religion.

He often laid his prayer book next to his Satanic bible, and thus beautifully expressed the frayed, ambivalent nature of his soul. The struggle between belief and disbelief ended in the creation of a substitute religion.

Corset fetishism is comparatively frequent. The chief point

is always the pressure of the article and the pain caused by it. This type of fetish addiction is often combined with shoe fetishism. Hammond reported an interesting and significant case of this kind:

Case 40. The patient is a well-educated and respectable man, the father of four healthy children, happily married. "Even long before puberty," he said, "I disclosed a preference for domestic activities, girl's games and even for feminine clothing, although I never expressed the last leaning beyond wearing women's shoes at times. I also admired the narrow waists of the ladies and even tried at fourteen to get a corset for myself. The older I got, the greater became my interest in feminine clothing, but, since I had no sisters, my sole source of gratification lay in reading novels which dealt with women, etc. I wrote several little stories entitled *Adventures in Crinoline* and also wrote some other short tales of a similar nature. They were published and greedily bought up. To this day, I never miss an opportunity to see a man playing a female rôle on this stage."

At twenty-one, he began to wear corsets himself because he liked them so well, and, although he laced himself rather tightly, he seemed to suffer no serious detriment to his health. He confessed, however, that this always afforded him a certain sensual satisfaction. At first he suffered some pain in the pubic region and also had erections, but he soon learned that whenever he tied the corset on tightly, the erections ceased and copulation as well as masturbation were quite impossible.

Fearing impotence and other detriments resulting from masturbation, he anxiously avoided any voluntary orgasm and remained abstinent to the day of his marriage. He recalls having had three involuntary emissions, once while he was riding horseback. The result was that he gave up this otherwise healthful sport. The other two emissions occurred while he was buttoning on a pair of tight women's shoes with French heels.

Following marriage, he never put on a corset nor wore any female clothing (with seldom exceptions), i.e., until the birth of two children convinced him of his potency. Then, however, the patient began to succumb again and dropped into his old habits. Here I will let him speak for himself: "I bought myself a pair of very elegant women's shoes with French heels which were at first so tight on me that I limped." He would wear these shoes publicly while promenading in fine weather and lift up his trousers,

THE BIBLE OF THE FETISHIST

so that the heels would show to better advantage. When the weather was adverse, he would put them on at home once a week and button them up in front of a mirror. This would always bring on an erection and sometimes even ejaculation.

When the novelty of this had worn off, he bought himself a corset, and whenever he could do so without being noticed, he would lace it on so tightly that he nearly fell in a faint. Both these articles of apparel, the button shoes and the corset, seemed to have a special appeal for him. Often in the horse cars, he would see a lady with a narrow waist and small feet opposite him and would experience a kind of idealized coitus with her or, as he put it, he felt a flow of his feeling towards her. Roubaud reports a quite similar case of a young man who was potent only with blondes who wore a corset, high heels and silk dresses. The last three objects also had a great effect on our own patient, regardless of whether the wearer were a man or woman.

He soon came to indulge his tastes more and more and even went so far as to buy himself, in addition to his already mentioned possessions, a black silk dress which fitted him very tightly. He was quite proud of it, too. Ringlets and hoops, false hair, earrings and brooches, everything female was grist for his mill. Indeed, he would sit tightly corseted for hours while a barber would curl and do up his hair in the feminine manner. Finally, he arrived at the point where he would wear his black silk dress on promenade and to church, lifting it gingerly on one side to display the white, pleated trimmings and the shoes with the high, French heels. With a well-padded bosom, closely gathered waist and enormous *cul de Paris,* with fantastically done up hair, earrings and extremely tight and uncomfortable shoes he could walk miles or dance for hours with the greatest of pleasure. It actually appeared as if physical pain were an integral part of his bliss and he gloated in it as long as it were caused by some feminine article of apparel. Although he aped the manners and habits of women, he never abused his dress for base purposes, with the exception of experiencing an orgasm in these clothes now and again.

As I have already mentioned, he recommended narrow waists highly and had not only read a great deal on this subject, but had also collected all the literature that had been written for and against the practice. He often tried to lace himself so tightly that he would faint but in this he was unsuccessful. He even succeeded in persuading his wife to lace herself closely and tied her corset tighter every day himself until her waistline had been reduced about six inches. This also gratified him sexually. A child which she soon afterwards bore was quite healthy and well formed.

"He showed me," said Dr. Hammond, who communicated the case to me, "several photographs which portrayed him in all conceivable forms of feminine dress: as a ballet dancer, as Queen Elizabeth, as a Polish peasant, as an old maid, the goddess of liberty, Juliet; or in a simple street dress which he had some time worn to church.

"He often resolved to give up his habits, but he invariably reverted to them. Sometimes he was able to abstain for weeks and months, but the old susceptibilities would return. He enjoyed a largely protein diet, but ate no fat. Only albumens satisfied him. I prescribed a vegetable diet for him, but he was so disgusted that I had to rescind my orders. He drank only weak tea and coffee. For a while he was given bromides in order to weaken his passions."

This case is not one of genuine fetishism and would doubtless be diagnosed by Hirschfeld as transvestitism. He nevertheless reveals two characteristic factors: the tight lacing in a corset and the wearing of tight-fitting shoes. It is significant that he himself chooses to wear the corset and the shoes. In every case that I have observed, these features of identification with the usual wearer of the clothing can be made out. I have always stressed this point. The pains express the invariable component of sado-masochism. I would call this man a case of "rudimentary fetishism." We are indebted to Abraham for another interesting case [7] of corset and foot fetishism which I shall discuss in detail later on.

IX

THE ANALYSIS OF A FOOT FETISHIST

It is not at all the purpose of this work to exhaust the symbolic possibilities of the various parts of the human body. The divers forms of partialism and fetishism, especially, show such a specifically individual etiology that one is tempted to forget the general symbolism involved. And yet the individual possesses a secret memory for symbols. There is a mnemonic system of recording symbols; so that in dreams and other hypnoic states we all sink back into the thinking and feeling of prehistoric times. It would be an interesting piece of work to demonstrate the signs of archaic thought processes in fetishism and to show that every paraphilia is really a regression to some aboriginal human level. I know that some schools of psychotherapeusis lay a deal of weight on such relationships, but have they any significance in psychoanalytical practice? Do they bring us nearer the solution of parapathias?

It is particularly in the case of foot fetishism that I could easily reveal the relationships between individual and general symbolism, but there is an exhaustive treatise by Dr. Aigremont (*Fuss-und Schuhsymbolik-und erotik,* "Folkloristische und sexualwissenschaftliche Untersuchungen," Leipzig, Deutsche Verlags-Aktiengesellschaft, 1909), which makes any special study of this kind superfluous. That learned author has come to the following conclusions: Sexual foot and shoe symbolism is very widespread and of age-old origin. The female foot is the symbol of fruitfulness because it touches the earth; the male foot, on the other hand, is the symbol of creation. The shoe is a symbol of the vulva, while the foot is a sign of the penis (there are innumerable corroborations in ethnographic and folk-lore studies). The old and holy symbols of the pagan world, however, where creation and birth were looked upon as mysterious and holy manifestations of supernatural power, were transformed in the newer spiritualistic thought of Christendom to evil and depraved concepts. As in the case of many sexual symbols, cynicism and a kind of frivolity also crept into these. In conclusion, Aigremont advises us not to forget the historical use of the foot and the shoe as sexual symbols in the direct sense.

We acknowledge the right of such conclusions, but we must ask how far would such research get us? It is certain that the instincts as the sum total of unconscious experience also play a part in the choice of a symbol and Binet has too greatly simplified the matter for himself, despite the fact that many observations appear to corroborate his thesis. We must simply admit that there are cases of fetishism and fetishism. The ones which I term genuinely fetishistic are all quite complicated and reveal their symbolism in divers forms.

Foot fetishism or, rather, the attractiveness of the foot and the shoe, the calf and the stocking, is so extraordinarily common that these parts of the body (and their clothing) could easily be reckoned among the so-called secondary sexual characteristics. Throughout literature, there are innumerable eulogies of the foot and the shoe and it would be easy to collect many such examples.

To illustrate this subject I shall choose that case of foot fetishism from among the number which I have observed, which I analyzed the longest. The observation dates from the period of my association with Freud, when I still believed in long periods of analysis. I analyzed this man for over a year and thus had plenty of opportunity to examine his parapathia carefully.

Case 41. Mr. Beta, a thirty-year-old independent scholar, suffers from divers parapathic symptoms of which I shall pick out only two because they irritate him most of all: his agoraphobia and his foot fetishism.

He cannot walk in the street alone, but must always be accompanied by someone. It is only along certain routes in the immediate vicinity of his quarters that he can navigate without the aid of his servant, but when he desires to go further, he needs company. The second part of his suffering is quite antithetical to the first mentioned part. He raves about feet and feels impelled to

run after persons with feet of the shape he delights to see. Should
he meet with his "ideal" in the street, he will follow it for hours
at a time, would like to speak with the person and beg him to
display the naked foot to him. During the first phase of his analytical treatment, he lost his anxiety and was able to walk quite
a distance alone. And what would he do on such a walk? He
would look for an "ideal" and follow it about without, however,
having the nerve to walk up to the person and talk about what
oppressed him. He could go through the streets for hours in this
wise and loved best to go for the Danube where there are often
numbers of men who pull off their shoes, unwrap the rags from
their feet and lie down to sun themselves or cool their feet in the
river. I must mention that Beta was not at all attracted to the
delicate, lovely and provoking feet of women. Nor was he in the
least animated by women's ankles, legs or lovely shoes, as many
of his fellow sufferers. He would always look first at a person's
feet, be they man or woman, and formed his opinions of them on
this basis. A woman as such did not interest him. He wanted
to see the shoe fit the foot tightly and the phantasy of whatever
was pinched and close was of elemental pleasure to him. He is
promptly enlivened by the sight of corns and envies every chiropo-
dist he sees.

He likes only male feet: red, swollen, dirty, sweaty and inflamed feet. Abraham, to whose publication I will return below,
explained foot fetishism on the basis of a repression of the olfactory pleasure in sweaty feet and Freud lends this theory considerable support. It is argued that man has developed from an
olfactory to an optic animal and the consequence has been a sad
reduction in the functional rôle of the nose. In this type of
fetishism, the repressed impulse breaks through (partial repression) and all foot fetishists are really fixated to the memory of
sweaty feet. In this case, where sweaty feet are preferred, the
tendency of the orthodox Freudian school to lay foot fetishism
to the repression of certain instincts would appear to have found
objective corroboration. We will soon see, however, that there
are much more important mechanisms in operation here. Our
patient—he felt himself ill and came to me to be liberated from
the tyranny of his fetishism—would have plenty of opportunity
to see men's feet at the bathing resorts if that were all that he were
really after. He would have only to go through the cure at
Wörishofen (a watering place) according to the Kneipp method
and would there be able to gratify his dearest wish without becom-

ing noticeable.[1] But such easily attained delights do not attract him. The feet of the rich leave him unmoved, but the foot of the working man, the man who is oppressed, the servant, the dependent, the man who must go bare foot, whose feet are subjected to such great pressure that the marks can be seen on the skin, only such a foot impresses him deeply.

I must pause here for a moment to emphasize this factor as a frequent point in the histories of fetishists. Whatever is exposed to pressure or a compression or compulsion increases the value of the fetish. This factor alone contains the symbolical representation of the whole fetishism. In such a case as this, the fetishism clothes the patient like a tight shoe and compresses him. It keeps the patient under constant constraint. From this point of view we are able to note the great similarity between fetishism and compulsion neuroses. In this form, the masochistic tendency of the fetishism betrays itself as a reaction to the never failing sadism of the patient.

As explained, Beta always sought out-of-the-way places for the gratification of his fetishism. On warm days, he goes to the Danube where poor working men may be found in droves, bathing their sweaty, swollen feet. It is the sight of these large, red feet which then gives him a thrill. He rushes home to masturbate. It is also important to find out in such cases just what the onanist adds to the scene in his phantasy. Whoever would suppose that Beta desired to touch the foot of a man or perhaps to have a homosexual relation with him would be sadly mistaken. Mr. Beta imagines that he is the poor workman with the red, sweaty feet and this picture is what provokes in him the most gratifying orgasm. Such a sign is also typical of the genuine fetishist. He identifies himself with his sexual object and it is by this process that Beta becomes the possessor of the red, swollen and sweaty feet.

Now, we could search here for infantile traumata and Beta actually related a host of details in this regard which I shall be able to report in the course of the dream analyses later on. He declared that as a child he had seen how a soldier who was the lover of their cook had pulled off his boots in their kitchen and the soldier's big, red feet had impressed him greatly. He also tells how the soldier rocked him on his knees and how this created a rush of pleasure in his veins. Such experiences cannot, however, explain the special mechanism of his parapathia, nor are they even accurately recalled. It is even probable that he sketched them into the story of his life in the telling of the tale. I believe that fetishists invariably make up a great part of their early life and add experiences to the story which lie in the direction of the fetish itself. Their so-called memories are false memories (screen memories, but not in Freud's sense [2]).

I therefore expected our foot fetishist to relate a story to me which would approximate the type of history which all fetishists and homosexual men tell one. They relate how there was a time when the whole woman or the whole man interested them, with especial reference to the genitals. Subsequently, gradual changes in their attitude allegedly took place. First they became interested in women's feet, then in men's feet in the course of time, until finally they developed a restricted attraction to red and swollen, sweaty feet. The sight of the soldier's feet should have determined the patient's subsequent interest specifically in that sense, but we see that the memory was hauled forth as a flight from sexuality and from woman (in this case from men, too). We must not forget how many children are exposed to these and similar experiences and yet how comparatively few become fetishists.

I repeat that this particular expression of taste developed only in the course of years and that, also, is a special characteristic of fetishism in general. But the individual's taste does not remain stable. The sexual goal keeps changing, but always in a progressively restricted and circumscribed sense. There are always new compulsion formulæ added to the original one, just as in a true compulsion neurosis. In this case, for example, it was the female foot which was the first step removed from the female genital and deflected all the interest from the genitals to the sexually indifferent foot. The next step was then the male foot, but the special condition of redness, swelling, perspiration, etc., came only later. As if Beta were afraid that he would achieve his sexual goal somewhat too easily. Artificial obstacles and difficulties which derive from a hidden ascetic tendency.

Beta, nevertheless, has intercourse with women or, rather, he is continuously trying to have intercourse with women. He belongs to that class of society in which one simply must have a mistress. His comrades go regularly to a brothel after the amusements of the club and he feels that he must go along. Once there, his conduct is quite characteristic. He quickly falls for the first girl who pleases him, but, strangely enough, pays little or no attention to her feet, looks only for her pretty face. He rapidly gets a strong erection which subsides, however, at the moment when he is about to effect the immisio penis in vaginam. We note here the operation of an inhibition which springs from deep seated moral tendencies. Just as if a voice were saying to him: "Don't do that. It's a sin!" Under the circumstances, Beta has the girl then phallus extra vaginam manu stuprare usque ad ejaculationem. This act meets with all the requirements of that tendency of parapathics which I have called "pleasure without guilt." The passivity of his part also portrays to him his guiltlessness. Such logic is, of course, infantile, but that is true of all parapathics. He virtually says to himself: "It's really not your fault; she did it." That is also the reason why any practice which necessitates passivity on his part is always more successful, an apparent paradox which is due to his essentially feminine attitude. Immissio penis has been successful only infrequently, and then generally in a half erect state. Once, however, he was able to carry out perfect intercourse, but in that case the prostitute gave him a slap in the face and told him he deserved to be beaten. A wave of anger poured over him, he wanted to beat her back, to choke her, humble her, show her his real strength; at that moment he got a strong erection, felt himself to be the complete male, took a properly aggressive attitude and was able to exploit his potency.

After such escapades and visits to prostitutes, he feels himself sullied and must take a bath. All his plans to find himself a beautiful mistress went wrong. Meretricious contacts and clear cut attempts by women of his circle to seduce him lost their effect in his indifference. He would begin the flirtation willingly enough, but never permitted the relationship to force a decision since that would necessarily have ended in a debacle for him.

The anamnesis and the psychoanalytical probing of the patient afforded much important material. At a very early age, Beta already showed signs of considerable erotic urge combined with quite an aggressive constitution. At seven he was the friend of a little girl who came daily from near by to play with him. Instinctively one day he tried to cohabit with her and injured the child. The punishment which followed—for the girl's English governess heard of the scene—and the ceaseless talk of his bad conduct promoted a gradual change in his character. This experience had the effect of an "eternal warning" and stood threateningly at the very beginning of his life.

But still his guiding principle led him towards the female. During the following years he had various little affairs with cousins, transient adventures with maidservants, etc. At twenty-one he fell in love with a dancer, and his father took this occasion to have a talk with him about women. His father believed that he should be absolutely unhampered in his activities, but he advised his son that one could not be cautious enough in life. Aside from the ever present danger of venereal diseases, there was the palpable possibility that he would fall into the clutches of an unscrupulous woman. He should therefore take hold of himself and try to keep from binding himself to any one woman. In short, Beta realized that any kind of an affair with this dancer would be unpleasant to his father whom he idolized and respected. He therefore resolved not to disappoint his father and never to have any intercourse as long as his father lived, except now and again with a prostitute to whom he would not be obligated. Such a resolve naturally resulted in his harboring death wishes against his father and the father actually died a few years later. Beta had, of course, pushed this thought aside, it was no longer in the center of his consciousness, but at the periphery; he dared not think it; he had to repress it.[3]

What did he do when his father died? First he assured the physician that he would never survive his father's passing, and then he promptly made a new resolution. He now swore that he would not have intercourse with any woman for the next three years. Succinctly, three years of strict abstinence. But he stuck to his resolution for only a year and then broke it with the motivation that it was, after all, not in accordance with what his father would have wished. His eruption took place under great resistance, however, and his impotence became more and more clear cut; the forms of his fetishism began to appear dimly in the background.

A cold sweat would break out upon his body when he would bring himself to sleep with a prostitute. Poisonous feelings of guilt appeared before his eyes in all kinds of shapes. He was particularly hounded by the fear that he had acquired a venereal infection.

Externally, one would take him for a freethinker, but he was quite devout at heart. He was the plaything of two rival tendencies. It had been well known that his father was a liberal and that had always been the tradition of the family. But a clerical tutor had instilled the fear of God in the boy and packed him full of all sorts of superstitions about guilt, sin and atonement.

The solution of his fetishism was achieved in a peculiar manner. One day he confessed to me that what really interested him in the line of feet was a *bloody* one. He would often phantasy that he had stuck a nail or splinter into his foot and that it bled. The picture of a foot with a nail in it appeared more and more frequently in his phantasies and day-dreams. In short, there appeared that phenomenon which I have found so often in parapathics: the Christ neurosis.

And now we can better understand his identification with the possessor of a sweaty foot. He was an impassioned hunter and for them "sweat" meant blood. His foot bleeds because it has been stuck through with a nail. He is Christ. It is with this picture in mind that he masturbates.

We must not mistake the fact, however, that fetishism performs an important function. It insures the fetish lover's chastity, guarantees the ascetic state for which he will be repaid in heaven. This circumscription gives him the right to expect sainthood. That is why he is specifically interested in the feet of the poor, the oppressed. Christ was not the king of the wealthy, for to them heaven had been closed. Christ was the Lord of the weak and the enslaved. And the more one humbled one's self on this earth, the surer one could be of achieving salvation and recompense above. Since, now, Beta was very pious at heart, there was but one cure for his fetishism, viz., marriage. In that state cohabitation is no longer a sin. This case thus shows clearly that his fetishism was nothing but a mask for his ascetic and devout tendencies, for as soon as he was married, he promptly lost all interest in red, swollen, sweaty feet and his potency was fully satisfactory after the first few erratic experiences usual in such cases.

I have already mentioned above that the fetishism must contain an indication of the compulsion. Whatever presses, laces, hurts; whatever is done under coercion serves to symbolize the parapathia. In no case of fetishism will one miss such an indication of constraint. It was with an iron obsession that Beta had forced his impulses into the Procrustes bed of his parapathia. He developed the agoraphobia in order to shield himself from the dangers of the street. He reduced and focussed his attention to the foot because he was in mortal fear of all the other depraved thoughts he might have.

Beta had the misfortune to have been the cause of his mother's death at birth and now he feels himself to be a born woman killer. He also had his own impulses to kill women, to choke them, be-

cause he hated them to the kidney. His father had been a Don
Juan and the boy had felt that women stood between him and his
father. Even as a youth he had a bipolar (ambivalent) attitude
towards the tutors and governesses in the house. He hated the
governess because she, too, was the mistress of his father while
he himself was also attached to her. She had strikingly big feet
which were almost the size of men's feet. His father's foot was
also his sexual object.

At this point I wish to demonstrate the accuracy of some of
the above statements and explanations on the basis of some of the
dream analyses of this case.[4] The analyses are built strictly on
the foundations of the patient's own associations; he was a thinking and intellectual person. He was the first case of fetishism
which I was able to study so carefully and it will doubtless interest others to follow the path I trod in gaining knowledge.

He dreamt:

I see a large wooden image of Christ before me and take a
piece out of it.

This dream is to be taken symbolically. The dreamer is still a
believer, a devout believer, as a matter of fact, despite his apparent pose as a freethinker. The day before the dream, he had
read a book entitled La folie de Jésus (Dr. Binet-Sanglée, Paris,
A. Maloine, 1908), but had to stop suddenly in the middle of
it. He could not say why. It was all like an obsession, like
a command: stop reading. The deeper causes for this experience
are revealed in the dream. He had taken something from his
godliness.

Second determination. He himself is Christ, but only a part.
He adapts a part of the life of Christ for himself. He is therefore no longer flesh and blood, but wood. He can no longer give
way to the passions of the flesh. Simultaneously he expresses his
bipolar tendency: he is made of wood, can easily burn and go
up in flames. What piece was it that he took out? He doesn't
know, but we shall learn in later dream analyses. That piece
which he took out of the image—might not that have been the
foot? His fetish? His personal religion? His atonement? A
later dream will afford us still further insight into this.

Another dream:

I read a complaint of a certain Mr. X. against the high school
principal Weihrich who died the same day. There were three
parts to his complaint and Weihrich was indicted only on the last

count. He had to walk in sandals and do something else, too. But I didn't understand that part of it.

Addendum: I saw a photograph of Gessmann and spoke with him about it.

The evening before, the dreamer had eaten a whole wheat roll with butter which, in Vienna, is called bosniak or Hadschi-loja after some Bosnian insurgent. A short while after eating the roll, he vomited and had terrific pains in the region of the kidney. He thought it was due to acid and alleges that any acid makes him sick. Whenever he eats ripe pears, he gets the same kind of griping and has a diarrhœa.

The analysis brought forth significant associations to the name of Weihrich. Weihrauch (incense)—Weihe (dedication)—Weiher (fish-pond)—Wow. Relating X (knock-kneed)—wow—and Gessmann, who is a notorious anti-Semite in Vienna, this was manifestly "knocking" the physician. He complains that the analyst has spoiled his pleasure in his perversions. He is being swindled (smoked out). Swindle makes him think of rocking. He recalls that as a child he was rocked on the knee of a soldier. That is one of the roots of his fetishism. There is, in addition, the fact stressed by Adler that he sucked his big toe as a baby.

His latent desire is thus to take a dirty, sweaty foot or a great toe into his mouth. Making a symbolical equation, we have the foot instead of the hand, the toe for the thumb, the penis and a breast. From here the path of associations leads to the paraphilia of fellatio and to the wet-nurse complex.

Bosniak is a Viennese expression for a Bosnian soldier and Hadschi-loja reminds him of the slang Viennese expression for walking-hatschen. The vomiting, the pains and the diarrhœa were provoked by the phantasy that he had taken a great toe (sweat—butyl acid—butter) into his mouth and had swallowed the acids contained in perspiration. Before we began the dream analysis, he had had waking phantasies of having swallowed a big foot.

Thus another root of his fetishism: the penis had been portrayed to him as something revolting, something one must be ashamed of. The result was a displacement of all his erotic libido to the foot.

Gessmann leads to guess. I'm the man who only guesses and knows nothing. The photograph (my picture) didn't please him at all. It was much too pale for him (Gessmann is dark). Light leads again to sweat and to his idiosyncrasy against rare roast beef. Blood is called sweat in the language of hunters and roast beef also reminds him of sweat which is considerably reduced if one uses sandals instead of shoes (symbolic equation: blood, perspiration, pus, mucus, urine, sperma, air, money, etc.).

The three parts of this dream are: (1) His English governess, (2) His brother, and (3) The sweaty foot. I have already severed him from his governess and his brother through the analysis and now I want even to separate him from his perverted delight in sweaty feet. That is the reason for the "knocking," the blame contained in the association Foot—flat foot—wow—. Further associations lead him to the "Wandering Jew" of Eugene Sue and that calls forth sweat again.

He himself is Ahasuerus, however. In his most delightful phantasies, he is Ahasuerus, the flying Dutchman or any other eternally damned soul. His foot images are all masochistically colored and represent ideas of expiation.

That which he could not understand in the dream is what he learns in the analysis. He doesn't want to understand it, for the moment he does have understanding, he is through with his obsessions. He derives too much pleasure from these infantile things, however, and doesn't want to give them up.

This dream also contains a number of serious emotional strivings. Among others, coarse calumniations of my own person which are so well disguised that the manifest dream content appears to contain no affect whatever.

Finally, he has me die, throws me among the corpses. That walk in sandals is a march into eternity. Sometimes he doesn't understand me at all. "There is something *spirited* about your thinking." He makes a spirit of me (Gessmann—Geistmann—Geist is German for spirit. Trans.). A spirit is light, white, pale. I'm much too dark for him. As far as he is concerned I could live only as a picture (photograph). This all leads to a new opening, his belief in the devil. I'm the devil in his eyes. I want to make him potent, i.e., to lead him into the arms of the female. But he wants to live an ascetic life and become a saint. He is always looking for situations in which he shall be unrighteously injured. He is invited to a party and the hostess has to call it off for one reason or another. He immediately makes a serious insult out of the whole thing. He thrives on unrighteous slights. He wants to suffer the pains of the pure. Thus, after the party had been called off and he had gone on a hunting trip, he wrote me the following very interesting letter:

"The calling off of that party; the invitation to another visit with a similar renunciation following, all this plunged me into a state of the direst depression, despite the fact that I should have been happy that the hunt was also called off because that always makes me nervous. Indeed, even the depression wasn't so despairing; I think I found it rather pleasant. It was all a frustration, an injuiry from which I gathered pleasures. I'm just a masochist, and a masochist is passive, and passivity means femininity, whereas the male is active. That is why the masochist possesses feminine feelings and desires to be overcome by a man, by an active individual. That is also the reason why masochists have a preference for soldiers, for active military men. The chief pleasure of the masochist, the passive one, is 'passio,' 'passion'; and thus the ideas of atonement. His greatest irritation is to be found in 'action'—coitus.

"There must have occurred some great injustice in my childhood from which I then derived gratification. I am still intent on gathering satisfaction from such a construed injustice.

"And do I not forbid myself everything even now? My illness is the apotheosis of a prohibition. I don't have intercourse, I'm asexual, see nobody, avoid the theatre, close myself off more and more behind a wall of books and don't even leave the house which is the first step one would have to take to do anything. My anxiety is a protection against pleasure.

"At times I feel as if nothing would give me greater pleasure than to die and be forgotten: the nth degree of masochism. During such a depression, I often have a curious day-dream:

"A man was unjustly sentenced for murder, but the peculiar thing about it all was that he hardly defended himself and heard the sentence with a composure which only those possess who are unjustly accused and feel as innocent as an angel. He was sentenced to life imprisonment. In prison, he appears so great that even all the jailers look upon him as a saint. He comforts the sick, heals them and seems to work wonders. In the course of years the fame of this holy criminal even reaches the ears of the emperor and he pardons him without rescinding the sentence. The saint in prison is notified, but he no longer understands the trifles of this world. He is completely transfigured, he is Christ himself. It is his chief triumph that in his sainthood he has lost his genitals, has become sexless and passes like a ray of light to heaven. The ruler is speechless, but is powerless even so much as to approach him. He, however, lives on in his usual manner."

This letter contains highly significant confessions, the most important of which are patently presented in the waking phantasy. It discloses to us the root of his asceticism. He indicts himself bitterly because of his murderous tendencies and is sorry that he has not led a saintly, but rather a sinful existence.

That name Weihrich is indeed an ingenious choice. It points to his satanic and olfactory complex (incense; the devil stinks). The incense also leads to his saintly complex. The principal is the father who had once unjustly whipped him. It is this infantile situation which constantly shadows him in life. "Blessed be the meek and they who suffer for the sake of justice; for theirs is the kingdom of heaven." That is his guiding motive.

He *wants* to reach the kingdom of heaven. He wants to excel his father, and his asceticism will assure him an even higher post in the skies. He wants to be a woman and lack a penis. These female tendencies alone will enable him to triumph over his father and in life eternal he will be over his father and gloat. He the saint; his father the sinner. Before the throne of God, he will fling three complaints at his father (the principle) and at the dead. But, we must ask ourselves, what is the source of this hatred against his father? An old rivalry—the English governess. This governess was his great love. When his wet-nurse left, this maid became everything for him. She dared not have anything to do with anyone else, otherwise he would become enraged. His father, however, was very sweet to this English child's maid and the boy witnessed many small and one important meeting which deeply mortified him. Was it possible? "His" Frances dared to kiss another man? That inflamed his sensitivity and his egoism to the thoughts of direst criminal revenge. But the child is impotent against adults. If only he had a poison, he could revenge himself on his enemy. Therefore the vomiting, the nausea and the diarrhœa after the Hadschi-loja. Father was a pasha and kept a harem. Beta's masochistic ideas are the atonement for the criminal phantasies of his childhood.

Here he clearly demonstrates his castration phantasies. He desired to castrate his father for having had intercourse with the Englishwoman. Then he wants to emasculate himself. The piece that he wants to take from himself (see the dream of the wooden image) is the genital. Then he can become Christ. He is the criminal, the mother killer who is innocent of the crime. We see also the root of his wandering impulse (marching in sandals) and the neurotic distortion of this impulse—the agoraphobia. He also wanted to murder his brother in order to have his father for himself.

The most important meaning of the dream is: He charges himself with three crimes and must atone for the third. He must become a wanderer and expiate his sins. What are the three crimes? What has he committed that he should desire to renounce all earthly happiness? The other dreams will give us the answer.

Another dream:

THE CLIMBING APE

It was in the Tyrol and the road was fearfully steep. Frances, my brother and I were together. Three trucks and an auto came uphill and a one-horse dray came down the hill. I climbed about like a monkey and had terrible fears. Then I tore out a tree branch with my left hand. They all marvelled at my strength.

An onanistic dream. He is the poor man who rides a one-horse dray, i.e., without a woman, and thereby comes down (a one-horse dray came down hill). He bears the heavy burden of his parapathia and always feels weak and beaten. The contrasting wish: "They all marvelled at my strength." His potency always fails with women; the path to woman is too steep for him. He can't find his way into the vagina. He can never effect immissio penis. He is no man at all and must satisfy himself with masturbation (the auto and pulling out the branch). His associations then take a singular turn. We will follow closely. The seven asses—branches—burden lead to depravity and syphilis. Many of his dreams deal with picking an ace—pickle—pimple—picking a pimple—pox. Infection.

What do those three wagons and the auto represent? Who are they? Three persons whom he loves and among whom his affections vacillate. He identifies himself first with one and then with another (the ape frequently expresses the capacity for "aping" or identification as well as the possession of a long tail (penis) and climbing). He apes everybody, even his brother who lives a loose life. The three wagons are his father, Frances, and the wet-nurse. He himself is represented by the auto.

His greatest fear is to fall. His climbing leads to his wet-nurse complex. A wet-nurse once let him drop and he is afraid that Frances might also let him go, i.e., stop loving him. She could also fall—for some one else. She could transfer her affections to his brother of whom he is bitterly jealous. He emasculates his brother, tears out his branch. One of his pet phantasies is that he is Zeus who emasculates Cronus. He has castrated his father and has become the stronger. He is jealous of his father. If his father is God (Cronus), then he is the son of God: Christ. He is the man who has overcome time (Cronus), he will live eternally. He is Ahasuerus: Damned, unhappily wandering forever, ever searching, but possessed of eternal life nevertheless.

That was his great discovery. He believed as a youth that he had discovered the secret of eternal life and divine power. This discovery (one must involuntarily marvel at the bipolarity of all parapathic phenomena) was masturbation. During the early years of his life, onanism was but a substitute for his nurse's breast. He had been nursed for thirteen months and the trauma of weaning played a major rôle in his phantasies. He had been abruptly weaned and he wants to do the same to others. He wants to cut off the breasts or the symbolical substitutes (penis, feet, everything paired, such as the ears, etc.). He wants to ape what was done to him.

We come again upon the castration complex. He tears a branch out with his left hand, his own penis from the tree of life. He rips his own sexuality out of his body. He always fears that his penis might be caught and cut off in a woman; she might bite it off. He gladly castrates himself, since he wants to have nothing to do with women and visits a brothel only under pressure and even then cannot effect anything. In order to execute this auto-castration, he needs such strength as will command universal attention and wonder. He wants to become a saint, like St. Francis. The apparently innocent word Frances contains a direct indication of his foot fetishism. He is a Franciscan, a Minorite, a begging monk who wanders barefoot from land to land and extols the virtues of poverty and chastity. That is why the dream takes place in the Tyrol, the land of the pious peasants. The road to heaven is a steep one and he has to drag the three conscious sins (the sinful truck) along with him. In addition to this, a fourth one, his worst and most difficult one: the auto. He sees the threatening burden bear down upon him. That's what will happen to you if you but leave the straight and narrow path. You'll come down more and more. You're not a human; you're an animal, an ape.

Above the entire dream there hangs the powerful anxiety. He is also the three persons in one: himself, his unconscious brother and his parapathia along with the female (castrated) component in him, the Franciscan. He feels that he must climb the heights, however, and overcome everything. He is fearful lest he fail to achieve his goal. He is afraid that he might fall to the bottom and lose his eternal bliss.

The polar tension between the conscious and subconscious tendencies which drive him into the drama of this paraphilia can best be perceived when we remember that in conscious activity he is a freethinker who hates monks and nuns (he could tear them to pieces) and chooses to read books which undermine religion (*La folie de Jésus*).

There follow three dreams which he dreamed in one night.

I had an old jacket and some old cloths in a box, but when I opened the box, it was full of red splinters and sawdust which represented a part of the cross and the blood of Christ. I was then able to close the box only with great difficulty and my right thumb and index finger were bloody. I became greatly frightened and had much trouble in washing the blood away.

Papa, my brother and I wanted to ride from Pest to Vienna in the Orient Express. We spoke with the conductor and ordered three seats. I said I'll sleep with papa and brother can sleep alone.

My friend M. telephoned me that I would be advised about the monotelephone.

The word monotelephone is another clever disguise for masturbation. One should read the dreams backwards. He must masturbate and has been told by M. how detrimental it is.

He is to die. He orders the seats from the conductor (usually the figure of death). *He sleeps* with father. His brother, who is a Don Juan, doesn't belong to father after whose death he, Beta, remained chaste for a year. He here atones for an old sin. He sinned grievously against his father (see the dream of the wooden image of Christ).

Blood sticks to his fingers. The blood of Christ. He can't wash it away. It is strange, however, that the cross which now enters his mind has a curious form. It consists of four hemispheres which are connected by cross-bars. From this cross he wanders to the image of four cups—hemispheres—filled with blood. Blood and milk. He drinks the blood of Christ. The Orient Express is also a leader to the Christ neurosis. As I have already explained, he vacillated between two extremes: Christ and Antichrist (Satan).

Masturbation was also the atonement and expiation of his desperate ideas of murder. Blood sticks to his fingers.[5] He would like to cleanse himself and become a saint. When he heard that onanism was detrimental to his health, he continued it in order thus to punish himself and finally kill himself. Then the semen (symbolical substitute for blood) stuck to his fingers. The box is Pandora's box. All his pleasures and desires flowed from the box that could not be shut.

All three dreams deal with his onanism. The fingers defiled with semen (self-pollution), the express train and the monotele-phone are but three variants of the same theme: masturbation. The old cloths refer to the handkerchiefs he used when mas-turbating.

The conductor leads the way across the viaduct of the dead to his death wishes. Everybody will die (sleep). He alone (monotelephone) will remain. The jacket leads to murder and blood phantasies via Jack the Ripper. He opened the box with bloody things with the aid of a knife (memory of ripped-up dolls filled with sawdust).

Most important of all: He is a woman and no man. He has a jacket and a box.[6] He is menstruating. He sleeps with papa, just as that Englishwoman did. He has a telephone with a re-ceiver. This phantasy also illuminates his position when mas-turbating. He must always lie supine otherwise he never ex-periences any satisfaction. He repressed his sadistic murder im-pulses as too male. As a female he could be passive and masochis-tic. He could suffer. This phantasy leads directly to the wish to be a woman, Christ nailed to the cross. His pet phantasy is that he is nailed (possessed).

The masturbation (mono) enables him to retain his feminine phantasies stubbornly. He is male on the right side and uses his left side. His phantasies during masturbation are distinctly bisexual and even in the next dream, we shall see that he is the horse and the rider in one.

He masturbates only with his left hand (he is left-handed), and we may recall that in the previous dream, he had torn out the tree branch with his left hand.

The most significant (functional) meaning of the dream is that the jacket and the old rags which he has hidden in a box, repre-sent his old piety, inculcated by that clerical tutor he had; the priest who had told him a lot of tales about the miracles worked by the blood of Christ. He has lost his belief, however. The warm and well-fitting jacket of devotion is gone. Only worthless remnants of Christ are left; sawdust. In another dream, he had cut something out of the wooden image of Christ. He had destroyed the holy image. And now the blood of his deed sticks to his fingers. He has turned against his religion.

He wants to be pious. He wants to leave Pest (pestilential sin) and go to his father, i.e., to his father in heaven. He will be advised—by God. He is the one and only, a chosen man, a part of Christ himself (monos). He awaits the miracle of enlightenment. He would like to experience such miracles as his tutor had related to him.

In vain will we search for traces of his paraphilia in his dreams. Only seldom does one hear of sexual pictures and never does he dream of naked men with sweaty feet. Consciously he is a paraphilic, but unconsciously he is a hypocrite.

Still another onanistic dream of Mr. Beta.

My brother, a riding master, and I had a ride in the Prater with a stable boy. The riding master and I were ahead and he thought I had better gallop ahead a little, but not too fast because otherwise the other horses would rush after. I did as he asked, but my horse, called Nana, crowded me somewhat, and I played with the reins as if they were elastic, pulling on them until I would bend far backwards and twice, I think, my knees went up and I nearly rolled over backwards. A little anxiety.

Again we have four persons. This is a death ride. The father died first, as we know, and advised his son not to ruin his life. His horse is called Nana—Oh, Nana—onanism. He plays with the elastic reins (his penis) and goes through the well known motions. He masturbates too much and will die as a result.

He will die first—gallop ahead. The horse is also a memory of the successor of his wet-nurse, a child's maid who played with his penis. After he was weaned, he was quite incorrigible and this nurse-maid quieted him by this new form of gratification. It is this same old infantile delight that he still seeks. He would like to have this form of affection from everybody and also desired it of his father.

Still more important is the functional significance of the dream. We have again the anxious emotion and the fear is that he might fall. His riding master teaches him how not to spend his life and not to ride too fast. But Nana crowds him. Nana is the well-known courtesan made immortal by Emile Zola. He is afraid the sorceress could catch him. He's not safe in the saddle and the reins are elastic. Horses are symbolic of passions. Will he be able to rein in his impulses?

In this dream, too, we miss any sign of feet or any indication of his perversions, but we do see the anxiety of woman (Nana) which plays such a leading rôle in his paraphilia.

The next dream:

I travelled with my brother to Reichenberg and there we looked for the station. Everything was German. We finally found the railway station, but there were no tracks. They were one floor higher. My brother wanted to go up in the elevator, but the machine stuck between the floors of the station and my brother jumped off. Then some porter or other went up and we were told that the railway formerly passed through the valley until the "great misfortune" occurred.

We shall try to follow the thoughts of the dreamer himself in analyzing this dream, reserving our interpretation for the last. He is struck first by the fact that Reichenberg is mentioned in the dream and this reminds him of a singer named Reichberg who died in an asylum of paresis. He had apparently had syphilis, just like another singer, G., and the poet Lenau. But Reichberg also means the fertile hill, the breast, the milk-laden udder of the cow. "I was always impressed," he said, "by Homer's use of the expression 'the udder of the earth.' I often used the expression myself many times a day. That makes me think of another hill, too: the mons veneris. And now another singer comes to my mind, that poor and tragic Reichenmann who died so young. Don't you think it's surely untrue that he was a homosexual? Reichberg is the opposite of Armental (rich hill—poor valley. Trans.) and that makes me think of an opera in which the lately deceased bass Hesch used to sing the rôle of D'Armental. Poor Hesch! He too died so young. I like all bass singers."

He also likes the expression "feet forward," [7] and thus reveals his real passion, his foot fetishism. Bass also calls the French word bas to his mind and that leads him again to foot. Every hill (Berg in German) has a foot, at the foot of the hill. And then from Reichenberg he passes to Reichmann, a certain Hermann whose feet attracted him when he was a child. He was only a very young boy and was greatly impressed whenever he saw the slightly older Hermann walking about the courtyard of the house with bare feet.

At this point his associations pass from the city of Reichenberg and we observe that his thoughts turn to certain bodily symbols. Behind Reichenberg there lurks the shadow of an important figure of his youth.

After a short pause, he comes to the statement in the dream: "and we looked for the railway station." He tells me that as a child he was in the habit of turning all words about. The German word Bahn (railway) thus made Nab and that leads him to navel. He feels certain that the railway represented the navel in this dream. Suddenly he thinks of the moon, and then recalls that the dream must have taken place under the light of the moon. The moon is a celestial station. The railway station was the navel. Yesterday he suffered an attack of anxiety while passing the hotel Oesterreichischer Hof and now recalls that his mother once lived there. His attack of fear is explained by associations which lead to the deepest factor of his paraphilia. The hotel is identified with the figure of his mother who lived there. "The other side of the station" (a statement in the dream) indicates the phantasies of his mother's womb which are so characteristic of him. The other side of the station (or navel) was where he also once lived. Via navel, tunnel, hall, dirt, he passes to divers railroad symbols. Trains come and go in the station. He recalls his onanism. Machine is also the French word for penis. Il a gaté sa machine. He has ruined his phallus. He is impotent. He recalls seeing a train stop in the middle of an open field once because the machine (the locomotive) had broken down. Masturbation has also ruined his machine. The prepuce is for him a symbolic expression of the hall of a railway station where trains move in and out. He is also subject to a definite form of anxiety, viz., that he may rub off his prepuce while masturbating. During coitus, too, he desires to leave the foreskin out, as if the phallus were a child which had to be kept in a protected place (symbolization of his phantasies of the mother's womb in the form of the phallus).

The day before, I had advised him to go out despite his great anxiety, and this he was able to carry out with the aid of the analysis he had already undergone. Again he had an attack of fear before the hotel Oesterreichischer Hof, and we see how correct Freud's rule is that a patient with an anxiety neurosis must always be forced into the situation which provokes anxiety. The phobia is a kind of mental moat, a protective wall of unconscious notions which the patient does not wish to give up or reveal.

Walking in this case has the effect of producing anxiety and the psychoanalytical examination of this emotion affords us a better understanding of the elements of the mental structure. At this moment, the patient produces an association which is of great significance. He says: "The smaller the room, the more comfortable I feel. I now know why. Because I have a covering for my head. The larger the space I am in, the more unpleasant I feel, especially if there is no roof or ceiling above me." We note here the classical identification with his attitude towards his phallus (the protective covering, the foreskin that dare not be pulled back because he will become anxious). What he feels in respect of his penis, he feels regarding his whole person. He likes it in the toilet best of all, because the room is small and has a low ceiling. That is also the room which interests him most of all in the house and the place where he often spends the most time (a very frequent occurrence with parapathics who suffer from phantasies of the mother's body).

The initiated reader will recognize that this clearly depicts the maternal womb phantasies which appeared in the form of the hotel scene. We now understand what he meant by "the great misfortune" which he mentioned at the end of his dream. It was his "great misfortune" to lose his mother at birth. He was the cause of her death and in his phantasy, returning to his mother's womb means, symbolically, going to the grave. The grave is a small and well-covered place. Some of his masochistic ideas, such as being unrighteously sentenced to a cell, also derive from these phantasies of a small and narrow space.

The anxiety he produces on the street is intimately connected with the act of walking. The "act" of walking reminds him of the sexual act. As a boy, he used to masturbate while walking, by rubbing his penis against his pants. That was also why he usually walked in a pigeon-toed fashion. (This manner of walking has been completely changed during the course of the analysis. He now points his toes outwards, as most people do [8]).

His anxiety is a fear of walking in the street. Mother Earth symbolizes his real mother and the walking thus indicates for him the accomplishment of an incestuous sexual act.

There is, however, still another parallelism between walking and erotism. He is not able to effect immissio penis, no matter how great his erection is at the time. The phallus collapses immediately. To-day he has captured the solution. "I should be tickled that I have got out of a woman alive. It would be foolish to try to get back in again." As he had learned later in life, there had been some talk at his birth of sacrificing him for the sake of his mother. But he is now really happy that they did not choose him for the sacrifice and is therefore actually thankful to all doctors for his being alive. After all, it would have been so easy. He thus denies any desire to get back to woman or even to go to heaven (this is, of course, just stage play on his part). He recalls a humorous verse he read recently in the *Fliegende Blaetter* wherein a child is supposed to pray for piety in order to get to heaven, but instead, says that it just came from there and doesn't want to get back.

Long pause. Then he remembers that as a young boy he wrote a little fairy tale about a fairy which changed itself to a hill (mons veneris?) and then fell apart again. The knight who saved her received such a munificent reward from her that he was able to marry her. This fantasy is a new lead for us. The figure of the fairy is first transformed to the mother and then to a governess who is, in reality, identified with the mother. Moreover, both these women had once lived together in that hotel Oesterreichischer Hof. From the psychoanalytical point of view, therefore, these first literary attempts are significant. Such products invariably contain the nucleus of the child's uneliminated psychic conflict and represent a sublimated attempt to digest the situation (Cf. my monograph "Dichtung und Neurose," J. F. Bergmann, 1909).

The governess represented mother to him, taught him how to pray and to say the Ave Maria. He was particularly impressed with that part of it which said: blessed be the fruit of thy body. For months and months he continued to turn over in his mind the question as to what that could be: the fruit of thy body. How did the fruit get in there? How did it come back out again? Could it be through the anus? From here he returns to his ideas about toilets and small spaces. In large rooms or spaces, he is afraid of tentacles that might reach out from the walls or ceiling and envelop him. He thinks of the houses along the street as immense women who could seize upon him. A part of his anxiety on the street is, however, ultimately a fear of prostitutes. Each house is to him a female.[9] Policemen are the tentacles of the law. In Reichenberg, the policemen are going to wear speared helmets as they do in Prussia. The helmets remind him again of the breasts—the cups—the pox—and from there he goes back again to lues and the ideas of infection he expressed at the outset of the dream as corroborated in the persons of Reichberg, G. and Lenau. The helmet also recalls to him an infantile sexual theory which has to do with being born in a hood. It is interesting in this respect that he always holds his hat on his head whenever he is seized by an attack of anxiety, as if the labor of the wind (birth labor) could blow it from him. In short, he could lose his magic hood. He expresses the infantile sexual theory that children are first laid as eggs and then appear in a skin (or amnion).[10] His foreskin is even now a representative of the amnion and at every coitus he thus repeats the act of birth.

From Reichenberg and helmet his associations travel over Prussia to Germany. Germany reminds him of the so-called German vice (le vice allemand, i.e., homosexuality). He flees from the female to the male. Coitus is a dangerous path which leads to woman, whereas the noble affection for a man preserves life. Other important relations are touched upon in this respect which may be due to the fact that his mother was a German whereas his father was an Austrian.

The first part of his dream thus means as much as: I have always been searching for the man but have invariably found the woman. His fear of syphilitic infection had a great deal to do with this attitude, of course.

Proceeding, we come to the analysis of the dream statement: "And then we found the station, but there were no tracks." This makes him think of a joke he once heard about a man who was sitting opposite a woman in the train coupé who had her legs crossed in such a fashion that one could see rather far up them. "What fine rails you have there," he said. She demanded a certain sum of money for the privilege of viewing the station to which the rails led, but he felt the fare was too high. He claimed that he could show her the station master standing at attention with a red cap on for less than half the price.

The rails are thus the road to woman, the road which he cannot find despite all his searching and seeking, simply because of his homosexuality. And now we come to that peculiar manifestation of the dream viz., the necessity for going up to the first floor of the station in order to find the tracks. He promptly associates the first year of life to the first floor. One must get as far back as the first year of life in the analysis in order to find the right track (the first floor is thus also the nurse's breast). There is still another interpretation which approximates the approach of Scherner. If the vagina is the mezzanine, then the navel is a

floor above it. Here the word navel reminds him of Naples, and
he recalls the adage: Vede Napoli e poi mori (See Naples and
then die).

He produces still another infantile sexual theory which derives
from these associations. "I thought," he says, "that babies came
out through the umbilicus." He is constantly plagued by the fear
that he may burst open at the navel, he permits no one to touch
him in that region. As a boy he did not believe that he was a
boy, but a girl, and that the female differs from the male only in
having a somewhat larger belly button. His navel was thus his
vagina. Later he believed that he was hermaphroditic. His persistent disorientation in respect of the female body, on which he
can never find the foramen vaginæ without the woman's aid, is
due to his chronic confusion of the vagina and the navel. He
always climbs a floor too high. His further associations led to
the wet-nurse who lifted him ("elevator") still another story
higher.

Strangely enough, and contrary to his feelings about the nurse,
he abhors elevators and suffers from the fear that they might
get stuck between floors and prevent his escape. We see in this
a revamping of his agoraphobia: he gets stuck on the street and
can't move further. The same is true of his heterosexual relations: his penis might get stuck in the vagina and he would lose
it; he would be caught in the caverns of the mother's body and
wouldn't be able to escape. Or the phantasy: he has committed a
homosexual act or has been unjustly accused of having committed
such an act and has been *locked* up.

He feels that his greatest despair would be to find himself
locked out on an open balcony with no covering above and a drop
below. This leads us back to the above-mentioned nurse complex.
There creeps through his memory a dim flicker of having been
dropped by his wet-nurse. The balcony, which is the most universal symbol of the nursing breast, accurately portrays the child's
position on the arm of the nurse: uncovered above and a drop
below. He was always breathlessly afraid of being swung and
lifted as a baby and felt best when safely tucked away in his
carriage or crib. He always preferred a bed with a canopy and
feels that every house is a woman. Comes again to the fear that
every house might reach down and swing him into the air. He
never shows any anxiety in the garden or on the street or if he
gets into a wagon or a car because the carriage symbolizes for
him the comfort and security of the baby carriage. He always

wants to feel his feet on the earth and finds that he cannot walk because that necessitates his lifting his feet. He thinks of an illustration he once saw in the *Fliegende Blaetter* in which the houses were all represented as humans. The houses are constant recollections of the "terrible" people who always swung him into the air. The elevator reminds him of his nurse because she always elevated him (lifted him) to the breast. It was in a lift that he experienced his first attack of anxiety.

Now he first feels certain that some woman had dropped him. Probably his governess. The "great misfortune" is thus not only the death of his mother, but also his "own fall." The word fall reminds him of the fall of Eve—omphale and phallus; then again to the fall on the street. He is especially anxious when the wind is blowing (he was also nearly blown out at birth). He recollects a picture from *Struwelpeter* (a German fable) in which the wind carries off a child.[11] He was greatly impressed by Rembrandt's Ganymede in which the seizure of a child and its flight through the air are depicted. The wind can lift one up just like the houses on the street, and there is such a thing as "the bride of the wind." We begin to see the connections ever more clearly. Throughout childhood, he was constantly in fear of being picked up and that is a reason for his appreciation of big feet. They stand solidly on the ground. He is also frightened by boat rides because the rocking of the boat on the waves reminds him of being rocked in his nurse's arms. He is also then forced to retire to the "narrow cabin" where only resting in the bed or bunk will quiet his nerves. He also abhors the idea of going up in a balloon or airplane. When Bleriot went up in his airplane, our patient was afraid that the flier was going to fall on his head. He says that he would jump out of any balloon he got into, just as his brother jumped out in the dream. He would not be in the least ashamed although he shamed himself whenever his governess was tender with him on the street. She always used to kiss him and people would laugh at him. That is also why he is able to go through the streets at night without fear, he is not able to see anyone laughing at him. Once when he was twelve years old, his governess awaited him at the school and kissed him when he came out. He fell into a bit of anger. He doesn't want to be a baby forever. He wants to stand on his own feet. He even learned to dance recently in order that he might mix more socially. This reminds him of the fact that his governess would always dance about with children in order to quiet them. He suddenly recalls being caught in an elevator in Reichenhall (a well-known German resort—Trans.) and almost being squeezed to death. That leads to a new anxiety, viz., his fear that his chest will be crushed. He even knows the basis for this particular anxiety, the infantile source of the phobia. His governess used to crush him to her breast and say: "Oh, I'll crush you to death, I'll just eat you up." The scene in the elevator in Reichenhall [12] happened in this wise: the elevator boy jumped out at a floor and he tried to jump after him while his father and brother stayed in to ride on up.

This incident represents another significant complex to us. He wants to have come out of the mother's womb before his brother and he manifestly envies his brother having been born first. The phantasy of the mother's womb thus again plays an important rôle in this mechanism. There is also another basis for the incident: father and brother can die (be carried off), but I'm going to save myself. He now recalls an experience from his fifth year: his father and brother were riding in an elevator which got stuck between two floors and he himself stood below and yelled insanely that father better look out, he could be crushed or pressed to death. He likes to ride in ex*press* trains, especially in the direction of *Press*burg. Sailors interest him because, as he hints, they are "pressed" into service. He always reads the *Neue Freie Presse* (a leading Viennese daily—Trans.) and finds it a good paper, whereas the Old Press did not satisfy him. He likes to watch wine pressing because it is still done with naked feet. He is more anxious than otherwise at the end of a walk or errand because he is "pressed" and he associates that masturbation also occurs by his pressing his penis. He likes to see soldiers who appear as if they had been compressed into their uniforms. "Pedem (or passum) premere" is the Latin expression for walking fast. Whenever he watches the review of cavalry, he looks for the boots of the leader because his feet are tightly pressed into them. He is thoroughly gratified libidinously if he has to press hard at defecation.

Whenever he has been examined by a physician, he has always emphasized to the doctor that he should not touch his navel as otherwise he might die.[13] This analysis thus shows us how far-reaching are the thought processes and associations which determine an apparently harmless dream picture and what widespread connections with it are set up. I have purposely gone into details (although not the exhaustive details) of this dream in order to show that the simple translation of dream material into the language of psychoanalysis is in itself not enough. The most important part of the solution comes from the dreamer himself.

We begin to see that the repressed wish may be formulated about as follows: If only my father and brother had died there in Reichenhall, just as my mother died when I was born. I would then be independent in this world. That is, in fact, one of his dearest desires. He wants to be the only pebble on the beach. He would like to see everybody die out. He would see a great misfortune strike the world, but leave him unscathed. He, the small, scared, bashful, anxious and oppressed patient would then be the One and Only.

We also learn what significance was attained by the infantile impressions of being swung and lifted through the air as regards the development of his anxiety. The governesses and other educing adults are indicated in the dream in the form of the "servants."

The matter of the servants then led to a still further association of importance. One of them was a kindergarten teacher from Prussia by the name of Deutsch (the word German in previous associations). She was called La Prussienne in the house. He comes back to the associations of Deutsch (German) with the German vice and Prussian helmets. He then brings forth the memory of another childhood experience from the deepest infantile level. The nurse carried him in her arms up to the first floor of the house where he involuntarily became the witness of a rather undisguised erotic scene between herself and a strange man. That was also a "great misfortune." He remembered an exhibitionistic act on the part of the man.

We now have an understanding of the dream. His brother is the penis that wants to jump out (before him). He once got a box on the ear from his father because as a little boy he wanted to take out his penis on the street and walk around with it hanging out. Now he has developed the lustful phantasy of walking about the main streets of Vienna with bare feet and great toes showing. His exhibitionistic tendencies have been displaced downwards.

Finally, his agoraphobia has been demasked and we see that it is but his anxiety of his own impulses. He would like best of all to open his trousers and walk about with his phallus hanging out, but he is afraid that he might actually do this in an insane moment (the insanity of Lenau, the institution at Reichenberg). That is why he would like to be insane, just for the pleasurable moment of gratifying his exhibitionism. The Hotel Oesterreichi-

scher Hof, before which he suffered an attack of fear, faces the
Old *Meat* Market. He would like to open up his meat stall. And
why? Because he is always reproducing the scene of his birth.
The phallus is the fassimile of the child. It is to be born without
accident. That is, he identifies himself with his mother and his
penis with himself, his mother's child. One of the two must
be sacrificed, either the mother or the child. The first idea is
emotionally represented by the castration phantasies and the second
by the fear of death. When a man takes his foot out of a shoe,
it is for him a symbol of birth. The great toe is the symbol
of the dirty, compressed and red child.

The attack of anxiety, however, plays the same scene except in
a displacement upwards. He is afraid that his hat might fly away
and convulsively holds it fast to his head. He is afraid to uncover his head, i.e., the head of his phallus.

The trains now travel up above. Everything takes place either
above (in the head) or below (the feet). Formerly, the masturbation took place below and it was while everything travelled
below that the "great misfortune" of the box on the ear took
place which he has not yet forgotten.

The causal scene here becomes more and more clear cut in his
memory. He was bathing with his older brother and they had
been playing with their genitals when their governess broke into
the room and threatened them with the direst punishment. They
would have their pipi cut off if they didn't stop. They would
get a "terrible disease" from such playing. Finally, he even got
a box on the ear from father. He himself had been the prompter
in playing with their genitals. His brother got off with a sermon.

In the dream, the railway is the onanism. He made a train
out of his phallus and ruined his machine by overwork. He must
die. He can still hear the horrible warning of his governess: "If
you don't stop playing with your pipi, it'll fall off and you'll die."
Then there was the trauma of that clap on the ear which was
truly a trauma for him because he had never before been punished.
He was unconscionably proud and sensitive.

His thirst for revenge and insatiable hate date from this experience. The true phantasy is that father and brother (the latter
derided him because of the box on the ear) should die. In order
to realize this wish, he makes use of the railway and the elevator in
the dream (he reproduces the dream elements of the elevator in
his own parapathia in that he cannot bring himself to get stuck
in a woman's vagina). He also presents his brother with a syphilis

in the dream from which he will soon die. Why? Because his brother is wealthy (Reichenberg) and he wants to inherit his money. The hill (his fable) should crumble apart and he should collect all the riches.

That is why he desires to be a woman. A woman cannot lose her pipi, it cannot fall off her, she does not sin, she is passive. He wants to be a woman, a saint, and thus triumph over his father. High above, in the eternal fields, he will be the conqueror and to that end he must be ascetic. He is not deserving of the enjoyments of life, especially because, in his heart, he has been a murderer. The railway and the lift were to have killed his father and brother and the governess to the end that he might have masturbated without interference. The railway and the elevator are thus death symbols here.

Finally, the dreamer considers the whole thing and says: "This picture represents a sort of cross-section. It expresses my ambivalent nature: half man, half woman. I masturbate as if I were a woman, and the most important thing, I think, is the fact that walking in the street alone also means masturbation to me. I am ashamed to be seen in the street because I have a feeling that everybody can see in my face that I have masturbated. That is why I desire always to be alone. I would like to see the whole world crumble and disappear and then I could exploit my pleasures without shame or fear. That is what I call my "psychic anarchism." [14]

This dream has demonstrated to us the sexual meaning of walking and also the divers uses which the foot has found in his phantasies. His anxiety in walking is anxiety of woman and his foot fetishism is a protection from woman. In his asceticism, he assures himself a final triumph over his brother. His fetishism also aids him in persevering in his asceticism. The foot admonishes him of his birth, of his sins, of the fact that he is a pious pilgrim, a Franciscan.

There then follow seven dreams. .

1. A very handsome young man was telling me and all the gentlemen and ladies that he was quite healthy except that he had sweaty feet. There was nothing to do about it because it was a disease he had inherited from his father and grandfather.

2. I went down into a valley and saw a sailor disappear into a country house. I searched for him, but didn't find him any more.

3. Papa, my brother, a certain Mr. F. and myself played bil-

liards. I played the balls as if I were playing golf, however, and continued a try until I had made a good shot. Then everybody was sitting down; Mr. F. ate up the contents of two cans of sardines and said that at midnight he was going to eat at a friend of his whom he liked a great deal, despite the fact that the friend had said: "I am a Christian Socialist."

Then father was suddenly taken deathly ill with some heart condition and they bought only half of the evening edition of the *Neue Freie Presse*, which I read. They said that he dare not move and that the whole paper would kill him. Then I saw that there was the entire first afternoon edition there and I thought: how can that be that father should die a second time after he has already died once.

4. I threw my watch to the floor, but it didn't break. Only the case sprang open.

5. An economist by the name of Christians and some fat man and myself were together in a small room. Christians had said: "We'll play the following game." He would bathe first and then would come I and then, if there were still another bathroom left, the fat man. He bathed in a single bathroom, but the one I used was for four people. The fat man left because there were no other bath rooms. Christians attracted me considerably. We were both naked and I wondered that he was larger than myself. Then my brother came along and asked me what I was doing and whether I hadn't seen his penis. "Not even so much," I said, and pointed to a part of my finger.

6. A woman with a staff or a phallus in her hand is bending over a child (Jesus?) in a cradle.

7. I wanted to go into the mausoleum at the Central Cemetery, but it gave me the shivers and an angel barred the way.

The first dream plainly emphasizes the foot fetishism which characterizes our patient. He is the "handsome young man" who feels himself completely healthy with exception of his sweaty-feet fetishism which is here represented by its own symbol. His first nursemaid suffered from perspiration of the feet and now he has repressed the contact and has a great disgust. He is, however, attracted by a livid or warm foot. We are also reminded of the second meaning of sweat in his mind, i.e., blood. A bloody foot and a foot covered with filth (wading in muck) play a leading part in his phantasies. Another meaning of this dream is: his guilt smells to heaven. All his personal blame in the matter is here displaced to his father and grandfather and comes to him only via heredity. Later we shall become acquainted with still another meaning of the dream which has to do with the fact that he also inherited quite a fortune from his grandfather and father.

The second dream refers to the serious trauma of his life. The sailor (his father, the master) used to visit a peasant (the Englishwoman in the country) every night. He has repressed this occurrence because he did not want to see it. The dream fulfills his desire; he searches (for the memory), but does not find it any more. In this second dream, also, his father dies again, disappears into the grave where he can no longer be found. The third dream is of fundamental significance in this series. His father is alive again, has been resurrected, and the patient wonders at this. A great miracle has occurred. Father has died twice. This second death is of great importance because, as we know, his father had not actually died within him. He was still the master over our patient's destiny. But now—and that is the wonder—Beta has become free, only now has his father actually died. In this we observe the weighty problem of the death of already deceased persons. Th second death is an expression of the dreamer's wish to eliminate them and actually know them to be among the dead.

The game with the billiard balls has a meaning of its own. He thinks first of flat feet and then of football. The ball of the foot is what interests him. He alleges that he is disgusted by feet with corns which he also calls balls.[15] But even other kinds of balls attracted his attention, e.g., the breasts. Golf reminds him of gulf and he thinks of the Latin name for gulf which is also the name for breasts or bay (sinus). His foot fetishism is also a displacement from above downwards. The balls of the feet represent both breasts. Mr. F. represents his father, F. is the "real anal erotic" as he calls him because his mouth is so full of blasphemy. These blasphemies are closely connected with the dream material, but I cannot take the trouble to follow this thread now.

His two delineations of father (Faustand Mephisto) are here indicated by the father and Mr. F. Father has two mistresses, the child's maid, i.e., the country house, and the Englishwoman. They are portrayed as cans without a head (tail). His association on sardine is Piedmont which easily resolves itself into piedmont, i.e., foot of the hill (see the dream about Reichenberg). We see that the dreamer goes to the bottom of the valley in the second dream, i.e., down to the foot of the hill. What the mean-

ing of this passage is we shall presently learn. Mr. F. is to visit
a friend of his who is a Christian Socialist for a midnight supper
(one of the political parties in Germany and Austria.—Trans.).
That is, this is the holy supper which Greek Catholics take after
midnight. The friend's name is Carpenter and immediately Beta
thinks of the son of a carpenter—Christ (the name in German
would be Zimmermann which thus would permit of the further
distortion to Frauenzimmermann—a not unusual pun on a common German name—indicating the figure of a Don Juan or a man
who loves the ladies). Father should turn Christian and become devout. The other determinant is: father should turn to
him (Christ).

This defines the real conflict of his life. As I have already
mentioned above, Beta's father and grandfather were confirmed
liberals, never prayed and never went to church. His own first
tutor was a fanatic clerical, however, and inculcated a point of
view into him which now makes him look upon the heritage of his
parental line as a stigma. He has inherited liberalism, i.e., heath-
enism from them. Externally playing the rôle of the freethinker,
he is inwardly a most pious clerical (i.e., Christian Socialist).

"Suddenly father was deathly ill from some heart disease."
Agnosticism was what had been gnawing at his heart and it was
high time that he should be proselyted and saved. That was why
he dared not read that "Jewish sheet" the *Neue Freie Presse*.
That is why only half of the paper, i.e., the "Press," as the conservative and almost clerical forerunner of the *Neue Freie Presse*
had been called, was permissible. The allusion to the paper is
also another indication of the female question. The free press
(the libertine which blackmails), a prostitute. The half press, a
demi-monde. A full-blooded paper might be detrimental to his
health. Furthermore, he doesn't want father to marry again or
have anything to do with "whole," i.e., with full-blooded women.
"Half the evening edition" leads to thoughts of the "holy supper,"
but "the first afternoon edition" was not susceptible of solution.
Probably an allusion to some scene between father and a nursemaid.

The fourth dream shows the watch as the representative of the
heart. His heart (the father) will not die. He throws it to the
floor, but it does not break. He only notes what time has been
struck (the watch sprang open). His father struck him after that
first scene. The opening of the case indicates the resurrection of
the dead, their release from the tomb.

The fifth dream appears to be the keystone of a series of dreams including some of the earlier ones. The analysis of this dream lasted about ten hours and I have set down only the net results. In respect of the economist, he thought of his brother, but there were no associations on the baths until I insisted that the dream must have some relationships with his religious complex. He denied this but soon came upon allusions to his own economy, his desire for money, the need for living economically. Further associations led to Aaron and the golden calf.

These disparaging ideas are apparently directed at the fat man who seems to be the imago of his father, despite the fact that he looked in the dream more like a common, ordinary cab driver. He also stood there as if stone dead, a description which fits well since his father is actually dead. (Coachman or driver also indicates the leader or driver of the family, i.e., the father. A coach indicates a pair, i.e., marriage.) He now thinks that it wasn't really a bath, but only a shower, they only wet their heads. Finally, he thinks that the economist was a man who suffered from a chronic eczema and that instead of economist it should be ecce homo. Aaron—John—Ko—Kohn and Christ. The bathing means baptismal (John the Baptist). Christ was the first to be baptized. He is the One and Only (see monos—monotheist). Beta had for some time considered whether he should have himself baptized or not and envied the courage of Constantine the Great who had himself baptized on his death bed and was thus able to enter heaven "pure" and enjoy eternal bliss (he calls his friend Kohn constant Ko). That "horrid fat man" rejected baptismal and the baptists and thus lost his chance of going to heaven.

The most important factor in the dream is, however, that the economist animated him sexually. We also begin to understand his brother's question as to whether he had seen his (the brother's) phallus or not. Christ was the patient's first religious and sexual ideal. The sweaty feet are the blood-stained feet of the son of God.

The patient's sins, however, are much, much greater than this. For a time during childhood, he had suffered from the grandiose delusion that he, too, was a son of God. He thought himself a sort of Christ, and the family was the holy family. Father was God, brother was the Holy Ghost, and he himself was the "Son of God." That is why he is surprised to find in the dream that Christ is larger than he is. He is the savior. He is atoning for the sins of his father and has nailed himself to the cross of his parapathia. His chief sin was that he had made an erotic ideal of his religious God. As a boy he had felt frustrated by the fact that Christ always wore a loin-cloth. Another sin was that he had once wanted to see his father's phallus and had asked his father to show him his "pipi." What he got was a beating, and that is what the brother's question in the dream really refers to.

The following day, he dreamed a variation on this theme—the sixth dream. He described the woman as follows: a heavy, common person, avaricious, lewd, repulsive; a cook who was the apotheosis of all the worst memories of his childhood. The bisexual character of the dreamer also becomes noticeable. The chief consideration here is that his father (the fat man of the fifth dream) has been represented as an old woman. He is the little Jesus. His father prevents him from masturbating.

In the last dream, he is seized with regret for having so calumniated his father. He wants to climb into his father's tomb.[16] Ideas of suicide. An angel (his physician) prevents him from the execution of the notions. The angel reminds him of a picture of the resurrection of Christ. This was also effected in the third dream (the miracle or wonder expressed as wondering). The springing open of the watch case is the opening of the door of the tomb when Christ was resurrected. The angel is also the angel with the fiery sword who drove the sinners out of paradise. We then realize that the deepest cause of his impotence is his feeling that he is unworthy of the possession of a woman. The angel drives him out of paradise (the cemetery—the tomb—the vagina). He shudders before woman who personifies sin in his mind. Every time he tried to enter the vagina, his phallus collapsed. Between him and woman stand death and sin.

He dreams of resurrection. That is the great miracle. He really awaits the renaissance of his potency. His phallus is to be resurrected. His member is his divinity. His true God is dead; he can neither pray nor believe—nor even possess a woman.

The second dream reviews the death of his father and the loss of his potency. He no longer possesses a phallus; only the foot. His foot fetishism is his atonement for the alleged sins of his father and for his own waywardness. But throughout all the dreams there is a growing hope of immanent recovery. The coup succeeds. His father dies. The watch falls to the ground and an angel saves him from annihilation.

There is also another form in which his belief in his parapathia appears. He suffers from agoraphobia, but this is, in a way, his fear of the resurrected. His father might be revived and meet him on the street. The devil might come after him.

It took a year of arduous work in the analysis to dig up this long-lost religious complex of Beta's. There is hardly a para-pathia in which this complex is not to be found, regardless of how enlightened and atheistic the patients may consider them-selves. They are all believers, hypocrites in feeling. Intellectually, they have overcome their religious leanings, but their infantile effects are eternally seared into their hearts to flame up again in their darkest moments. It is the heart, unflinching child's heart which still believes when the mind has thought itself beyond all religion and piety.

This dreamer, too, who sees the Bible in place of his mother, is ostensibly a fanatical freethinker and an ardent follower of Haeckel. A "monist" of the strictest sort. But all skin deep. The religious complex usually is firmly soldered into one piece with the parent or Œdipus complex. The sins against the parents be-come the sins against God and religion.

It is astounding how frequently we meet with the Christ neu-rosis in the case of this patient. In the last series of dreams it was sufficiently indicated by the words Christian Socialist and the name Christians. In addition to this there was a hint at the child Jesus. The foot is for him a melting pot of his religious and sexual symbols. Such a consolidation is characteristic of all cases of fetishism and one can observe the same to be true if one only analyzes them with sufficient care and depth. Dream analysis is, to be sure, an art which demands perseverance and patience as well as the probing of even the most complicated ramifications in the patient's mind. These complexes are more or less dis-guised in Beta's first dreams and it is only after the analysis of the later dreams that we are able to gain insight into them. But even in them the whole problem of his parapathia was present.

It is now, towards the end of this analysis, that I wish to bring the first dream which this patient produced. Such initial dreams are very important because they generally contain the whole para-pathic problem *in nuce*.

I saw a play at the royal theatre. It seems that I was with a couple of friends (M. R. and K. R.). They played a piece with two actors. One of them was Kainz and the other Gregori (two famous Viennese actors of a generation ago—Trans.). It seems that the action took place in the middle ages, because we were all dressed in togas or things that looked like bathrobes.

Suddenly one of the actors (Gregori) talked a lot and then ran off after having spoken very loudly. The other one continued talking and then, suddenly calling out: "Now everybody must look at me!," he pulled off his toga and stood there with his trunk naked and a sort of towel about his loins.[17] The most curious thing about the whole scene was that he had a triangular piece of brown wood stuck on the end of his penis. When we saw that we were all disgusted and left the theatre. The act was over.

I also recall that someone said the next act begins in ten minutes. We took a little walk in a long street and then wanted to return for the next act.

It is difficult to convey a true impression of the amount of condensation represented in this dream. The most significant and definitive experiences of his life are reproduced in its various parts. The reader who has studied the foregoing dreams of this patient will already have recognized some of the unconscious dream motives without further analysis. Before going into the chief meaning of this dream, i.e., into the experience represented, I would like to set down at least fragmentarily some of the dream analysis.

As we already know, the play in the royal theatre indicates the family situation. He was not alone in the audience there either; there were, in addition to him, his brother, the governess and the tutor. The two actors, Kainz and Gregori, are special references to the two souls within his breast. He first saw them, too, in "Faust," when Gregori played Faust and Kainz, Mephisto. They were the incarnation of the cleavage in his soul, the devil and Faust. Gregori reminds him of the Greek word for awakening and also of Gregorius, the pillarist, of the pope Gregory, etc., etc. Kainz is also an allusion to Cain which permits of divers relationships to his brother, etc. The scene is staged in antiquity, i.e., his own early age or childhood. The actors are dressed in bathrobes, a scene which looks funny to him and somehow reminds him of the old Roman togas. Then came the curious scene with the wooden covering of the phallus, a picture which was resistive to solution for some time. The most important feature of this element is doubtless that it expresses his castration complex, one of the chief bases of his whole neurosis.

But now to the trauma which is cloaked by the dream. Once after a bath, he and his brother crept up to the room of the English governess. They were both dressed in bath robes. They dragged up a chair and then alternately climbed up on it to look

through the keyhole where they were able to observe diverse provoking scenes (coitus) in which the actors were the persons to
whom their rearing had been entrusted. Suddenly his brother
became frightened and ran away yelling. He also began to shriek,
but was so paralyzed with fright that he remained standing in
the next room. His brother had already reached the safety of
the bed before he had been able to collect himself. When he was
caught, he was soundly beaten and boxed. He remembered the
punishment for the rest of his life. That was the worst beating
of his childhood. That scene when he was caught before he
could reach the haven of safety is reproduced by him now in his
agoraphobia. It is one of the deepest roots of his anxiety. The
second meaning of the dream derives from Kainz and passes to
the theme of Cain and Abel, i.e., the murder of his brother. He
was always the cat's paw for his brother and even in this case,
he was the one who got whipped whereas his brother got off
without a scratch and laughed up his sleeve. That is the source
of all his dark hatred against his brother. Still another interpretation derives from Abel. As children, the two of them were
present at a ballet given for children called "The Sun and the
Earth." A certain Mrs. Abel played the part of the sun. She
had thin jersey tights over her naked body and for months thereafter the boys amused themselves by going around saying, "Old
Abel has no pipi, old Abel has no pipi!," i.e., she was castrated in
their eyes. But it was Beta's idea that brother also should have
no pipi. It was the aim of his sadistic desires for revenge to effect a castration of his brother.[18] The punishment for such a
desire is now his psychic impotence. Again we note the bisexual
character of this dream. The actors wore bathrobes which also
make them look like women (the clergyman's gown, robes, dressing gowns, etc., are also made use of for the same purposes in
dreams). It was also in a bath that certain homosexual scenes
took place between himself and his brother. This act he had
staged "alone" with his brother. Now he is Kainz, the man who
has nothing. He would like to be a woman. The next trauma
occurred ten years later when the English governess began to
have affairs with another of his tutors; they took place so frequently that the tutor soon had to leave the house. The last sentence about the long street in which he spends some time, the
"endlessly long trail," is a figure of the path of his life. The
wood instead of the breast. The governess was as flat as a board
where he expected her to have full, round breasts. (There is

also the board-like flap in the pants of the Styrian mountain folk, which the patient knew very well.) Another determinant derives from the wet-nurse, after whose discharge he had cried bitterly and was implacable for weeks. This is the trauma of weaning which, according to Staercke, is the apotheosis of castration.

A few months later, Mr. Beta finally brought me the concluding solution of this dream. That story about the coitus scene was right, except that it originally dealt with two other persons (the soldier and the nursemaid). It was an act of revenge that he had displaced the action to his father and the governess. The real traumatic scene had taken place as follows: After their bath, both the boys had gone to bed together and there began to play Mama and Papa. Beta was on the bottom and was pushed in the navel by his brother. Then they played all kinds of little tricks with each other. Suddenly their father appeared and gave it to both of them. Such experiences preclude the development of the individual's aggressiveness and lead to the fixation upon a female rôle in life from sheer obstinacy (Adler). Such was also the case here. He wanted to be a woman and that is why he suddenly finds himself in the dream with a piece of wood instead of a penis.

It is important that he is playing on the stage, he is an actor and is doing splendidly. He is Faust, the God seeker and Mephisto the God hater, both in one. As Mephisto he plays the fetishist, the paraphilic, the degenerate; as Faust he is the pious believer, the chosen one who yearns for salvation. The toga-like dress is his monk's garb.

And what does he make himself look like? First he prattles about piety and then we see him standing in a loin cloth. We begin to understand this figure. He is Christ. But Christ without a phallus. He wears a piece of wood as a covering for his penis and this hides and hinders its function. It is the same piece of wood he took out of himself in the first dream about the wooden idol. His Christ neurosis is a protective mechanism against his sexual activity. He wants to while away more time in the dark street of life and then return to his piety.

This is a consideration of the most fundamental of this patient's dreams. I have mentioned the trauma which was woven into the dream. The following communications are extracts from further dreams of Mr. Beta. They are instructive because they show us how significant materials return over and over again.

On the other hand, they will disclose to us divers variations of the original trauma.

The first one is a dream of his brother's.

I was supposed to appear in some vaudeville as a woman. I was horribly surprised to see myself dressed only in a bathrobe and feared that it might open and that then everybody would see me. I then sat down among the audience.

The brother, too, is a serious case of a parapathia. We see here a dream which is almost identical with the one Beta had and note how the same environment, the same mistakes in bringing up, the same trauma have been able to produce almost identical results in two different boys. We find here the vaudeville stage (Silvester Schaeffer), the bathrobes, the acting and the dread.

I was at a cinema and there we saw pictures of a glacier on which a couple and a guide were coming towards us. First came the woman, who had on a long hiking coat that looked like a bathrobe. Then came the man with a hood over his head. Suddenly the guide was no longer there and in his stead there was a cross. The cross then changed to a white ghost. I wanted to run out of the cinema, but I was suddenly frozen to the spot with the ghost coming after me. I awoke with fright.

Here we see the figures which were such good stock in other dreams. He looks into the moving picture of his own soul. He sees the glacier which is doubtless the symbol of his own icy sex‐uality. His guide is Christ himself who turns into the cross. The couple represent the two components of his own soul, the female and the male. Again we see the bathrobe and the hood, the latter indicating the hood of the monks, the Franciscan hood. The spirit of Christ chases and threatens him. He awakens in a fright that he may transgress the commandments of religion.

At the end of this dream he had a very clear-cut hypnagogic dream. I phantasy that my life should be one great expiation. First would come a public confessional in the Franciscan church and following that a protracted atonement and penance with the monks, chief among the punishments being public whippings on the cross, etc. Then I asked myself why I should want to suffer so, and my answer was that I had killed my father and mother. The first crime was forgiven but the second was not. Then I asked myself how had I wished to kill my father and the answer was that I had wished to kill him because I did not wish him to put his thing in. I recalled the scene at Aussee and heard the thundering voice of God calling: "In punishment for not having wished him to put it in, thou also shalt not be able to put it in. Thy seed shall fall fruitlessly on the ground. Thy suffering shall be the eternal lopping off of thy phallus and it shall always grow back again, an eternal torture. For thou hast the desire to cut off thy father's phallus." Whenever I was whipped thereafter, I always got an emission and the semen was left as a sacrifice on the cross. But the monks found me too evil for them and I was turned over to worse company, the soldiers. With them I went to war, came to Africa and was there captured by natives and tortured fearfully. At the last moment I was saved, but I never saw my home again. Christ appeared in the clouds and, reaching down, took me to his bosom. He is always pure and said to me: "Thou hast conquered, my son, for thou hast overcome the flesh."

This hypnagogic dream speaks such a clear and unambiguous language; it comprises all the elements of his Christ neurosis in such an unmistakably unified whole that I can doubtless spare myself the trouble of analyzing it.

All these dreams are variations on the one theme of the great traumatic scene of his early childhood. His father came upon the brothers in the bath just as they were playing with each other. That is why all the dreams reenact a play (theatre, cinema, vaudeville, cards, games, etc.). This early experience was the great misfortune of his life. Every time there arises within him a tendency to aggression, he recalls the beating he received at that time and a still, small voice says to him: "Hands off!"

The day after that scene in the bath, their father came to the boys and spoke quietly and considerately with them about the terrible consequences of masturbation. The results would be death, softening of the brain, diseases of the spinal cord, the nerves, paralyses, etc. One would then be unable to walk and would have to be pushed in a wheel chair or ride in a carriage. This sermon appears to Beta to be the most deeply impressive of his life and doubtless entered into the provocation of his agoraphobia. He cannot walk; his father's prophecy has come true.

His father was the black crow who prophesied his ill fortune. Because of this and the fact that his father was also the intruder who broke up the erotic games with his brother, Beta succumbed to the audacious ideas of revenge. This gives us an even deeper understanding of his foot fetishism. It is a pleasure and a penance in one. The fetishistic manifestations can also be determined by infantile criminal phantasies. That may perhaps be the usual mechanism behind the development of fetishism, but only more analyses of such cases can enlighten us. In Beta's case it happened as follows: After a bath, he ran about in his room barefoot. The English governess came into the room and yelled at him: "You'll catch your death of cold." Going barefoot thus took on an association with dying. His passive (criminal) wish then became a desire to see his father catch cold; that would be his revenge for the scene after the bath and the father's chastisement for his having masturbated. The wish then turned to anxiety, i.e., he could not see his dear father walking about the house without slippers. He feared that he would catch cold. Another cause of his anxiety was the notion that he could be infected by a splinter. This fear also derived from a repressed criminal desire.

His father's death was a serious trauma for him. Father had caught a cold and died as the result of pneumonia. He had been warned against his affair with that dancer, but he knew that when father would die, he would be free to do as he wished. Old death wishes arose in him anew and he desired to see his father die and liberate him. The reaction to the wish was, however, that he became anxious and feared that his father would die. We recall that after his father's death he actually threatened to take his own life, and that he swore not to have any intercourse for three years. This oath he broke, however. But, although he made attempts, they were invariably failures. His foot fetishism became progressively more marked.

We know of three sins, three burdens, which he always carried about in his soul. The death of his mother, the death of his father and—the most serious—his masturbation. These three sins he had to expiate.

He wants to castrate himself and, spiritually, has already done so. He has even played with the thought of having himself actually castrated, so that he may prevent his onanism and become a saint. His paraphilia is still further determined and directed by his castration complex as we shall see directly.

The analysis then came upon the following dream.

Although the mustache which I had was quite short, I cut it still shorter, using a scissors. Finally, it looked so short that I might just as well not have had any mustache.

He himself interpreted the dream. He wants to be a woman and have no penis. Mustache is a well-known and universal symbol for the phallus. Women fall for a fine mustache. Like a large nose, it is the sign of a large penis. (Bluebeard, the historical woman eater, was described by Grimm as a very potent man with a large, black beard.)

Beta gets a thrill from cutting his finger nails. He also dreams frequently of manicuring himself. What is the purpose of the castration? Suddenly he falls asleep during the analysis but awakens again in a few seconds. He had a curious dream-picture. He saw a man within a mandolin; but this man was himself, he finds. He sketched the picture as follows:

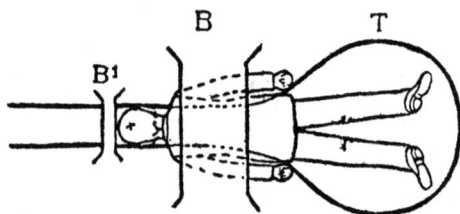

The dream is:

I stood in the round belly marked T and fell forwards through the Bridge B to the cross-board B′. I couldn't extricate myself Before that I thought of a certain man named Triasangoli who had had a fight with a porter.

On the basis of all that we have already heard, this is manifestly a phantasy of the mother's womb. Some of the parts of the dream-picture are well known to us, e.g., the bridge and the wooden board. The belly of the mandolin is his mother's belly, the bridge the vagina—the bridge to life. The cross-board blocks the way.

Mr. Beta, however, is also the man who killed his mother at his birth. Now he phantasies himself back in that position—i.e., with some variation. He can't get out. One of his infantile birth theories (with especial reference to his own birth) was that he had ripped open his mother's belly with the toe nail of his great toe.

This makes everything more clear to us. The nail of the great toe is the penis and he feels at bottom that with his erect penis he injured his mother. That is why he is afraid ever again to put his penis back into a woman. His erection always collapses under a wave of anxiety. (Such anxiety often arises from the observation of copulating dogs who, after copulation, frequently cannot come apart. Beta insists that he has never seen such an incident, but says that he had early witnessed such occurrences in June bugs, flies and butterflies.)

His anxiety in the street is equivalent to his fear in the vagina. He never has any fears when he is out in the open country and out there he also experiences persistent erections (outside the vagina).

The fight he mentions indicates the injury. Triasangoli makes him think of trias and angle—the characteristic trinity which we know to be the symbol of the phallus. Angle has to do with that which catches and hooks fish. He thus symbolizes his penis as an angle; it has a catch which can injure a woman. That's why he prefers to castrate himself. That's why he takes the scissors to cut off his mustache. These sadistic and castrating phantasies appear directly in his consciousness. Beta has every reason to repress his sexuality. He hates women, is a woman murderer. He would like to possess a giant phallus with which he could bore them through and kill them. Jack the Ripper. That's why he has to avoid women and circumscribe his interests to the foot.

His inability to put it in also has a definitely criminal source. We may remember that he wanted to stab his father to death. For the sake of a woman (that English governess) and his desire to be undisturbed in his relations with his brother, he wanted to remove his father. The beating and that intrusion after the bath had inflamed his hate. Now, however, he suffers from the imperative tyranny of penance. Instead of his original desire, he symbolizes it, as it were, on himself by removing the points of his mustache. That is the reason for the mention of Mr. Triasangoli in the hypnagogic dream-picture. He had a terrific fight with a porter. The sexual act is altogether too closely identified with the criminal act to suit the patient. Every coitus is murder. Murder is forbidden.

He has, on the other hand, every reason to desire to live his life over again and that is the reason for the phantasy of the mother's womb. He is compressed within his fetishism just as that figure in the mandolin. He can't even move. The figure he drew is thus a symbolic representation of the compulsion which he has brought upon himself.

Further than this, I must also call attention to a significant infantile theme which enables us to appreciate all these disturbances as a form of psycho-sexual infantilism. The first compulsion which we suffer in life is being pressed within the womb and then immediately upon birth being rolled in a diaper. It was once a common habit to see babies done up and bound in strips, but this has long gone out of fashion, especially in England and

America. The diapered child is often the prototype of all later
binding and swaddling phantasies. In the sketch he has given
us, Beta presents a remarkable resemblance to a child swathed in
diapers. In short, he is a perennial nursling, as we have already
had occasion to observe in his dreams.

Beta's psychic impotence is not only infantilism, it is also a
punishment for his criminal thoughts. Almost every impotence is
to be explained on this basis. That is why such patients always
dream of revolvers and rifles which never go off. This is, furthermore, another reason why young persons so frequently commit suicide. As long as the revolver is to go off, it had best be
directed at one's own breast.

The hypnagogic picture is intimately related to these thoughts.
The two Bs together give BB which leads him to baby, and such
he really is, both in the picture and in his unconscious. He re-
verses the process of his birth and reappears as a girl, without a
penis. The result is that his mother may live yet. He is not
the murderer of his mother (he also does not wish to be his
father's murderer consciously).

The belly of the instrument is his mother's belly and the servant
represents the father. As a child, he had to bow before his father
and they had a slang expression for that about "being your
servant." That evil piece of wood which we saw in the dream
about Kainz and Gregori retains a connection here, too, in that
his head is nailed down under it. Playing the mandolin (masturbation) caused his parapathia. A woman cannot injure herself in masturbation because she loses no semen. This dream-
picture reveals to us how quickly the complicated and ramified
thought processes of a parapathic can transform themselves into
the elements of a dream. The phantasy of his mother's womb
quickly possessed him for but a few seconds as if he were thus
ventilating his wish to start his life over again.

We must approach such hypnagogic dream-pictures as transitional stages between day-dreams and true dreams. Sometimes
individuals are subject to such hypnagogic pictures during full
consciousness and are then much surprised to learn that they are
subject to such phantasies altogether. All these patients have
two kinds of thought. Beside their stream of consciousness there
flows an uninterrupted stream of phantasies. These phantasies
can often be fished to the surface of consciousness by means of
a method which I have called the production of "artificial dreams."
The method consists in having the person make up a dream, create

a pure phantasy. The product of such creation will then frequently reveal all the individual's innermost complexes and wishes, and its structure will be found to deviate in no respect from that of the so-called genuine dreams. One can thus often arrive at the most important and definitive analytical material with a minimum of effort. The following is such an artificial day-dream of Mr. Beta and I must add that this phantasy afforded me even deeper insight into the structure of his unconscious than most of the true dreams he produced. For the hour just previous, nothing had entered his mind, and I requested him to produce an artificial dream which should comply with but one condition, viz., that it should be told promptly and without hesitation. The day-dreamer closed his eyes and began to speak so quickly that I could scarcely follow him.

I was in a labyrinth consisting of innumerable passages. I saw somebody in front of me, but try as I would, I couldn't catch up with him. I arrived at the end of the passage far behind him and had a hard time getting out, too. I seem to think that I got out a little too fast. I was on the Isle of Crete and saw Minos. He had a crown on his head and a great, thick snake about his trunk. He clubbed the labyrinth with the snake and it crashed to pieces under one blow. Then I climbed aboard a little ship and was driven about the whole Mediterranean Sea by a storm until I found succor and peace at the pope's. He commanded me to make a barefoot pilgrimage to Jerusalem and that would make me well again.

The difference between a true dream and this psychic creation may, perhaps, be looked for in a certain logical cohesion of the day-dream. It lacks the grotesque and senseless manner of the dream and also reveals a triumphant optimism unknown to dreams of sleep. The initial phase is a clear-cut phantasy of the mother's womb. The man ahead of him is his brother whom he envies because of his primogeniture. He came after him, but was never able to catch up with him. There was also another feeling about this scene. He wanted to catch up with this somebody as fast as possible and the result was that he came out with a rush and killed his mother. We are already acquainted with this phantasy of the innocent murder of his mother. The subsequent picture is a continuation of the phantasy of the mother's body with the father appearing as Minos (Cf. "The Elfenking with Crown and Sword"). He has a terribly thick phallus. The statement about clubbing the labyrinth with the snake betrays an idea of cohabi-

tation as a sadistic act whereby the mother is killed. He himself
is not guilty of the death of his mother. It is his father who
killed her with his great thick snake. He also produces more
direct phantasies about his father having removed his mother for
the sake of other women, to get her money, etc. He then regrets
such baseless suspicions dejectedly. Many of his acts of atonement are obedience and regret after the fact.

Then again the phantasy of his mother's body bobs up (small
ship—Mediterranean Sea), but along with this there appears the
unified consolidation of the various motives of salvation: the flying
Dutchman, Ahasuerus, Tannhäuser, etc. His religious ideas of
atonement are condensed into the one trip of penance to the pope
(who is also the father; his name in Italian is papa). The pilgrimage to Jerusalem is variously determined and its importance
is also indicated by the plural determination. (1) It is the Holy
Grail. (2) It has to do with the physician who is a Jew. (3) He
has been reading a novel by a certain Else Jerusalem called *The
Holy Scarib*. It deals with prostitutes. Religion, medicine and
the prostitute will cure him. At the same time, however, the penance which the pope places upon him is also a pleasure. For him,
walking with bare feet would be a permanent thrill, the greatest
delight. The snake in the dream points, also, to the story of the
garden of Eden and the fall of Adam and Eve. Like Morel's
patient (see Vol. VI), he seeks the paradise of virtue. The earth
is his mother—mother earth—and walking with bare feet he will
always be close to her.

Considered from the functional point of view, the plasticity of
this dream picture is nothing less than marvelous. His soul is a
labyrinth of innumerable passages and before him walks the man
whom he cannot overtake—Christ, the pure and noble man. He
strives towards a divine goal, but is judged otherwise. Minos is
the judge of the nether regions, and I also was the judge who reflected to him his true inner structure. The whole labyrinth of
his parapathia crashes about his head and that I break up the
labyrinth with a snake is the expression of his anxiety that I
might conduce to his sinfulness. In the language of Silberer, he
is seeking for an anagogic orientation. He feels that I am setting
him free too early. He still wants to do penance and save himself
by conscious religiousness.

In reviewing the totality of this case, we see, first of all, that
this alleged paraphilic (pervert) has chosen a disease which per-

mits him to avoid women and successfully exploit his asceticism. For every one of these patients the female is an instrumentum diaboli, the incarnation of sin. Even masturbation is a lesser evil. As a matter of fact, Beta took to masturbation as a punishment and expiation, an original discovery for shortening his life. The idea is that as long as I must have pleasure, let me pay for it with my life and vitality.

His sadistic attitude towards the female—and how often shall we meet with it in this book!—drove him to impotence and permitted the progressive development of his paraphilia. The foot became a symbol of his sin and his striving. The foot which was compressed into a narrow and tight-fitting shoe, the tortured, pressed, heated, swollen and wounded foot—that is what provoked his fancy more than anything else. The foot became a symbol of his illness, his spirit, his constrained impulses, his whole ego. Whatever impulses he had to fear were nullified by his fetishism. He was accomplished in the art of reversal or opposition. His limitless ambition, finding no satisfactory outlet because his capacities were insufficient for real creation, plunged him into the opposite habit of self-denial. Everything could be attained through self-abnegation. Become a second Christ. He, the hater and murderer, would become another saint. Such a goal was really buried deep within his unconscious, whereas outwardly he played the agnostic, the monist, the atheist, the freethinker, and looked sarcastically upon all religious ceremony. His fetishism, however, was a true religion which he had formed for himself. His God was —the foot.

It is a matter of interest that he left the analysis unimproved. He was much too obstinate in his attitude towards the physician and would not suffer another's triumph. He preferred to be treated by a masseur who, after two weeks of general massage, discharged him as cured. He sought an excuse against cure and preferred to hand the prize to a masseur than to a psychoanalyst. Shortly thereafter he married and is to-day the father of several handsome children. His foot fetishism, the agoraphobia and several other neurotic symptoms have completely disappeared. He has, however, become quite pious and has no compunctions about the exercise of his religious devotion. He no longer needs his fetishism, for he has found a more direct path to his God.

He has given up his hopes of fulfilling some historical mission and has adjusted to the search for a more tangible happiness. His guilt feelings evaporated as soon as he came to learn in the analysis how universal his impulses and feelings were. He is neither a sadist nor does he fear his sadistic eruptions any more. It has been overcome by means of the one antidote I recommended to him: love. Previously he had avoided love and had been incapable of falling in love because he depreciated women and fled as soon as he felt that he was endangered. It became necessary for him first to change his attitude towards women and thus to correct his adjustment to the world at large.

Fetishism is a religion of hate. The hatred is well disguised, but breaks forth at various moments. Every compulsion leads to the formation of hatred against the compulsion and this hatred finally is transformed into a hatred of everything and everybody. The obsessional neurosis is the apotheosis of a hate neurosis.

Man's original attitude towards the world in general is hate. Any loss of pleasure or gratification provokes the aboriginal reaction of hatred. In Beta's case we were able to observe the significance of the "weaning complex" which, by the way, is an expression to be preferred to the more biassed and one-sided expression "castration complex."

His first frustration took place when he was weaned at thirteen months. I might say here that I consider it a great mistake to wean children from the breast so late. The result is that they react all the more strongly and remember with hate the brutal disturbance of their pleasant situation.

His second frustration occurred when his father and the English governess forbade him to masturbate. Onanism was a practice filled with satisfaction in his stage of life and the threats of his environment forced him to desist from this his glorious discovery. The reaction, of course, was hatred of his environment.

The third frustration was his father's warning against the

dancer when he was twenty-one. Beta had sought a normal sexual contact and was certainly wealthy enough to keep this dancer, just as many of his social equals kept other women. But the weighty voice of his father put an end to the first awakening of love in his heart. It was this that reactivated the earlier hatred of the young man and caused him to wish that man dead who had so persistently intruded upon his life. His dilemma was, however, that he loved his father quite as passionately as he hated him (bipolar attitude). The line of reasoning here was: you have robbed me of so much pleasure that you should really recompense me in some way.

It is rather characteristic that the real development of his foot fetishism took place after his twenty-first year. He still had an opportunity to make heterosexual contacts, but when his father fell ill his first thought was: "If he dies now, I'll be free and the road to some girl is open." The reaction was, however, that a pathological fear arose that his father might actually die. He told the doctor that if his father died, he would commit suicide. He talked and acted like an insane man. Nevertheless, he was unable to squeeze forth a tear at his father's grave.

It was now that he was ready for penance. Now he could indulge in his fetishism and create the swollen foot as his ideal. He was quite a linguist and, as the analysis showed, knew well the meanings of all ancient and modern languages. The "swollen foot" was Œdipus.

He had killed his mother and perhaps also his father, since he had wished him death. He had also desired to kill his only rival, his brother. These are the three crimes for which he must do penance. His foot fetishism enabed him to combine his ideas of expiation with a complicated paraphilia. The foot became the sign of the genitals and religion, sin and lust, punishment and praise.

This shows us how complicated are the psychic structures of fetishism. The chief factor in this case was the "Christ neurosis."

Dr. Missriegler has made the following illustrative plan of this case.

Father

Love of father ——→ Because of his faithlessness / Because of his prohibition of love —————→ Hate for the father

Homosexual Love — Transformation to a woman

Hail-Father — Fear of Woman — Agoraphobia — Fear of Infection

Nailed Foot (with traces) — Dirty Foot

Fetishism

Constraint ——→ Compressed Foot

Send him to heaven (God the Father) — Christ — The bloody Foot

Death Wishes (Cold, etc.) — Repenter, Monk — Naked Foot

Castration — Asexual Saint — Foot as an asex object

Fetishism

COMPULSION

Woman

Penis in vaginam

Anxiety in pulling back foreskin

Injure Woman

Child in the uterus

Birth Anxiety

Kill Mother

Open Spaces / toilet / Baby Carriage

Foot in the Shoe

Anxiety with shoes

(Shoes tearing?) Agoraphobia

Woman

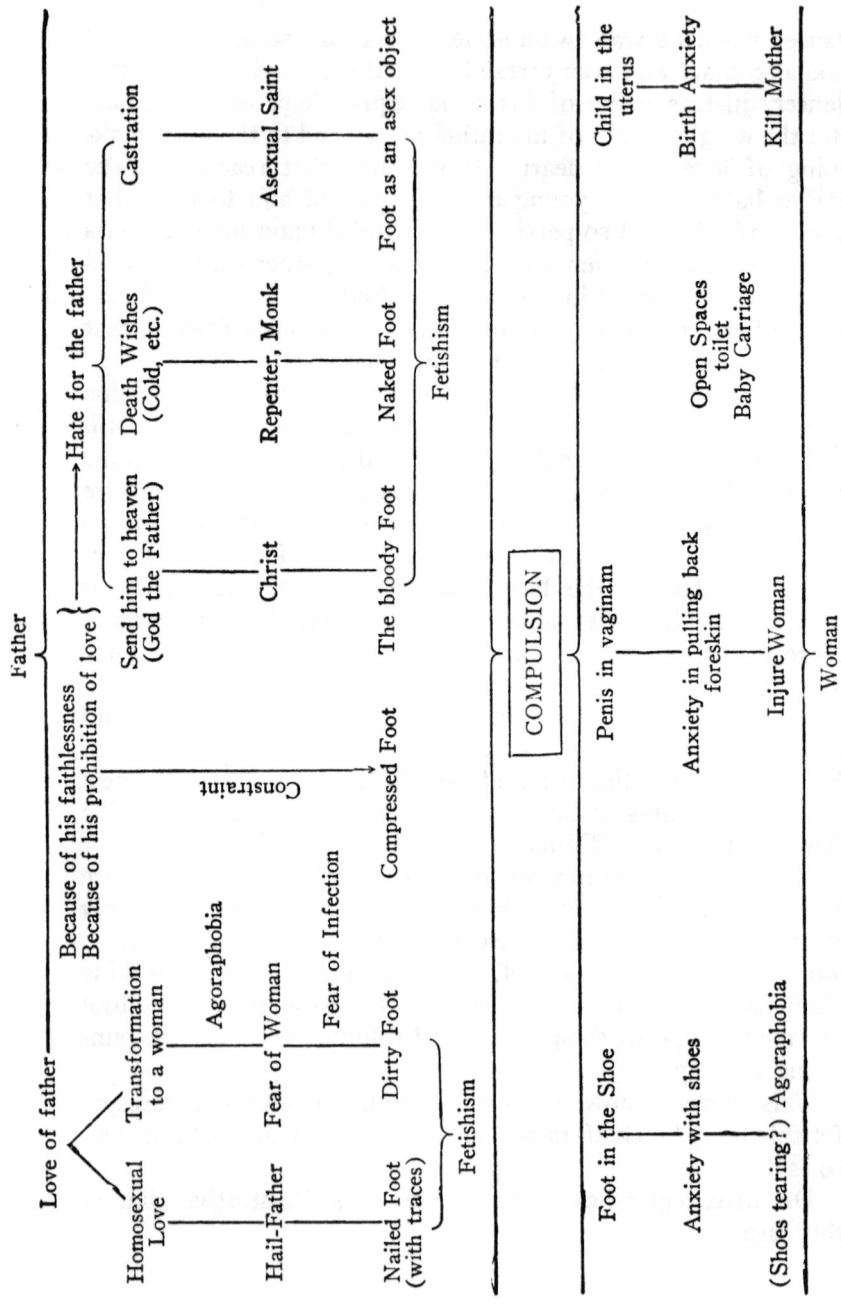

The compulsion leads from father to the woman and the reaction is the obsessional neurosis. "Others" constrain him to give up his love and choose another. He tries at first (the female foot), but always falls back upon his original sexual ... He ends with a sublimated realization. Religion (God, Father)

If we attempt a resolution of this complicated foot fetishism of Beta's, we will find that foot signifies:

1. The Genital.
   - (a) The phallus and foreskin (shoe).
   - (b) Lingam: phallus and vagina (shoe).
   - (c) Erection.

2. His Paraphilia.
   - (a) His fetishism.
   - (b) The Child.
   - (c) Birth (taking off the shoe).
   - (d) Symbolization of the obsession.

3. The Criminal Ideas.
   - (a) The foot as a weapon.
   - (b) The nail as a weapon.
   - (c) The gory man (object and subject).
   - (d) The swollen foot (Œdipus—patricide).

4. His Religious Ideas.
   - (a) The foot of Christ—nailed to the cross by the feet.
   - (b) The repenter (Ahasuerus—the pious pilgrim—flying Dutchman).
   - (c) Punishment for his hatred.
   - (d) Ideas of salvation.
   - (e) The martyr.

5. Phantasies of the Mother's Body.
   - (a) Birth (taking off the shoe).
   - (b) Protection in the womb (regression—retrospective tendency).

See plan on page 274.

See plan on page 274.

We meet here with the phenomenon of symbol condensation. The following chapters will enlighten us on this as well as other manifestations of fetishism.

X

THE SYMBOLISM OF COMPULSIONS

In the foregoing chapter, I presented a case which shows us how powerful is the impulse to look upon a compressed foot. Beta was not in the least animated by the sight of a foot in a broad and comfortable shoe. The foot must bear the signs of mistreatment, pain, compulsion and compression.

It is thus that the parapathic symbolizes his own parapathia. The tightly laced shoe is the symbol of his tightly laced and artificially constraining parapathic system.

Every case of true fetishism that we analyze will disclose these signs of obsession and compulsion. Indeed, the object or part of the body in question can become a fetishistic symbol only when it exerts an obsessional force or when a compulsive influence can be exerted upon it. We must remember this bit of knowledge well. It has been corroborated again and again in experience. It reveals to us the playful exploitation of the symbol itself, for that which the fetishist compresses and constrains is his own sexuality. He makes it appear as if he is elevating himself above the normal, but in reality he is receding from the normal and natural in sexual activity; he is abstinent and, as we shall see further, pious, ascetic, suffering.

The following case is an unusual one which I take from Havelock Ellis with his express permission.[1] I have had to shorten the highly interesting case history to some extent, but the plenitude of perspectives which it affords us is preserved. I know of hardly a case which presents such a wealth of human and symbolical material in such concise form.

Case 42. C. P., thirty-two years old, good heredity. He masturbated between the ages of nine or ten and fourteen because he felt the desire and need. He had discovered the act for himself. Otherwise he was quite naïve, ignorant of sexual matters and had never been enlightened by either servants or other children.

"If I meet a woman who appears attractive to me," he writes, "it is not my wish to have sexual contact with her in the usual sense of the word, but rather to lie down prone on the floor and have her walk over me and tread me underfoot. This curious wish occurs seldom and only when the woman in question is a real lady and well built. She must be elegantly dressed, preferably in evening clothes with low shoes which have very high heels. The shoes I like to see either open, so that the instep is visible, or fitted with a single ribbon or strap. The dress should be high enough for me to get a good view of the shoes and also of the ankle, but not necessarily as high as the knee, for then the effect is not quite the same. Even though I may appreciate the spiritual or beautiful qualities of a woman, there is, after all, nothing about her that could arouse me like that part of her from the knee down, especially the foot. She must also be carefully dressed. Under this condition, my desire for sexual gratification can increase rapidly, but can be satisfied only by contact with that part of a woman which really attracts my interest. Comparatively few women have a leg or ankle or foot beautiful enough to command my undivided or permanent attention. If such nevertheless turns out to be the case, I lose no time or energy in trying to get under her feet and then await being trod with most anxious anticipation.

"The treading must last several minutes and must include the chest, abdomen, inguinal region and, finally, the penis which is by then far too stiffly erect to suffer any damage thereby. I might say that I am also thrilled when a female foot compresses my throat.

"When, then, the lady faces me and places one foot suchwise on my penis that the high heel sinks into the root and the sole covers the rest of the phallus while the other foot is placed upon my abdomen so that I can see and feel her shifting her weight from one foot to the other—then I experience an almost instantaneous ejaculation. Such a moment, under the conditions I describe, is for me the outbreak of a storm of rapture which culminates when the lady bears down upon my phallus with her whole weight.

"One of the reasons for my special delight in this kind of contact seems to be that first the heel and then the sole of the slipper prevents the immediate passage of the semen and thus protracts the period of my enjoyment. In addition to the physical aspect of the experience, there is also a curious psychic accompaniment. I imagine that the lady who treads upon me is my mistress and I her slave, and that she does it as a punishment for some transgression I have committed or perhaps out of pure pleasure for herself.

"The natural and accurate conclusion is that the greater the mistreatment and harshness I 'suffer,' the greater is my pleasure. The phantasy of 'punishment' or 'enslavement' appears less frequently when I have difficulties in realizing my wish or if the lady is lovelier or heavier than usual and the treading is merciless. I have often been trod so sedulously and long that I have tried to avoid the pain of every tread and afterwards was black and blue for days. I strive especially to induce women to do this to me when I feel that I sha'n't insult them, and it is surprising how much luck I have in this. I must have lain under the feet of at least a hundred women already and many of them were from the best strata of society. They would never have dreamed of permitting normal sexual intercourse, but the idea of effecting it in this form so provoked and caught their fancy that they gladly repeated the process. I hardly need to emphasize that in achieving orgasm in this fashion neither my own nor the clothing of the ladies were ever in the least opened or ruffled. On the basis of divers and long experience I can say that the weight I prefer is about ten-eleven stone, and that black shoes or slippers and brown silk stockings appear to call forth in me the deepest gratification and the strongest desires.

"Ordinary boots or street shoes give me nowhere near the pleasure I find otherwise, although on occasion I have been trod satisfactorily with them. Naked women repel me, nor do I find any joy in women dressed in trousers. I do not reject normal sexual intercourse and have occasionally cohabited. The pleasure I derive therefrom is, however, considerably less than that I find in being trod by women. I have also found considerable delight—and have often had a strong erection—in seeing women, clothed as I have described above, trodding some other, inanimate, thing under foot, such as a cushion in a carriage or the foot rest before a chair. Often at picnics or garden parties I have followed a couple of pretty girls only for the sake of seeing the grass straighten up again after they had trod it down. Even the sight of a carriage step under the foot of a lady gives me pleasure; it is something which demands the pressure of a foot.

"And now I can explain how my feelings were bent in this direction. When I was a boy of about fourteen years of age, I was visiting for some time with close friends of my parents. The daughter of the house—and the only child—was a pretty and robust girl about six years my senior. She was my chief companion.

"This girl was always prettily dressed; she had well-formed feet and ankles and was also well aware of the fact. Whenever she could, she dressed herself so that her virtues stood out well, i.e., with short dresses and small, low shoes with high heels. Nor was she averse to showing these advantages off in a very coquettish and inspiring manner. She seemed to have a *penchant* for treading on things which gave way before her feet, e.g., flowers, grass, fallen fruit, acorns, hay, straw, etc. On our walks about the garden, which were quite informal, I had become accustomed to watching her tread things down and would even scold her. At that time, also, it was one of my chief pleasures—and still is—to stretch out before a roaring fire on a thick carpet. One evening I was in this position and we were alone when A. came through the room to get something from the fireplace mantel. Instead of stretching her hand out over me, however, she playfully stepped up on me and said that was the way she did in the grass and hay. I naturally complied with the jest and laughed with her. After she had stood on my body for a minute or two, she gingerly lifted up her dress and, holding on to the mantel piece, stretched her lovely foot and brown silk stockinged leg towards the fire to warm them, meanwhile laughing at my heated face. She was quite an ingenuous and charming girl and I am rather certain that, although she was quite pleased at my animation and the feel of my body under her feet, she had not yet understood my feelings at this first experience. Neither do I recall that, although I was nearly bursting with sexual desire, she manifested the slightest sign of a corresponding feeling. I grasped her uplifted foot, kissed it passionately, and pressed it in irresistible ardor against my erect penis. At almost the same instant that her foot bore down upon my phallus, I had the first real and complete orgasm of my life. No description can convey a conception of my feelings at that moment. I only know that from that time on the focus of my sexual desires was displaced and forever fixed.

"Innumerable times afterwards I felt the pleasurable weight of her delicate slipper and nothing will ever equal my memory of that delight. I know, too, that A. derived as much pleasure from treading on me as I from being trod. She was in a position to buy whatever articles she desired and when she had recognized what thrills she afforded me, she acquired more and more lovely stockings, delicate shoes with high, sharp heels. She would then demonstrate her new goods to me by demanding that I lie down and get the feeling of them for myself. She confessed that she was pleased to see her slippers sink into my body and to hear the crack of the muscles whenever she would turn her heel in my ribs. After a few minutes, I would invariably press her shoe to my penis and then she would cautiously bring her whole weight, about nine stone, to bear upon it, meanwhile watching me with glistening eyes, red cheeks and trembling lips as she would feel the pulsation of the phallus beneath the sole of her slipper, as must surely have been the case. I am not in the least doubtful that she also had an orgasm, although we never exchanged a word on the subject.

"This took place at every suitable opportunity for several years, and after a separation of four or five years we did it about four or five times a day. A few times I masturbated in her absence, using her shoe to press my penis as hard as I could. I imagined thereby that she were treading upon me. Naturally, the pleasure I derived from this surrogate was considerably less than with her. Never did we mention normal sexual intercourse, especially since we were both satisfied with things as they were.

"When I was about twenty, I began to travel and upon my return, I found her married. Although we met frequently, our former habits were never mentioned and we remained good friends. I confess that I frequently looked surreptitiously at her feet and would gladly have accepted the pleasure of resuming the curious practices which she was able to afford me. But my wish was never realized.

"I then resumed my travels and now both she and her husband are dead.

"From time to time, I had occasional relations with prostitutes but always in the above-mentioned manner. I nevertheless prefer to make use of a woman of my own or a better station, but such a wish is fraught with difficulties.

"Of the one hundred women, more or less, who, both at home and abroad, have stood upon me, at least eighty or eighty-five percent were not prostitutes. Ten or twelve at the most also derived sexual gratification thereby, but even though they manifested excitement, the majority of them were not really excited. As far as I can remember, A. alone derived complete gratification therefrom. It has never been necessary for me to waste many words in inducing a woman to tread me (prostitutes excepted). On the contrary, it has always been my purpose to achieve my aims in a joking or playful way and it is more than doubtful whether any but a few married women have really been cognizant of the situation even when they have been affording me the deepest sexual satisfaction; especially since the movements of my body and my excitement at the time could just as well have been laid to the effects of the treading. Those women who did it to me more than once (and most of them complied but once) naturally understood the second time what it was all about, and although neither the women nor myself ever so much as mentioned the real nature of the proceeding, they were never averse to complying with my wishes as often as I wanted. I can hardly believe that they derived the least sexual delight from the business, although they could patently see that I was achieving it, and yet they never refused to afford me the pleasure. In the case of many a woman it has taken me over a year to achieve my goal, but I finally gained my wish. In most cases, however, my plans have failed. I never risk the request until I am practically sure of acceptance and have never yet experienced a really serious reversal or refusal. In very many cases, I must confess, compliance with my request has often been a sort of giving in to a joking whim which, aside from the novelty of treading on a man, promised little excitement for the woman. Just as in the case of normal seduction, one of the chief sources of gratification for me is winning the woman over to my desires without arousing any resistance in her. The higher the social standing of the woman, the more difficult does this seduction become and the greater is then my satisfaction. I have found three prostitutes in my experience who had had the same sort of contact with other men and were well informed on the method. It is not without interest to remark that these three women were all of fine, strong build—one of them about five feet, ten inches tall and weighing about fourteen stone; but they had nondescript faces. The weight, the build and the dress of the women I meet are all of equal importance to me. I find that a sudden kick at the moment of the very pitch of sexual excitement is capable of enhancing and protracting my gratification. My emotional pleasure is due especially to the fact that when the woman stands with her full weight upon my erect penis and presses it into the soft and giving abdominal wall, the period of ejaculation and the time of the orgasm are considerably protracted. That is also why I prefer low shoes with high heels. The semen must also be pressed through two separate barriers:

first at the root of the penis which is crushed under the weight of the heel and then again past the ball of the foot which compresses the forward part of the phallus; between the two there is only the space under the instep of the shoe. My pleasure is further increased by a retention of urine and that is why I like to have as full a bladder as possible when being trod. The weight, the build and the dress greatly enhance my desires, especially when the woman is one whom one would love to have tread one."

I have presented this case here despite the fact that it is a mixed form. We must not forget that this man actually cohabits with women, he needs them for his purposes and uses the shoe for onanistic practices only in cases of emergency. The paraphilia has not yet isolated the man nor has it yet repelled him from women. He is neither impotent nor asocial and the conquest of a woman excites his libido. His sense of reality easily overcomes his phantasy.

And yet this case reveals the power of the original impression. Or perhaps not? What would have been the effect of this first impression in the case of any other man whose phantasies were directed in some other direction? We are also not at all helped in this question by Mr. C. P.'s early history. We cannot say whether or not there may have been a much more important, more infantile impression behind this early one.

Aside from these points, however, this case illustrates the struggle against libido and the power of a compulsion. His sensuality is stronger than his urge to purity (James' antisexual instinct). The female, the personification of sin, is stronger than the male who symbolizes the resistance of virtue. The deeper meaning of this scene will be revealed particularly in our discussion of masochism (in *Sadism and Masochism*). One thing is true, however, and that is that this man strove to resist the supremacy of woman and stages her conquest only as an apparent one. He lets them go, unsatisfied, as if he had only wanted to make fools of them; as if he were to say: "So, now you're all excited and probably think that I'm going to cohabit with you. But you're mistaken. I'm satisfied and that's all that worries me." That is probably the reason why most of the women complied with his requests but once.

Women can, after all, be induced to almost any sort of procedure if they can be made to feel that they will be recompensed
by a considerable potency in the partner.   If they do not get
this satisfaction, they lose all interest in the "erotic symbolism"
(Havelock Ellis) of their partners.

I would also like to call attention to the special emphasis of
the lustful objects of these patients. All fetishists circumstantially describe the special conditions which their objects must
possess and the more eccentric and wild these are, the more
proud the patients are of themselves and their leanings.   I
have observed that they always watch the physician closely
when telling him about their tastes and are downright insulted
if he does not express the greatest astonishment at the singularity of what they relate.   I once saw the man in Vienna who
was known to all as the individual who visited prostitutes and
had them stick a feather in his anus, at which he would crow:
"kikeriki!"   I listened to him relate his story and then thought
I would joke with him.   I answered, "Oh, you're not the first
one who has told me this.   There has been quite a number of
men who have played the rooster."   He was deeply insulted,
manifestly dejected and had difficulty in assuring me hypocritically that he was relieved to learn that there were others like
him.   Of course, I never saw him again.

But this shows us that the true fetishist lives in the delusion
that he is "the only one," the chosen one.   The surface of his
illness is thus a distorted reflection of the idea of the historical
mission which is to be fulfilled.

C. P. also reveals the peculiar pride of the parapathic in his
abstruse form of sexual gratification.   The thought which dom-
inates him at all times is: will I be able to induce this woman
to accept the rôle I wish her to play?   Once he has inveigled
her into it, he triumphs over her.   I know of men who consider women only then as convincingly theirs when the women
have performed fellatio on them.   Under the guise of supremacy the women are depreciated.   It is with extraordinary clever-
ness that this situation has been turned to the use of a woman
hater.   The real motto of his life reads: All women are bad
and can be made to do what one wants them to do if one is only

persevering and patient enough. The naked woman as such does not interest him; indeed she repels him. He was on the road to becoming a true fetishist, but stopped midway.

It is not without significance that pressure on the throat is able to provoke the same type of deep orgasm in him. It is here that the criminal root of his paraphilia shimmers through. In principle it is similar to the lex talionis (the phantasy of choking a rival. The penis a symbol of this rival and his paraphilia a displacement from above downwards). The woman with a high heel appears to be but a bisexual representative: the woman with the penis, the original ideal of many men. Functionally, his paraphilia is to be looked upon as a symbolic concession to his homosexuality. The woman in him conquers the male. The male is the subjected, humiliated, constrained one.[2]

The pressure on the penis, as well as the pressure of a corset (we have already heard of such a case), the pressure on a hand, the pressure of some article of clothing (tight trousers), a tightly fitting vest or glove—all these articles can become specific love conditions.

Great interest must be accorded those cases in which the object itself is rejected for the sake of the circumscribed interest in the pressure itself. The compression is the thing which effects an orgasm. It is, however, not always necessary that the pressure be exerted directly on the penis as in the foregoing case; often it is sufficient if exercised against an arm or a leg.

Again, such a pressure may be able to direct the patient's attentions to coitus itself. Thus, a man once told me that he had vainly courted a woman for a year. One day he suddenly grasped her firmly by the arm and said: "I could hurt you, you cruel thing." At that instant she became pale and sank into his arms. "You shouldn't have done that," she said, "it completely overcomes me." The following day, he again approached her, but in vain. When he remembered what had transpired the previous day, he again grasped her arm so firmly that she was terribly pained. But the result was again the same; she succumbed to his will. Subsequently he never forgot that this trick was the key to her body.

A genuine pressure fetishist, however, forgoes the possession of a partner and seeks only the opportunity to be pushed or pressed in some part of the body. In the street car, in omnibuses or trains, there are always a few pressure fetishists who revel in the happy hunting ground of a crowd.

The following is the classis case first published by Féré. It is doubtless in a class by itself as a clear-cut example of this type of fetishism.

Case 43. M. V. was a thirty-eight-year-old distiller who had revealed divers neurotic symptoms even in childhood. While teething, he suffered from convulsions and until puberty had pavor nocturnus and wet the bed. Even now he will awaken occasionally soon after falling asleep and feel anxiously oppressed, but he generally lays this to exhaustion or stomach trouble. While at school he had manifested industry and intelligence and at eighteen he successfully passed two academic examinations. At the school where he was only partly boarding in (because of his enuresis), he was given the nickname of Miss V. because of his delicate complexion, his smooth skin and girlish appearance. He never took part in the activities of the other boys and always sought to be alone. He insists that he never was so much as animated sexually during his school days and only occasionally did he have a nocturnal emission attended by some dream or other. Afterwards he was invariably tired and more than ever disgusted with his comrades' talk of sexual matters. He never felt especially attracted to the boys with whom he was thrown together and the sight of a girl was a real scare for him, especially when, because of his shy and delicate appearance, they were more than usually nice to him. Even the memory of such experiences caused him to become red with shame.

The first time he ever sensed a sexual lust which was accompanied by pleasurable feelings was when he was eighteen. Along with a very large family, he went on an outing in a buggy which was much too small to permit all of them to sit down. Many of the children stood between the adults' legs. One of the girls, about twelve years old, stood in front of him with her back turned towards him. In the course of a little while, what with the jarring of the buggy, she slid in between his legs. At first he was quite ashamed of the situation, but when he saw that no one had taken any note of the fact, he was calmed. The rubbing, however, soon called forth an erection and whenever the buggy jarred on the road, the girl stepped on his foot and he noticed that this pain or pressure enhanced the quality of his lust and excitement. At one point where the wagon went over a great bump and the girl came down hard on his foot, he had a sudden ejaculation. He experienced with that a sudden sexual relief which was not at all accompanied by lassitude and disgust as had been the case after nocturnal emissions. On the way home, a little girl of about six or seven took the first girl's place between his legs, nor did she have any greater respect for his feet or for his comfort. Again he was sexually provoked, but this time he did not achieve an orgasm. The lack of this natural climax to his desire kept him in a state of constant excitement throughout the day and the memory of the extraordinarily pleasant pressure on his feet persisted.

From that time on these feelings have repeated themselves often, the only addition being that he would sometimes become ticklish and cold in the feet whenever they were compressed. From then on he was no longer intimidated by the presence of women as had previously been the case, nor did females excite the slightest sexual desire in him. Whereas his nocturnal pollutions had formerly been attended by only vague dream pictures, they were now more frequent and clearly accompanied by the vision of women treading on his toes. Ever since that buggy ride, he has not had another opportunity to be in a crowd, nor has he experienced the same intense feelings he had then. For several years his paraphilia expressed itself only in torturing thoughts and dreams, but the other sex did not exert any attraction for him.

At twenty-seven he went to Paris and for many years now he has been the passive sufferer of those passers-by in the auto bus who step on his feet. At first he experienced a thrill only when the bus would bump over the heavy cobblestones, but soon he was affected even when in the tram. Whereas he was initially thrilled only when young women or girls would step or stand on his feet, he soon was excited when any kind of woman touched his foot and continued to seek the opportunity for this contact although it never lasted sufficiently long for him to achieve an orgasm. Frequently, however, such experiences would produce dreams the same night with the result that he became more and more tired.

One day while riding on the bus, he saw that the platform was filled with women and offered one of them his seat, but not so much out of courtesy as to seize the opportunity to be among the others. With every bump in the road and every change in the direction of travel, the little group had to shift its weight from one foot to the other with the result that he succeeded in being stepped on and thus achieved his end. He was quite thrilled and soon experienced an orgasm. He then began to stand only near the exit whenever he would ride in the street car and would stick out his foot to be stepped on (accidentally, of course) by every woman who got ready to get off. He was thoroughly frustrated whenever the lady would avoid him or first excuse herself and then avoid him. He noticed, however, that this occurred much less frequently than one would expect and that the women showed no compunction about treading on his feet. In the event that the person treads on his toes twice or more, he may even be promptly relieved. He was thirty-one before the thought entered his mind to try normal sexual intercourse, i.e., he came upon the notion more out of curiosity than because of a real urge. He visited a prostitute and after the ejaculation, which came only after a protracted period, he felt very tired, heavy with lassitude and disgust. His disgust was especially astonishing in view of the fact that the girl called forth his sincere and heartfelt sympathy and admiration by a heart-throbbing story of her life. As a matter of fact, he cannot yet forget the effects of her tale. The second time he visited her, he was again unsatisfied and then decided to have her tread upon his feet, but even this was a failure. Apparently, the desired result is achieved only when he is trod upon in a certain way and publicly. Ever since these failures, he has been plagued by the thought that he is different from other men and that the fact might be noticed, especially by the women. He became subject to fits of depression and gave up his position in 1894. There began the habit of drinking, although he did not give way excessively to alcohol. Soon, however, he began to suffer from insomnia and epileptiform seizures at night. When he heard that alcohol was able to call forth new diseases in man, he abruptly gave up drink and simultaneously broke off all his other relationships and withdrew into seclusion where he gave himself over to the execution of religious ceremonies.

He was thirty-four at the time the epileptiform convulsion began. His small stature, the enuch's voice, the pale skin and his blond hair made him look like a very young man from a distance. He was nevertheless very well proportioned and disclosed no deformities with the exception of slight webbing between two or three toes of both feet. His genitals were of normal size and not deformed. He had sufficient hair in the axilla and about the genitals, but the rest of his body was quite devoid of hair and the beard over his chin was very sparse. Since falling into the depressive state, he has begun to look like an aged man, his body is bent, his skin wrinkled and shrunken and his eye dulled. (L'instinct sexuel. Evolution et dissolution. Charles Féré, Paris, Félix Alcan, 1899, pp. 262-265).

Unfortunately this very interesting case was never analyzed, but we can nevertheless see that the pressure fetishism was accompanied by a simultaneous incapacity for heterosexual intercourse. Furthermore his life ends in a religious twilight state.

All these patients suffer from the deepest of guilt feelings, for without a sense of guilt there is no fetishism. The fetish itself is at once a symbol of pleasure and punishment. Initially, the pain is supposed to drive out the pleasure, for the patient really wants to castigate himself for his pleasures by means of these pains. He wears narrow shoes in order that the pain may make him forget his fetish. Here we see sexuality creeping into the very medium which was to have repressed it, it overcomes the pain, displeasure turns to delight and finally the two are inseparably welded. The chief goal has been reached, however. The woman has been avoided (i.e., as a sexual partner). These men are all infantile characters for whom coitus, putting the penis into the vagina, is a cardinal sin. Pleasure derived from other erogenous or sensitized zones is not depraved nor even looked upon as sinful. The sinful wishes and ideas are eliminated by means of hysterical or epileptiform seizures or in dreams and dream-like states. The patient mentioned above, a palpable degenerate, also fled into the arms of religion and expressed his sexual strivings in his epileptiform attacks. Whether or not the pressure on the foot which he experienced was a psychic correspondent in his mind of the nail which bore through the foot of Christ is a question I cannot answer. On the basis of analogy with the case before it, it would seem so. The paraphilia is, as it were, a kind of religion. The enuresis from which he suffered until adolescence points to the "urine sexuality" which deeply motivated his conduct. Like the case just before it, the last one appears to me to be intimately connected with phantasies of the mother's womb. It is remarkable, too, how late this man's paraphilia began; so that we must say that the case probably concerns the parapathic super-structure superimposed on a much older system. What could have been the infantile sources of this paraphilia?

The next case of my own observation throws some light on the genesis of such paraphilias.

Case 44. Mr. A. L., a twenty-six-year-old technologist, relates that it is only in a very unusual manner that he can achieve an orgasm. He tries normal intercourse frequently, but, despite his utmost efforts, he has not been able to get an orgasm or ejaculation. Only when the woman touches his phallus with the tip of her foot does he experience complete gratification, and it is to this end that he always lays himself in bed with a woman in the opposite position, i.e., with his head towards the foot of the bed. I immediately recalled the fact that brothers and sisters not unusually lie in bed together in this fashion and, surely enough, he confessed that he had for some years slept in bed with a sister in this manner. She had also repeatedly pressed against his phallus with her feet, whether accidentally or purposely, he cannot say. At the time, he claims not even to have thought about it and insists that he recalled the facts only when I questioned him about it.

It is not impossible that a similar etiology was present in the foregoing case as well as in others like it. It need not surprise us then that these persons continue to repeat one and the same situation throughout the conduct of their lives. The parapathic simply happens to be the individual who has not overcome his past. The limits between phantasy and reality have become vague to him and the symbol becomes the dominating influence of his life.

In some later cases, we shall become acquainted with even more characteristic causes for paraphilic development, but at this point I might with profit to the reader call attention to the cases in Volume V of this series (Psycho-sexual Infantilism) wherein the infantile source of the parapathia is more clearly outlined than in these cases. We must not forget that in diapers and cradles, babies are protractedly wrapped in tightly, and that this circumstance undoubtedly has something to do with the psychogenesis of fetishism. All fetishists are, after all, pronounced infantilists as the obstinate retention of an infantile impression alone shows.

We must also bear in mind that a parapathic symptom is never determined solely by a single fixation. The symptom represents a plurality of causes which may be of the most heterogeneous nature. Every symptom is a compromise between the most diverse impulses, and the compromise is the very essence of the parapathia. The fetish is the future and the past of the individual, childhood and divinity, compulsion and freedom, appearance and reality.

Can it really be true that each man retains the memory of the time when, wrapped in diapers, he delighted in his infant state?[3] I recall, in this respect, the case of the man (Vol. V, No. 19) who wound himself in linen sheets and then defecated as a representation of the child. I believe that the essential causes are somatic in nature, constitute the primary nucleus of the disease, as it were. But later, there is added a psychic super-structure; so that the pressure of the system symbolizes the compulsion which is taken upon one's self or suffered at the hands of the world. The parapathia is the reflection of an inner struggle. It expresses a psychic conflict and its compromises.

The following case is one of Löwenfeld's and also affords us interesting points of view.

Case 45. "I noticed the first traces of perverse tendencies in myself during my earliest boyhood or youth. At that time I was particularly attracted by other youths in riding boots with stiff shanks, preferably of patent leather. I must digress to mention that my father was a shoemaker by trade and that this offered me considerable opportunity for visual gratification. I can distinctly recall having often surreptitiously followed some schoolmate or other who wore such boots. But these leanings began to broaden their horizon and soon included girls who wore white stockings and spangled shoes (such as one saw frequently in those days). One of my father's customers was a certain Prof. H. who had three charming daughters often seen chatting in our establishment.

"At that green age I already had developed divers means of finding just the right place or position from which I could observe these girls with all the sensual concentration of an adult,

watch their feet in all the various stances they took, see them try
on shoes, etc. I also masturbated at that age. I could lie in bed
in a certain sensual position, concentrate my thoughts upon shoes
and achieve the heights of lascivious rapture. Later I got hold
of a book on onanism and read about the masturbation of youths,
about the secretion of a sort of semen and then recalled my former
practices. Whenever there were shoes in the store belonging to
any of these girls, I couldn't have enough of touching, smelling
them or putting my hands inside them.

"Thus years passed. My terrible leaning to shoes only increased and finally I was interested, also, in button shoes and high
shoes of all kinds. My tastes became not less than discriminating
and I began to pay special attention to boots and shoes belonging
to young women and girls, shoes that were yet tainted with little
perspiration. In my mind, I compared such shoes only with an
'angelically pure chalice.' I confess to a special susceptibility to
button shoes which were lined with white flannel; the odor of
them almost made me sensually drunk.

"During my early school years, I also suffered from frequent
and apparently unprovoked erections; but these erections were not
at all attended by any feelings of lust or desire, rather they were
accompanied by a feeling of general unpleasantness in the abdomen and a sort of burning in the phallus. I was also enuretic,
but that disappeared in the course of some time. In addition to
my passion for shoes, there developed in me about this time an
even more terrible and persistent one, an indulgence which has for
the past twenty years afforded me the most painful experiences
of my life. When I was about ten or twelve years old I began to
be attracted to such girls and boys as wore stiff collars. In those
days, the children wore sort of Lord Fauntleroy collars and cuffs,
and to scratch these starched linens was pure delight for me. I
can still see a relative of mine who was then a handsome little
boy. He complained to me one day that his collar was too tight
and then showed me a chafed spot on his neck. I experienced a
sudden and overpowering sexual irritation and ever since then I
have been spellbound as by a hellish influence. The thoughts of
such collars monopolized an increasingly greater share of my
mind and the sight of a girl with one of them on could drive me
nearly crazy. My heart would begin to palpitate and the blood
would rush through my body in a wave of sensuality. If the collar stood high, I would become dizzy with excitement. In addition
to this, there was, of course, my occasional flair for shoes, boots,

etc. I already had an idea of the nature of the unhappy passions which had possessed me as early as my thirteenth year, but I had as yet no notion of the word perverse. But I firmly felt that my habits and desires were singular, and thought that I was incurable, an idea that I still retain. Of course, I read several things about self-tainting, and the like.

"At about that time, it also behooved me to think of choosing some trade, but because many masters always warned me against taking up their trade or profession, it came about that I drifted into my father's business. Strangely enough, I had no real desire in this direction, despite my passion for shoes. I didn't like the idea of a constantly cooped-up, sitting position, in addition to which I feared that the trade would expose me to frequent irritation, chafing, repression and frayed nerves. Nevertheless, I could discover no other special inclination within me and remained with my father.

"Dr. Moll's book came into my hands when I was about twenty-two and I might mention here that at that time I also visited a prostitute in the company of one of my friends. The result was the usual one; I was not able to do more than get an initial erection. Even on the way there, I felt as if I were going to be impotent and, like the persons in Krafft-Ebing's book, I had no more desire to visit one of them.

"Among the various methods I undertook at that time to control my passions, I might mention specially the long walks which had the purpose of making me as tired as possible. It is my enjoyment of the beauties of nature which even to-day makes it easier for me to bear my cross.

"Whenever I would see a woman on the street (preferably one dressed in black), who wore a high collar, I would follow her until I would see her either adjust it with her hand or make some movement of the head which indicated that the collar was chafing or otherwise irritating her. In that instant, I would feel as if struck by lightning, a feeling which I can often compare only with a sudden rush of blood. As soon as this movement or action had taken place, another thought intruded upon my mind: 'The spell is strong and you are lost.' It was immediately thereafter that I would feel the sinking feeling, that rush of blood through my veins. To-day just as years ago.

"I once bought a girl a high starched linen collar, a pair of cuffs to match and then got ready for what I looked upon as a supremely enjoyable evening. She manifested considerable understanding for my inclinations and I couldn't see enough of her that evening. I got her actually to go through the almost endlessly repeated movements of loosening with her finger the collar which I had purposely tied tightly about her neck until I noticed that she had chafed her skin. My joy and gloating was nothing short of the delight of a sadist. Every time her hand went to her collar, I suffered a pleasant jolt in the pit of my stomach. The same was repeated when she bought a pair of button shoes another time. When I saw them, I instantly imagined the fun that awaited me when I would be privileged to pull them off her feet. The sad ending was that my relations with this girl were not permanent."

There followed a third affair with a girl who turned out to be pregnant and deserted by her lover. The patient writes further: "I must also not forget to mention still another passion which formed itself at about this time, viz., an interest in narrow sleeves. Of course, it was not too hard to interest the girl in these, too. She was rather a full figure and it was a rare treat for me to grip her under the arm where I could feel the perspiration; especially when she also wore a belt. I had no trouble making the girl dance to my music. Impassioned words, subtle compliments, unceasing flattery of her physical charms all aided in making her more compliant with my perverse desires. I must say that I succeeded, too. In the course of a few months we were involved in a correspondence which fairly exuded the most extravagant phantasies on my part and corresponding replies from her. I burned these letters some time ago because I couldn't stand the irritation of them. I have never forgotten their contents, however.

"I must also mention still another group of feelings I developed. I could never stand women who wore a *pince-nez,* not even if they possessed all the perverted virtues I have mentioned. It has always seemed peculiar to me that these horrible pictures nevertheless pursue me into my dreams, and not only once, but many times and, curiously enough, always with the same actions.

"I must digress to mention the fact that I visit a certain part of the country at least once or twice a year regularly. It is a place which appeals to me as an absolutely ideal retreat from all impure things of life. The dream I mention invariably produces a house somewhere in this region and as I am hesitatingly coming around one corner of the house I meet with a middle-aged woman accompanied by three pretty girls who disclose precisely that which I came to this place to be rid of.

"There are times when I feel that I have a firmer grip on myself and yet again moments when I am possessed by a deep and harassing depression. Anything which touches upon this chosen countryside idyll can also plunge me straightway into fright or sensual excitement.

"What seems to me to be the most important and significant part of the whole thing is the feeling of a splitting of my ego whenever these perverse feelings come over me. As I have already mentioned, I am always striving to overcome and suppress these perverse impulses and the depraved habits connected with them, but there are then the inevitable periods of relapse. I live in phases. There are times when my perverted desires press me more than usual, my body seems to burn with an unrelenting fever. I am oppressed and paralyzed by the pressure of a passion which is looked upon by normal persons only with undisguised sarcasm, and fear that even the best physician might, after all, have the same attitude towards my condition. And yet when a particularly charming female crosses my path, the terrible moment is upon me again and I realize to the full how deeply this frightful evil has taken root in my soul." (Extract from Löwenfeld, *Sexualleben und Nervenleiden*, 5 ed., I. F. Bergmann, Wiesbaden, 1914).

This case also shows us how that which "oppresses" so easily becomes a fetish. The patient's infantile impression of those three pretty girls also recurs in his dreams. He raises his fetish to a divine position as is shown by his calling the shoes "angelically pure" receptacles. His abhorrence of sweaty feet may be due only to a repression and would then corroborate Abraham's theory of the rôle of sweaty feet in the psychogenesis of the fetishism.[4] The relationships of this case with homosexuality are also rather plain. Always his interest generates in boys and then passes to girls, and it is a debatable question whether a fetishism can develop altogether without a considerable admixture of homosexuality. We invariably observe the avoidance of the woman and the interest in boys. In this case, he is always running after boys and only later does he transfer his interest to girls. The high, starched collars attract his attention when worn by either boys or girls. His impotence is revealed not only in his plain avoidance of women, but also by the fact that he cannot effect intercourse with prostitutes. First he succumbs to the foot fetishism, then to the collar habit and finally to a mania for narrow sleeves. Before a wave of homosexuality and the fears of woman he retreats into a parapathia; he fixates upon a symbol. He is also subject to those curious sleeplike and dream-states which we stressed in our discussion of infantilism and impulsive conduct. His split personality is fairly distinct, but it has not reached the stage of epileptiform seizures.

This case presents the interesting feature of the displacement of the paraphilia from the foot to the neck. That is somewhat analogous to Havelock Ellis's classical case in which the compression of the throat was as gratifying as the compression of the phallus. It is most certain that sadistic-criminal phantasies, of which the patient has no conscious knowledge, play a considerable rôle in this mechanism. Is it, after all, possible that the sadistic, the actively criminal, attitude of fetishists may be the reason why we see so few female fetish lovers?

Mrs. H. Hug-Hellmuth has put such a case of female shoe fetishism on record.[5]

Case 46. This case concerns the daughter of a general who from her youth has manifested a special attraction for the shiny riding boots of her father. "A man clad in boots and sitting atop a horse is the only man." She rejected divers suitors and finally engaged herself to a lieutenant thirty years her senior (father imago). She was deaf to all the arguments of her family and invariably countered with praise of his attractive feet (riding boots). Her fiancé died before she married and she chose in his place a strikingly ugly old major just because he wore very high riding boots. She is fatally infatuated with his charming boots and any civilian in his "run down" low shoes is no man at all in her eyes. "One can get the shivers at the sight of riding boots and yet love them, too," she says. The marriage, of course, was a failure. Perhaps because she is frigid. She advised a girl friend of hers not to marry because naked feet are ugly. A man with his feet naked is a gruesome sight. "I shudder even at the thought of the great toe [manifestly a phallic symbol in her mind]. And the nails that are crippled and crooked, and the little toe which cannot grow, it is all a frightful sight for me." She herself preferred to wear high shoes because of the virile and erect appearance it gave her and also because of the *pleasant sensation of being tightly laced in.* High shoes are charmingly decent because they clothe the form of the calf, but leather puttees and calf braces only accentuate these features of the leg. As a child she had wanted high riding boots and was thrilled when her father gave her a present of a pair on one of her birthdays (identification with her father).

Hellmuth remarks on this case: "The genuine character of this girl's fetishism is indicated by the fact that her complete and sole interest in a man was ultimately dedicated to his boots, the man was, as it were, the necessary accessory to the fetish, a fact which she herself quite clearly recognized in so many words. She not only rejects the normal goal of sexuality, but she takes umbrage in the thoughts of her fetish in order to make her wifely duties at all bearable."

If this case had concerned a man, he would probably have been impotent. A woman can still bear children and be a party to sexual intercourse, no matter how anæsthetic and frigid she may be. We nevertheless observe a marked flight from normal sexuality in this case. She chooses old men and avoids the young ones, not alone because this enables her to gain a father imago for herself, but also because it protects her from the stormy passions of youth. She, too, reveals the symptom of "symbolical compulsion" in her delight at being laced in high shoes. Her disgust with the naked foot is doubtless the symbolical abhorrence of the naked phallus. It is not at all proven, however, as Sadger and Hellmuth believe, that the fetish or boot in this case is a phallic substitute. The case was unfortunately not analyzed, but it is characteristic and transparent enough to be mentioned here.

An excellent example of how the symbol can completely displace the genitals is presented in Löwenfeld's next case which also concerns itself with high shoes.

Case 47. "As regards the sexual question, I must have seen some equestrienne wearing high boots as a child. It might have been in the theatre or on the street, I can't recall. But it left a lasting impression upon me, nevertheless, for even as a boy I had a curious desire to see equestriennes whenever I could, either *in natura* or on pictures. The chief factor was the boots, of course, but I was interested only if women were wearing them. When I grew to be a little older, such a sight would produce an ejaculation and I must confess that whenever and wherever I was able to gain the sight of a riding woman, whether in the theatre, the circus, a riding academy or in the park, I could not withstand the impulse to get near her. I invariably got an orgasm.

"As a result I never cultivated normal sexual intercourse, but preferred to gratify my desires in this manner. And since no other person took the trouble to advise me in the matter, I continued to follow these impulses until I was twenty-six years old. At that time, I sought the advice of an Italian psychiatrist, Prof. A. R. in M. He advised me to find myself an attractive girl, dress her in conformity with my phantasies and then to try sexual intercourse with her. I followed his advice and was successful. In that way, I gradually became accustomed to coitus, but when I began to attempt intercourse without the dress and shoes, it would succeed only sometimes and sometimes it would not. It is simply because I am more sure of myself when the woman has the proper clothing on. The female genitals as such interest me little.

"In the course of time I developed the habit of observing the shoes of women on the street. Elegant high shoes provoke a prompt erection which can persist until ejaculation if I follow the woman.

"When I see such high shoes in the display windows of shoe stores, I am mildly interested, but I never get an erection nor ever an orgasm. It is only when a woman is wearing the articles that I am affected.

"Since I have found a way to effect normal intercourse, however, I try to control my perverse desires and have heterosexual intercourse about once a week. This desire of mine is of the greatest detriment to me for I am easily susceptible to phantasies of equestriennes, and my business suffers from lack of attention. I have a business of my own and it would soon be advantageous for me to marry, so that I might have some aid. At present my father is still helping me out, but he is old. Marriage will doubtless be an impossibility, however, as long as I am afflicted with such ideas. The Italian professor advised me another time to marry an equestrienne, an idea which might be of theoretical value, but practically it could not work. For what would I do with such a woman in my financial condition? In addition, I would first have to get acquainted with one. The very sight of such a female would so excite me that I would become orgiastic and thus weaker than ever." (From Löwenfeld, l. c.)

All these cases reveal an hyperbolic development of a specific sexual taste which may look absurd as long as psychoanalytical insight has not solved their eccentricities. The one loves only women who wear *pince-nez* and the other hates women who wear *pince-nez*. This negative attitude is a trait which Hirschfeld once erroneously named "anti-fetishism." [6] Aversion must, of course, be looked upon from the same point of view as the desires. Whether the fetish is of a negative or a positive value in the mind of the patient is an irrelevant matter to the psychologist. He finds in both forms of expression one and the same force. I could therefore no more accept Hirschfeld's anti-fetishism as a separate paraphilia than I can his transvestitism. Psycho-sexual partial aversion [7] is nothing more than a specially marked psycho-sexual partial desire. One of his patients has an insurmountable aversion to female breasts and even avoids the word breast in his speech. Hs is a physician and avoids percussing or auscultating women's chests in front, not to speak of palpating the mammæ. That was the reason why he became a pediatrician. He says he does not know the cause for this antipathy and then he adds a phrase which is so typical of parapathics and especially of parapathic physicians: "I have probed myself carefully and find nothing which could be blamed as the cause of this aversion." Such a statement is, of course, no proof at all, as I shall be able to demonstrate in my own case of anti-fetishism described later on. Another patient, a woman, hates men who wear beards; a third despises brown or yellow shoes and even damages them in hotels whenever he comes across them before the doors of guests. The following case is such a one from the collection of Hirschfeld. It is a revealing study and shows that behind the anti-fetishism there lurk objects which are despised because they are unconsciously valued as sexual symbols, just as we learned was the case in the discussion of kleptomania.

Case 48. A thirty-one-year-old mechanic suffers from a "real hatred" of mother-of-pearl buttons. He cannot recall ever to have been free from the spell of this hatred of underwear or shirt buttons, but it was only later in life that he came to realize that it had anything to do with his sexual life. He had otherwise always had normal and uneventful heterosexual intercourse. P. said: "All

kinds of buttons on underwear, shirts, etc., appear indecent to me
and, according to my personal and by no means definitive opinion,
they are also immoral. The larger and shinier they are the uglier
and more disgusting I find them. Those covered with some white
cloth disturb me less. I can still remember how furiously I went
after the buttons on the underthings of my sister when I was between seven and twelve years old. I couldn't tear them off because I couldn't get hold of them, but I cut them off with a scissors
and then kicked them about. My parents frequently punished me
for such bad habits, but I could not refrain from the impulse,
although I was otherwise quite a well-behaved boy. Even to-day I
hate such buttons wherever I see them. If I see a woman who
pleases me and then follow her, I find her quite uninteresting as
soon as I discover a deficiently covered row of buttons on her dress
or at the back of her blouse. The most monstrous example of ugli-
ness for me are those new types of corsets which have buttons instead of hooks and eyes. A woman swaddled in one of those
things would repel me, even if she were a paragon of female
physical beauties. The more a collection of such repulsive buttons
looks as if it were in a row, the more disgusted do I become.
Curiously enough, ever since I have been seventeen or eighteen, the
sight of such a row of buttons makes me think of a row of swine's
or dog's teats. I should much prefer to see women's underwear
and blouses tied or hooked, although I am not at all fetishistic
about strings or ribbons; neither are hooks and eyes or snaps
irritating to me, but I am revolted by the disgusting sight of open-
ings in the blouses or dresses of some women. And yet despite
my indescribable antipathy to these objects, I am always on the
lookout for them and see them frequently enough. And if I
happen to discover a naked, shiny button through the opening of
the blouse or dress, the woman appears viler in my eyes than if
she were naked. My disgust becomes acute at times and I could
certainly never cohabit with such a woman, nor even speak with
her."

It is easy to recognize that these buttons are only the symbols of nipples for this man and the anti-fetishist admits it
himself in his phantasy. It is precisely in the case of fetishism
that we can observe the colossal sexual significance of the symbol. The sadistic component is sufficiently portrayed in his cutting off the buttons on his sister's things with a scissors. He
also kicked the buttons about afterwards. It appears that his

conduct reveals a displacement of hate from the sister to the buttons, his sister having been his rival for his mother's love. "The mother swine" speaks for itself. That he is a repressed peeping Tom is clearly betrayed by his very emotional reaction to involuntary exposure.

Hirschfeld (*Sexual Pathologie,* Vol. III) reports the female counterpart to this case.

Case 49. "A most singular case of my observation concerns a woman who suffers from a fetishism of collar buttons. Her basic feeling is an intense hatred of these articles, and she is greatly irritated both by the sight of such buttons and also of the rings which their pressure so frequently leaves in the skin. But if her sexual appetite is aroused by a man—usually a 'pure line' roué, as she puts it—her fear of the buttons and her aversion to them transforms itself into a passionate curiosity to see them. She would like to put them in her mouth if possible and destroy them. This case is very instructive on the question of the transformation of a feeling from a negative to a positive type."

This case is quite as transparent as the one before. The fetish hate is ultimately shown to be a fetish love. In this case it is the repression of a fellatio phantasy.

I would also like to mention that in this treatise Hirschfeld has also mentioned the novel *Fetish-Hass* (Fetish Hate) by Gustav Adolph Weber (Berlin, York Verlag). That novel describes the life of a woman who had a decided aversion to full dress suits. She experiences all kinds of quarrels and troubles with waiters and the like, nearly chokes with her own passions and finally—falls in love with a full-dressed valet. The author then proceeds to describe how her hatred of his clothing struggles with her desires until she succumbs to the positive tendencies. When, after the first intimate scene between them, she opened her eyes and saw her lover again clothed in his black dress, she was "seized with a fit of terrible anger, a rush of hatred filled her brain. Like red tongues of flame through which the black suit shimmered sarcastically at her, the passion danced before her eyes, and before she could realize what she was doing she had seized a revolver from out of the dresser drawer and had fired a bullet at Reinhard's head."

The analyst clearly understands such cases. They constitute one's psychological a b c's. One could easily cite a long list of such apparent cases of anti-fetishism. I recall a woman who once told me that she had but one real aversion: large, strong, self-possessed men with a "Wilhelm II" mustache. Her first lover who had betrayed her was of this type and it was evident that her anti-fetishism was a self-protective mechanism for her.

I shall close the series of these cases with a history which Hirschfeld would certainly label with "anti-fetishism."

Case 50. For the past few months the eighteen-year-old patient W. B. has been suffering from a complete inability to study. He had always been an industrious and good student and had even found time for other things. For some time now he has found it difficult to absorb knowledge and to pay attention to his work. He cannot progress unless his tutor or his mother sit with him while he is studying. He is irritable and hypochondriacal, always dejected, shows no brightness and no interest in anything. He complains of pains in the back, sleeps poorly and only long after he has gone to bed, awakens late and is usually tired, and also complains of headaches which begin in the neck and radiate down into his back.

Since such complaints are frequently heard after some sexual abstinence, I questioned him about his sex life. He states that he has never masturbated because he was early enlightened by an uncle who described to him the terrible results of this practice. He has also never cohabited with a woman. At fourteen he was sexually enlightened by a schoolmate, told his mother about it, and she then referred the matter to his uncle again for the proper explanations. The uncle then preached to him about the frightful consequences of early intercourse. He said that nervous diseases would be the result, one succumbed to libertinage, there were frightful venereal diseases in store for one which would either kill one early or cause one to suffer for life. He had best control himself and wait until he could marry.

Latterly, however, sexual phantasies had overcome him at times and he was perplexed. He had frequent wet dreams, always about women and never about men. He looks after every woman on the street and weaves a romantic robe of phantasy about each and every one. Suddenly he said: I have one great aversion: women with large feet. They make me sick. I could never be tender to such a woman and when I accidentally note that some woman has big feet, I'm through with her.

He lays this anti-fetishism to one of his earliest infantile impressions. When he was twelve, a schoolmate of his pointed out a Slavish woman to him, one out of so many that are to be seen in Vienna. They wear short, peasant skirts, and their calves are exposed. His schoolmate said: "Look at those classy legs." He looked, but what he saw were thick legs that "hung almost over her shoes." Ever since then he has been conscious of an aversion to large feet in women.

"Does your mother or your sister have large feet?"

"No. My mother has lovely feet which are rather small."

He then related how as a child he was quite devout and went to church every morning. They had a very strict professor of religion whom he didn't like. He hated this teacher and after some contact with a proselyted Jew, he became completely independent of the church and religious habits. He preserved a firm belief in God, but did not observe the forms of the Catholic church. He is, also, very superstitious and is the butt of all the family's jokes because of this. He has his unlucky days, believes in the dire influence of the number 13, the dangers of a Friday and the like. He also believes in lucky omens as, for example, that the teacher would always examine him on just what he had studied.

He claims to be distrustful and suspicious of everybody. His mother, he claims, supervises him constantly and does not believe him. He takes a walk every day, but his mother believes that he is sitting in some café or other or is wasting time with a colleague. He is easily influenced. He realized this for the first time when his friend weaned him away from his religious practices. He was easily turned against his family. Once he let himself be hypnotized and fell asleep quickly.

He likes art and is especially fond of the old pictures. He can't stand modern paintings and considers them to be a hodgepodge of paints. The old paintings, however, are full of lovely, soft colors and a delightful quiet. The modern ones are noisy and cannot elevate the soul.

He hates everybody. He is much attracted by the anarchistic literature and considers their tenets as self-evident and true. Any authority disturbs him and provokes his animosity. He is pleased whenever he hears that some anarchist has attempted an assassination somewhere. I explained to him that this attitude was manifestly derived from a hatred of his father and this he promptly corroborated.

He is an illegitimate child and does not know who his father is. His mother has never mentioned his father's name to him, but he hates him passionately, nevertheless, and would kill him if he could only learn his name. How is it possible to bring a child into the world and not worry further about it? It is his deepest shame that everybody in school knows that he is an illegitimate child. But he can't help that. He is especially afraid that his father may turn out to be a Jew. He is an ardent anti-Semite and hates all Jews. He has convinced himself that his father is really a Jew. He fears that people may think he looks like a Jew and likes to wear a cross, so that his Christianity may be noticeable.

After a few hours of further analysis, he related how jealous he is of his sister. He counts the minutes whenever she goes out and says that he will kill the man who tries to become intimate with her. Finally, he confessed that he loved her himself and that he has often had to fight back the desire to make her his mistress. He is even conscious of the incestuous phantasies in regard to his mother and frequently dreams of intercourse with his mother or his sister. He is afraid to have intercourse with any other girl. Since he does not know his father, it might barely be possible that the girl he slept with would be his sister (parapathics love to travel in such roundabout paths when they see their sister in every woman). All these factors are driving him to homosexuality. He has become interested in handsome men and can follow and rave about a trim-looking officer just as if he were a girl. He is particularly jealous of his sister in respect of officers because he believes that their wooing is irresistible.

"Yesterday," he says, "I saw an officer who attracted my attention and followed him for about a quarter of an hour."

"Did you also look at his feet?"

"I never see them. I never look at boots."

"Why not?"

"Because . . . well, I can't say."

"Is it so unpleasant that you must hide the fact?"

"Well, yes. I have never said anything about that. Men really don't animate me. It's only a Platonic attraction I have to them. But if a man has a well-formed foot or wears elegant boots with spurs, then I become sexually excited. I am then afraid that I could become a homosexual."

"Must the officer's foot be large or small to excite you?"

"To tell you the truth, it is only a large foot or a large nose which excites my passion. A colleague of mine once told me that men with large feet or large noses also had a large penis."

I may close the case at this point. The anti-fetish is really the memory of the large male foot. The analysis also showed that as a little boy he had been interested in the large feet of his mother. He tried to wear her shoes and would attempt to put his little feet into them. Although his mother had fairly small feet, her shoes were then always too large for him and that frustrated him. He wished to have a foot which was large enough for him to wear mother's shoes. This case also indicates an erotic symbolism, the fetish representing the phallus. His anti-fetish is a protection against his incestuous thoughts and the homosexuality which resulted from their repression.

In this case, which is distinctly one of partialism, we can observe the infantile roots of the illness (anti-partialism, Hirschfeld would say). His mother's foot appeared very large to him when he was a child. There is also a marked homosexual component. He hates a woman who reminds him of a man. It is the unknown foot of his unknown father that he seeks and hates. He would kill his father, he says, if he could only find him. He only knows that his father is rich now and is living in luxury. His mother had said this. She, too, had lived in luxury as long as she was the mistress of this man, but now she has to live from the interest of the hush-money he gave her. Every woman who looks elegant and appears to be living in the lap of luxury provokes in him the thought that she, too, is a kept woman. He is afraid his sister might become a kept woman also.

He is particularly animated by the sight of officers when he sees them tightly buttoned into their uniforms. Hussars are his special delight because they have plenty of braid, tight and narrow breeches and high riding boots. The large foot he likes to see compressed into a narrow boot. His preference for officers is a derivative of his persistent infantilism. Women's susceptibility to the colors is also partly due to an infantilism and partly to the belief that officers and soldiers are characterized by a specially great potency. The love for the colors is also to be found among homosexuals who disclose all kinds of partialisms. I have again and again heard patients praise the attractiveness of a tightly fitting uniform. The soldier is, of course, the very apotheosis of compulsion which is euphemistically called "discipline."

So-called fetishistic leanings are to be found quite as frequently among homosexuals as among heterosexuals (we shall later on become acquainted with such a case). The particular case can be either one of partialism or of true fetishism, the fetish in this event then replacing the man in the homosexual's mind. The fact that soldiers are a singular object of these types points to the infantilistic root of the condition. Everyone knows what a tremendous rôle the soldier plays in the life of every child. The uniform is enough to provoke the senses and excite the phantasy. The criminal instincts of the child thus also gain expression since the soldier is after all the paramount carrier of weapons. Stabbing and shooting can best be played as a soldier without the oppression of growing social constraint. Hirschfeld has stressed these traits of the homosexual and I find his discussion sufficiently interesting and important to include it here.

"But even here there are also very marked differentiations within each group. Thus, among the soldier lovers, we may find those who deal only with infantrymen, others who fall for non-commissioned officers, still others who desire officers' aides and those who strive only after officers of higher rank. Besides, the kind of troops also plays an important rôle. Some look with favor only upon the infantry, others upon the cavalry, etc. I knew of a homosexual who became interested only in the special Uhlan guard, whereas the rest of the German army did not exist for him. Not long ago I had to examine a physician who displayed a love for cavalry officers only. Since his profession in no wise brought him together with them, he sought to entice them to his quarters by starting up some financial business or other with them. It seems apparent that fetishism plays a great part in all these cases and it would not be difficult to find indications of the same tendencies in almost any homosexual.

"That we are here actually dealing with fetishism may appear from the fact that whenever there is no fetish, the homosexual manifests indifference to the sexual object or even an aversion.

Thus, for example, some soldier lovers have told me how 'completely cool they were towards former soldier friends of theirs when they afterwards saw them as civilians or reservists.' The latter, on the other hand, are just as astonished at the conduct of their former lovers, once they have returned to that long-awaited state of the civilian. A young priest wrote me: 'I am a thorough homosexual and my type is a strong, handsome man of about twenty-five to forty. I am not interested in whether this man be blond or dark, but he must have sympathetic features and wear a mustache. Men with full beards or clean-shaven faces leave me cold. Just how much the mustache has to do with it may be illustrated by the following. My uncle, an important Catholic clerical with whom I lived during my student days, had a chaplain who possessed just the features I have described to you, but as a Catholic cleric he was not permitted to wear a beard. We were both quite friendly without my being in the least sexually animated by him. One day I bought a false mustache at a barber's and took it home. I gave it to him and begged him to try it on. He complied with my request and I must say that I was overcome with a rush of sexual excitement which cost me great efforts of self-control to keep from embracing him and kissing him.'

"Just how detailed and specialized the tastes of a homosexual can become may be illustrated by the following infrequent cases. I have known homosexuals who have displayed an interest only in policemen, others who have loved only fraternity men. One of my patients loved only shepherds. He searched for them far and wide. 'Once,' he told me, 'I was in San Remo and spied a shepherd at the top of a hill among his sheep. I had unfortunately left my binoculars at home, but since he appeared even at that great distance to be a young man, I set out for him, although the road passed into the valley first and then became very difficult. It took me over an hour and when I got to the top I saw that he was a very old man. I have often been fooled like that.'

"Another man was always attracted by a specially prominent seventh cervical vertebra and still another by bald heads. I made the acquaintance of two homosexual brothers in Brussels once, the one of whom loved only hunters and the other chauffeurs.

"One of my patients never had anything to do with any men but those from the Rhineland, Westphalia or Pomerania. Saxons, Hamburgers and Alsatians were taboo for him. One man was excited only by men who smoked short pipes. Some homosexuals and Lesbians have told me that handsome men left them cold whereas revoltingly ugly men attracted them. I must stress the fact that the differentiation in taste goes just as far among the Lesbians as it does among homosexuals. One of my patients was interested only in married women, another only in house-maids, a third was attracted by furs and large earrings and a fourth loved women 'not under 200 pounds in weight.'

"When the former minister of war, von Einem, said of homosexuals, 'I have read in papers and scientific treatises that such men always look for men who manifest strength and physical perfection, as, for example, porters, drivers and beer wagon drivers,' he showed how one-sided his orientation on the matter was.

"A speculating military tailor in Berlin whose establishment was a frequented resort of homosexuals, kept a collection of all kinds of uniforms in his closets with which he was able to transform any kind of Uhlan or infantryman into a sailor or marine. There were also many other perquisites for the demands of homosexuals, e.g., apache bandannas, priest's collars, boots and spurs, etc. To follow the causes of such individual eccentricities as far as the endogenous limits set by the personal constitution, we must resort to psychoanalysis. On the basis of a rather exhaustive statistical study of the traits desired in the love object as compared with the homosexuals own make-up, I have found that about fifty-five percent look for characteristics which coincide with their own, whereas about forty-five percent seek traits of an opposite nature as a complementary consummation of their own ego." (Hirschfeld, *Die Homosexualität*, p. 282.)

The author has made an absolutely accurate observation. The last patient we considered had large feet himself and was greatly pained by the fact. The very little foot of the child had become a very large foot later. Originally he had been very proud of this size, but then his polar attitude came to the fore. The psychoanalytical study of these cases will invariably disclose an infantile cause of the individual's personal tastes.

Some of Hirschfeld's cases have nothing in common with true fetishism. They concern cases of partialism, the fixation of infantile impressions. But even such cases reveal the phenomenon of the compulsion. The partialist is, after all, caught in the corner of a certain and definite condition. He often fights against this obsession but he cannot overcome it. Is it possible that a single infantile impression should be capable of

acting as a compulsion throughout an individual's existence?
I am skeptical about Binet's theory ever since I have examined
these cases analytically. It is too easy.

That the essence of partialism and anti-partialism is not to
be explained in this manner is clearly demonstrated by the psychogenesis of our last case. There the large foot was the
symbol of a mistress. Indeed, we also find a direct sexual
interest in the foot and the indication of his mother's large
feet. But an analytical examination of these cases shows how
dangerous it is to bind one's self to a certain theory. Thus,
e.g., there was no basis for the opinion that a sweaty foot had
been etiologically important in the development of the partialism in the last-mentioned case. Nor is it *a priori* to be assumed. I have seen many cases of hand partialism which were
not a whit less intense than the cases of foot partialism. And
in no case was there any evidence of the rôle of a perspiring
hand. It was the mother's hand which had played with the
phallus during infancy, or the hand of a governess. Or the
hand was an indication of masturbation and many other mental associations. Such cases are not to be confounded with
fetishism. It is, of course, entirely different in the case of a
glove fetishist with a *penchant* for kid gloves, who puts the
ladies' gloves on only to feel their tightness and produce the
phantasy that his finger is inextricably clamped into the glove.
It is noteworthy that this patient was able to achieve an orgasm
only when his penis, too, was tightly pressed.

But I would have to repeat myself endlessly if I were to
trace the manifestations of hand fetishism as I have done for
foot fetishism.

Both forms have the common feature of the compulsion,
the phantasy of compression and being tightly laced in; the
avoidance of and retreat from the woman and the harem cult.

The need for a coerced situation may often lead the patient
to compress his own penis and we have frequently heard of
parapathics who have bound their phallus with string or ribbon.
Some do it at night in bed and others wear such articles by
day.

Many otherwise puzzling phenomena find a solution by
means of such an approach. Maresch once demonstrated a

pathological case in the Vienna Academy of Medicine ("Ein Fall von jahrelanger Einschnürung des Penis durch einen Fingerring," Wiener klinische Wochenschrift, 1920, No. 5). At a post mortem a man was found with a ring around his penis. The wearing of the ring there had led to the development of an urethral fistula.

The catamnestic study of the case disclosed that the deceased, who was married, had not had sexual intercourse for the past ten years and that he had at that time, i.e., ten years ago, complained of unpleasant and painful erections. His wife had advised him to consult a physician and when she later asked him about his condition, he told her that he no longer needed the aid of a physician. The woman knew nothing of the ring. We are therefore not far from the truth if we surmise that the deceased applied the ring to his penis at about that time, especially since the anatomical examination of the region discloses nothing which would stand in the way of such a supposition. The man suffered the not inconsiderable consequences of the incarceration of his penis without the desire to consult a physician, nor did the urethral fistula seem to bother him either. For if he had gone to a doctor, he would have been freed from the ring at least. The nurse and the fellow patients in his ward also stated that he had visited the toilet with remarkable frequency during his residence in the hospital and that he had used up a great number of towels with which, as the pathological specimen shows, he had successfully protected himself against the development of an eczema.[8]

Simple persons choose a simple tool for the execution of their compulsion. The greater the individual's differentiation as a personality, the more complicated does his obsessional mechanism become.

One other circumstance necessitates a separate discussion. We have seen that the chief factor in all these cases is the impulsive conduct. Many of these foot fetishists are kleptomaniacs, they steal the shoes they desire, make a whole collection of them; steal gloves, corsets, and all the rest. What is the relationship between these impulses and the compulsion?

First of all, every civilized person would feel such an irresistible impulse as an unpleasant compulsion. The civilized person struggles against his instincts, he wants to overcome them, he wants to save himself from these compulsions and coercions. That inner freedom and independence which is the highest ideal of every individual can be attained only through the conquest of compulsion and constraint. The original compulsion can no longer be recognized in the fetishism itself. The impulse has become transformed, the affect is displaced, the compulsion has been transferred from a sexual to a symbolical object. The patient no longer strives towards the possession of a desired person; he succumbs to his passion, his compulsion, but in a symbolical garb. His ascetic tendencies are pacified by the fact that his striving avoids sexual intercourse or at least reduces it to a minimum. He has opposed an anti-compulsion to the original one. Obsessional symptoms are reactions to an unrealizable instinctual striving, the deeper, more primitive reaction changing to a quite atypical reaction of the civilized man. He succumbs to a compulsion, indeed, but it is an obsession which he has forced upon himself, only in order to avoid the demands of his own sexuality. The fetishist has forced himself into the clutches of one compulsion only as a means of freeing himself from an earlier one. He plays the paraphilic and remains ascetic. For him the compulsions of civilization, education, religion and ethics remain triumphant. This constraint, however, is no longer foreign to him because the paraphilia is his very own creation. In reality, he is not at all attracted by the foot. He acts only as if the foot were his sexual object (Vaihinger). He accepts the fiction only to flee from the reality of his own sex. The bipolar tendency of being a Don Juan, Satan, libertine, faithless husband on the one hand, and the priest, saint, and savior on the other, is fully expressed in his own creation. Once his system has been erected, he looks upon the instincts, the impulses as foreign elements and the fetishism is the heart's desire. The impulse is inactivated by the fetishism, as it were, and made forever innocuous. But the power of that original impulse is never lost. It is only deflected in its course and exerts an influence which is opposed to its original purpose. It becomes a part of that system which seeks evil and yet achieves good.

In the symbol of compression the patient thus expresses both tendencies: the impulses of his instincts and the compulsions of his obsessional neurosis.

I thus return to my old formula: fetishism is nothing but a kind of compulsion neurosis. Its psychic structure can be understood only in the light of an obsessional neurosis. Erotic symbolism expresses this constraint in its choice of a fetish which is the manifest and visible symbol of the compulsion.

XI

CASE MATERIAL.

The result of our study thus far is the knowledge that fetishism is a kind of compulsion, which the patient forces upon himself out of the motive of atonement. It seems to be a paraphilia, but it is really a religion, a cult. The lords of this religion are the gods of childhood. The fetish itself must be capable of representing the compulsive character of this religion, which invariably bears the stamp of constraint, symbolically.[1] It must be something protective, covering or compressive. It is for this reason that shoes are so suitable as symbols because they do clothe and protect the foot from dirt. That is also the reason why tight trousers or corsets are so often chosen, simply because they cover or compress the body. It is understandable, too, how several fetishes may be used simultaneously as long as they all express the same tendency. It is as if the same thing were being expressed in different languages. A shoe fetishist could thus also reveal other forms of fetishism and it is just such a case which Abraham has reported.[2] I should like here to discuss his case.

Case 51. Abraham described a twenty-two-year-old university student who in puberty had already differed from others of his age by the fact that he displayed no interest in the opposite sex. He considered himself impotent. When he was 14, he began to bind himself in divers ways. At fifteen he began to observe the more elegant shoes of some of his schoolmates. And then came the typical change. He proceeded to transfer his interest from male to female shoes and was particularly fetched by the thought of how uncomfortable walking in such shoes must be.

He put the left shoe on the right foot and the right on the left just to find out on his own person what such discomfort could mean. This interchanging of left and right is a wonderful symbolic act. It means that he would like to make a woman out of a man, and that is probably derived from a deep identification with his mother. When he was sixteen he took one of his mother's old corsets, laced himself into it and then went out for a walk. Here again we meet with a case of fetishism in which the necessary implements are taken from the mother's arsenal. The patient related: "When I see women and girls wearing corsets and then think of the pressure which is being exerted upon their breasts and abdomens, I get erections." Contrary to the cases which I have seen, however, his dreams, too, often deal with corsets and lacing them up, etc. He displays a marked coprophilic olfactory lust which is derived from his infantilism. One of his most frequently recurrent memories is a picture in which he sees his mother wading in some water. For me that seems to contain the nucleus of his foot fetishism. Until his tenth year he was very tender with his mother and often went to her bed. He yearns to be a woman and this desire palpably has something to do with his strong castration phantasies. He also manifests the typically infantile habit of retaining his excrements, and it was always in the toilet that he used to bind himself. These habits doubtless were due to the persistent effect of phantasies about being swaddled in diapers. Moreover, he used also to bind up his genitals.

Abraham also reported a dream from this patient.

He finds himself together with his brother on a ship which is passing through a harbor. In order to pass out of this harbor it is necessary for them to ride under a barrier which looks like a house built hanging over the water. They are then out in free water, but suddenly find themselves on land with the ship passing down a street, without, however, touching the earth. They seem to be riding in the air. A policeman was watching them.

The dream was not recognized by Abraham in its fundamental light since the author did not at the time of the publication know of the so-called spermatozoa dreams. The important association which the patient produced on the barrier; the Colossus of Rhodes, explains the dream. The Colossus of Rhodes represents a giant who stands with outspread legs across the entrance to the harbor of Rhodes. It reminds him of his father urinating. The dream represents the patient himself as a spermatozoon riding through his mother's body, and that is also the basis for the curious flying found later in the dream (Cf. also the womb dream of a previous case). The meaning of the dream is: I'd like to be born again and start my life over. I'd like to be a child again. Once this patient also dreamed that his shoes were so run down at the heels that his heels showed through. Among other determinants, this dream means also that he feels himself losing his parapathia. Such is more frequently the case in an analysis than psychoanalysts themselves believe. The reason is that, once the patient has begun to reveal the details and secrets of his parapathia, it loses its supreme value for him. The parapathia is his most intimate secret, and once he has decided to betray it, he has practically decided to give it up. Indeed, Abraham is right when he interprets the heel as a genital substitute, but every fetish replaces the genitals and is produced in the first place only because some erogenous zone is involved. But that does not explain the essence of the fetishism, as we have already shown.

For the present, we shall leave Abraham's case at this point. I shall have an opportunity of discussing his theory of foot fetishism later on. We must remember one thing, however, and that is the tendency: I want to be a woman. It is a striving which is present in every case of true fetishism. It gives us insight into the curious avoidance of the woman. Whenever the fetish lover collects women's shoes, he phantasies how they might fit him. The same holds true of chemises, corsets, aprons, petticoats, hats, etc. The homosexual basis of the fetishism also achieves its ends in this powerful wish. Even the patient's spermatozoon dream might conceivably have had this wish as a basis, i.e., if I only had the opportunity to live my life over again, I should like to be a girl, like mother or sister. It is only a short step from such a wish to the transvestitism of Hirschfeld. As a matter of fact, all transvestites reveal the characteristics of fetishists. They collect female articles of apparel, cultivate a harem of such goods, and disappear into an otherwise inaccessible realm with all the power of a frenzied phantasy.

The following case displays all these signs in addition to some other interesting ones. It was reported by Otto Walther.

Case 52. M. K., a journalist, was thirty-six years old when admitted to the psychopathic pavilion of the general hospital. Nothing was elicited concerning hereditary stigmatization. He was only a fair pupil in school and graduated from high school at twenty. He then studied law in the Universities of Berlin and Marburg. After failing twice in his bar examinations in Kassel, he became a journalist upon the death of his father and managed to keep himself in rather fair pecuniary circumstances. His family had not supported him too well nor had they left him much.

He was usually affiliated with the conservative papers, thus in W. where he was rather looked up to, moved in the best circles, became a member of the Conservative party, etc. In 1895 he married, but the marriage was not fruitful. For this reason, he adopted a little girl in 1898 at the urgent request of his wife. He had not cultivated sexual intercourse with his wife. 1899 to June, 1900, he was the managing editor of the paper in R. and appears to have done well according to the publisher.

K. was arrested and charged with repeated attempts at fraud, it being claimed that he tried to acquire a farm in Silesia under false pretences and that he had approached wealthy persons for loans with false promises of collateral.

It was only when the prosecuting attorney had asked a sentence of three years in prison and the judge had postponed passing sentence that he confessed to his attorney that he had not sought the acquisition of the farm solely for financial or economic reasons, but that he had hoped to satisfy his other desires easier in the country. He then related that he was possessed of an impulsive attraction to aprons and linens and that he believed his wife would find it easier to clothe herself according to his desires out there than in the city. He then confessed to the possession of diaries, letters, and to some episode with the police in Dr. where he was charged with disorderly conduct. The patient's attorney then asked for a stay of sentence and the psychiatric examination of the defendant. The plea was granted and K. turned over to an institution.

He dates his susceptibility to aprons from a very early period in his life and believes that one of the exciting causes was the fact that his nurse used to place aprons in his crib to quiet him. At first his passions centered on the aprons of his mother and sister. He would even take them clandestinely and hide them away. Despite frequently painful punishments for his habits, he continued to indulge his impulses and even as a student later in life he manifested these tastes. When as a student, he became engaged to his present wife, he would often take some of her aprons surreptitiously on visits to her home and bring them back to Berlin with him. It was during this period that his interest in washable goods awakened in him, allegedly because his fiancée and her sister wore them. But to this day his special delight has been aprons.

The aprons must be made of washable goods and must also be printed in certain colors and patterns. He prefers articles which have been worn and are dirty; and he cannot suffer his fetishes to be washed. The thought that his "dear little aprons" are not carefully handled, even mistreated by washing, provokes almost physical pain in him. As a matter of fact, it even hurts him to see aprons and linens to his taste worn by strangers because the thought then bobs up that they are not being properly cared for. For this reason, and also because these articles simply captivate his fancy, he has often followed the wearers of them and has bargained for their purchase, despite the fact that he possesses trunks and closets full of them at home. It was during such an episode in Dr. that he was suspected of attempted disorderly conduct. He had seen a little girl wearing an apron which attracted his attention, followed her home and then told her to ask her mother whether she wouldn't like to sell him the apron. He said that he would come back in the evening and get the piece. When he returned, he was arrested. He explained to the police that he had only wanted to buy the apron for a collection he had. The police made a search of his quarters and actually found a pile of similar articles, the origin and fate of which were carefully noted in books which looked like business books or diaries (beginning with the year 1897). In B. he had given an order to a junk woman, Mrs. U., to buy him an apron he had seen on a little girl and there was evidence of other orders for aprons, too. But he was not interested in old or worn goods alone. He would never miss the opportunity of buying new ones if he saw satisfactory ones in a store.

He gave the following information on his vita sexualis. He masturbated only during his student days, and then without much gratification. He cannot recall just how he came to begin the practice, but declares that his aprons had nothing to do with it. Soon, however, he gave up the habit after having read a book on the subject of the "terrible detriments" which follow it. He has never had heterosexual intercourse, not even during the eight years of his matrimony. That was, of course, a frequent cause of marital difficulty, especially since his wife wanted very much to have a child. That was the reason why he complied with his wife's desire to adopt a child. He feels that his doings with his aprons and linens has been a substitute for intercourse and that his desires have been spent in the one direction rather than the other. He feels tenderly bound to his wife, but his relationship has no more to do with sexuality than his interest in the women who wear aprons he desires. He is ultimately attracted only by the objects which they wear. He states that he has frequently thought of meeting his wife's demands if only to have an heir to the farm he intended to acquire, but the aprons formed an obstacle to his intentions. It was as if they had spoken to him and said that he dared not do so for their sake.

He described his practices with the aprons and linens as follows. The sight and possession of his aprons and washable goods affords him a feeling of pleasant comfort and satisfaction. He never becomes sexually excited by these objects nor does he ever use them for onanistic purposes. He is pleased simply by the sight of a woman or girl wearing them. He also piles his bed full of these articles at night and takes the apron which is dearest to him at the moment into bed with him without, however, masturbating with it. By day he hangs them about the room, strokes them, kisses them and talks to them "like to a wife or child." Even while travelling, he invariably has several of these pieces with him, thus also on his last trip to Pomerania (he actually had two aprons in his possession when arrested).

He was also happy in keeping books and diaries about the acquisition and qualities of his goods (ever since 1897).

Because his wife and daughter began to refuse to put the rather old-fashioned and often dirty aprons on, he conceived the idea that if he lived in the country, they would probably not need to be so ashamed and would not be reluctant to wear what he desired them to put on. That was the beginning of his plans to acquire a farm. But, in addition to the hope of achieving his desires in the solitude of the country, his plans were also motivated by a host of other notions which had developed in him during the past few years. He believes that the possession of a large piece of land will enable him to realize many of his ideas for the improvement of man's social lot. At first he was reluctant about discussing these ideas, but finally he was cajoled into betraying some of them. As a landed gentleman, he feels that his party connection would bring him in touch with the most influential of cabinet circles and that perhaps he might even receive a special dispensation from the Reichstag. He talked of ministerial affairs and even hinted at the possibility of becoming minister himself. Arrived at such a level, he would be able to carry out the plans for progress and social improvement which lodge in his mind. What they are, he is not yet ready to reveal. He did not speak of his activities as a managing editor of a newspaper with any shadow of boastfulness, but stated simply that he thought he had executed his position with thoroughness and satisfaction.

The history of his further residence in the institution reveals that for about two years (1898-1899) he suffered from periodic attacks of headache which affected the frontal and occipital regions especially. He was a regular addict of about three headache powders a day. For the past two or three years, he has suffered from disturbed and irregular sleep and often awakens with fright. He is always begging to be given the children's aprons to be found among his things and claims that he cannot live without them. He is frequently lachrymose.

The following is an extract from his diaries.

"Dark brown apron with the blue striped border. Upon my request, tied it on again early this morning after it had been put on. But only to-day, after she had washed and dressed Marga; so that the horror of seeing her washing Marga in the sweet apron was spared me. Breakfasted in it and then carried the dishes into the kitchen in it. Wore it while washing and rubbing Marga's hair with bay rum. Had it on when I put on Marga's puttees and rubbers and she touched the apron with her arm, so that it was again folded and creased. Much to my greatest pain, the little apron again hangs full of creases and ruffles. It is all crumpled and pulled and even the blue striped border is just covered with wrinkles and crumples left and right. I'm all disconsolate that the dear little apron has been so mistreated by being put on again.

LITTLE DARK BROWN APRON

"Sunday. J. made me completely happy to-day by tying on that little brown apron. On a Sunday, too, despite the fact that it's not washed and I had never expected her to put it on here in N-Str. The lovely little apron has not been washed or cleaned since the days in R., W., St., Dr., and St., nor even since that day in O. twelve years ago when she put it on the first time. When she put it on, she reminded me of the fact that that was one of my oldest aprons, etc. To my deepest chagrin J. then continued by saying that the apron appeared shoddy and would probably soon fall apart from decay." He then describes a quarrel with his wife about the wearing of the apron and his wife gives in to him.

There follow some tales about some other aprons, thus, e.g., the white, ribbed apron with the little trimmings, the blue striped and ribbed apron, the dark blue ribbed apron with the red-ribbed hem and shoulder straps, the little blue one with the red flowered border, the light yellow ribbed apron with the blue ribbed border, etc., etc.

Among other things his descriptions of his washable goods: blue striped blouse with the sailor collar, the blue striped and ribbed washable dress, the dark blue washable dress, etc., etc.

Even his letters to his wife indicate his worry about his dear little aprons and washables. He wrote her that she shouldn't dare to put on his lovely, dear, little aprons while he was away.

At the taking of evidence, his mother stated that as a boy and also during the period of his later high school days, he had manifested a peculiar leaning towards aprons, especially blue ones. She had frequently noticed that some of her own wearing apparel was missing, and later would find the articles crumpled away or laid out in some corner of one of her son's drawers. Admonishing or punishing him was of no avail. Her deceased husband had looked upon it as a sort of fooling, at least soon after the boy had displayed these tendencies. She herself believed that the whole thing derived from an old nursemaid who used to place these aprons in his crib with him and let him play with them. How his habits developed and whether he continued them later on, she was unable to say. She recalled, however, that her son's letters to her deceased husband at the time that he was going with his present wife showed that he was also subject to these tastes in respect of her (his fiancée), too. She was unaware that her son displayed a passion for any other form of clothing. She had not seen him for the past eleven years.

The patient's wife corroborated her husband's information in regard to his passion for aprons and dresses in almost every detail. She also agreed that that was the cause of much disaffection in their relationships, particularly whenever she had refused to dress the way he had wanted her to. She feels certain that his desire to have them dress themselves on the farm without feeling ashamed was the sole basis for his plans and attempts to acquire it. She described her husband as an industrious and saving person. As long as he had not had the idea of buying a farm, she said, they had been able to live free from debt on the income he had and had even been able to save a little money. It was only the loss through paying the brokers which had plunged them into debt. She repeats that she believes his desire for an unhindered enjoyment of his passions led him to think of buying the farm and not the hope of a more comfortable independence as a landed person. She also stresses the fact that in addition to the color, the aprons must also possess certain satisfying patterns. It has occurred that despite a satisfying color, such as blue or blue stripes, he has rejected an apron because the pattern did not meet with his requirements. He has also spent a good deal of money on such articles as have caught his fancy, a thing he usually never does. The only substitute for normal intercourse could be this relationship with his aprons and dresses and this enables him to gratify his leanings, his sexual desires, albeit in an unconscious form, without the necessity of exposing his genitals. It is the sight, the possession and the handling of his goods which alone afford him pleasure and the gratification which the normal individual can find only in direct sexual intercourse. The female as such is quite negligible as far as he is concerned and even his wife is a sexual entity only in the secondary quality of being the wearer of one of his aprons. (Fetischismus und Psychose. Ein Beitrag zur Kasuistik. Innaugural Dissertation. Otto Walther. Rostock. Carl Boldt'sche Hof-Buchdruckerei, 1905.)

This quite singular case reveals to us a pure culture of a typical case of genuine fetishism with all the traits and characteristics.

1. The fetish has completely deposed the value of the female. It has even displaced onanism and permits the patient to live in a state of comparative chastity.

2. The cult of the harem is particularly marked.

3. The infantile root of the evil is manifest. The first fetishes were some of mother's and sister's aprons. The inhibition which prevents him from approaching a woman appears to be a secret incest motive.

4. He himself wears the aprons, wants to be a woman, identifies himself with his mother.

5. He did not take the road to homosexuality, but the result was the development of the fetishism.

6. His belief in a great historical mission does not reach the heights of divinity, etc., but he nevertheless has a secret hope of becoming a minister or a cabinet member. It is not definite whether or not a careful psychoanalysis would not have revealed the Christ neurosis and we have, unfortunately, none of

the patient's dreams at our disposal. It is my experience, however, that the apron here might stand for the apron which Christ so often wears in pictures. I would suspect that the patient had once seen a picture of the Savior dressed in an apron (blue, the color of heaven). This is, of course, only a guess and cannot be proved, but it is possible to conclude by analogy on the basis of a similar case which will soon follow. The very fact that he kept a diary creates in us the suspicion that he nursed an inner delusion of grandeur.

7. He possesses a secret which he is afraid to divulge to others, a sacred treasure.

His fear that his aprons will wear out deserves special comment. The apron is his symbol of the parapathia. It protects him from the dirt of the world and he dare not lose this protection. His fetishism must never wear out, for otherwise he will lose his chastity. I am also of the opinion that his love for his mother played an equally important rôle here. The fact that he did not see her for eleven years means nothing. The apron stood for the mother and had already begun to replace her. And I feel that at bottom he also wanted to buy the farm in order that his mother might be able to come to visit him. I must admit that the plasticity expressed in this case excels any other that I know. It is actually a triumph of human phantasy, a stubborn struggle for chastity, an indulgence in a symbol to an extent that is seldom observed. K. even became a criminal for the sake of his symbol and it was only then that his awakening anxiety drove him to confess his secret.

I myself am in the favorable position of being able to present a similar case which has the advantage of having undergone a rather thorough analysis. I shall set it down somewhat later and it will show us how much more complicated the ramifications of a fetish lover's soul are than we suspect.

This patient also discloses an animistic tendency in his relations with his aprons. The aprons live and speak with him, they suffer on being washed. He does not look upon them as inanimate, but as a part of his own person.

The next case leads us still further into the labyrinth of fetishism and shows us how wonderfully constructed is the system upon which the parapathia is founded. It will show us how impossible it is to explain these cases simply on the basis of an infantile experience. A dream analysis here will also afford us greater insight into the psychogenesis of this disease.

Case 53. A twenty-seven-year-old man of considerable physical strength by the name of Kappa manifested a special interest in sport breeches. He consulted several physicians who had no good advice to give him and finally went to Schrenk-Notzing, who tried to hypnotize him and then in the poorly effected hypnosis gave him the suggestion to try a prostitute. He tried a prostitute, but with what miserable success! As soon as he got into the brothel, a cold sweat broke out upon his brow, he was shaken as if with the chills and fevers, and finally ran out of the place in agony. He nevertheless repeated his efforts several times, but always with the same result, either half successful or a complete failure. But it would be best to have Mr. Kappa speak for himself, for he has been suffering greatly because of his sport breeches fetishism. In addition, he is a masochist and cultivates flagellation. We have asked Mr. Kappa to give us as detailed an account of his difficulties as possible because only a careful analysis of the situation will be able to aid us.

"I experience sexual excitement whenever I see a man up to thirty years of age or so wearing trousers or any kind of clothing which give the impression that their wearer is chafed or incommoded by them and appears to be suffering in them as under coercion. My thoughts turn particularly to trousers or jackets or even whole suits of corduroy, but other cloths or imitations, such an imitation leather or genuine leather, animate me also. Schoolboys clothed in suits of cheap goods are specially preferred.

"The provocative effect is increased when, in addition to the kind of cloth, the cut of the clothing is considered, i.e., when the article is tight fitting to such a degree that the buttocks, the thighs or the knees are plastically revealed. The parts of the clothing which may be tightened beyond their natural position, such as belts and the like, are highly delightful to me. The same is true of the knee straps of sport breeches, high boots, boots with hobnails or leather puttees. The effect of tightly fitting clothing is, however, quite independent of the kind of cloth the article is made of. This is of distinct advantage in the case of soldiers.

"The clothing which makes up my fetish takes on a still greater attractiveness when it shows the marks of considerable wear, my attention being riveted usually on the seat of the trousers. If I see a bicyclist going by I am provoked by the very phantasy of his anus coming in contact with the saddle. I must add, too, that even when such clothing has never been used and is on display in a store window, my interest is undiminished.

"But, quite apart from the conditions made by these fetishistic articles of clothing, my sexual desires are also aroused by any individual who looks like a member of a hard-working or serving family. I frequently try to examine the hands of soldiers surreptitiously to see whether or not their skin shows signs of their belonging to a social stratum not in accordance with their three years of service.

"I am, further, attracted to look upon boys and young men whose facial expression meets with certain of my requirements. They must have a countenance which reveals either something forward or reflective. They may be either clean-shaven or wear mustaches. Thick or interestingly drawn eyebrows, long eye lashes, small or lively or large dark eyes, dark brown color of the skin, wrinkled forehead, a row of regularly set and white teeth, hair which runs together in the nape of the neck to a point, all these are charming details for me. I prefer brunettes to blonds. A narrow waist is more desirable than any other advantage. Whenever I see such an individual, I have a desire to be as handsome and as young as the one I happen to be looking at.

"Another one of my sexual eccentricities is to put on some of the fetishistic pieces of clothing which I may have bought and show myself in public. These articles of clothing never titillate me for long, however, and I am soon searching for novelties. I am invariably looking for corduroy of an ever new color, this cloth being my unimpeachable favorite. I have seen and used all the shades of brown, grey, green, blue and black. I feel that the highest raptures of these fetishistic clothes will never be reached until I am forced to wear them every day. That would determine their wearing quality and would also soon delight me with marks of their use. At present I make up for this deficiency in my fetishes by rubbing my buttocks on a chair or the floor and always avoids sitting on a well-upholstered chair when I am wearing my fetish trousers. But I am invariably disappointed in the wearing qualities of my fetishistic clothing. The coarsely ribbed corduroy is better in this respect than the narrow ribbed variety and it possesses the added virtue of shining more, too. Its odor it shares, however, with even less valuable cloths. I experience the supreme delight in a pair of long corduroy trousers when they are worn with well-shined black shoes. A further advantage of these common goods in my eyes is the fact that they are heavier than the better grades.

"As regards my leanings to flagellation, I can say that I usually like to see an ordinary stick being used, and often the very sight of the stick is sufficient to enliven me. When doing it myself, I hit myself on the buttocks if I can, but usually on the thighs; my parts are usually naked, but I get the greatest pleasure out of wearing a pair of riding breeches during the act. I pay especial attention to the skin lesions caused by the beating.

"An indispensable component of sadistic phantasies is the requirement that no utterance of pain or sign of wincing should be expressed during the process of being beaten. Frequently it may appear as if suffering these beatings is a form of becoming accustomed to suffering pain in general. A further part of the phantasies is that prior to the beating the one being beaten prepares for the act by taking off his underwear or putting on a pair of tight trousers thinner than the usual kind, in short, donning whatever uniform happens to accord with the desired category of his partner. In my mind I have constructed fantastic beating machines and benches with a strapping arrangement. I am excessively thrilled by phantasies of whacking someone on the buttocks who has submitted only half willingly and half resistively. Afterwards, and this is the acme of my pleasures, I think of him still bearing the marks of the beating underneath his clothing, but this all unknown to any but himself."

This description in the patient's own words clearly demonstrates the systemization. There are, of course, many rather confusing details here which demand a careful analysis. There is also manifest a tendency towards the formation of a harem of fetishes. Our patient has, for example, quite a collection of fetishistic trousers and breeches which he uses at his leisure. We also observe that the notion of compulsion is the specially provocative feature of the mechanism, just as was the case in the former patient. Kappa, too, must feel that the trousers are ill and tight-fitting. Even the fetish is a patent symbol of his own disease. He finds his illness just as constraining and irksome as he wants others to find their trousers. Here we also meet with the preference for low-class cloths and people. The unused trousers, on the other hand, are a symbol of his own unexploited manhood, the virility which he has been saving, and this thought, too, is animating. The important point is that the fetish wearers must be servants or relatives of hard-working families or low-class soldiers, the present standing of the latter being a contrast to their former level. We must understand this attitude as follows. If he notices that men with delicate hands and well-formed features have been serving three years as common soldiers, he becomes impassioned to a high degree. But this is also a portrayal of his own life and his own tendencies. He is the son of a wealthy man, possesses good intelligence, literary talents and has nevertheless arrived nowhere in life. He forcibly keeps himself back from any respectable or high station in life and serves as an example of the ordinary —in every sense of the word. His goal is different from the usual ones of this world. We see, too, the inevitable identification with the fetish itself. He imagines himself to be just as handsome and as young as the particular favorite he happens to be looking at. His avoidance of upholstered chairs is a symbolical representation of his wish to make life hard for himself, not to have a soft bed. He is the expiator, the half-hearted sufferer who offers his buttocks to the stick. And yet he is tickled that no one knows the suffering he has gone through or the kind of life he leads, quite in accordance with his own phantasy about suffering the marks of a beating alone, because they are hidden from the world under one's clothing. His parapathia delights him, he constructed it, it is his and no one knows a thing about it.

This patient was analyzed for fourteen months by an experienced pupil of Freud's and led through the whole gamut of all the sexual symbolism. But what was the result? Discouraging enough. The hunt for infantile experiences, for a "trauma with short pants," had to be given up as a lost cause. The patient was disconsolate and the physician even cast blame upon him, claiming the psychoanalyst cannot do anything if the patient produces no material. The material this patient did bring consisted of a long series of dreams to which he had no associations. The patient finally came to me and I had the opportunity of analyzing him. This offered me the opportunity of analyzing his dreams and checking the associations which had been noted stenographically. That was an amusing collection to read, nor did it lack for a tragic thread either. Some of the dreams he had produced before served only to express his sarcastic attitude towards his former analyst. Thus, one dream read:

"I am lying on a sofa and behind me sits Dr. X. dripping water on my head. I think to myself: as long as my helmet sits tightly on my head, he can pour the water as long as he likes."

The stenographic notes reveal the fact that this dream is to be looked upon as an expression of "urine erotism." An infantile desire to drip urine on the analyst's head. Hardly conceivable and yet true for all that. The dream means: I lie on your sofa and the luke warm water of your talk pours over my head. My parapathia, however (the helmet), is well deserved and I shan't listen to your talk.

An examination of his psychic life permitted the following facts to be elicited as significant for the psychogenesis of his parapathia. There was one very important impression in his childhood. If we look carefully, we shall always find that at some time early in the life of these parapathics some significant person has died and this individual was the source of the parapathia. That person was the source of the patient's guilt feelings. The secret belief in the omnipotence of one's own thoughts, the trust in one's own supernatural powers, provokes the thought: that person's death is the result of your own wishes. You are really the murderer. And we must even assume that these mental mechanisms operate in earliest childhood. They appear along with the criminal thoughts and phantasies of the child and form the heart of the parapathia. In this case, one of the patient's little sisters died of diphtheria when he was hardly three years old. He had unwittingly infected her. He must have greeted her death with unmixed malicious pleasure for even at that early age he had already manifested markedly sadistic trends. He beat on cushions and even on other little boys. He liked to kill insects, revelled in gruesome games and once bound a schoolmate of his when he was eleven.

As a reaction to this early and well-formed sadism, there

developed his masochism. As early as his sixth year he was tying himself in bed with straps and ropes and at thirteen he was beating himself on the thighs and buttocks with a stick. His tieing and binding habits clearly indicate infantile phantasies of the crib, just as his habits of retaining his excrements are typical examples of the psychic infantilism we observe so frequently in fetishists.

He also reveals a characteristic of fetish lovers, viz., his desire to stand in front of display windows and gloat over the collection of whatever fetishes he may observe therein. This habit, as well as standing before a mirror, is expressive of his looking backwards into his childhood. He passes into a dreamy state.

His fear of bed bugs is also revealing. It discloses his unconscious fear of infection, his anxiety that his conscience may bite him, that spots may appear in his clothing. He actually trembles at the sight of these insects because they symbolize all the faults he fears.

He masturbates excessively, has continued since early childhood and sometimes practises this habit as many as six times in a night. There are also periods of protracted abstinence.

Although he is quite proud of his fetishism, he displays a highly emotional repression of his homosexual components. This resistance to their homosexuality is typical for many male fetishists. Even more than the female, the homosexuality is for them the sign of sin and depravity. As I explained in the last chapter, the fetishism is often a method of avoiding the homosexuality by flying into the arms of a compulsion. For our patient, too, the chief factor of delight is the thought that someone may be compelled to clothe himself in a common cloth. The pleasurable accent lies on the humiliating coercion. In the pregnant words of the patient himself, the parapathia is an over-compensation, a most consequential symbolization in which the symbol has totally replaced reality. The parapathia is a roundabout road to asceticism of which the patient is an ardent devotee. He is not really the man he appears to be. One might take him to be a paraphilic, but at bottom he is the pious ascetic. That is demonstrated beyond all doubt in a dream he had. He calls a black poodle towards him only to see the poodle change to a man with a black corduroy suit on. The black poodle is the symbol of evil, of carnality, as in Faust. He, however, transforms sin into atonement.

I could exploit the entire dream book of this patient in corroboration of my thesis. Each and every dream contains some reference to his struggle for purity and chastity and also betrays his secret wish—the divine transformation of his carnal spirits.

His paraphilia also consists of beating himself. It is significant that he had often been beaten by his mother and these experiences are still retained in pleasurable dreams which desire a repetition of the old days. But, like the heroes of antiquity, the pain must be suffered without wincing.

One of his earliest impressions is of the first pair of pants he received. They were of velvet. He had envied his brother the fact that he had for some time been wearing pants and now that he had a pair, too, he felt somewhat outstanding as the only boy in velvet pants. This joy in singularity, this pleasure in being the only one, has marked his make-up to this very day and has entered into his parapathic system. But we note that he has transformed the tendency to valuable goods into its opposite just as his primary sadism was changed to masochism. He also senses a degree of haughtiness in this masquerading: "I'm not at all the poor devil in cheap clothes for whom you take me. I'm a gem beneath all this dirt and filth."

And now I shall present one of this patient's four dreams. It unfolds before our eyes a panoramic view of the structure of his parapathia and the motives of his fetishism. I must add, however, that I first analyzed this dream without the aid of the patient's associations, although the associations which I then later had him produce under my immediate control more than verified my conclusions. This shows us distinctly that Freud's method of dream analysis is an insufficient weapon in the case of most dreams and that the method with which I work through the material is indispensable. It is, indeed, much easier to wait for the patient's own associations than to achieve the correct interpretation by means of one's own ability, but neither can it be said that every analyst is capable of the latter form of analysis. In addition, I must emphasize the fact that this

dream material was in no wise influenced by me and that is
what constitutes its special value.[8] The reader will recall my
repeated mention of the fact that patients dream in the jargon
and dialect which they have learned from us and then exploit
the dream analysis to laugh at and triumph over us.

The dream reads:

"We moved out into the field for military manœuvers and I received the written command to report to the major at 7.50 o'clock
at that point south on the Elster (a river—Trans.) where the road
branches off towards the dragon's cave. I immediately stepped
out of rank to straighten something on my uniform, and the company continued to march in the direction that I was to take. I
would have to arrange myself quickly if I wanted to overtake
them and get to the appointed place before them. The time is so
short that it seemed I would hardly get there at 7. Moreover, the
changes I was making were progressing so slowly that it seemed
as if I were being constantly inhibited in my movements. Finally,
however, I was all ready with exception of having to change my
shoes. In view of the lack of time and even in the face of the
danger of wounding my feet in the attempt, I desisted from this
change and decided to chance it. But I didn't know where I
should leave my extra pair of shoes. Before me stood a soldier,
perhaps my aide. He had a knapsack into which I had already
stuffed divers things. There was no room for more. On the
road, troops kept moving by.—I am with the major in a room
which looks like a hall. He spreads a map before me which also
contains a diagram for the reports of the coming battle. Some
of the data on the map, such as dashes, marks, and the like, were
very carefully drawn in red ink or colors (doubtless the work of
the regimental clerk, I thought to myself; my own hand would
have failed completely in that job). The first printed question on
the map asked about 'culture.' A heavy, red line signified the
answer. That, explained the major, meant that his side was the
enemy. That was his notion of the correct answer to the question about culture. There followed on the map some letters and
numerals which apparently indicated the troop groups constituting
the detachment. I knew that, but didn't have the courage to speak
up when the major asked me about the significance of the signs.
He then had me turn to that section of the manual which explained them, and I thought that even if I was not so clever in
hiding my lack of knowledge I was at least quick in finding the

right place in the manual of arms. But I felt pretty well cowed, nevertheless, and my discomfiture increased the more I came to realize that the major was manifestly taking me over the bumps. And then I saw that his aide was also present, a rather handsome fellow with a blond mustache. It was held against me that he was there much more promptly than I. I protested against any depreciation in this particular, however, by affirming that I had appeared at the stroke of 7.—Then strange soldiers burst into the hall. It seemed to me that some of them were wearing yellow leather breeches. They made a prompt about face as soon as they saw us. The major, however, was greatly wrought up by their intrusion for some reason or other, and commanded me to lead them away. They, on the other hand, paid little attention to me although I yelled 'halt!' to them several times. Some of them did halt half-heartedly, but most of them pushed on through the door. I was altogether uncertain what I should command them to do, and before I could call out anything, like 'Company—about face!' or 'At ease! March!' the major got after me and proceeded to make a fool of me before the whole crew for the way I was commanding.—For a moment some men and women from Quedlinburg appeared on the scene, very much as I had seen them once at a congress of the Red Cross in Munich. They wanted to demonstrate the fact that they were idling.—Then, like some hatcheck woman, the major was standing behind a counter and circumstantially explaining to me on a map where I was to meet him. I heard something about a wall and a zigzag path, but, although I understood very little of what he was saying, I didn't ask him to repeat and managed to snap out my 'At your command, major.' When he hesitated and wondered whether I wouldn't miss him after all, my knees sagged. His women were standing in front of the counter, and as I was withdrawing from him in strictly military fashion, I sort of bowed to them, too (and then thought that if that were altogether necessary, they would surely have noticed by the awkward manner in which I bowed that it might also have meant the opposite of the courtesy for which it was intended).—I then ensconced myself somewhere on the road, half hidden by a knoll, and was busy writing out a report of the progress of battle, that now being my chief duty. The major appeared and promptly found fault with the spot I had chosen. He claimed it was not the point he had ordered me to take up. He pointed to the group of houses in the right background and said that that would have been the most advantageous place to establish my lookout. A tall chimney which rose above one of the houses should easily have convinced me of that. The major then executed his duties as a leader himself after ordering me to make my notes in a prone position and thus make myself unseen. I thought of some low desk or slanting board which might have served me well as a base for writing. The major on his horse then sprang up some stairs which led almost perpendicularly up a hill. He did this in a peculiar fashion, leaping up the stairs left foot first while the horse pulled ahead. All of us were astounded at this feat of the old man. He halted half way up, and the Quedlinburg crowd appeared again. There was talk about the possibilities of getting home. Some mentioned a train which took a circuitous route (there was mention of stations in Schleswig-Holstein). I thought of recommending that train, having once ridden on it, but I kept quiet.—I began my report of the battle by first looking up on the map which I luckily found in my coat pocket the name of the place where I found myself. It sounded something like Vita or Zita.—I had left my observation post for a while and now returned to it. I was worried about being seen by the enemy. My glistening helmet seemed especially betraying to me. God protect me from bringing the major down on me again by betraying our position. I live in the hope that they won't see a lone man. But to cap the climax, I now appear as a civilian with a straw hat on and a cane in my hand. The major general von Ende and his adjutant, von Festenberg-Rackisch, come galloping over the field. The former was very angry and swore about an 'idiotic despatch.' How is it possible that the fellow knew the name of the major two days in advance! The major then rode past me. I heard the words: 'Such an ass!' but thought that they might just as well have referred to the man the major general meant as to me. Back at my post, I started to finish the unhappy despatches, although I didn't know what to say and had to ask others about their observations. Several men were sitting at a table and my place was taken by a certain Sontje who, rather unwillingly, of course, gave it up when I asked him to.— Again the major appeared. He wanted to light a cigar and had already pulled out the box of matches. I hurriedly offered him a light and heard him mumble something like: 'Well, at least you can show me this favor.' My hands trembled fearfully, one match went out and another broke in two. He seized the box out of my hands, but I was of service in opening my coat and guarding the fire from the wind. Contrary to my expectations, he seemed not in the least annoyed by the odor of perspiration which radiated from my body. Suddenly he asked me: 'You're a homosexual?' He was evasive when I looked nonplussed and asked him how he could tell. The Stuarts died from that, he added warningly, and advised that I beware of death. He withdrew and the thought flashed through my mind: 'Well, as long as the cat's out of the bag, there's nothing left but to commit suicide.'"

Such a singular dream demands a thorough analysis. Once we have found the key, the whole thing is easy. But there is no better way than to go at the dream sentence for sentence, and in that way we shall learn that sexual symbolism alone cannot completely clear up such structures.

"We moved out into the field for military manœuvers and I received the written command to report to the major at 7.50 o'clock at that point south on the Elster where the road branches off towards the dragon's cave."

The manœuvers represent his life. That is corroborated by the word "Vita" which appears so suddenly later on. The major is a symbol for the major power, i.e., God. The "written order" means the written word, the scriptures, the Bible. He is a Protestant and is thoroughly acquainted with his Bible. His life is, in other words, a manœuver towards another life. The dragon's cave symbolizes hell. The significance of the number 750 is apparent to him. He secretly believes that he will live to be seventy-five years old. The first sentence thus takes on the following sense: "At the end of my allotted span of years, I shall stand before the judgment of God, as is written in the Bible, and it shall be decided whether I am to enter heaven or be damned in hell."

To continue:

"I immediately stepped out of rank to straighten something on my uniform, and the company continued to march in the direction I was to take. I would have to arrange myself quickly if I wanted to overtake them and get to the appointed place before them."

He secedes from the ranks of the pious who appear here as the legions of the Lord, i.e., as soldiers, and goes his own way. His clothes are not in order. It is here that we notice that his clothes [4] form a symbol for his parapathia and his beliefs. The rendezvous or meeting place is heaven, i.e., the place where mankind is tested and judged. He wants to overtake all his companions, i.e., excel them and be first. He wants to manifest an unusual and exemplary piety.

"The time is so short that it seemed I would hardly get there at seven. Moreover, the changes I was making were progressing so slowly that it seemed as if I were being constantly inhibited in my movements. Finally, however, I was all ready with exception of having to change my shoes. In view of the lack of time, and even in the face of the danger of wounding my feet in the attempt, I desisted from this change and decided to chance it. But I didn't know where I should leave my extra pair of shoes. Before me stood a soldier, perhaps my aide. He had a knapsack into which I had already stuffed divers things. There was no room for more. On the road, troops kept moving by."

Solution: All the troops march in one direction: towards heaven. Life is short. He must change his clothing. That requires a careful explanation. In real life he pretends to be a follower of Nietzsche and a freethinker. Now he must become converted and wander through life as a believer [5] (other shoes). But he is inhibited by his intellect which permits him to wander through the world as an atheist (the extra pair of shoes); he has another religion in reserve. That reserve religion is his fetishism. His aide is a symbolization of his parapathia, his other consciousness, his alter ego. Indeed, he has loaded him with so much that nothing more can be put in (the full knapsack). This is plainly the most revealing point of the dream. It betrays the whole structure of the parapathia. What didn't he force into that bag! Religion and sexuality, assurance of his chastity and his entire psychosexual infantilism.

The dream proceeds and he appears before God, who informs him of what he wants to hear about the struggles of his life (the skirmish despatches).

"I am with the major in a room which looks like a hall.[6] He spreads a map before me which also contains a diagram for the reports of the coming battle. Some of the data on the map, such as dashes, marks and the like, were very carefully drawn in red ink or colors, doubtless the work of the regimental clerk,

I thought. My own hand would have failed me completely in that job. The first printed question on the map asked about 'culture.' "

Like a teacher, the major underlined the mistakes with red ink. The colors indicate the blemishes which so frequently spot the life of man. The notion of the regimental clerk is prettily introduced. Many religious dreams contain the idea of God having a clerk or amanuensis keep a big record book of all the sinners. Our dreamer sighs at his lack of knowledge of his own life. He cannot answer God's very first question about culture which is underscored in red. God is very merciful, however, and tells him that culture is the enemy of God and the pious. This reveals the dreamer, who strives for as rich a cultivation as possible, as a hypocrite at bottom; he conceives all the things of civilization as the work of the devil.

"There followed on the map some letters and numerals which apparently indicated the troop groups constituting the detachment. I knew that, but didn't have the courage to speak up when the major asked me about the significance of the signs. He then had me turn to that section of the manual which explained them, and I thought that even if I was not so clever in hiding my lack of knowledge I was at least quick in finding the right place in the manual of arms. But I felt pretty well cowed, nevertheless, and my discomfiture increased the more I came to realize that the major was manifestly taking me over the bumps."

The numerals and letters are the section references to the Bible, which is here represented as a manual of arms. He knows his scriptures well, but fears the questions of God. nevertheless, because he is to be taken over the bumps and asked about his sins.

"And then I saw that his aide was also present, a rather handsome fellow with a blond mustache. It was held against me that he was there much more promptly than I. I protested against any depreciation in this particular, however, by affirming that I had appeared at the stroke of seven."

Who is this strange, blond fellow who was there before him? It is doubtless his elder brother who came before him (the old theme of primogeniture). The religious element is, neverthe-

CASE MATERIAL 335

less, the more important determinant. The aide of the major, who was there ahead of him, is Christ. This patient, too, suffers from what I have so often called the Christ neurosis. He believes in his great historic mission and will not give it up. He envies Christ for having become the Savior of man. He is forever recalling Schiller's verses:

> "It is no vain, deluding thought,
> Which from disordered fancy springs.
> By hope our hearts are plainly taught
> That we are born to better things.
> That inward voice, if we believe,
> The hoping soul will not deceive."

The expression "brothers in Christ" and being there ahead (primogeniture) are the bridges which lead to Christ. He also wants to suffer as Christ did and his parapathia is the cross upon which he has crucified himself. Later we shall have the opportunity of stressing the specific attributes of the parapathia which are due to the identification with Christ. Now we may continue with the dream analysis.

"Then strange soldiers burst into the hall. It seemed to me that some of them were wearing yellow leather breeches. They made a prompt about face as soon as they saw us. The major, however, was greatly wrought up over their intrusion for some reason or other and ordered me to lead them away. They, on the other hand, paid little attention to me, although I yelled 'Halt!' to them several times. Some of them did halt halfheartedly, but most of them pushed on through the door. I was altogether uncertain what I should command them to do, and before I could call out anything like 'Company—about face' or 'At ease! March!' the major got after me and proceeded to make a fool of me before the whole crew for the way I was commanding."

This episode becomes understandable only when we look upon each of the thoughts as the soldiers which are struggling against each other.[7] The hall thus becomes the symbol of his brain in which piety is struggling with the intellect. Strange thoughts crowd into his soul and demand enlightenment and renunciation of the old feelings. He wants to call a halt to these

rebellious ideas of civilization. They, on the other hand, conduct themselves diversely. Some seem to have taken root in
his intellect. God, however, demands the whole truth, his whole
soul and a complete purification of his mind. God is also dissatisfied with the lukewarm manner in which he fights off civilization and enlightenment. The feeling of vacillation, uncertainty, is beautifully depicted in the dream here. It is this
which makes it difficult for him to orient himself properly in
life and forces him to construct the paraphilia as a protection.

*"For a moment some men and women from Quedlinburg
appeared on the scene, very much as I had seen them at a congress of the Red Cross in Munich. They wanted to demonstrate the fact that they were idling."*

The Red Cross is an indication of the religious background
of this organization. In addition to this, he recalls a pietistic
church society in Quedlinburg which is very active in religious
propaganda. The tone of the dream picture is well preserved
throughout and the inexperienced interpreter could easily be
misled into believing that this is nothing more nor less than
the harmless and repetitive dream of a reserve officer. The
others are the ones who do not have to undergo such a strenuous examination as he.

*"Then, like some hat-check woman, the major was standing
behind a counter and circumstantially explaining to me on a map
where I was to meet him. I heard something about a wall and
a zigzag path, but, although I understood very little of what
he was saying, I didn't ask him to repeat and managed to snap
out my 'At your command, major!' When he hesitated and
wondered whether I wouldn't miss him after all, my knees
sagged."*

A connection with his paraphilia appears. The major, God,
is a check woman. He hands out the clothes that one wears.
He decides the station, figure, confession, in short he decides
on the costume we shall wear on earth. It is only a loan for
the short duration of our lives, like the mask or costume we can
get at a costumers for the ball. But, although God has handed
out the dress, it is not easy to find the right path to him again.
He shows us the way in the holy scriptures, but how are we to
understand them and know our way about? What is the right

path, after all? Whatever it may be, our dreamer certainly
does not follow any direct road. He is bound to get to heaven
by all manner of tricks and artifices. Here again he weakens
at the thought of missing God and bliss because of his sins.

*"Before the counter were standing his women and as I was
withdrawing from him in strictly military fashion, I sort of
bowed to them, too, (and then thought that if that were altogether necessary, they would surely have noticed by the awkward manner in which I bowed that it might also have meant
the opposite of the courtesy for which it was intended)."*

The women of this family are Mary, the mother of God,
and some of the female Catholic saints. Like all parapathics
who are not Catholic, he displays a singular leaning towards
Catholicism, apparently because, for all of them, its mysticism
possesses something very attractive. He manifests somewhat
of a taste for Mary's position (the half bow), but also makes
fun of this leaning. Whoever does not become acquainted with
this singular form of religious symbolism, the type which de-
thrones its gods and brings them nearer human kind, as was the
case in the days of antiquity, that person will never be able to
decipher the religious sense of such a dream. Here he has
hidden the Catholicism which for him is the one and only path
to the blessedness of the church. He would also like to change
religions like changing clothes and thus undress the man he was.
In addition, his (half-hearted) attitude towards woman is
cleverly interwoven with the religious motif.

*"I then ensconced myself somewhere on the road, half hidden
by a knoll, and was busy writing out a despatch of the battle,
that now being my chief duty. The major appeared and
promptly found fault with the spot I had chosen. He claimed
it was not the point he had ordered me to take up. He pointed
to a group of houses in the right background and said that that
would have been the most advantageous place to establish my
lookout. A tall chimney which rose above one of the houses
should have convinced me of that."*

The path he took is false and doesn't lead to God, God himself is dissatisfied with it. His secret devotion doesn't please
God at all.[8] He should stick to the right party (right background), i.e., the conservatives. The high chimney is a symbol

of the church tower.   Back to the church, is what this part of
the dream really means.

*"The major then executed his duties as a leader himself,
after ordering me to make my notes in a prone position, so that
I could remain unseen.   I thought of some low desk or slanting board which might have served me well as a base for writing.   The major on his horse then sprang up some stairs which
led almost perpendicularly up the side of a hill.   He did this in
a peculiar fashion, leaping up the stairs left foot first while the
horse pulled ahead.   All of us were astounded at this feat of the
old man.   He halted half way up, and the Quedlinburg crowd
appeared again.   There was talk about the possibilities of getting home.   Some mentioned a train which took a circuitous
route (there was mention of stations in Schleswig-Holstein).
I thought of recommending the train, having once ridden in it,
but I kept quiet."*

The war despatch, which is the confession of his life, is not
finished yet, and God, as his teacher, shows him the right path.
He should hide his piety and devotion, and do his writing lying
down.   This is a clever play of words because what the words
really mean is: by lying.   Let him lie to the whole world, declare himself a freethinker; at heart he is the devout cleric.[9]
The desire for some "slanting board or desk" indicates his unconscious thought of the altar and the hassock.   The major's
feat is nothing more nor less than Odin's ride (as depicted in
the ballad of the same name) to the bright heights of heaven.
He is shown how one can do it even with the left foot, i.e., sin,
forward.   It is at this point that erotic elements begin to mingle
with the religious ones.   The experienced interpreter will already have noted that the spermatozoon and womb phantasies
here permit of other than religious determinants).   The riding
feat of the old man commands the admiration of his pupil.[10]
Need I explain this further?   The ladies appear again and there
is a conference as to what would be the surest and quickest way
to God (home).   The dreamer betrays himself by knowing of
a rather circuitous route.   Indeed, the train he has made up is
one of the most complicated one can imagine.

*"I began my report of the battle by first looking up the name
of the place where I found myself on the map which I luckily*

found in my coat pocket. It sounded something like Vita or Zita."

Now he knows that this deals with his own life (vita). Zita is an indication of the other determination present, viz., the ex-empress who had married at that time.

"I had left my observation post for a while and now returned to it. I was worried about being seen by the enemy. My glistening helmet seemed especially betraying to me. God protect me from bringing the major down on me again by betraying our position. I live in the hope that they won't see a lone man. But, to cap the climax, I now appear as a civilian with a straw hat on and a cane in my hand. The major-general von Ende and his adjutant, von Festenberg-Rackisch, come galloping over the field. The former was very angry and swore about an 'idiotic despatch.' How is it possible that the fellow knew the name of the major two days in advance! The major then rode past me. I heard the words: 'such an ass'! but thought that they might just as well have referred to the man the major-general had meant as to me."

The glistening helmet of his devotion is his parapathia,[11] the paraphilia which protects him against all dangers. It is the purpose and plan of his life not to betray his real piety until just the day or so before he dies, and then only to confess his faith in God. The major-general "von Ende" (of the End) is death itself. The names are taken from the military superiors he has known. The straw hat, an easily inflammable article, is a symbol of his paraphilia which, beneath the appearance of depravity, hides a life of devotion. He will confess his faith two days before he dies, and that enrages death who here assumes an even more important rank than God. Even God, who has more and more taken on a resemblance to his father, chooses to call him an ass, and this, too, he conceives as directed at himself. Indeed, it is manifestly an asinine business to play the libertine and freethinker and be a hypocritical believer at heart.

"Back at my post, I started to finish the unhappy despatches, although I didn't know what to say and had to ask others about what they had observed. Several men were sitting at a table and my place was taken by a certain Sontje who, rather unwillingly, of course, gave it up when I asked him to."

He is having more and more difficulty getting through his confessional, the story of his life. He has continued to stress the fact that he understood little, was poorly oriented in life and depended greatly on the leadership of others. Like a flash, he thinks of his brother [12] (Mr. S.) who, being the first born, has always stood in his way. Now he struggles with him for a place at the table, but we recognize this as another mode of expressing the spermatozoon phantasies mentioned before. As Silberer has so succinctly put it, all these phantasies mean one and the same thing: The beginning of a new life.

"Again the major appears. He wanted to light a cigar and had already pulled out a box of matches, but I hurriedly offered him a light and heard him mumble something like: 'Well, at least you can show me this favor.' My hands trembled fearfully, one match went out, the second broke in two. He seized the box out of my hands, but I was of service in opening my coat and guarding the fire from the wind. Contrary to my expectations, he seemed not in the least annoyed by the odor of perspiration which emanated from my body. Suddenly he asked me: 'You're a homosexual?' He was evasive when I looked astonished and asked him how he could tell. 'The Stuarts died from that' he added warningly, and advised that I beware of death."

This portion is particularly important in the study of the dream analysis because it shows how strong is the patient's tendency to make fun of the physician and pull the wool over his eyes. It would be easy to take this last part for a homosexual expression, and the other analyst, to whom the earlier portions of the dream had been an impenetrable darkness, actually fell upon this scene with zeal, thinking it to be a transparent symbolization of the homosexual relationship between father and son.

We must be very cautious in the handling of the situation, however, when an intelligent patient suddenly broaches a trauma or sexual theme awaited by the analyst. And this patient was certainly intelligent; he stood head and shoulders above his former physician. It is a trap into which the analyst will fall unless he is on the lookout.

The meaning of this part of the dream derives from the

sense of the whole structure. It can be only a religious one
and such it is despite the presence of the sexual component. He
desires to inflame himself in God. He wants to believe, and
God demands but this one service or favor of him: faith. He
wraps himself well in his clothes in order to protect himself
from the wild winds of modern times which threaten to blow
out the little spark of his faith. He trembles for the sake of his
bit of faith. By the sweat of his brow he is supposed to be
earning his living, but the paraphilia and his masochism have
made life sour enough for him. Such bitterness cannot but
please God and does not disturb him.

But now comes the unveiling. That question: Are you
homosexual? Behind it lurks a cunning play of words. The
homo is nothing but a certain homo, viz., Christ. His most persistent memory is about the painting by Titian called "Ecce
Homo." He even believes himself to be another Christ. He,
too, suffers the sorrows of mankind and would like to be a
savior. The question thus really means: Do you love Christ?
Are you Catholic? The Stuarts died of it. A mysterious sentence the interpretation of which did not at first succeed. It may
have alluded to Mary Stuart, who was reputed to be both an
artist in love and a very pious woman.[18] This also indicated
reminiscences of Schiller's drama on the subject. God's added
warning that he should beware of death now takes on a definite
meaning, particularly since he now wants to become religious,
i.e., openly to confess his faith.

*"He withdrew and the thought flashed through my mind:
'Well, as long as the cat's out of the bag, there's nothing left
for me to do but commit suicide.'"*

God has finally recognized him as a devotee, a believer in
Christ and the mother of God, sees that he was always a believer. His faith has finally been revived and now he can die
in peace.

It is not difficult to see how the solution of this dream is
essentially the solution of his whole parapathia and paraphilia.
Never has a case more clearly refuted Freud's contention that
the neurosis is the negative of the perversion. The perversion
(paraphilia) is itself a neurosis (parapathia) and manifests
the selfsame mechanisms as the latter. This patient's whole

life was bent in the direction of heaven; he wanted to attain God's love.   His entire conduct is explainable in terms of an identification with Christ whom he envies and manifestly wishes to outshine.   It is simply that his secret wish, his faith in his "great historical mission" is imperturbable.

What factors in his parapathia corroborate our point of view?

His paraphilia is a self-made punishment for his faithless-ness and the sins he has committed.   It fits him poorly, like an ill-fitting suit.   That is the reason he becomes so animated by the thought of someone wearing clothing which discomforts them, compresses them.   The cloth must be cheap, just as his illness makes him look like a sick, bad, cunning, cheap person. The cloth must be wearable, just as his parapathia is durable and lasting.   The paraphilia completely surrounds him, so that he is removed from life.   It is a self-inflicted compulsion.   It is for this reason that any piece of clothing which laces him and binds him also animates him; thus, belts, boots, etc.   We have seen these objects appear in dreams before as symbols which describe the parapathia.   In short, the patient is animated by his own parapathia, he derives sexual pleasure from it, he revels in himself and his own clever constructions.   Serving and obeying satisfy him because, as a soldier, he looks upon himself as a servant of the Lord.

Why, we must ask ourselves, has he, however, picked on sport breeches of all things?   Is this choice really determined by some infantile experience?   Was he so deeply impressed by his brother in little pants?

We shall not be able to comprehend this phenomenon unless we understand that the fetish degenerates in the course of time. It metamorphoses, so that it may better mask its real purpose. We have already seen how, in a previous case, the nailed and gory foot of Christ became a livid and sweaty foot and that, later, the other important attribute, viz., the nail, was dropped.[14] In the same manner, this patient has also transformed the origi-nal character of his fetish.   Initially, he had been provoked by cloths such as the orientals wear about their loins.   Upon ex-amination, we found that this cloth derived from the phantasy of the loin cloth Christ wore.   The helmet also has a double symbolical meaning, viz., that of his faith and that of the crown of thorns, the unseen thrusts thereby being translated in a physical sense.

The meaning of the parapathia is thus: I am Christ, the Savior, and when I identify myself with Christ I derive the greatest pleasure.

Still another source of his difficulties is his magnified narcissism. He loves himself and even admires himself. He looks for and finds himself in every earthly manifestation. His self-love and egotism is almost limitless. He sees himself reflected in fresh and musing boys, in young men, and desires to be as handsome as the others. In short, he identifies himself with those objects which appeal to him.

Through the masochistic procedures we can still catch a glimpse of his ideas of atonement. He is punishing himself for the sexual pleasures he is getting and the punishment itself becomes a pleasure. Then he controls himself, but that brings him more suffering; the suffering, however, returns him even more gratification when he bears it without wincing. He is, after all, continually bucking the obstacles of life. He denies himself the least joy of living and the slightest success; he has chained himself to his paraphilia as to a torturing instrument. He voluntarily kneels before God and willingly offers his body for punishment.

His secret pride in his cleverly framed parapathia is betrayed by the sentence: "I am particularly provoked by the thought that the beaten person conceives the marks of his whipping, hidden beneath his clothing from all others as they are, as a sign of distinction." That is his pride, too. He beats himself, suffers, and yet no one realizes what a devout and pious man lives among men, an individual who has been chosen for great deeds and the salvation of mankind.

The question arises as to how such a parapathia originates and what are the forces which consolidate it. The paraphilia is essentially a distorted caricature of up-bringing, with its compulsions, beatings, bindings, etc. The child's pants indicate the infantile period. The condition is at bottom a facet of infantilism. The patient would like to be a child again and wear boy's pants. Such wishes (which are also indicated by the determination of his dream as partly derived from spermatozoon phantasies) indicate a deep dissatisfaction with his life to date and a great regret. He would like to live his life over again and then he would have an entirely different report to write out. This dissatisfaction derives from the period in which he had wished his father dead. He felt that father's death would liberate him from every compulsion in life and make him independent. He hated his brother in the same way because the brother was an obstacle and rival in his struggle to gain ever more affection from the parents. He had therefore also wished his brother dead. It was only the full realization of these evil thoughts of his which provoked his feelings of inferiority and guilt; then he began to feel that he deserved neither happiness nor freedom. His religious habits whirled him ever deeper into the treacherous eddies of his guilt feelings and soon there was no other form of salvation but the renunciation of his faith. He became an atheist and freethinker. The success of this step is sufficiently exposed in his dream and his parapathia. Inwardly, however, he continued to become more and more pious the more anti-clerical his external conduct appeared.

It seemed, however, that his parapathia was insoluble because of a certain condition he had made himself (Adler). As long as he would indulge this form of sexual gratification, his father would live. This condition naturally had the effect of removing him completely from any relations with women. It furthermore proved to be the source of added conflicts. He had to wish the father renewed death if he were ever to achieve a woman. His anxiety of the female as the symbol of sin,[15] however, was so strong as to make this protective mechanism bearable. That is, even if his father were to die, his freedom would be only an apparent one, because it was not an inner freedom. His guilt feelings would reappear, i.e., for example, you are guilty of your father's death (Freud's notion of the omnipotence of thought). He would lay new years of atonement upon himself and thus continue to avoid the female who symbolizes death for him, too, as in the dream figure of Mary Stuart. One of the secret imperatives of his soul is: beware of woman!

In another dream he said: "Some man had treated others cruelly. The avenger appeared in the form of another, somewhat older man. The latter commanded me to pick up a box which was so large that I had to carry it with both hands and, driving the evil doer before him, went up a flight of stairs which seemed to lead to the attic. On the way, he continued to beat the guilty one. Arrived at the top, the avenger took a large leather billy out of the box I was carrying and proceeded to flay the evil doer with it in a most cruel fashion."

He himself is the sinner and the box symbolizes the brain box which is the cupboard of all cruel punishments. The same is symbolized by the attic. The box is also a representation of his brain-child, the parapathia. He is his own avenger and judge, the source of his own chastisement.

He has finally found the key to his suffering and symbolizes it in his dream as his brother. Thus, in another dream, he says:

"I found the key to the closet in which my brother's things were kept. That was rather unpleasant to me because I feared that the key would be needed and looked for."

The first analyst conceived the key as a phallic symbol and overlooked the significant meaning which it indicated: I fear that the doctor might find the key to my parapathia and try to make me well. That would rob me of the chance for heavenly bliss. In other words, the dream really shows us his anxiety of being cured and his pride in his parapathia.

A fairly careful examination of his whole paraphilia will reveal the fact that it is really not a paraphilia. It is a sort of frame-up in the sense that Adler means the term, an arrangement, a truce. He conducts himself as if he were a paraphilic. His fetishism is an artificial construction, a second religion which is intended to replace the first, a substitute for the joys of this world; it promises him heaven for his rejection of honor, fame and woman. The cohesive force behind this paraphilia, or rather caricature of a paraphilia, is a resolve. That must be stressed. His father will continue to live as long as he continues to avoid women. A similar resolution was to be found in all the other cases I analyzed. It is this condition which makes the parapathia insoluble. This is the source of the punishment for all the criminal death wishes. Woman is the symbol of sin, but behind the fear of depravity there hides also the fear of woman herself, the apprehension that he may fail in the sexual struggle. It must be emphasized, on the other hand, that this case reveals no trace of any organic basis for the parapathia. I want to stress again the fact that this part of Adler's theory is, in my opinion, wrong and insufficient. The feeling of inferiority is solely due to the sense of guilt as far as I can make out, and not to any organ inferiority.

How remarkably our patient knows how to play the pervert and yet remain pious! As I have already mentioned in my paper on "Der Neurotiker als Schauspieler" (The Neurotic as Actor).[16] "The neurotic is the actor and audience in one and the same person. His parapathic symptoms represent a definite scene." Thus this patient appeared to himself as a parapathic, he was a hypocrite hiding behind the mask of a satan. His paraphilia protected him from woman and sin, and in this manner his fetishistic sin became a religious and pious act, and the devotion, furthermore, a sin against his better intelligence.

We see, in short, how complicated the proper analysis of such a case of fetishism becomes. It is probable that this case, too, would reveal threads running back to a primary incestuous attitude. He emphasized the fact that corduroy smelled like urine and frequently mentioned his relationship with his mother. It is possible that he once saw his mother sitting in a pair of tightly fitting pantalets. Unfortunately, he mentioned nothing of the sort and his dreams contain nothing more than suggestions that he is cherishing some secret, but they do not disclose the nature of it.

Even granting this, however, the paraphilia of this patient is such a complicated structure that it is not to be resolved with such a simple key formula as incest. Nor does the strongly developed olfactory sense of the patient offer a satisfactorily exhaustive explanation of the religious superstructure. We can only say that there is here an irresistible tendency to cover up sexual activity with an appearance of sexuality.

Abraham emphasized the reduction in the sexual activity of his patient. I was able to find the same to be true in all of my cases. It was too great an activity which led to the choking off of sexuality by means of a fetishism. It was the patient's anxiety of his own sexuality which caused the apparent destruction of it; that was the beginning of his deviation from his own sexual guiding principle, the principle which always looks for the whole man and the whole woman. In agreement with such cringing tendencies, he produces castration phantasies, the mark of all fetishists. As a matter of fact, all of them have effected a sort of ideal castration on themselves, they even play with the thought of actual and physical castration, a step which would be equivalent to complete self-denial and the realization of their highest ascetic and hypocritical ideals.

Abraham has, however, already recognized the mixture of parapathia and fetishism and feels that Freud's theory—that the neurosis is the negative of the perversion—cannot be absolutely retained. He looks upon the parapathia as being caused by the foot becoming a genital substitute. "Scoptophilia and ophresiolagnia, instincts which always have been directed at the excrements, have, in this case, undergone a marked although unequal transformation. The ophresiolagnia has been largely repressed, but the scoptophilia, on the other hand, just as markedly emphasized. It has naturally been deflected from its original path, however, and idealized, so to speak. This process, to which only one of the two instincts is subject, deserves Freud's title of 'partial repression.'"

That's how far the strict Freudians will go in reducing all of the symptoms of a parapathia to the terms of repressed instincts. How would Abraham explain our case of sport breeches fetishism with his olfactory lust or a case of strict corset fetishism? We see how important it is to understand the religious motives involved in every one of these cases and also the mechanisms described by me. I am not afraid to declare that I have achieved a psychological understanding of these patients, whereas the concept of partial repression is nothing more than a clever hypothesis which has made a not unimportant factor the chief consideration in the question.

Abraham also mentioned the fact that his therapeutic efforts were of no avail and that the analysis would only have produced greater resistance to the powers of the fetishism. But that only proves that such a method of analysis which cannot disclose the basic mechanism underlying the sense and the purpose of the parapathia, the secret ideal of the patient, cannot possibly be effective, just as I have pointed out in the case of Kappa, who was analyzed fourteen months.

Fetishism is not only a second religion, it is also a disease. It is a spiritual parasite which incapacitates its host for any other form of mental endeavor. Everything is exploited in the service of the fetishism and everything is expressed in its terms. Finally, the fetish lover is so totally bound up in the mesh that he is incapable of doing any fruitful work. He sinks beneath the surface of his dreams, cannot turn his attentions either to his social or business duties, all for the simple reason that, as Bleuler has expressed it, his emotions are bound up in other things. It is just such a circumstance which brought me the following interesting case.

Case 54. A thirty-year-old government official who was unable to continue with his duties because his pathological fetishistic notions gave him no peace and undermined his concentration.

His case is doubtless one of the most singular which has ever been reported. Our patient—we may call him Mr. Lambda— has become deeply interested in men who display a swollen or injured cheek or jaw and likes to see it bandaged. He prefers to see young, beardless men in such a condition or at least men who show only the earliest growth of a beard. When he sees a man with a swollen face, he begins to act rather queerly. For example, he may be sitting in a café and suddenly sees a man outside who has a turban or black cloth around his head; or perhaps someone with a bandage around his face or head. He promptly yells to the waiter for the bill, and if the waiter doesn't come on the run, he becomes upset, frothy, irritable, leaves the change on the table and runs out to look for his desired object. If he has lost sight of him, he becomes dejected and disconsolate, excited and very tense. He will retrace his steps, wait, search the same street for hours at a time, in the hope that the man will return or come that way again. Indeed, he has often stood in the same place for as many as six hours, hoping that his object would return again. He will then return to the same spot or street the following morning and keep this up for a week until a new object deflects his attentions from the old one. He is invariably convinced that the new object had particular and special sensations and thrills in store for him.

To take the case that he has not lost sight of his object. He then follows the man, proceeds ahead of him, at one side and then the other, in short, looks the man over from all angles as unobtrusively as possible. If the fetish walks into a store, he waits patiently, even for hours, until the man comes out again. Then he approaches under some pretense or other. Usually he says that he is a stranger and is looking for the right road to somewhere.[17] At this point, he takes the opportunity to sympathize with his informant, to ask whether he is suffering great pain or not and what he does for himself. In this wise, he tries to pass as much time as he can in the man's company, and is particularly pleased when the man tells him that he (the object) will accompany him a distance in the same direction. As soon as he has left the company of the other, he goes into a store and buys himself a cloth or bandage similar to the one his late acquaintance had on. The lower the class and the simpler the caste of the fetish, the greater is our patient's libido. There is, however, a faintly bitter and empty taste about the whole experience, as if a yearning had remained unfulfilled. He has not the least desire to be alone with the fetish or to have a homosexual relationship.

Quite the contrary! It is now that he makes use of this meeting with the fetish to provide himself with the most delectable ecstasy of his experience. He stands before a mirror, dresses his head or face as nearly as the fetish was bandaged and imagines himself to be the other man. As soon as he has consummated this mental identification, he fixates the bandage and proceeds to masturbate. He has collected a whole harem of such dressings and cloths, but they usually lose their charms for him within a few weeks or less. He then must find new ones or dig up one of the old favorites. His desire for such fetishes is insatiable and irresistible. He will jump from a moving omnibus, a street car, any vehicle, as soon as he spies such a fetish. He may have gone to some extreme to get a theatre or concert ticket, but that he will give up unconcerned if he notices such a fetish on the way to the performance. He will miss his meals, appointments, even his work for the sake of such an experience. He may be walking with some woman or a superior, but he will leave them abruptly. But it is interesting to learn that the compulsions of military service were stronger than his own inner demands. He never missed a single exercise during his year of service nor was he deterred from following a single fetish. That only proves to us that the only law under which these patients live is the law of least resistance. We will find this fact always to be true. Military service is the apotheosis of iron rule. Its pressure replaces the compulsions of the parapathia. The patient's own imperative is displaced by the military imperative.

This patient discloses many other curious phenomena besides his fetishism. The first day he was in Vienna, his father took him for a walk through the center of the city and past the cathedral of St. Stephen. For months afterwards, he could not bring himself to take any other route through the city, and it was some time before he began to walk in other streets. He finally found the Mariahilferstrasse (Street of the Good Virgin) also pleasant. He is always looking for streets with churches at one end. He denies, however, that he is pious and states that he never goes into a church "except when I want to hear lovely church music." He took an active part in the anti-clerical movement of his home country and was even furiously attacked in the church newspapers.

His sudden outbursts of anger are terrific. He himself fears his passions. For two years he was given to gambling and lost quite a tidy sum of money. His office banishes him to the solitude of the country and whenever he wants to indulge his fetishistic passions he has to ride to the next town. On such occasions, he puts on entirely new dress, goes through a regular masquerade. He is, after all, an official and must look to his position. For that reason, he disappears from the small town whenever the urge comes upon him, sneaks away to the next larger city, stands guard at some hospital or dentist's office, and awaits the appearance of satisfactory objects.

Transiently he wanted to become a drunkard, but was never able to become drunk, and so gave up the idea. He finds no pleasure in alcohol.

His one real delight is masturbating before a mirror after he has bandaged his head or face or bound some kind of cloth around it. But even without a mirror, he can drop off into hours of phantastic dreams. He gets a little thrill at the end of every urination. He had been an enuretic for a long time and disclosed the bladder troubles typical of fetishists.[18]

His conduct with women is eccentric. He knows plenty of them and likes to talk with them, but the slightest indication of sexual contact stampedes him. He once had a vivacious interest in girls and was infatuated with a cousin at twelve. Six years ago he had fallen in love with a girl who liked him, too, and let him know by her attitude that she would never say no. He was about to be

ingaged to her and decided to test her devotion by introducing a
gallant officer to her. In a few months, the officer had fallen in
love with the pretty and well-to-do girl, but he had to wait some
time for her, because she continued to wait for Lambda to make
a move, expecting all the time that he actually wanted to marry
her. When she finally decided to marry the other, Lambda fell
into a protracted and serious depression. He felt unhappy, betrayed, cheated and alone. The playful and hypocritical nature of
these patients is here well manifested. He himself had brought
on the whole debacle by cleverly introducing the officer. Why?
Only to avoid the necessity of coming to grips with the situation
himself, to find a way of hiding his real fear of woman and marriage, to retain the right to be unhappy. He wanted to say to
himself: You have done your best to marry, but you can't be
blamed when girls are so unreliable and fickle, so false and faithless.

At the time when I saw him, he confessed that he was in a
similar position with regard to his cousin. He could marry
her, too, if he wanted, and believed that he would be potent with
her (he hadn't the slightest doubt of his potency although it was
never tested). But—marry? That would mean giving up his
paraphilia, a thing that would be out of the question. An inner
voice told him that marriage would be the right means of finding the way to woman, but he hadn't yet the courage to mind
this advice.

Such singular attitudes are naturally characteristic of fetishism. The artificial structure of the paraphilia was originally
intended to protect the possessor only against extra-marital
coitus (sin), but in the course of time the sexual guiding principle is totally obscured, the road to woman is altogether blown
over and the chances of reaching marriage become more and
more distant. Marriage is nevertheless the one method of helping these men and I have seen two cases find their salvation in
matrimony. It is absolutely false to base any therapy of fetishism upon any kind of intercourse with prostitutes, public or
clandestine. The great, inner moral sensitivity of these men
abhors the step, and whatever success seems to be gained in this
manner is only transitory. The advice is usually followed by
outright failure, however, and that more than ever shakes him

in the belief in marriage. Sometimes the doctor is asked for a guarantee of potency or they themselves will suggest trying themselves out with a prostitute in order to make sure. Such attempts fail. And so they did with this patient, also. His family physician even went to the brothel with him, ostensibly to examine the girl because the patient feared he would be infected. Afterwards he wailed that he was unfit for marriage and thus again avoided a decision.

He did not want to give up his paraphilia, however, and manifested considerable pride in his illness. He was, after all, the only one he had ever heard of who displayed such an abstruse form of sexual gratification. This resistance immediately expressed itself in the course of the treatment in that the very first day he told me that he had little expectation of being cured. I had not, of course, been so rash as to promise him that, but I had assured him that he would be enabled to work again. I wanted to give him no opportunity of triumphing over me at the end of the treatment or of finding fault with me for not having kept my word. I nevertheless expected that he would be cured because I knew that this disease would collapse as soon as the patient had achieved insight.

The third day he had already run out of associations and later confessed that he had thought to himself: "I'll tell that doctor nothing, just to show him. What'll he do then? Let him cure me if he can, but I won't keep up this infernal talk talk talking." The fourth day he didn't even turn up. He had overslept. We changed the hour to the afternoon because he would oversleep every other day, but even then he came too late. He managed to sleep into the afternoon out of sheer resistance. The whole analysis was a constant struggle which inevitably showed him that he had but one goal in mind: to preserve his fetishism and triumph over the physician.

We must try, however, to answer the question as to how Lambda came to choose this one mode of expression for his parapathia and no other. His family doctor reported to me that as a child Lambda had a pretty governess who suffered frequently from toothaches. She often had a bandage about her jaw. The boy's attention was thus very early directed to this phenomenon. But how many beloved mothers and governesses are there who have toothaches and bandaged faces without their children being thus singularly fixed in their sexual habits? The causes must be of a much deeper nature. Such an explanation as this would be far too superficial.

We learned the following about his early childhood and youth. He manifested an immense and insatiable desire for tenderness. Unfortunately for him, his brother was always ailing and invariably attracted the affections and attentions of the parents. The father especially was always taking care of that brother. He was sent to baths and resorts of all kinds to restore his health and the patient suffered pangs of envy every time he returned to tell of the wonders and beauties of the new place. This brother always irritated and depreciated him. Whatever *he* did was childish and unimportant, but whatever his brother did was *a priori* important and clever, although the one was only a year older than the other. The result of this situation was that Lambda anxiously avoided any contact with his brother; he had his own toys and was unhappy whenever his brother disturbed him or them. Once he became so angered with his brother that he attacked him with a toy gun and nearly put out his eye. As a result, the brother had his eye and face bandaged for some time, and he himself was painfully punished for his conduct. They also chastised him by telling him that he would be a criminal yet, everybody would be ashamed of him, God would punish him severely for his ways, etc. In short, it appears that a determinant is possible on the basis of his guilt consciousness. The *lex talionis* demands that the memory of his criminal act shall always remain fresh in his mind and always persist in annoying him. In addition to this, one of his younger brothers had died then and at the time this filled him with malicious satisfaction. The memory of this malice clouded his conscience and the idea that there were such things as retribution and the revenge of the dead began to take on a prominent rôle in his fetishism of which we shall speak later on as soon as we have completely unravelled the mystery of his religion and suffering.

At five he contracted erysipelas and was constantly attended by his parents for a week. Like all dangerously ill children, he was showered with tenderness and affection and each of his slightest wishes was promptly fulfilled. That was the most happy and delightful time of his life and he yearns for those days even yet. We have already mentioned that he always liked to walk the old paths and streets. He is really always looking backwards at his past.

He would enjoy those childhood days again when he was passed from one arm to another. His face was then smeared with salves and bulging with bandages. His fetishism is thus a yearning for himself and his childhood. The old ways and paths are the ways of youth. We shall soon see this corroborated by other material. He would like to pass his whole life as he did in those infant days, always to be ill and always to be coddled by the parents. In secret, he was tickled that his present serious illness had so worried his parents. His brother had long since become strong and healthy and filled a respected official position. He was now the handicapped one, perhaps he was even incurable. The family physician had communicated the severity of the patient's condition to his father, the latter had to support his son, had to give him a long period of rest and vacation, came through with the costs of the treatment, etc. In short, the patient was beginning to taste the sweets of long-awaited revenge and victory; he was now the source of anxiety in the house. Everybody at home began to pour out their sympathy. Parapathics blackmail their relatives for every ounce of love and affection they can get, all in the form of sympathy. It gives them the deepest gratification when their parents spend money on them. It is thus that parapathic children easily become spendthrifts by persistently testing the patience and affection of father or mother. In this case the same thing took place. He was ill; the most handicapped member of the family; he could not work; father had to support him. But he had a disease which presented a form the like of which his brother had never had. Nobody as a matter of fact had ever heard of such a curious condition. His illness became a feat, he was proud of it.

Still another experience had affected his youth. His sister, who was two years his junior, was passing by a store when she was eight and was injured in one thigh by a sudden explosion from within. The wound, which he saw later in the room as the doctor came to dress it, made a great impression upon him. There had been talk about her having been exposed to the danger of blindness if the explosion had chanced to strike her face. Whether or not this statement discloses what Freud calls a displacement from below upwards, is more than I can say. He mentioned nothing about it himself. But he did speak about another form of displacement.

He had cherished many phantasies about the process of birth and pregnant women always appeared to him as swollen. When he had a tooth pulled one day, he suddenly thought that perhaps they had brought him into the world by means of a forceps and that he thereafter must have had a swollen head for a long time, just as, now, his jaw was swollen. He is greatly interested in the subject of reincarnation, and has often considered whether or not the great pressure of being born may not have injured his brain permanently and whether or not, as a result, his present condition is the forerunner of insanity. The swollen jaw thus reflects upon his birth phantasies and the question of reincarnation which so captivates him.

Sometimes he is possessed of very curious notions. He does not know, for example, whether he is still alive or has already died. He thinks at times that he sees ghosts or cadavers on the streets. He then recalls what a terrible impression the sight of a dead man made on him. They bound up the face or the jaws of the dead brother. Indeed, he recalls that they always bandage the face of the dead in order to prevent dropping of the jaw.

He's looking for his dead brother on the street, the dead who are to be resurrected from their graves. On the one hand, his death wishes against his brother, his ideas of revenge and the various methods by which he would have had his brother die provoked him; he was, on the other hand, shaken by the fear that the dead would return like vampires to revenge themselves upon him. Moreover, a superstitious nursemaid had told him all kinds of such blood and thunder stories and they had become engraved in his heart. He was really looking for such a resurrected person. He was looking for a miracle on the street. He was looking for his dead brother, i.e., for himself, that lovely and devout part of him which had long since died.

His parapathia was conditionally bound by his guilt feeling, however, and this made it almost indissoluble. I have already pointed to the fact that the death clause is lacking in no case of compulsion neurosis or obsessional ideas. Nor was it missing in this case of Lambda and I shall have to present it here. His father had lost his first wife and married the dead woman's sister. The child had often heard the father arguing with the family physician about mother's constant ailment and weakness. Father was always in mortal fear of her life. The boy had heard his father saying: "Doctor, I'll never stand the death of this woman. I'll send a bullet through my head on her grave." His brother had also heard this, and that was the one moment of brotherly harmony in their lives, that night when they whispered to each other in the dark about what father had said. For weeks he was sleepless, thinking about it. When mother again became ill, he was

already twelve years old. He promptly recalled what his father
had once said and remembered the shudder that passed up his spine
when he considered what would happen if both parents died. He
would then have come to live with his grandfather, everybody in
school would feel sorry for him, all the friends in town would
sympathize with him. Something like a desire for this experience
had raised its head within him. Now, when his mother lay again
in bed, those terrible phantasies of earlier days returned to him
and he resolved never to touch a woman as long as God would
give his parents life. He offered God the sacrifice of his sexuality
for the preservation of his parents. He had faith in this condition, too. He, the freethinker and atheist, tells me that he cannot
give up his "perversion" as he calls it, because then his father
or mother would promptly die. It is this condition which bars
the road to his cure. That is also the situation which I have
chosen to call the puzzle picture of the parapathia. Even if his
father should die, he would promptly produce another resolve and
the female would then finally be so surrounded with fences and
the barbed wire protections of his conscience that it would be impossible to overcome the obstacles.

We must not forget that such resolutions play a most important rôle in all compulsive conduct. They are seldom revealed by the analysis, for obsessional patients are geniuses in
the art of dissimulation. They can talk for a year with a physician without telling him anything of real importance. Thus,
Abraham's patient kept on telling him endless details about his
excremental interests as soon as he noticed that the analyst was
looking for just such information. Indeed, the patients will
even invent material in order to keep from talking about those
things which are really basic for their condition, viz., their religious problems. Our own case illustrates that very well.

The reader will recall that Lambda was distinctly anti-
clerical. He had attended a parochial school where he had
been taught by Catholic priests. Up to the age of fourteen, he
had been devout and pious. He had fled from his aggressive
and criminal tendencies into the arms of God and religion. In
high school, he had been especially impressed when his religion
teacher told of the saints and their miracles. The desire to
become such a saint and also work miracles began to grow upon

him. He would kneel for hours before an image in the church, ecstatically praying and begging for a miracle to be done, for his salvation from sin. The biological awakening which took place in puberty and the stories of his schoolmates about their relations with girls made his conflicts more acute, in addition to which the onanism which he practised and about which he had heard the most blood-curdling tales of punishment, enhanced his guilt feelings. He was pleased then to imagine that he were ruining himself by masturbation, robbing himself of the future and happiness.

In his fourth term of high school, he became acquainted with a boy whose father was a very enlightened person. Through this boy, he secretly became acquainted with all kinds of books of a modern trend. It was not long before he threw his whole stock of superstitious baggage overboard, but only apparently and not completely as we shall soon learn. He was soon reading the philosophers and holding long conversations with his friend's father. In his sixth term, that is, at sixteen, they had founded a secret philosophical society in which Nietzsche, Haeckel, Darwin, and the like were read, studied and explained. It was thus that he finally turned out to be a fervent anticlerical.

We know, nevertheless, that every passion of this sort is suspicious. Such transformations are to be looked upon as attempts to liberate oneself from the all-powerful authority of God. The individual revolts against the monarchy and omnipotence of the Lord. It is all a heroic attempt to shake off the feelings of guilt and become free. In the last analysis, this is a struggle to shake off every form of compulsion. Every parapathic struggles against authority and is almost dedicated to psychic anarchy.

The analysis of this case revealed, however, that all this freethinking was, at bottom, only superficial. Lambda disclosed many traits which made it almost certain that he was simply hiding his essential piety, as I have explained in my paper on "Masken der Religiosität" (Masks of Religion).[19] Up to a short time ago, he was still wearing the scapular which he had worn in school as a charm against evil influences. His path always led him past churches and whenever he was tired he was in the habit of going into a church for rest. During the course of my treatment, he never failed to retrace that first walk of his in Vienna, simply because it led him past the St. Stephen's cathedral. He really wanted to retrace his first steps in life, the path of childhood faith, the road that led to God. In youth, he had been greatly impressed by the stories of the martyrdom which the saints had suffered. Subsequently he had tried many similar tortures on himself. For example, he would suddenly touch a burning cigarette to his hand without wincing. He hit his teeth with a hammer and became angry that he never suffered toothaches. He would have been happy to train himself in the suffering of pain. We note, also, that he carefully questioned his objects about the pains they suffered and what they did about it. He had beaten himself with a stick and often lay down upon the floor to sleep.

His chief interest was, however, dedicated to Christ himself. This was the figure which always ignited his emotions and he said: "I admire Christ as a man and not as a God. He was the greatest of men." It was plain that he envied this son of man who had been able to become a God.

In the course of the analysis, his inner piety came closer and closer to the surface. It was as if an old and hidden painting were being restored and the features of the ancient religious figures were beginning to shimmer through the fading colors of the false covering. The most important insight was achieved through the question of miracles. It was a miracle that he was awaiting from God, a wonder which should restore his faith to its former strength. The religion teacher had told them that the days of the wonders were not at an end; they had been seen only a few years ago and he proved it by reading of the miracles of Lourdes from his thick book. Why, thought Lambda, should he not experience a miracle.

It appeared that he was still awaiting the great miracle. Christ walks among men, and he shall some day see Christ. The man with the swollen jaw is revealed as a distortion of the suffering Savior, God with a crown of thorns. It was him whom he hoped to find among the suffering on the street.

What he really sought was Christ. It was Christ with whom he was identifying himself during onanism. His peak of libido was produced by his imaginations of the suffering he was enduring.

Besides this anagogic tendency, there was another, satanic, trend as disclosed by the analysis. He manifested both heterosexual and homosexual incest wishes and a distinct psychosexual infantilism. Many of his dreams clearly displayed a very strong fixation to his mother and sister. His deep homosexual attachments were expressed in his ambivalent and bipolar attitudes towards his brother and father. Love and hate.

The following dream, taken from the stock of this patient, will further our understanding of the secret motives of the fetishism.

"On Easter Sunday I was invited with my entire family to take dinner with the bishop. We arrived at the bishop's palace and were admitted. They said, however, that the bishop was still at church. As we gave up our clothing in the hall, I noticed that my mother wore a curious apron of fur which she also laid away. 'What's that for?' I asked. My father answered me that it was to prevent colds. I looked at myself in the mirror hanging in the hall and saw that I was unshaven and unkempt. My clothes were dusty and my shoes dirty. I said: I must get a shave and have my clothes brushed. Looking at the clock, I thought I still had time to do this before dinner. I then left the palace with my parents and as we came out upon the street I saw a herd of pure white sheep and lambs coming out of the cathedral and thought to myself: the services are now over. I looked for a barber shop, but they were all closed. I then went home to find the house in great disorder. I looked in vain for a clothes brush but finally got one from my brother. I talked with my brother and said that our invitation to dinner with the bishop was probably due to our close acquaintance with the canon. We then returned to the palace and went immediately into the dining room where dinner was just being served. The bishop got up from his seat and, in all his regalia, went to the open window where in a thin feminine voice he began to call out commands in German. I was at first surprized, but then I thought that the bishop certainly had the right to give commands to the guard of honor which had appeared at the services."

Without delving into an exhaustive dream analysis, I want
to point out the essentials of this dream and also to call attention
to the resemblances to the dream of Mr. Kappa. The keystone
of the dream is the fur which the mother wore. It would be
easy to impute a sexual meaning to this. But the mother is
really the representative of his parapathia here.[20] She wears
a fur which is to be cast off in the anteroom, i.e., she must put
away a covering, a shell. He has the phantasy of a wolf in a
sheepskin and then interprets it laughingly: I'm just the opposite: a lamb in wolfskin. And that is precisely the riddle of his
parapathia. How delicately does this dream express his guilt
consciousness, too! He is dirty, unshaven, covered with the
dust of the earth. Meanwhile the lambs and the sheep come
out of the cathedral and he hardly finds time to change himself
from a wolf to a lamb. The dinner to which he was invited
represents the Holy Supper.

Again we come upon the picture of military service in this
religious dream. Ecclesia militans! Just as the major commanded in Kappa's dream, so the bishop does the commanding
here.

But we have had enough of this analysis. It is not my purpose here to exhaust the possibilities of dream analyses, but to
demonstrate the hidden and undisguised signs of religious tendencies in these patients. The patient's description of himself
as a wolf in sheepskin is the best characterization of these cases
of fetishism.

We are conviced, however, of the complexity of these cases
of fetishism and the difficulty of confronting them with any
of our former methods. We have nevertheless been able to
come to some very important conclusions about them.

*Fetishism is a substitute for religion. In the form of a para-
pathia it offers its possessor a new religion in which he can
express his desires according to his faith. Fetishism is thus
not a paraphilia, it is only a caricature, the fiction of a paraphilia. It derives from a compromise between insurmountable
sexual strivings and a deep-seated piety. It offers its possessor
the opportunities of a more or less complete asceticism. Under
the guise of Satanism and libertinism there is hidden a piety
whose goal lies far beyond the boundaries of this world. The*

fetishist finds himself in open struggle with every form of authority, especially with God to whom, secretly, he submits and whom he hopes to appease by his divers forms of self-denial.

My own cases distinctly reveal the picture of a Christ neurosis. Further studies are, of course, desirable before we can decide whether this is a generally operative law or not. The fetish lover expects to find compensation in heaven for all his sufferings on earth. Fetishism should not be looked upon as the result of a degenerative constitution, but rather as the attempt of a strongly sexed individual to deviate from the path of his sexual guiding principle. The apparently primary fetishistic instinct later appears as a secondarily transformed and distorted but primarily normal sexual instinct.

It must be emphasized again and again that these fetish lovers try their best to make the parapathia indissoluble. The basis of this is often a secret clause according to which the life of dear and near relatives is made dependent upon the continuance of the fetishism. The penalty for breaking this secret oath is death and eternal damnation. The condition originally was formed by the patient having wished some rival death in childhood. It is this very individual who is then later absorbed into the condition in order that the asceticism of the patient may be protected. It is at this point that threads of an incestuous nature appear and I have never found them missing in any case. Fetishism is an infantile religion, but it is also an obstinate preservation of infantile sexual ideas.[21]

Our therapy must take cognizance of these facts. The analysis must lay bare the secret piety and religious trends of the patient; we must bring about a truce between the patient and reality and turn his eyes from heaven back upon this earth. The result will then be either open piety or unclouded atheism. The patient must make a decision between out-and-out religiousness or real inner freedom. The only sexual gratification which seems feasible for most cases is the consummation of marriage.

NOTES TO VOLUME ONE

CHAPTER I

[1] It would be more correct to say: retreat from the other sex.

[2] Cf. the chapter "The Struggle of the Sexes" in my book *Das liebe Ich* (Otto Salle, Berlin, 1913).

[3] Binet, *Du fétichisme dans l'amour. Revue philosophique*, 1877.

[4] *Ueber sexuelle Perversionen. Ztschr. f. Sexualwissenschaft*, Vol. I, No. 8, 1914.

[5] Paul Garnier characterizes the fetishist as follows: "Timide dans les choses de l'amour, le fétichiste, bien loin d'être un excité sexuel au point de vue des plaisirs vénériens, ets bien plutôt un insuffisant que rien n'attire vers l'union des sexes, le plus souvent. Génitalement, il pèche bien plus par défaut que par excés."

[6] "Die Lehre von den Geschlechtsverirrungen (Psychopathia sexualis) auf psychoanalytischer Grundlage," F. Deuticke, Vienna, 1922.

[7] "This is not to be confounded with the vague, general and absolutely unspecific concept of 'nervous disposition.' In this case, it is a very definite erogenous zone, the irritation of which is naturally more pleasurable than usual" (Sadger).

[8] The reader will doubtless have noticed that I always speak of male fetishism. I have observed a case of jewelry fetishism in a woman and other rudiments of fetishism in females. Fetishism is, despite such cases, generally a male disease, but it is natural that the same points of view hold good in these cases as for male fetishism. Howard has described cases of female clothing fetishism, a thirty-nine-year-old woman who stole trousers, a twenty-one-year-old woman who coddled the drawers of her dead husband, a seventeen-year-old girl who possessed a veritable harem of men's garters (*Ztschr. f. Sexualwissenschaft*, Nr. 3, January, 1914). There are further examples of female fetishism in Chapter III of this book. In the last chapter I have exhaustively discussed the question as to why fetishism is largely a male disease.

[9] In some cases of this sort, I have been able to observe a secondary psychic mechanism which I have called the principle of the "finished product." I borrow this curious title from a well-known joke which I must insert here because of its psychological value in reference to our theme. A match-maker offers the hand of a rich girl to a young man, but the young man reminds the match-maker that the offer suffers by the fact that the girl once broke her leg and now limps. "What of that!" said the match-maker; "just imagine that you were already married to the girl. You take your wife for a walk. Along comes an automobile and your wife is run down. You immediately call an ambulance and have to take your wife to the hospital. The professor comes in. You go through a few weeks of the greatest excitement, and finally you have to come through for the big bills. But here you have a finished product!" This principle of the finished product plays a leading rôle in some cases of pseudo-fetishism, e.g., in the following case. A man meets with the wife of a friend of his. The woman had always left him cold. Now he finds her quite banged up from a beating her husband had given her. At this moment his entire sexuality rose up in a wave of passion and he practically fell upon her. The woman, on the other hand, nursed a

rankling desire for revenge against her husband. They both enjoyed a tremendous satisfaction during intercourse, but the enravishment did not cease with this experience. The man in the case was a sadist who had never permitted his cruel instincts to become conscious. When he met this woman he came upon a "finished product." Fetishists who search for women with amputations have also repressed that bit of sadism which calls for the dismemberment of the woman. The amputated arm or the missing leg is then that reality which offers an anchorage for their phantasy. It is the make-believe of red blood for the animation of their colorless schemes. It is also possible to gain new insight into the psychology of sympathy from this point of view. This feeling also operates according to the principle of "pleasure without guilt." The cruel deeds have been accomplished by someone else or by destiny, and we derive our enjoyment therefrom in a form compatible with our ethical conscience. The malicious joy which so frequently precedes our sympathy and secretly accompanies it is the conscious expression of the same tendencies.

¹⁰ *Les Fétichistes*, Paris, Bellière et fils, 1896.
¹¹ Infantile psycho-sexuality.
¹² *Peculiarities of Behavior*, New York, 1925.

CHAPTER II

¹ Cf. *The Language of Dreams*, Chapter X.

CHAPTER III

¹ De Clerambault, Passion érotique des étoffes chez la femme. Archives d'anthropologie criminelle et de médicine legale, 1908, 1910. I was unable to see the original, but have cited from an excellent critical paper by the sexologist, Dr. Kurt Boas: "Ueber Hephephilie, eine angebliche Form des weiblichen Fetishismus." H. Gross' Archiv, Vol. LXI.
² Ueber Warenhaus Diebinnen Mit Besondrer Berücksichtigung Sexueller Motive. H. Gross' Archiv, Vol. LXV.
³ One thinks here of Ibsen's Nora ("A Doll's House"). The playwright appears to have taken his observation from life.
⁴ *Journal de Médicine de Paris*, 1914.
⁵ Reported by Kurt Boas in H. Gross' Archiv, Vol. LXVII, "Kleinere Mitteilungen." "Weitere Beiträge Zur Forensischen Bedeutung des Puppenfetischismus."
⁶ Laquer, "Department Store Thefts," *Sammlung zwangloser Abhandlungen aus dem Gebiete der Nerven-und Geisteskrankheiten, Halle a.S.*, 1907, Vol. VII, Nr. 5.
⁷ Vinchon's literal reproduction reads: "Le fétichisme est une perversion sexuelle obsédante et impulsive conférant tantôt à un objet auquel nos usages prêtent une signification sexuelle (fétichisme impersonel), tantôt à une partie du corps (fétichisme corporel), le pouvoir exclusif de l'orgasme génital, le fétiche étant soit directement, soit par évocation ou réprésentation mentale l'élément à la fois nécessaire et suffisant de l'excitation sexuelle."
⁸ Cf. the very important case of Féré cited in Vol. II.
⁹ Une observation de fétichisme des étoffes chez la femme. Thèse de Montpellier, 1912. Nr. 51.
¹⁰ 4 l. c.

CHAPTER V

¹ Zentrlbl. f. Psychoanalyse, Vol. IV, 1914.
² Cf. the chapter on urine sexuality in *Infantile Psycho-Sexuality* in this series.

³ Three contributions to the theory of sex.
⁴ l. c., p. 328.
⁵ Cited after Dr. Veriphantor, *Der Fetischismus.* Berlin, Singer & Co.

CHAPTER VI

¹ This girl's analysis appears in *Sadism and Masochism* as a case of masochism.
² His attorney wrote Elise that his wife would sue her for adultery. Having taken his money, she would have no case in court.

CHAPTER VII

¹ Gabriele D'Annunzio dedicated his drama "Giaconda" to the lovely hands of Leonora Duse.
² Cf. Freud, *Totem and Taboo;* and Levy-Brühl, *The Psychic Life of Primitive Peoples.*
³ Cf. the chapter on "The Race on the Street" in *Masken der Sexualität.* Paul Knepler, Vienna, 1922, 2 ed.
⁴ *Onanism and Homo-sexuality,* the chapter on "Don Juan and Messalina."
⁵ *Medical Jurisprudence,* Vol. I, 1860, p. 732.
⁶ l. c.
⁷ Cf. also Dr. A. Hagen, *Ueber die Geschlechtlichen Gerüche* (on sexual odors). H. Barsdorf, Berlin, 1900.

CHAPTER VIII

¹ "Mr. B. is a fifty-year-old business man with a distinct preference for red-headed women. He is not satisfied with the pleasures of the moment, however, and looks to the refreshment of his memory in the future by cutting a lock of pubic hair from every red-head with whom he copulates. The trophy is curled, bound with a black silk cord and pasted in an album where the treasured spoil of happy hours is labelled with name and date. His future gratification consists in paging the leaves of his fetishistic reminiscences."
² A vulgar Viennese expression for vagina.
³ A vulgar Viennese slang description of a cohabitatio inter mammas cum quinque ejaculationibus et cum erectione permagnarum mammarum.
⁴ Fellatio.
⁵ Titillare locum minoris resistetiæ.
⁶ While this book was in the press, the patient came for another appointment. If the analysis succeeds, I shall publish it in another edition.
⁷ *Jahrbuch für Psychoanalytische Forschung,* Vol. III.

CHAPTER IX

¹ How often are medical fashions derived from fetishistic leanings! Foot fetishism is unusually widespread and many of these fetishists make a pilgrimage to Wörishofen or such places. Exhibitionists rave about sun baths and the cult of nakedness. The masochists become devoted teetotallers of all kinds, vegetarians, apostles of chastity, prohibitionists and the like.
² Freud's use of the term screen memory implies an important experience in the shadow of a harmless scene, but these false memories I mention create important occurrences out of unimportant events The archives of memory are searched and suitable scenes borrowed and revamped.

³ I no longer say that this wish was "unconscious" in Beta's mind. *Freud* looks upon repression as an ejection of material into the unconscious, as "not knowing." For me, however, repression is simply ignoring of material, "not wanting to know." At one of the congresses for medical psychology, *Klages* asked, "Is repression concerned with that which is unknown or with that which is not thought?" I declared for the opinion that repression is not thought material and defined the process as that psychic mechanism by which we refrain from thinking something we don't want to know because it is associated with certain unpleasant features. Such a thought or, rather, image, is pushed out of the center of consciousness by our inner judge, our conscience, as an undesirable. The thought *must* not appear and if it does, it is either in the negative form of astonishment, anxiety, etc., or in some symbolic shape. It is thus that Beta did not want to see that he had been waiting for the death of his father, so that he could live his life as he wished to live it.

⁴ A part of these dreams is also contained in *The Language of Dreams.*

⁵ His mother died at his birth.

⁶ He used to call his governess an "old box."

⁷ For the sake of greater clarity in English, the translator has taken insignificant liberties with the German in some instances.

⁸ Aigremont also considers walking as a symbol of the sexual act. All languages also reveal some indications of this fact. Thus, the Latin coire for cohabit really means to go together. Congressus also means coming together. To go with a boy or girl has a sexual background both in English and German. The expressions misstep, go straight, go after, all have sexual meanings, as well as certain other movements such as climb, jump and dance. This is true of the dream as well as of social usage. The French word marcher means as much as go after in English. Le vieux marcheur: the old masher. This collection is, of course, arbitrary, but it nevertheless indicates the basic connection between walking and erotic ideas.

⁹ In this respect, I would like to cite a characteristic sample from *Das Leben des Traumes* by Karl Albert Scherner. "The general fantastic expression for the human body is that thing which we build of bricks, mortar and beams, i.e., a house. It is easy to see that our universal fantasy has chosen an apt symbol in this expression, in that the house, like the human organism, possesses an architectonic structure and also a number of hollow spaces and rooms. In addition to this, one could say that the soul lives in the body as in a house. Finally, it must have been perceived that all man's real activity is directed by the needs of house and hearth, just as the spiritual activities take place within the human structure. All these apperceptions together must have contributed to the choice of just this symbol."

¹⁰ Another determinant leads from the shape of the egg to the egg-shaped head of the phallus. The phallus is as brittle as an eggshell and might break if he put it in. Or, he thinks, some vein might burst. That also indicates an infantile sexual theory. He thought that the man lost a part of his penis every time he cohabited with a woman. It is the lost part which is put in the vagina. This particular infantile theory derives from comparisons with botanical processes and the method of inoculation. The connection is not at all seldom and frequently constitutes a basis for psychic impotence. The practice of circumcision, so mysterious to most children, is also connected with this theory. As a child, our patient had seen a picture called "The Circumcision of Christ" which had made a lasting impression upon him (castration complex).

¹¹ Struwelpeter was quite a trauma for him. Especially the part in which the tailor or cutter (circumciser) cuts off the thumb-sucker's thumbs filled him with horror and trembling (castration complex).

¹² His father died in Reichenhall from a pulmonary disease. That was

his "great misfortune." Following his father's death, his guilt consciousness began to show its head, reproaches pained and lashed him with the feeling that he had foregone something which might have saved his dear life. These reproaches derived their emotional strength from childhood experiences in which the father had prevented his masturbation and thumb-sucking by means of threats (castration). At that time his thought had been: when father dies I can masturbate all I want. Furthermore, we already know of the relationship which existed in his mind between the awaited death of his father and his sexual freedom.

[13] The homosexual attitude towards the physician as a father imago.

[14] The symbols of "above" and "below" which Adler has so strongly emphasized as meaning male and female, find a simple explanation in this case as in so many others. Children are little and adults big; children must look up to them from below. Psychic infantilism finds its expression in "below." It is the burning desire of all children to "be big," and being "bigger than the grown-ups" is expressed in dreams by situations in which the dreamer is "above." Another determinant for "above and below" is to be found in the religious complex of heaven and hell. On the balcony he always saw heaven above and hell below.

[15] Later it was found that the ball of the foot and the corns also provoked him sexually. His disgust was positive only in the early stages of the analysis. Corns were for him an anti-fetish which soon changed to a pro-fetish.

[16] Indication of Nekrophilia. He even loves his dead father.

[17] Addendum: This reminded him of an actor he had seen in a cabaret once, dressed in a thin jersey shirt. His name was Silvester Schaeffer.

[18] Also his father.

CHAPTER X

[1] Taken from the German edition prepared by Dr. Ernst Jentsch. "Die krankhaften Geschlechtsempfindungen auf dissoziativer Grundlage," Würzburg, Kurt Kabitsch, 1907.

[2] This case shows distinct signs of urine sexuality (see Vol. V). The full bladder enhances his pleasure. May not the original impulse have come from the bladder? It is probable that he has suppressed information about such tricks with his bladder.

[3] A mother communicated the following relevant observation to me: "My little six-year-old son has, since his earliest infancy, had the habit of binding his feet up under his knees. He then tries to walk, but this is, of course, hardly possible; nevertheless, he derives the greatest fun from trying it. He loves to play with belts which he ties about his body in all kinds of ways. He is always pestering me to bind him. He likes to dress himself up in other clothes, especially in my things and finds powdering his face a rare treat. It is his ideal to be dressed up like a baby and he is always begging to be done up in diapers, put under a quilt and carried about on my arm. It is doubtless of importance that my boy clings to me and unfortunately continued to sleep with me until he was two years old. He was very tender with me. Until recently he suffered from enuresis and pavor nocturnus. Since reading your books, I know that much of this is my fault because I gave him so much of my tenderness and thus bound him to me. He was also specially attached to the game of tying the awning rope around his neck and then calling: 'Look, mama! I'm hanging myself!'"

[4] His active delight in odors and the significance of perspiration are demonstrated by the fact that axillary perspiration excites him sexually and that he likes to grip a girl under the arm pit, so that he can feel the sweat.

[5] Ein Fall von weiblichem Fuss, richtiger Stiefelfetishismus. Int. Zeitschr. für ärztliche Psychoanalyse. 3 Jahr, 1915. No. 2.

[6] *Pince-nez* (pinching) can also serve as a symbol of the compulsion.

[7] Über Horror sexualis partialis (sexuelle Teilaversion, antifetishistische Zwangsvorstellungen, Fetischhass). Neurologisches Zentralbl., 1911. Nr. 10.

[8] In the June number of *L'Encephale,* 1921, Jeanselme reported a similar case of self-mutilation. A twelve-year-old boy had so incarcerated the glans penis by a stricture about the suclus that it became gangrenous and fell off while the boy was urinating. In the Int. Zeit. f. Psychoanalyse, Vol. VIII, No. 3, 1922, Saussure adds some interesting remarks on the case. He considered the possibility of castration ideas, but rejected this theory because the boy would otherwise have constricted the penis at the root. It is my opinion that this was a case of symbolical compulsion which derived from the penis and had to be expiated on the penis. One must also think of protective mechanisms against masturbation in such cases.

CHAPTER XI

[1] Cf. my discussion on the representation of the parapathia in the dream. Zbl. f. Psychoanalyse, Vol. III, p. 66. The shoe is a very frequent symbol for the parapathia, as is also the glove.

[2] Psychoanalyse eines Falles von Fussund Korsettfetishismus. Jahrb. f. psychoanalytische u. psychopathologische Forschung, Vol. III, 1912.

[3] I possess four dream books of this patient which were written during the fourteen months he was analyzed. He was particularly interested in this dream because his physician was not able to analyze it.

[4] As I have frequently found. The suit representing the individual's character.

[5] As a barefoot pilgrim, like Beta, the foot fetishist.

[6] Church.

[7] The soldiers dressed in leather breeches symbolize his paraphilia. God is incensed at them and blames him. These legions of his do not obey him and he is uncertain just how or whether he should command them.

[8] His fetishistic stand is also frowned upon by God.

[9] Lying down is also the position of humiliation and submission.

[10] One must also remember that the analyst is a major or father imago, and the patient the pupil.

[11] Cf. the dream about the water dripping on his head.

[12] In a determinant we have mentioned before, the same as his ideal: Christ.

[13] I came upon the interpretation later: Stuart is woman.

[14] We recall that the other patient had a pet phantasy: walking on the main street in Vienna with a giant nail through his foot.

[15] Nietzsche also emphasized the "eternal cowardliness of man before the eternally feminine."

[16] Zentralbl. f. Psychoanalyse, Vol. I, 1911, p. 38.

[17] This statement betrays the religious tendency of his parapathia. He is looking for a leader who might lead him in the right path. He has left the straight and narrow road.

[18] Hitschmann was the first to point out connections between the bladder and compulsions.

[19] Zentralbl. f. Psychoanalyse, Vol. III.

[20] Cf. my paper on Die Darstellung der Neurose im Traume. Zentralbl. f. Psychoanalyse, Vol. III.

[21] It is not self-contradictory when I previously wrote that fetishism is a compulsion neurosis and now state that it is a kind of religion. The compulsion neurosis is itself a religion. (Cf. Freud, *Imago,* Vol. I, p. 332: "Hysteria is the distortion of a work of art, the compulsion neurosis a religion and the paranoid delusion a distorted philosophical system.") It is also true

that in both the compulsion neurosis and religion, the heart of the matter is to be found in the relationship of the individual to his father.   But in each individual case of obsessional neurosis or fetishism, we are not merely interested in the basis of the situation, but in the whole structure which has crystallized about this nucleus, in the colossal psychic superstructure built upon the general foundation.

SEXUAL ABERRATIONS